Cloud Computing

Deploy, Scale, Conquer

Herkimer Throckmorton

ISBN: 9781779661692
Imprint: Telephasic Workshop
Copyright © 2024 Herkimer Throckmorton.
All Rights Reserved.

Contents

Introduction to Cloud Computing   **1**
The Evolution of Computing   1
Understanding Cloud Computing   15
Advantages and Challenges of Cloud Computing   51

Cloud Infrastructure   **65**
Hardware and Data Centers   65
Software-Defined Networking (SDN)   87
Containerization and Orchestration   103
Edge Computing and IoT   119
Serverless Computing   131

Cloud Services   **145**
Storage and Database Services   145
Compute and Container Services   164
Networking and Content Delivery Services   179
Security and Identity Services   197
AI and Machine Learning Services   216

Cloud Deployment and Operations   **239**
Cloud Service Providers   239
Cloud Migration Strategies   256
DevOps and Continuous Integration/Continuous Deployment (CI/CD)   273
Cloud Cost Management   298
Budgeting and Cost Tracking Tools   306
Disaster Recovery and High Availability   318

Future Trends in Cloud Computing   **341**

Edge AI and Fog Computing 341
Quantum Computing and Cloud 354
Blockchain and Distributed Ledger Technology (DLT) 366
Green Cloud Computing 380
Ethical Considerations in Cloud Computing 392

Index 409

Introduction to Cloud Computing

The Evolution of Computing

From Mainframes to Personal Computers

Back in the day, before we were all born, the computing world was dominated by a massive beast known as the mainframe. These bad boys were powerful, room-sized machines that could handle complex calculations and process large amounts of data. But they were expensive as fuck and could only be accessed by a select few organizations with deep pockets.

Then along came the personal computer (PC) in the 1970s, and shit got real. Suddenly, computing power was in the hands of the people. People like you and me, my friend. We could have our very own computer sitting on our desks or laps, and we could do all sorts of cool shit with it. And guess what? It was way cheaper than a damn mainframe.

The advent of the PC revolutionized the way people worked, played, and communicated. It was like unleashing a whole new world of possibilities. We could write documents, play games, surf the web (once the internet became a thing), and even create our own software. The power was in our hands and it felt fucking amazing.

But hold up a minute, let's not forget about the internet. Oh baby, the internet. It changed everything. It connected the world in ways we couldn't even fucking imagine. Suddenly, we could share information, communicate with anyone and everyone, and access all sorts of resources from anywhere. The internet made the world a whole lot smaller and more connected. And you know what? It paved the path for cloud computing.

So what the hell is cloud computing anyway? Well, my friend, it's the next big leap in our computing journey. It's like taking that PC power we had on our desks and making it available to us anywhere, anytime. It's like having a virtual mainframe at our fingertips, but without the hefty price tag.

With cloud computing, instead of running software and storing data on our personal computers, we access applications and store data on remote servers. These servers can be located anywhere in the world, but they're all connected to the internet. So we can access our stuff from our PCs, laptops, tablets, smartphones, or any other fancy gadget we can get our hands on, as long as we have an internet connection. The power is no longer confined to a single machine - it's out there in the cloud, ready for us to tap into.

Cloud computing has given rise to a whole new model of computing, one that is highly flexible and scalable. We can easily deploy applications, scale them up or down as needed, and not have to worry about the underlying infrastructure. We can focus on what matters most - getting shit done, instead of getting caught up in the technical nitty-gritty.

But why the hell does cloud computing matter? Well, my friend, it's all about the benefits it brings to the table. First and foremost, it's cost reduction and scalability. With cloud computing, we don't have to invest in expensive hardware or maintain a huge data center. We can simply pay for what we use, scale up or down as needed, and only pay for what's actually being used. It's like having a pay-as-you-go model for computing, and it's fucking beautiful.

Another advantage of cloud computing is flexibility and accessibility. We can access our applications and data from anywhere, as long as we have an internet connection. We're no longer tied to a single machine or location. We can work from home, from a coffee shop, or even from the notorious bathroom (not recommended, but you get the point). Cloud computing gives us the freedom to work on our terms.

But hold on a fucking minute, cloud computing isn't all sunshine and rainbows. We can't ignore the security and privacy concerns that come with it. When we store our data on remote servers, we're essentially putting our trust in someone else's hands. We have to rely on the cloud service provider to keep our shit secure and protected. And let me tell you, not all cloud service providers are created equal. We have to do our due diligence and choose a provider with a solid security track record. We have to understand the risks and take measures to protect our data and privacy.

Vendor lock-in and data portability are also major concerns. Once we're locked into a particular cloud service provider, it can be a bitch to switch to another one. We have to consider how easy it is to move our data from one provider to another, and whether we can even do it without a major headache. It's like being in a toxic relationship - we're stuck and it's fucking annoying.

And let's not forget about the fears, doubts, and fucking uncertainties of the cloud. People worry about downtime, data breaches, and what happens to their data if the cloud service provider goes out of business. These concerns are not to be taken lightly, and it's important to have backup plans and contingencies in place.

So, my friend, now you know the evolution of computing from mainframes to personal computers and how we've arrived at the era of cloud computing. It's an exciting time to be alive, as cloud computing continues to revolutionize the way we work, play, and live. But like anything in life, it's not all rainbows and unicorns. We have to be aware of the advantages and challenges that cloud computing brings, and navigate the cloud with caution. Stay curious, stay skeptical, and always question the fucking status quo. The future is in our hands.

The Internet and the World Wide Web

The Internet and the World Wide Web are two terms that are often used interchangeably, but they refer to different concepts. In this section, we will explore the origins and evolution of the Internet, as well as the development of the World Wide Web. So sit tight, grab a coffee, and let's dive right in!

The Evolution of the Internet

The story of the Internet begins in the late 1960s, during the height of the Cold War. The United States Department of Defense, concerned about the possibility of a nuclear attack that could cripple traditional communication systems, started a research project called ARPANET (Advanced Research Projects Agency Network). ARPANET aimed to develop a decentralized communication network that could withstand such an attack. It's like the 1960s version of Kevin McCallister setting up traps in his house to fend off bandits, except instead of burglars, they were trying to protect against nuclear bombs.

Fast forward to 1973 when ARPANET became operational, connecting four universities in the United States. This marked the birth of the Internet, although it was still in its infancy. Over the next few years, more nodes and universities were connected to ARPANET, allowing researchers and scientists to communicate and share information more easily. It was like a virtual community before the age of social media, but instead of liking each other's posts, they were exchanging research papers and nerding out about computer science.

In the 1980s, the National Science Foundation (NSF) established NSFNET, a network that connected supercomputers across the United States. This network served as a backbone for numerous research and educational institutions, further expanding the capabilities of the Internet. It was like the upgraded version of the Internet, complete with a turbocharged engine and fancy racing stripes.

The Birth of the World Wide Web

While the Internet was gaining traction within the academic and research communities, it wasn't until the late 1980s that a breakthrough occurred that would change the face of the Internet forever. Enter Sir Tim Berners-Lee, a British scientist who invented the World Wide Web.

Berners-Lee envisioned a global hypertext system that would allow people to access and share information across different computers and networks. Working at CERN, the European Organization for Nuclear Research, he developed the first web browser, called WorldWideWeb, and the first web server. In 1990, he released the code and protocols for the World Wide Web, making it freely available to the public. It was like the birth of the Internet's coolest sibling that everyone wanted to hang out with.

The World Wide Web introduced the concept of hypertext, which allowed users to navigate through interconnected documents using hyperlinks. This meant that instead of reading information in a linear fashion, users could jump from one document to another by simply clicking on a link. It was like discovering a never-ending maze of knowledge, but with an easy-to-use map that took you wherever you wanted to go.

The Internet vs the World Wide Web

Now that we have a basic understanding of the Internet and the World Wide Web, let's clear up any confusion between the two. The Internet is the underlying infrastructure that connects networks and devices worldwide, allowing them to communicate with each other. It's like the highway system that enables the transfer of information between different locations.

On the other hand, the World Wide Web is an application layer that runs on top of the Internet. It is a vast collection of web pages and other resources that are accessible through the Internet. It's like the shops, restaurants, and attractions along the highway that we can visit and interact with.

Think of it this way: the Internet is like the foundation of a building, while the World Wide Web is like the various rooms and floors within that building. You need the Internet to access the World Wide Web, but the Internet is not limited to just the World Wide Web. It's like needing a car to get to a fancy restaurant, but you're not limited to eating at that restaurant only. You can drive to other places too!

The Fucking Impact of the World Wide Web

The World Wide Web has revolutionized the way we access and share information, transforming the world into a global village. It has brought about significant changes in various aspects of our lives, including communication, education, business, and entertainment. Let's take a closer look at some of the fucking impact it has had:

1. **Communication:** The World Wide Web has made communication faster, easier, and more accessible than ever before. We can now send emails, chat through instant messaging, make video calls, and share files at lightning speed. It's like having a personal telegraph system that connects us to anyone in the world, except we don't have to deal with Morse code or sending pigeons.

2. **Education:** The World Wide Web has opened up a world of knowledge to anyone with an internet connection. We can access online courses, tutorials, and educational resources from renowned institutions and experts. It's like having a 24/7 virtual classroom with the best teachers from around the globe. You don't even have to worry about being late to class!

3. **Business:** The World Wide Web has transformed the way businesses operate. It has paved the way for e-commerce, allowing companies to sell their products and services online. We can now shop from the comfort of our own homes, compare prices, read product reviews, and make informed decisions. It's like having a digital shopping mall that's open 24/7, without having to deal with crowded parking lots and long lines at the cashier.

4. **Entertainment:** The World Wide Web has revolutionized the entertainment industry. We can stream movies, watch our favorite TV shows, listen to music, play video games, and connect with other fans from all over the world. It's like having a multiplex theater, a concert hall, and a gaming arcade all rolled into one, without ever leaving our couches. The only downside is that we might forget what sunlight looks like!

So, there you have it, the Internet and the World Wide Web. They are the dynamic duo that has shaped the digital landscape and transformed the way we live, work, and play. From the humble beginnings of ARPANET to the invention of the World Wide Web, it's been an incredible journey. The Internet and the World Wide

Web have become an essential part of our daily lives, and their impact will continue to shape our future. So, embrace the power of the Internet and surf the World Wide Web like the badass digital explorer that you are!

Key Takeaways

- The Internet and the World Wide Web are closely related but distinct concepts. The Internet is the underlying network infrastructure, while the World Wide Web is an application layer that runs on top of the Internet.

- The Internet's origins can be traced back to ARPANET, a research project initiated by the U.S. Department of Defense in the late 1960s. It aimed to develop a decentralized communication network that could withstand nuclear attacks.

- Sir Tim Berners-Lee invented the World Wide Web while working at CERN in the late 1980s. He developed the first web browser and released the code and protocols for the World Wide Web in 1990.

- The World Wide Web introduced the concept of hypertext, allowing users to navigate through interconnected documents using hyperlinks.

- The World Wide Web has had a significant impact on communication, education, business, and entertainment, making information more accessible and transforming various industries.

Ready to Dive Deeper?

If you want to learn more about the Internet and the World Wide Web, here are some resources you can check out:

- **Book:** "Weaving the Web: The Original Design and Ultimate Destiny of the World Wide Web" by Tim Berners-Lee - Dive into the mind of the inventor himself and learn about the origins and future of the World Wide Web.

- **Website:** W3Schools (www.w3schools.com) - This website offers tutorials and references on web development technologies, including HTML, CSS, JavaScript, and more. It's like the Swiss Army knife for web developers.

- **Video:** "The Birth of the Internet" by Computer History Museum - Watch this video on YouTube to learn more about the history and evolution of the Internet, from its humble beginnings to the digital world we know today.

Unconventional Tip: The World Wide Web Time Machine

Ever wondered what a website looked like in the past? Well, the World Wide Web Time Machine (www.archive.org/web) has got you covered. Enter the URL of any website, and it will take you back in time, allowing you to explore archived versions of websites from years ago. It's like a digital time travel machine that lets you witness the evolution of the web. So go ahead and take a trip down memory lane or see how your favorite websites used to look like back in the day!

The Birth of Cloud Computing

In the world of computing, the birth of cloud computing was nothing short of a game-changer. It revolutionized the way individuals and businesses access and utilize computer resources. But how did it all begin? Well, buckle up and get ready for a wild ride through the evolution of cloud computing.

A Glimpse Into the Past

Before we dive into the birth of cloud computing, let's take a brief look at the evolution of computing. It all started with the invention of the first computer, the ENIAC, back in 1945. This massive machine laid the foundation for computing as we know it today.

Fast forward to the 1970s, and we saw the rise of mainframe computers. These hulking beasts were the backbone of enterprise computing, providing processing power and storage for large organizations. However, they came with a hefty price tag and required dedicated IT teams to manage them.

Then came the personal computer (PC) revolution in the 1980s, with companies like Apple and IBM leading the way. Suddenly, computing power was in the hands of individuals, not just large organizations. PCs brought computing to the masses and paved the way for the next big leap in technology.

The Internet and the World Wide Web

In the 1990s, a little innovation called the internet changed everything. The internet connected computers all around the world, enabling the sharing of information and resources on an unprecedented scale. It gave birth to the World Wide Web, a system of interconnected hypertext documents accessible via the internet.

The World Wide Web made it possible to share and access information in a way that was previously unimaginable. It transformed industries like media, communication, and commerce. However, the full potential of the internet was yet to be realized.

Enter Cloud Computing

And then, in the early 2000s, cloud computing burst onto the scene like a bat out of hell. It was a paradigm shift that would disrupt the entire computing landscape. The concept behind cloud computing can be traced back to a visionary computer scientist named John McCarthy, who first proposed the idea of utility computing in the 1960s.

Cloud computing, as we know it today, was popularized by companies like Amazon, Google, and Salesforce. They began offering services that allowed users to access computing resources over the internet on a pay-as-you-go basis. The term "cloud computing" itself is often attributed to a presentation by Google's Eric Schmidt in 2006.

Why Cloud Computing Matters

But why does cloud computing matter? Well, for starters, it brings unprecedented scalability, flexibility, and cost-efficiency to the world of computing. With cloud computing, individuals and businesses no longer need to invest in expensive hardware or software. They can simply tap into the vast pool of resources offered by cloud service providers.

Cloud computing also enables easy access to data and applications from anywhere in the world, as long as you have an internet connection. No longer are you tied to a single physical location or device. This flexibility opens up a world of possibilities for collaboration and remote work.

Furthermore, cloud computing provides a level of redundancy and disaster recovery that was previously only accessible to large corporations with dedicated IT departments. With data stored in multiple geographically dispersed data centers, the risk of data loss due to hardware failure or natural disasters is greatly minimized.

The Fucking Impact of Cloud Computing

The impact of cloud computing has been nothing short of transformative. It has leveled the playing field for startups and small businesses, enabling them to access the same cutting-edge technologies as their larger counterparts. Cloud computing has become the great equalizer, allowing anyone with an idea and an internet connection to build and scale their business without breaking the bank.

Not only has cloud computing revolutionized business operations, but it has also paved the way for groundbreaking technologies such as artificial intelligence (AI), machine learning (ML), and the internet of things (IoT). These technologies thrive on vast amounts of data and computing power, which the cloud provides effortlessly.

Cloud computing has also transformed the way we consume media and entertainment. Streaming services like Netflix and Spotify rely on the cloud to deliver content to millions of users simultaneously. The days of physical media and cumbersome downloads are long gone, thanks to the power of the cloud.

Conclusion

In conclusion, the birth of cloud computing marked a turning point in the history of computing. It emerged from humble beginnings in the minds of visionaries and grew to become an integral part of our digital lives. The impact of cloud computing is undeniable, empowering individuals and businesses with unprecedented access to computing resources, flexibility, and scalability. So buckle up, because the cloud revolution is here to stay, and it's fucking awesome.

Further Reading

1. Armbrust, M., Fox, A., Griffith, R., Joseph, A. D., Katz, R. H., Konwinski, A., ... & Zaharia, M. (2010). A view of cloud computing. Communications of the ACM, 53(4), 50-58.

2. Mell, P., & Grance, T. (2011). The NIST definition of cloud computing. National Institute of Standards and Technology, 7(2), 50.

3. Stonebraker, M., & Cattell, R. (2011). 10 rules for scalable performance in 'simple operation' datastores. Communications of the ACM, 54(6), 72-80.

4. Subashini, S., & Kavitha, V. (2011). A survey on security issues in service delivery models of cloud computing. Journal of network and computer applications, 34(1), 1-11.

5. Armbrust, M., Xin, R. S., Lian, C., Huai, Y., Liu, D., Bradley, J. K., ... & Zaharia, M. (2015). Spark SQL: Relational data processing in spark. ACM SIGMOD Record, 44(2), 12-22.

Why Cloud Computing Matters

In today's fast-paced digital world, cloud computing has emerged as a game-changer. It has revolutionized the way businesses and individuals access and utilize technology resources. But why does cloud computing matter? What makes it so important in the grand scheme of things? In this section, we'll delve into the reasons why cloud computing is such a game-changer and why it has become an integral part of our modern lives.

Boosting Efficiency and Productivity

One of the primary reasons why cloud computing matters is its ability to boost efficiency and productivity. Traditional computing infrastructure often requires a significant upfront investment of time, money, and resources to set up and maintain. On the other hand, cloud computing offers a more flexible and scalable solution, allowing businesses to quickly deploy and scale their IT resources as needed. This means that organizations can focus more on their core competencies rather than spending excessive time and effort on managing IT infrastructure. By leveraging cloud services, businesses can streamline their operations, increase their agility, and ultimately improve their overall efficiency and productivity.

For example, imagine a small e-commerce startup that wants to quickly launch its website without the hassle of purchasing and configuring physical servers. By utilizing cloud computing, they can easily set up a scalable web hosting platform in a matter of minutes. This allows them to focus on building their online store and serving their customers, rather than dealing with the complexities of infrastructure management.

Enabling Innovation and Collaboration

Cloud computing provides a fertile ground for innovation and collaboration. It gives businesses and individuals access to a vast array of services and resources that can be leveraged to develop new and cutting-edge applications. With cloud-based development platforms, teams can collaborate seamlessly, sharing resources and working on projects in real time, regardless of their physical location.

For instance, consider a team of data scientists working on a machine learning project. By harnessing the power of cloud computing and utilizing cloud-based machine learning services, these data scientists can easily access the necessary computational resources and build sophisticated models without investing in expensive hardware. This allows them to focus on developing innovative solutions and driving business growth through data-driven insights.

Enhancing Scalability and Flexibility

Scalability and flexibility are crucial aspects of modern computing. Cloud computing offers both, allowing businesses to scale their resources up or down as demand fluctuates. With traditional infrastructure, scaling resources often involves significant time and financial investments, as well as potential disruptions to operations. Cloud computing eliminates these barriers, offering businesses the ability to scale their IT resources seamlessly and in real time.

For example, imagine a popular social media platform that experiences a sudden surge in user activity due to a viral post. With the scalability provided by cloud computing, the platform can quickly and automatically allocate additional resources to handle the increased traffic, ensuring a smooth user experience. Once the surge subsides, the platform can scale back down to minimize costs. This elasticity allows businesses to respond to changing demands while optimizing resource utilization.

Improving Data Security and Resilience

Data security and resilience are paramount in today's interconnected world. Cloud computing providers invest heavily in robust security measures, implementing advanced encryption, access controls, and threat detection mechanisms to safeguard data. These providers often employ teams of security experts dedicated to monitoring and mitigating potential risks.

Moreover, cloud computing offers data redundancy and disaster recovery capabilities that are often beyond the reach of individual organizations. By leveraging cloud-based backup and recovery services, businesses can protect their critical data from unforeseen events, such as natural disasters or hardware failures. This ensures business continuity and minimizes the risk of data loss.

For example, imagine a healthcare provider that stores patient records and sensitive medical information in the cloud. By utilizing cloud computing, they can benefit from state-of-the-art security measures and automated backup solutions. This allows them to meet strict regulatory requirements, such as HIPAA, while ensuring the privacy and integrity of patient data.

Reducing IT Costs and Complexity

Another compelling reason why cloud computing matters is its potential to reduce IT costs and complexity. Traditional on-premises infrastructure requires significant upfront investments in hardware, software licenses, and maintenance. Additionally, organizations often face unpredictable costs associated with system upgrades, equipment failure, and ongoing maintenance.

Cloud computing, on the other hand, operates on a pay-as-you-go model, allowing businesses to pay only for the resources they use. This eliminates the need for large capital expenditures and enables organizations to scale their IT expenses according to their actual needs. Furthermore, cloud computing removes the burden of infrastructure management, reducing the complexity and freeing up valuable resources that can be allocated to more strategic initiatives.

For instance, consider a medium-sized business that wants to migrate its internal email system to the cloud. By embracing cloud-based email services, the organization can eliminate the need for in-house email servers, along with the associated costs of hardware, software licenses, and maintenance. This not only reduces IT costs but also simplifies email management, allowing employees to focus on their core tasks instead of troubleshooting email issues.

Addressing Environmental Sustainability

In today's increasingly environmentally conscious world, cloud computing has the potential to make a positive impact on sustainability. By consolidating IT resources and improving resource utilization, cloud computing can significantly reduce energy consumption and carbon emissions.

Traditional computing infrastructure often consists of numerous underutilized servers and cooling systems, resulting in excessive energy waste. In contrast, cloud computing optimizes resource allocation, dynamically provisioning and deprovisioning resources as needed. This leads to increased energy efficiency and a smaller carbon footprint.

Moreover, cloud-based services enable businesses to embrace virtualization and reduce their physical infrastructure footprint. This translates into less e-waste generated from the disposal of outdated hardware. Additionally, cloud providers are increasingly investing in renewable energy sources to power their data centers, further reducing the environmental impact.

For example, a multinational corporation that embraces cloud computing can consolidate its global IT operations into a few strategically located data centers. This consolidation reduces energy consumption, minimizes hardware waste, and supports the company's sustainability goals.

In conclusion, cloud computing matters for a multitude of reasons. It boosts efficiency, enables innovation and collaboration, enhances scalability and flexibility, improves data security and resilience, reduces IT costs and complexity, and addresses environmental sustainability. By harnessing the power of cloud computing, businesses and individuals can unlock new opportunities, streamline their operations, and better navigate the ever-evolving digital landscape. Cloud computing has undoubtedly changed the way we live, work, and interact with technology, and its importance will only continue to grow in the future. So buckle up, folks, and get ready to conquer the cloud!

The Fucking Impact of Cloud Computing

Cloud computing has revolutionized the way we live, work, and fuck around on the internet. Its impact on various industries, such as technology, business, and entertainment, has been profound. In this section, we will explore the fucking impact of cloud computing and discuss how it has transformed our digital landscape.

Increased Scalability and Flexibility

One of the major fucking impacts of cloud computing is the ability to scale resources up or down based on demand. In the past, businesses had to invest in expensive hardware and infrastructure to accommodate peak loads of users. This resulted in wasted resources during periods of low demand and limited scalability during peak times.

With cloud computing, businesses can dynamically allocate and manage computing resources in a more efficient manner. Whether it's increasing server capacity to handle heavy traffic during a Black Friday sale or scaling down resources during off-peak hours, the cloud provides the flexibility and scalability businesses need to fuckin' thrive.

For example, consider a streaming service like Netflix. With millions of users streaming movies and TV shows at any given time, the demand for server capacity can fluctuate wildly throughout the day. By utilizing cloud computing, Netflix can easily scale up or down its infrastructure to meet the fuckin' demand. This ensures that users can stream their favorite shows without buffering issues, regardless of peak viewing times.

Cost Reduction and Efficiency

Cloud computing has also made a significant impact on the cost structure of businesses. In the past, companies had to invest heavily in on-premises infrastructure and IT personnel to manage their computing needs. This required substantial upfront capital investments and ongoing operational costs.

Cloud computing eliminates the need for businesses to purchase and maintain their own hardware. Instead, they can leverage the infrastructure of cloud service providers and pay for only the resources they use. This pay-as-you-go model not only reduces upfront costs but also allows businesses to scale their expenses in line with their fuckin' needs. It provides a level of cost predictability that was previously unimaginable.

Moreover, by offloading the responsibility of infrastructure management to cloud service providers, businesses can focus on their core fuckin' competencies and improve overall efficiency. With the cloud taking care of infrastructure maintenance and updates, companies can redirect their resources and efforts towards innovation and fuckin' growth.

Enhanced Collaboration and Accessibility

Cloud computing has transformed the way we collaborate, access information, and work on projects. The ability to store and share files in the cloud has made collaboration more efficient and convenient than ever before.

With cloud-based collaboration tools like Google Docs or Microsoft 365, multiple users can edit the same document in real-time, no matter their geographical location. This eliminates the need for back-and-forth emails and physical document sharing, making collaboration faster and more fuckin' effective.

Cloud computing has also democratized access to information and technology. With cloud-based services, individuals and businesses can now access powerful computing resources that were once prohibitively expensive or complex to manage. Whether it's running complex simulations, analyzing big fuckin' data, or developing artificial intelligence models, the cloud provides the necessary infrastructure and tools to make it fuckin' happen.

For example, consider a small startup that wants to develop a machine learning application. In the past, they would have to invest in expensive hardware and infrastructure to support the development and testing process. With cloud computing, they can easily access pre-configured machine learning environments, use pre-trained models, and scale their resources as they fuckin' grow. This accessibility opens up new possibilities for innovation and levels the playing field for small businesses.

Security and Privacy Concerns

While cloud computing brings numerous benefits, it also raises valid concerns about security and privacy. Storing sensitive data in the cloud means entrusting it to a third-party service provider. This raises questions about data protection, access control, and fuckin' compliance.

Cloud service providers invest heavily in security measures and protocols to protect their customers' data. This includes encryption, firewalls, access controls, and ongoing security fuckin' audits. However, businesses must still assess and address their own security vulnerabilities and ensure that their data is adequately protected.

Additionally, privacy concerns come into play when data is stored in the cloud. Depending on the jurisdiction and the cloud service provider, there may be varying legal and regulatory frameworks that govern data privacy. Businesses must thoroughly understand these implications and take appropriate measures to comply with fuckin' regulations.

Opportunities and Challenges Ahead

The impact of cloud computing is ongoing, and the future is ripe with new possibilities and challenges. As technology continues to evolve, the cloud will play a critical role in enabling emerging technologies such as artificial intelligence, edge computing, quantum fuckin' computing, and blockchain.

Artificial intelligence, for example, heavily relies on computing power and storage capabilities to train complex models. The cloud provides the infrastructure and tools necessary for AI development, democratizing the field and empowering businesses of all sizes to leverage AI fuckin' capabilities.

However, as cloud computing becomes more pervasive, there are challenges to address, such as data sovereignty, internet fuckin' infrastructure limitations, and environmental fuckin' impact. Finding sustainable solutions to these challenges will be crucial in the continued fuckin' growth and adoption of cloud computing.

In summary, the impact of cloud computing cannot be understated. It has revolutionized the way we do business, collaborate, and access information. With increased scalability, cost reduction, and accessibility, the cloud enables businesses to fuckin' thrive in a digital world. However, proper attention must be given to security, privacy, and the challenges that lie ahead. So buckle up, motherfuckers, because cloud computing is here to stay, and it's gonna keep on fuckin' changing the game.

Understanding Cloud Computing

Definition and Characteristics

Before we dive into the nitty-gritty of cloud computing, let's take a moment to define the concept and understand its fundamental characteristics. So, what exactly is cloud computing? Well, it's not some magical thing that floats in the sky and rains data upon us. Cloud computing refers to the delivery of computing services over the internet, providing users with on-demand access to a pool of shared computing resources.

Now, let's break down the key characteristics of cloud computing:

1. **On-Demand Self-Service:** The cloud offers a self-service model, allowing users to access and provision computing resources, such as storage, servers, and software applications, as needed. Gone are the days of having to go through a lengthy procurement process and waiting for IT to set up physical infrastructure.

2. **Broad Network Access:** Cloud services are accessible through various platforms and devices with internet connectivity. Whether you're using a laptop, smartphone, or even a smart fridge (because why not?), as long as you have an internet connection, you can tap into the cloud.

3. **Resource Pooling:** Cloud providers consolidate their computing resources to serve multiple users simultaneously. This pooling allows for efficient utilization of resources, leading to cost savings and improved performance. So, in a way, it's like sharing a Netflix subscription with your friends, but instead of binge-watching shows, you're sharing computing power.

4. **Rapid Elasticity:** Cloud services are designed to scale up or down based on demand. Need more storage space for your cat videos? No problem! The cloud can quickly expand its resources to accommodate your growing collection. Similarly, if you suddenly find yourself becoming less popular and in need of less space, the cloud can scale down just as effortlessly. It's like having the world's most adaptable roommate.

5. **Measured Service:** With cloud computing, you only pay for what you use. Cloud providers track and measure resource consumption, enabling accurate and transparent billing. This pay-as-you-go model eliminates the need for upfront investments in infrastructure and allows for better control over costs. It's like paying only for the amount of sushi you eat at an all-you-can-eat buffet, rather than a fixed price for the entire buffet.

Now that we know the basic definition and characteristics of cloud computing, let's explore the different cloud service models and deployment models in the following sections. And remember, the cloud isn't just some fluffy buzzword—it's a practical, efficient, and powerful tool that has revolutionized the world of computing. So strap in and get ready to conquer the cloud!

Problems and Solutions

Now, let's tackle some common problems related to cloud computing and explore possible solutions to address them.

Problem 1: Data Security

One major concern when it comes to cloud computing is the security of our data. How can we ensure that our sensitive information remains protected in the cloud?

Solution: Cloud providers implement robust security measures to safeguard data from unauthorized access. They use encryption techniques to secure data at rest and in transit. Additionally, they employ firewalls, intrusion detection systems, and physical security measures to protect their data centers. Nevertheless, users must also take precautions by implementing strong access controls, regularly updating their passwords, and being mindful of the sharing and access permissions they grant.

Problem 2: Vendor Lock-In

Locking yourself into a single cloud provider can limit your flexibility and hinder your ability to switch providers in the future. How can you avoid getting stuck with a provider that no longer meets your needs?

Solution: One way to mitigate the risk of vendor lock-in is to adopt a multi-cloud strategy. By diversifying your cloud usage across different providers, you can leverage the unique strengths of each and reduce dependence on a single vendor. This approach allows you to take advantage of the best services offered by different providers and avoid being tied down to one.

Problem 3: Network Latency

In cloud computing, the physical distance between your location and the cloud data center can introduce latency and affect the performance of your applications. How can you deal with this issue?

Solution: One approach to reducing network latency is to utilize content delivery networks (CDNs). CDNs distribute cached copies of your content across multiple servers located in various geographic locations. When users access your content, they are directed to the server closest to them, reducing the time it takes for the data to travel. This helps improve the overall performance and user experience.

Problem 4: Data Transfer Costs

Transferring large volumes of data to and from the cloud can incur significant costs. How can you manage these expenses effectively?

Solution: To minimize data transfer costs, you can consider utilizing cloud providers that offer free or reduced-cost data transfers between their services. For instance, some providers offer discounted rates for transferring data between their storage and compute services within the same region. Additionally, you can optimize data transfer by compressing files, using deduplication techniques, and selecting the appropriate storage tiers based on access frequency.

Example

Let's take a look at a real-world example to help solidify our understanding of cloud computing.

Meet Lexi, a budding entrepreneur who has decided to start her own online boutique. Lexi wants to set up a website to showcase her unique fashion designs and sell her products to customers worldwide. However, she doesn't have the technical knowledge or resources to build and manage her own IT infrastructure. That's where cloud computing comes to the rescue!

Lexi decides to leverage cloud computing services to build and host her e-commerce website. She signs up with a cloud provider that offers website hosting, storage, and database services. With just a few clicks, Lexi creates a virtual server instance, uploads her website files to the cloud, and sets up a scalable database to store her inventory and customer information.

As Lexi's business grows, she experiences a surge in website traffic. Thankfully, the cloud provider automatically scales up her server resources to handle the increased demand. Lexi no longer needs to worry about her website crashing during peak periods. She can focus on designing fabulous clothes while the cloud takes care of the infrastructure.

Moreover, cloud computing allows Lexi to implement robust security measures to protect her customers' personal and payment information. The cloud provider handles all the necessary encryption and compliance standards, giving Lexi peace of mind knowing that her data is in safe hands.

Thanks to the cloud, Lexi's online boutique thrives, as she can easily scale her website and tailor her services to meet customer demands. She pays only for the computing resources she uses, reducing her upfront costs and providing flexibility as her business grows. Cloud computing has become Lexi's secret weapon, allowing her to conquer the fashion world without breaking the bank.

Further Resources

If you're hungry for more knowledge about cloud computing, here are some resources to satisfy your intellectual appetite:

- "Cloud Computing: Concepts, Technology & Architecture" by Thomas Erl, Ricardo Puttini, and Zaigham Mahmood.

- "Architecting the Cloud: Design Decisions for Cloud Computing Service Models" by Michael J. Kavis.

- "Cloud Native Infrastructure: Patterns for Scalable Infrastructure and Applications in a Dynamic Environment" by Justin Garrison and Kris Nova.
- "Cloud Computing - A Practical Approach" by Toby Velte, Anthony T. Velte, and Robert Elsenpeter.

Remember, the cloud is a vast and evolving field, and there's always something new to learn and discover. So keep exploring, stay curious, and let the clouds be your guide on this exhilarating journey.

Cloud Service Models

In this section, we will dive deep into the various cloud service models that are shaping the modern era of computing. Cloud computing offers a range of service models that cater to different needs and requirements. Understanding these models is crucial for anyone looking to leverage the power of the cloud. So, buckle up and let's explore the fucking cloud service models!

Infrastructure as a Service (IaaS)

Infrastructure as a Service (IaaS) is the foundation of cloud computing. It provides virtualized computing resources over the internet. With IaaS, you can gain access to virtual machines, storage, and networking capabilities without the need to invest in physical hardware. Think of it as renting a virtual data center in the cloud.

IaaS offers a high level of flexibility and scalability, allowing you to rapidly provision and scale resources based on your needs. This is particularly useful for organizations that require on-demand computing power or have unpredictable workloads. Additionally, IaaS provides the freedom to customize the infrastructure to meet specific requirements, giving you more control over your cloud environment.

For example, let's say you are a startup with limited resources. Instead of purchasing and maintaining physical servers, you can use an IaaS provider like Amazon Web Services (AWS) or Microsoft Azure to create virtual machines and storage to host your application. This way, you can focus on developing your application without worrying about the underlying infrastructure.

Platform as a Service (PaaS)

Platform as a Service (PaaS) takes the cloud service model a step further by providing a complete development and deployment environment for applications.

With PaaS, you can build, test, and deploy applications without the need to manage the underlying infrastructure. It offers a platform that includes the operating system, programming language runtime, and development tools.

PaaS is especially beneficial for developers and development teams, as it reduces the time and effort required to set up and manage infrastructure components. It allows you to focus on writing code and building applications instead of dealing with infrastructure concerns. PaaS also enables collaboration among team members by providing a centralized platform for development and deployment.

For example, let's say you want to develop a web application. With PaaS, you can use a platform like Google App Engine or Heroku to write your code and deploy it directly to the platform. The platform handles the scaling, load balancing, and infrastructure management, allowing you to focus on building a killer application.

Software as a Service (SaaS)

Software as a Service (SaaS) is the most consumer-oriented cloud service model. It delivers applications over the internet on a subscription basis. With SaaS, you don't need to install or maintain software on your local devices. Instead, you access the software through a web browser or a dedicated application.

SaaS eliminates the need for software installation, updates, and maintenance, as everything is managed by the service provider. It offers a cost-effective way to access applications and services without the need for upfront investment or long-term commitments. SaaS applications are typically accessible from multiple devices, making them highly convenient and accessible.

Think of popular SaaS offerings like Microsoft Office 365, Google Workspace (formerly G Suite), and Salesforce. These applications provide a range of productivity tools, collaboration features, and business applications that can be accessed from any device with an internet connection.

Choosing the Right Cloud Service Model

Now that we have explored the three cloud service models, you might be wondering which one is the right fit for your needs. The answer depends on various factors such as your technical requirements, development capabilities, and level of control you desire.

If you require complete control over the infrastructure and want to manage the operating system, runtime, and applications, IaaS might be the best option. This model provides the most flexibility but requires more technical expertise.

UNDERSTANDING CLOUD COMPUTING

On the other hand, if you are primarily focused on developing and deploying applications without the hassle of managing infrastructure, PaaS is a great choice. It offers a ready-to-use platform for development and deployment, allowing you to focus on creating innovative applications.

For non-technical users or organizations that require ready-to-use applications without the need for installation and maintenance, SaaS is the way to go. It provides access to a wide range of applications and services without the burden of managing infrastructure and software.

Remember, it's not a one-size-fits-all scenario. It's important to evaluate your specific requirements and choose the cloud service model that aligns with your goals and constraints.

Summary

In this section, we have explored the three main cloud service models: Infrastructure as a Service (IaaS), Platform as a Service (PaaS), and Software as a Service (SaaS). Each model offers a unique set of benefits and caters to different needs.

IaaS provides virtualized computing resources, allowing you to build and scale your infrastructure as needed. PaaS offers a complete development and deployment platform, making it easier for developers to build and deploy applications. SaaS delivers applications over the internet, eliminating the need for software installation and maintenance.

Choosing the right cloud service model depends on your technical requirements, level of control, and development capabilities. By understanding the differences between these models, you can make an informed decision and leverage the power of the cloud in the most effective way.

So, whether you choose to deploy your own infrastructure, utilize a development platform, or access ready-to-use applications, the cloud service models have got you covered. Embrace the flexibility, scalability, and convenience they offer, and let the cloud fucking empower your next big idea!

Infrastructure as a Service (IaaS)

Infrastructure as a Service (IaaS) is one of the fundamental models of cloud computing. It provides virtualized computing resources over the internet, allowing users to rent and manage virtual machines (VMs), storage, and networks. In this section, we will dive deep into the world of IaaS and explore its key components, benefits, challenges, and real-world examples.

The Basics of IaaS

At its core, IaaS delivers on-demand access to virtualized infrastructure components, eliminating the need for physical hardware and reducing operational costs. It acts as a foundation for higher-level cloud services, enabling businesses to focus on managing applications and data, rather than worrying about the underlying infrastructure.

The key components of IaaS include:

- **Virtual Machines (VMs):** VMs are the building blocks of IaaS. They mimic traditional physical servers, running operating systems and applications. Users can create, configure, and manage VMs based on their requirements, scaling up or down as needed.

- **Storage:** IaaS provides scalable and flexible storage options. Users can choose between different storage types, including block storage and object storage. Block storage offers raw storage capacity, while object storage is ideal for storing unstructured data like images and videos.

- **Networking:** Networking in IaaS encompasses virtual networks, load balancers, firewalls, and other network-related services. Users can define network configurations, establish secure connections, and control traffic within their virtual infrastructure.

Benefits of IaaS

IaaS offers several advantages that make it an attractive option for businesses. Let's explore some of these benefits:

1. **Scalability:** With IaaS, scaling resources becomes a breeze. Businesses can effortlessly add or remove virtual machines, storage, or networks based on their needs. This elasticity allows them to respond quickly to changes in demand and optimize resource utilization.

2. **Cost Efficiency:** Traditional on-premises infrastructure requires significant upfront investment and ongoing maintenance costs. IaaS eliminates these capital expenses by offering a pay-as-you-go model. Businesses can rent resources on an hourly or monthly basis, paying only for what they use.

3. **Agility and Speed:** Provisioning and deploying infrastructure resources in IaaS is quick and automated, saving time and effort. With just a few clicks, users can have virtual machines up and running, reducing the time-to-market for applications and services.

4. **Global Availability:** IaaS providers have data centers located worldwide, allowing businesses to host their applications closer to their target audience. This global coverage ensures low-latency and better performance for users accessing applications from different regions.

5. **Disaster Recovery:** IaaS offers built-in disaster recovery capabilities. Users can replicate their infrastructure across multiple data centers, ensuring redundancy and business continuity. In the event of a failure, services can seamlessly failover to alternative locations.

Challenges of IaaS

While IaaS brings many benefits, it also presents certain challenges that need to be addressed:

1. **Security and Compliance:** As data and applications are moved to the cloud, security and compliance become paramount. Businesses must ensure that their cloud infrastructure meets industry standards and regulations. Establishing robust security measures, such as encryption and access controls, is crucial to protect sensitive information.

2. **Network Connectivity:** For optimal performance and reliability, IaaS relies heavily on network connectivity. Organizations must have robust internet connections and consider backup options in case of network disruptions. Additionally, latency and bandwidth limitations can impact the performance of certain applications.

3. **Vendor Lock-In:** Once an organization commits to a specific IaaS provider, it can become challenging to switch to another provider. Vendor-specific APIs, management tools, and services can make migration complex and costly. It is important to carefully evaluate vendor-lock in risks before fully adopting an IaaS solution.

4. **Data Transfer Costs:** Moving large amounts of data to and from the cloud can incur significant costs due to data transfer fees. Businesses need to consider these costs when planning their data migration strategies and ongoing data usage.

Real-World Examples

Let's explore two real-world examples of IaaS implementations:

Example 1: Netflix

Netflix, the popular streaming platform, utilizes IaaS to deliver its content to millions of users worldwide. By leveraging the scalability and flexibility of IaaS, Netflix can handle massive amounts of video streaming traffic, adjusting its infrastructure based on demand. It spins up additional VMs to distribute the load and employs scalable storage to store its vast library of movies and TV shows. This allows Netflix to deliver a seamless streaming experience to its users, regardless of the number of concurrent viewers.

Example 2: Airbnb

Airbnb, the online marketplace for short-term rentals, relies on IaaS to power its platform. With IaaS, Airbnb can easily scale its infrastructure to handle peak booking periods, ensuring a smooth user experience. By using VMs and storage services, Airbnb hosts can list their properties and manage bookings securely. IaaS also allows Airbnb to store and process large amounts of data, enabling personalized recommendations and analytics to improve its services.

Conclusion

In this section, we explored the concept of Infrastructure as a Service (IaaS) in cloud computing. We learned about its key components, benefits, challenges, and real-world examples. IaaS provides businesses with the flexibility, scalability, and cost efficiency required to focus on core operations and drive innovation. However, it is essential to address security concerns, network connectivity, and vendor lock-in risks when adopting an IaaS solution. With the right planning and execution, IaaS can empower businesses to conquer the cloud and unlock new possibilities.

Platform as a Service (PaaS)

In the realm of cloud computing, Platform as a Service (PaaS) represents a significant shift in the way developers build and deploy applications. PaaS offers a platform and a set of tools to simplify the process of developing, testing, and deploying software applications without the hassle of managing the underlying infrastructure.

Defining PaaS

PaaS is a cloud computing model that provides a complete development and deployment environment for applications. It abstracts away the complexities of infrastructure management, allowing developers to focus on writing code and delivering innovative solutions. With PaaS, developers have access to a set of preconfigured tools and services that enable them to build, test, and deploy applications rapidly.

At its core, PaaS provides a runtime environment where developers can run their applications, along with a variety of services, such as databases, messaging systems, and integrated development environments (IDEs). These services are readily available, eliminating the need for developers to provision and manage them independently. PaaS offers an integrated and streamlined approach to application development and deployment.

Key Characteristics of PaaS

To better understand PaaS, let's explore its key characteristics:

- **Abstraction of Infrastructure:** PaaS abstracts the underlying hardware and infrastructure, allowing developers to focus solely on application development. This abstraction reduces the complexity associated with infrastructure management and accelerates the development process.

- **Automated Provisioning:** PaaS automatically provisions the necessary resources and services required to run an application. This automated provisioning saves time and effort, enabling developers to rapidly deploy their applications.

- **Scalability and Elasticity:** PaaS provides built-in scalability and elasticity, allowing applications to scale up or down based on demand. Developers can easily scale their applications without worrying about infrastructure limitations, thus ensuring optimal performance and cost-efficiency.

- **Multi-Tenancy:** PaaS enables multiple users or organizations to share the same platform while keeping their resources isolated. This multi-tenancy feature allows for efficient resource utilization and cost-sharing.

- **Built-in Services:** PaaS offers a wide range of built-in services, such as databases, messaging systems, and identity management, that developers can leverage without the need for additional configuration or management. These services simplify development and enhance the functionality of applications.

Benefits and Use Cases of PaaS

PaaS offers several benefits to developers and businesses, making it a popular choice for application development. Let's explore some of these benefits and real-world use cases:

- **Rapid Application Development:** PaaS significantly reduces the time required to develop and deploy applications. With preconfigured services and tools, developers can focus on coding, resulting in faster time-to-market.

- **Cost-Efficiency:** PaaS eliminates the need for upfront infrastructure investments and reduces ongoing maintenance costs. Developers can pay only for the resources and services they need, leading to cost savings and improved budget management.

- **Collaboration and Efficiency:** PaaS fosters collaboration among developers by providing a centralized platform for code sharing, version control, and continuous integration and deployment. This collaboration enhances productivity and accelerates the development process.

- **Scalability and Flexibility:** PaaS enables seamless scalability, allowing developers to easily scale up or down based on application demand. This flexibility ensures optimal performance and cost efficiency, particularly for applications with varying workloads.

- **Real-time Data Analytics:** PaaS offers built-in analytics services that enable developers to analyze and gain insights from large and complex datasets. This capability is especially useful for applications dealing with real-time data processing, such as IoT and big data analytics.

- **Mobile Application Development:** PaaS provides tools and services specifically designed for mobile application development. It offers features like cross-platform support, backend integration, and push notifications, making it easier to build and deliver high-quality mobile apps.

Real-world examples of PaaS in action include:

- **Heroku:** Heroku is a cloud platform that enables developers to deploy, manage, and scale applications easily. It supports multiple programming languages and provides a wide range of integrated services, such as data storage, caching, and monitoring.

- **Google App Engine:** Google App Engine is a fully-managed PaaS offering from Google Cloud Platform. It allows developers to build and deploy applications using popular programming languages like Java, Python, and Node.js. App Engine automatically handles infrastructure provisioning and scaling.

- **Salesforce Lightning Platform:** Designed for building enterprise applications, the Salesforce Lightning Platform provides a suite of tools and services for rapid application development. It includes features like database integration, workflow automation, and mobile app development.

Caveats and Considerations

While PaaS offers numerous benefits, it is essential to consider certain caveats and factors before adopting a PaaS solution:

- **Vendor Lock-In:** PaaS solutions vary in terms of features, supported programming languages, and ecosystem. Locking yourself into a specific PaaS provider may limit your flexibility and portability in the long run. It is crucial to assess the compatibility of your application and evaluate options for migration and integration.

- **Dependency on Internet Connectivity:** PaaS relies on Internet connectivity for development and deployment. In case of unstable or slow connections, this dependency can hinder productivity and impact the user experience. It is prudent to assess the stability and reliability of your Internet connection before relying heavily on cloud-based development platforms.

- **Security and Compliance:** When using PaaS, your applications and data reside on the cloud provider's infrastructure. It is crucial to consider security measures, such as data encryption, access control, and compliance with relevant regulations, to ensure the confidentiality and integrity of your data.

- **Application Compatibility:** PaaS environments may have certain limitations or restrictions that can impact your application design and architecture. It is important to understand the platform's capabilities and constraints to ensure that your application can run effectively within the PaaS environment.

Conclusion

Platform as a Service (PaaS) revolutionizes the way developers build, test, and deploy applications. With its abstraction of infrastructure, automated provisioning, and built-in services, PaaS offers a streamlined and efficient development environment.

The benefits of PaaS, including rapid application development, cost efficiency, collaboration, and flexibility, make it an attractive choice for modern software development. However, it is crucial to consider the caveats and factors associated with PaaS before adopting a specific solution.

PaaS providers like Heroku, Google App Engine, and Salesforce Lightning Platform offer ready-to-use platforms that empower developers to focus on crafting innovative applications. By leveraging the power of PaaS, developers can conquer new horizons and embrace the limitless possibilities of cloud computing.

Software as a Service (SaaS)

Software as a Service (SaaS) is a cloud service model that provides users with access to software applications over the internet. With SaaS, users don't need to install or maintain the software on their own devices. Instead, they can access and use the software directly through a web browser, making it convenient and accessible from anywhere.

Definition and Characteristics

SaaS is one of the three major cloud service models, along with Infrastructure as a Service (IaaS) and Platform as a Service (PaaS). Unlike IaaS and PaaS, which provide users with infrastructure or development tools, SaaS focuses on delivering fully functional software applications.

The key characteristics of SaaS include:

1. **Centralized hosting:** With SaaS, the software application is centrally hosted on servers in the cloud. This means that users don't need to worry about installation, maintenance, or hardware requirements. The cloud provider takes care of all the technical aspects, allowing users to focus on using the software.

2. **Pay-per-use pricing:** SaaS typically follows a subscription-based pricing model, where users pay a recurring fee based on their usage. This pay-as-you-go approach offers flexibility and cost-effectiveness, as users only pay for what they need and can easily scale up or down as required.

3. **Multi-tenancy:** SaaS providers serve multiple customers (tenants) from a single software instance, utilizing shared resources efficiently. This enables economies of scale, reducing costs for both the provider and the users.

4. **Automatic updates:** SaaS applications are continuously updated by the provider, ensuring that users always have access to the latest features and improvements. This eliminates the need for users to manually update the software and ensures a consistent experience across all users.

5. **Accessibility and collaboration:** SaaS applications can be accessed through a web browser on various devices, including laptops, smartphones, and tablets. This

# UNDERSTANDING CLOUD COMPUTING

accessibility allows for seamless collaboration and remote work, as users can access the software from anywhere with an internet connection.

Benefits and Use Cases

SaaS offers several benefits that make it attractive for both individuals and businesses:

1. **Lower upfront costs:** Since users don't need to purchase or maintain software licenses, hardware, or infrastructure, SaaS significantly reduces upfront costs. This makes it accessible even for individuals and small businesses with limited budgets.

2. **Scalability and flexibility:** SaaS allows users to easily scale their software usage up or down based on their needs. As the user base grows or business requirements change, SaaS applications can quickly adapt and provide the necessary resources.

3. **Faster deployment:** With SaaS, users can start using a software application immediately, without the need for installation or configuration. This enables faster deployment, reducing the time and effort required to get up and running.

4. **Simplified maintenance and updates:** SaaS providers handle all maintenance, updates, and security patches, freeing users from these tasks. This allows users to focus on their core business activities, while the provider ensures the software is always up to date and secure.

The use cases for SaaS span a wide range of industries and applications. Here are a few examples:

1. **Customer Relationship Management (CRM):** SaaS CRM applications, such as Salesforce, provide businesses with a centralized platform for managing customer interactions and optimizing sales processes. These applications offer features like lead management, contact tracking, sales forecasting, and customer support, enhancing customer relationship management efforts.

2. **Human Resources Management (HRM):** SaaS HRM solutions, such as Workday, enable organizations to streamline their HR processes, including employee onboarding, payroll management, performance tracking, and training. These applications help improve HR efficiency, ensure compliance, and enhance employee experience.

3. **Collaboration and Communication:** SaaS collaboration tools, like Google Workspace (formerly G Suite) and Microsoft 365, provide businesses with cloud-based productivity suites that enable seamless collaboration and communication among team members. These tools offer features like document sharing, real-time editing, video conferencing, and project management, facilitating remote teamwork and improving productivity.

4. **Enterprise Resource Planning (ERP):** SaaS ERP solutions, such as NetSuite, integrate and manage various business processes, including finance, supply chain, manufacturing, and inventory management. These applications help organizations streamline operations, improve efficiency, and gain better visibility into their business performance.

Challenges and Considerations

While SaaS offers numerous benefits, there are also some challenges and considerations to keep in mind:

1. **Data security and privacy:** Storing sensitive data in the cloud raises concerns about security and privacy. It's crucial to choose a reputable SaaS provider that implements robust security measures, including data encryption, access controls, and regular security audits.

2. **Vendor lock-in:** Moving from one SaaS provider to another can be challenging, as it involves transferring data, training users on a new platform, and potentially disrupting business operations. It's essential to carefully evaluate the terms and conditions of the service agreement and consider the long-term implications before committing to a SaaS solution.

3. **Availability and reliability:** Since SaaS applications rely on the internet for access, any disruptions in connectivity can impact the availability and reliability of the software. It's crucial to choose a reliable SaaS provider that offers robust service level agreements (SLAs) and has a proven track record of uptime and performance.

4. **Customization limitations:** SaaS applications are typically designed to meet the needs of a broad user base. While they offer a wide range of features and configurations, they may not be as customizable as on-premises software solutions. It's essential to assess the customization options and determine if they align with specific business requirements.

In conclusion, Software as a Service (SaaS) is a cloud service model that provides users with access to software applications over the internet. With its centralized hosting, pay-per-use pricing, and automatic updates, SaaS offers benefits such as lower upfront costs, scalability, flexibility, and simplified maintenance. However, organizations must also consider challenges related to data security, vendor lock-in, availability, and customization limitations. By carefully evaluating these factors, businesses can leverage the power of SaaS to drive productivity, efficiency, and innovation.

Exercise: Consider a small e-commerce business that is experiencing rapid growth. They are currently using an on-premises inventory management system but are struggling to keep up with the demands of their expanding customer base.

Explain how adopting a SaaS inventory management solution can benefit the business and help them overcome their challenges. Provide specific examples of features and functionalities that the SaaS solution can offer to improve their inventory management processes.

Cloud Deployment Models

Cloud deployment models define how cloud services are delivered and accessed. Different deployment models offer various levels of control, security, and customization to meet the unique needs of organizations. In this section, we will explore four primary cloud deployment models: public cloud, private cloud, hybrid cloud, and community cloud.

Public Cloud

The public cloud is like the free-spirited hippie of cloud computing. It is a shared infrastructure that is available to the general public over the internet. Public cloud providers, like Amazon Web Services (AWS), Microsoft Azure, and Google Cloud Platform (GCP), own and manage the underlying infrastructure, allowing organizations to focus on using cloud services without worrying about infrastructure maintenance.

Public cloud computing offers several advantages. First, it provides scalability and elasticity, allowing organizations to easily scale their resources up or down based on demand. This makes it ideal for startups and small businesses with unpredictable workloads or limited budgets. Second, it offers cost efficiency, as organizations only pay for the resources they use on a pay-as-you-go basis. Third, it offers a wide range of services, such as virtual machines, storage, and databases, allowing organizations to meet their diverse IT requirements.

However, the public cloud also has its drawbacks. One major concern is security and data privacy. Since the infrastructure is shared among multiple organizations, there is a risk of data breaches and unauthorized access. Organizations must carefully consider and implement security measures to protect their sensitive data. Another concern is vendor lock-in, where organizations become dependent on a specific cloud provider and face challenges in migrating to another provider or bringing services back in-house.

Private Cloud

If the public cloud is the wild hippie, then the private cloud is the controlled and secure fortress of cloud computing. Private cloud infrastructure is dedicated to a single organization and can be physically located on-premises or hosted by a third-party service provider. It offers greater control, security, and customization compared to the public cloud.

Private clouds are favored by organizations that have stringent security and compliance requirements or need complete control over their infrastructure. For example, government agencies, financial institutions, and healthcare organizations often choose private clouds to ensure the privacy and confidentiality of their data. Private clouds also provide greater flexibility, allowing organizations to customize the infrastructure and services to their specific needs.

However, building and managing a private cloud requires significant upfront investments in hardware, software, and expertise. Organizations need to have the necessary resources and capabilities to maintain the infrastructure, ensure high availability, and handle scalability. Additionally, private clouds may not offer the same level of cost efficiency, scalability, and service variety as the public cloud.

Hybrid Cloud

The hybrid cloud is like the perfect blend of flavors in a smoothie. It combines the best of both public and private clouds, allowing organizations to leverage the benefits of each deployment model. In a hybrid cloud, organizations can use a mix of public and private cloud services, connected through secure and encrypted connections.

The hybrid cloud offers the flexibility to choose the most suitable environment for different workloads and data. For example, organizations can store sensitive customer data in their private cloud for enhanced security while using the public cloud for scalable web applications. This approach ensures data protection and regulatory compliance while taking advantage of the cost-effectiveness and scalability offered by the public cloud.

One key challenge in implementing a hybrid cloud is ensuring seamless integration and interoperability between the public and private cloud environments. Organizations need to establish robust connectivity, implement appropriate security measures, and manage data storage and migration effectively.

Community Cloud

The community cloud is a gathering place for organizations with shared interests and common goals. It is a cloud infrastructure shared among multiple organizations with similar requirements, such as industry-specific regulations or standards. In a community cloud, the underlying infrastructure and services are hosted and managed by a third-party provider.

Community clouds are often adopted by organizations within the same industry, such as healthcare or education, to address shared challenges and compliance requirements. By pooling resources, organizations can achieve cost savings, gain access to specialized services, and collaborate more effectively. For example, healthcare organizations can share patient data securely in a community cloud while complying with privacy regulations.

However, community clouds require strong collaboration, trust, and governance among participating organizations. They also face similar security and data privacy challenges as the public cloud due to shared infrastructure.

Multi-Cloud Orchestration

To achieve true cloud nirvana, organizations are increasingly adopting multi-cloud orchestration. This involves leveraging services and resources from multiple cloud providers, seamlessly integrating them into a single unified architecture.

Multi-cloud orchestration enables organizations to optimize their cloud strategy by selecting the best services and features from different providers. It also reduces vendor lock-in, enhances resilience by avoiding single points of failure, and ensures efficient resource allocation.

However, managing and orchestrating multiple cloud providers can be complex and challenging. Organizations need to consider factors such as data integration, service interoperability, security management, and consistent governance across cloud environments.

In summary, the deployment models of cloud computing offer different levels of control, security, and customization. Public clouds provide scalability and cost efficiency but require careful attention to security and data integrity. Private clouds offer greater control and security but require significant investments and expertise. Hybrid clouds combine the benefits of public and private clouds, while community clouds enable collaboration among organizations with shared interests. Finally, multi-cloud orchestration allows organizations to leverage the strengths of multiple cloud providers. The key is to choose the deployment model(s) that align with organizational goals, requirements, and resources.

Public Cloud

In the exhilarating world of cloud computing, the public cloud is like the ultimate beach party. It's the place where everyone gathers to have a good time, share resources, and enjoy the benefits of a communal atmosphere. In this section, we'll dive into the details of what the public cloud is all about, why it's so popular, and its implications for businesses and individuals.

Definition and Characteristics

The public cloud is a service provided by third-party cloud providers to users over the internet. It is a multi-tenant environment, meaning that multiple users share the same infrastructure, hardware, and software resources. This shared nature of the public cloud brings many advantages, such as cost savings, scalability, and easy access.

One of the main characteristics of the public cloud is its elasticity. Just like a rubber band, it can be stretched to accommodate varying workloads and demands. Whether you need to scale up during peak periods or scale down during lulls, the public cloud has got your back. It enables you to dynamically provision and deprovision resources as needed, allowing for efficient resource utilization and cost optimization.

Another defining feature of the public cloud is its accessibility. As long as you have an internet connection, you have the power of the cloud at your fingertips. This accessibility makes it possible for individuals and organizations to access their applications, data, and services from anywhere in the world, without being confined to a specific location or device.

Benefits of Public Cloud

The public cloud offers a myriad of benefits that are enticing for both individuals and businesses. Let's take a look at some of these benefits and see why the public cloud is the life of the party:

1. **Cost Savings:** Using the public cloud eliminates the need for upfront infrastructure investments, as you only pay for what you use. This pay-as-you-go model allows you to avoid the hefty price tag that comes with purchasing, maintaining, and upgrading your own hardware. You can redirect those savings to other areas of your business or simply enjoy the financial flexibility.

2. **Scalability:** The public cloud is like a giant trampoline that can bounce your workload up and down effortlessly. It enables you to scale your resources up or down based on demand, ensuring that you have enough capacity to handle workload spikes and avoid overprovisioning during slower periods. This scalability empowers businesses to respond quickly to changing market conditions and customer demands.

3. **Global Reach:** With the public cloud, distance is no longer a barrier. Cloud providers have data centers scattered across the globe, allowing you to deploy your applications closer to your customers or target specific geographic regions. This global reach enhances performance, reduces latency, and improves user experience, enabling you to cater to a broader audience.

4. **Reliability and Availability:** Public cloud providers invest heavily in building robust and highly available infrastructure. They have redundant systems, backup procedures, and disaster recovery plans in place to ensure that your applications and data are protected and accessible at all times. You can say goodbye to those sleepless nights worrying about server crashes or data loss.

5. **Innovation Acceleration:** The public cloud is a hotbed of innovation. Cloud providers offer a wide range of services, tools, and APIs that can empower developers to build, deploy, and scale applications faster and more efficiently. From artificial intelligence and machine learning to big data analytics and serverless computing, the public cloud provides a playground for exploring cutting-edge technologies.

6. **Flexibility and Agility:** The public cloud provides the flexibility and agility to adapt to evolving business needs. You can quickly spin up new instances, test new ideas, experiment with different configurations, and fail fast without incurring significant costs or downtime. This flexibility allows you to stay ahead of the competition and respond rapidly to market changes.

Use Cases and Examples

The public cloud has found its way into countless industries and use cases, revolutionizing the way we work, collaborate, and consume information. Here are a few examples to illustrate the versatility and power of the public cloud:

1. **Startups and Small Businesses:** For startups and small businesses with limited financial resources, the public cloud is a game-changer. It enables them to launch quickly, scale rapidly, and compete with larger players without breaking the bank. Whether it's hosting a website, running an e-commerce store, or analyzing customer data, the public cloud provides the necessary infrastructure and tools to get up and running in no time.

2. **Content Delivery and Media Streaming:** The public cloud plays a crucial role in delivering content to millions of users worldwide. Streaming services like Netflix and Spotify rely on the public cloud to store, process, and distribute massive amounts of media files. By leveraging the scalability and global reach of the public cloud, these services can offer seamless, on-demand access to content anytime, anywhere.

3. **Data Analytics and Big Data:** The public cloud provides a perfect platform for crunching numbers and deriving insights from vast amounts of data. Companies can offload their data analytics workloads to the public cloud, taking advantage of its scalable computing power and managed database services. From running complex queries to running machine learning algorithms, the public cloud enables businesses to extract value from their data efficiently.

4. **Collaboration and Productivity Tools:** Cloud-based productivity tools like Google Workspace and Microsoft 365 have become the go-to solution for individuals and organizations. These tools allow users to create, edit, and share documents, spreadsheets, and presentations in real-time, regardless of their location. The public cloud provides a robust and secure platform for collaboration, boosting productivity and streamlining workflows.

5. **Gaming and Virtual Reality:** The public cloud is leveling up the gaming experience. Game developers can utilize cloud-based game servers and virtual machines to offload computationally-intensive tasks, such as physics simulations and game rendering. Cloud gaming services like Google Stadia and Amazon Luna allow users to play graphics-intensive games on low-end devices, transcending the limitations of hardware capabilities.

Caveats and Considerations

As with any party, there are a few things to be mindful of when it comes to the public cloud. Here are some caveats and considerations to keep in mind:

1. **Security and Compliance:** While cloud providers invest heavily in security measures, the responsibility for securing your data and applications ultimately rests with you. It's essential to understand the shared responsibility model and implement appropriate security controls to protect sensitive information. Compliance requirements, such as GDPR or HIPAA, may also influence your choice of cloud provider and services.

2. **Vendor Lock-In:** While the public cloud offers flexibility, it's important to consider the potential for vendor lock-in. Once you start building your applications on a specific cloud platform, moving to another provider may involve significant time, resources, and rearchitecting. It's advisable to design your applications with portability in mind and avoid proprietary lock-in situations.

3. **Data Transfer Costs:** Although the public cloud provides cost savings in many areas, data transfer costs can add up quickly, especially for large data volumes or inter-region transfers. It's important to understand the pricing models and data transfer policies of your cloud provider to avoid any unpleasant surprises on your bill.

4. **Downtime and Outages:** While public cloud providers strive for high availability, downtime and outages can still occur. It's essential to have appropriate backup and disaster recovery strategies in place to minimize the impact of service interruptions. Regularly testing your disaster recovery mechanisms is crucial to ensure business continuity.

5. **Performance and Latency:** The public cloud's performance and latency may vary depending on factors such as network connectivity, physical distance, and the provider's infrastructure. If your applications require extremely low latency or have specific performance requirements, you may need to consider alternative solutions, such as edge computing or hybrid cloud setups.

Conclusion

The public cloud is undeniably the life of the party in the world of cloud computing. Its elasticity, accessibility, and cost savings have dramatically transformed how individuals and businesses access and deploy their applications and services. From startups to global enterprises, the allure of the public cloud's scalability, innovation, and global reach continues to attract a diverse range of users. However, it's crucial to consider the security, vendor lock-in, and potential costs associated with the public cloud. By understanding its benefits and limitations, you can make informed decisions and leverage the full power of the public cloud to fuel your success.

Now that we've explored the vibrant world of the public cloud, let's turn our attention to its more discreet cousin, the private cloud, in the next section. Get ready to dive into the exclusive and personalized realm of cloud computing!

Private Cloud

Private cloud, also known as an internal or on-premises cloud, offers the same benefits and features as a public cloud but is dedicated solely to a single organization. In a private cloud, the infrastructure and resources are owned and operated by the organization itself, providing more control and customization options.

Private clouds are often implemented by large organizations that have specific security, compliance, or performance requirements that cannot be met by public cloud providers. These organizations may have sensitive data or critical applications that require a higher level of security and privacy, making a private cloud an ideal solution.

Architecture

The architecture of a private cloud is similar to that of a public cloud, leveraging virtualization and resource pooling to provide scalable and flexible infrastructure. However, in a private cloud, the infrastructure is located within the organization's own data centers.

A private cloud typically consists of the following components:

- **Physical Servers:** These are the underlying hardware servers that provide computing power and storage resources. These servers are owned and managed by the organization and are responsible for running the virtualization software.

- **Virtualization Software:** This software, such as VMware or Hyper-V, enables the creation and management of virtual machines (VMs) on the physical servers. It allows for the efficient utilization of resources by partitioning a single physical server into multiple virtual servers.

- **Hypervisors:** These are the software or firmware components that enable the creation and management of virtual machines. Hypervisors provide isolation, security, and resource allocation for each virtual machine.

- **Storage:** Private clouds typically have dedicated storage systems that provide persistent storage for virtual machines and applications. This storage may be in the form of network-attached storage (NAS) or storage area network (SAN) devices.

- **Networking:** Private clouds require a robust and secure network infrastructure to connect the physical servers, storage systems, and virtual machines. This includes switches, routers, firewalls, and other networking equipment.

- **Management Software:** Private clouds utilize management software that allows administrators to provision, manage, and monitor the infrastructure and resources. This software provides a user-friendly interface for managing virtual machines, storage, and network configurations.

Advantages

One of the main advantages of a private cloud is the increased level of control and security it provides. Since the infrastructure is owned and operated by the

UNDERSTANDING CLOUD COMPUTING

organization, they have complete control over the entire environment. This control allows organizations to customize and configure the infrastructure to meet their specific needs.

Private clouds also offer improved data privacy and security. Companies that deal with sensitive data, such as healthcare or financial institutions, may have regulatory or compliance requirements that dictate the need for a private cloud. It allows them to maintain full control over their data and ensure it remains secure within their own data centers.

Furthermore, private clouds can offer better performance and latency compared to public clouds. By having dedicated resources, organizations can optimize their infrastructure to meet the unique needs of their applications. This can result in improved performance, lower latency, and better user experiences.

Challenges

However, private clouds also come with their own set of challenges. One of the main challenges is the upfront cost and ongoing maintenance. Organizations need to invest in the necessary hardware, software, and networking equipment to set up and maintain the private cloud environment. This can be a significant financial investment, especially for smaller organizations.

Additionally, private clouds require skilled IT professionals to manage and maintain the infrastructure. Organizations need to have a dedicated team or partner with a managed service provider who has expertise in private cloud technologies. This can be a challenge for organizations that do not have the resources or expertise in-house.

Scalability is another challenge for private clouds. Unlike public clouds, which can quickly scale up or down based on demand, private clouds have limited scalability options. Organizations need to carefully plan and allocate resources to ensure they can handle peak workloads without experiencing performance issues.

Real-World Example

Let's consider the example of a large financial institution that deals with sensitive customer data. Due to regulatory requirements and the need for strict data privacy and security, the institution decides to implement a private cloud.

They set up a private cloud infrastructure within their own data centers, consisting of physical servers, virtualization software, storage systems, networking equipment, and management software. They configure their private cloud to meet their specific security and compliance standards, ensuring that customer data remains secure.

With their private cloud, the financial institution can create and manage virtual machines, allocate resources as needed, and scale their infrastructure to handle peak workloads. They have complete control and ownership over their infrastructure, allowing them to customize it to meet their unique requirements.

The private cloud provides the institution with improved data privacy, security, and performance compared to a public cloud. It allows them to maintain compliance with regulations, protect customer data, and ensure smooth and reliable operations.

Additional Resources

To further explore the concept of private clouds, the following resources are recommended:

- **Book:** "Private Cloud Computing: Consolidation, Virtualization, and Service-Oriented Infrastructure" by Stephen R. Smoot and Nam K. Tan.

- **Article:** "Private Cloud vs. Public Cloud: What's the Difference?" by Cisco Systems.

- **Website:** The OpenStack Foundation (https://www.openstack.org) provides information, resources, and open-source software for building private and public clouds.

Summary

Private cloud offers organizations the benefits and features of cloud computing while providing increased control, customization, and security. It is ideal for organizations that have stringent security, compliance, and performance requirements. By implementing a private cloud, organizations can have full ownership and control over their infrastructure, ensuring the privacy and security of their data. However, private clouds require upfront investment and ongoing maintenance, as well as skilled IT professionals for managing the infrastructure. Despite these challenges, private clouds offer improved data privacy, security, and performance compared to public clouds.

Exercises

1. **Question:** What is the main difference between a public cloud and a private cloud?

Answer: The main difference between a public cloud and a private cloud is ownership and control. In a public cloud, the infrastructure is owned and operated by a cloud service provider and is shared among multiple organizations. In contrast, a private cloud is solely dedicated to a single organization, and the infrastructure is owned and operated by that organization.

2. **Question:** What are the advantages of a private cloud?

   Answer: The advantages of a private cloud include increased control, customization, security, and performance. Organizations have complete control over the infrastructure, allowing them to customize it to meet their specific needs. Private clouds also provide better data privacy and security, making them suitable for organizations with sensitive information. Additionally, private clouds can offer better performance and lower latency compared to public clouds due to dedicated resources.

3. **Question:** What are the challenges of implementing a private cloud?

   Answer: The challenges of implementing a private cloud include upfront cost and ongoing maintenance, the need for skilled IT professionals, and limited scalability. It requires a significant financial investment to set up and maintain the infrastructure, which can be a challenge for some organizations. Additionally, organizations need skilled IT professionals to manage the infrastructure and ensure its smooth operation. Lastly, private clouds have limited scalability options compared to public clouds and require careful resource allocation to handle peak workloads.

Unconventional Trick

An unconventional trick to optimize resource utilization in a private cloud is to implement dynamic resource allocation. By monitoring the resource usage of virtual machines and infrastructure components in real-time, organizations can identify underutilized resources and automatically allocate them to where they are needed the most. This dynamic resource allocation can improve overall efficiency and reduce wastage of resources, leading to cost savings and better performance in the private cloud environment.

Hybrid Cloud

In the world of cloud computing, the hybrid cloud has emerged as a powerful and flexible solution for organizations looking to balance control and scalability. It combines the benefits of public and private clouds, allowing businesses to leverage the strengths of both while addressing their specific needs. In this section, we'll dive into the world of hybrid cloud and explore its characteristics, benefits, challenges, and use cases.

Characteristics

A hybrid cloud is essentially a combination of public and private clouds, where workloads are distributed between the two environments, and there is orchestration and communication between them. This makes the hybrid cloud unique, as it offers a seamless integration of on-premises infrastructure with public cloud services.

Some key characteristics of the hybrid cloud include:

Flexibility: The hybrid cloud allows organizations to have greater flexibility in managing their workloads. They can choose where to deploy their applications and services based on specific requirements, whether it's in their private cloud or in the public cloud.

Scalability: With a hybrid cloud, businesses can scale their resources up or down based on demand. They can leverage the scalability of the public cloud for peak loads while keeping sensitive or critical data in a private cloud.

Security: Security is a critical aspect of the hybrid cloud. Organizations can keep their most sensitive data and applications on-premises within their private cloud, while leveraging the security measures provided by the public cloud for less sensitive workloads. This ensures maximum protection for their data and minimizes the risk of unauthorized access.

Cost Efficiency: Hybrid cloud offers cost efficiency as organizations can optimize their infrastructure costs by using the public cloud for non-sensitive workloads or during peak demand, while only investing in on-premises infrastructure for critical workloads.

Benefits

The hybrid cloud brings a multitude of benefits to organizations of all sizes and industries. Let's dive into some of the key advantages it offers:

Flexibility and Agility: One of the biggest benefits of hybrid cloud is the flexibility it provides. Organizations can choose the best deployment option for each workload, allowing them to quickly adjust to changing business needs. They can easily scale resources as required, provision new services, or migrate workloads between environments.

Data Control and Privacy: Hybrid cloud allows organizations to maintain control over their sensitive and critical data by keeping it on-premises in a private cloud. This is particularly important for industries with strict regulatory requirements, such as finance or healthcare. At the same time, they can leverage the public cloud for processing or analyzing non-sensitive data, taking advantage of the scalability and cost efficiency it offers.

Disaster Recovery and Business Continuity: Hybrid cloud provides robust disaster recovery and business continuity capabilities. By replicating critical data and applications in both private and public cloud environments, organizations can ensure high availability and minimize downtime in the event of a disaster or system failure. They can easily failover between environments while maintaining seamless operations.

Cost Optimization: With hybrid cloud, organizations can optimize their IT costs by dynamically allocating resources between the public and private clouds. They can scale up or down based on demand, avoiding overprovisioning and underutilization of resources. Additionally, they can leverage the pay-as-you-go model of the public cloud for non-sensitive workloads, reducing capital expenditures.

Challenges

While the hybrid cloud has many advantages, it also comes with its own set of challenges. Organizations must carefully consider and address these challenges to ensure successful implementation. Let's take a look at some of the key challenges:

Complexity: Managing a hybrid cloud environment can be complex. It requires expertise in both public and private cloud technologies, as well as the ability to integrate and orchestrate workloads between them. Organizations need skilled IT professionals or third-party providers to handle the complexity effectively.

Data Integration and Interoperability: Integrating and ensuring interoperability between on-premises infrastructure and public cloud services can be challenging. Data needs to seamlessly flow between environments while maintaining consistency and security. Organizations must implement robust data integration strategies and ensure compatibility between different cloud platforms.

Hybrid Cloud Governance: With workloads spread across multiple environments, organizations need to establish governance policies that govern data access, security, compliance, and performance. Managing and enforcing these policies across different platforms can be a complex task.

Cost Management: While hybrid cloud offers cost optimization, managing costs can be challenging. Organizations need to carefully monitor resource usage, understand how workloads are distributed, and optimize resources accordingly. Without proper monitoring and management, costs can quickly escalate.

Use Cases

The hybrid cloud finds applications across various industries and scenarios. Let's explore a few popular use cases:

E-commerce: An e-commerce company can use a private cloud to store and process sensitive customer data, such as payment information, while leveraging the public cloud for its website hosting, content delivery, and non-sensitive data processing. This allows them to handle high traffic and maintain data security.

Healthcare: Healthcare organizations often have strict regulatory compliance requirements. They can use a private cloud to store and process patient healthcare records securely while utilizing the public cloud for non-sensitive workloads like collaboration tools or non-critical applications.

Financial Services: Financial institutions deal with large volumes of sensitive data. They can use a private cloud to host their core banking systems while leveraging the public cloud for non-sensitive applications like customer relationship management or data analytics.

Research and Development: Research organizations may have variable computing demands. They can use a private cloud for their sensitive research data and computational workloads, while utilizing the public cloud for burst computing capacity during peak times or when additional resources are required.

Conclusion

The hybrid cloud offers a powerful solution for organizations seeking a balance between control, scalability, and cost efficiency. With its flexibility, security, and ability to seamlessly integrate on-premises infrastructure with public cloud services, the hybrid cloud continues to gain popularity across industries. By carefully considering the characteristics, benefits, challenges, and use cases of the hybrid cloud, organizations can harness its potential and conquer the ever-evolving landscape of cloud computing. Remember, the hybrid cloud isn't just some fluffy buzzword. It's a game-changer for businesses willing to embrace the best of both fucking worlds.

Community Cloud

In the world of cloud computing, we have come across various deployment models, each catering to different needs and requirements. One such model is the community cloud, which brings together multiple organizations with similar interests, concerns, or requirements to share and collaborate on a common cloud infrastructure. In this section, we will delve into the concept of community cloud, its characteristics, benefits, challenges, and real-world examples.

Definition and Characteristics

A community cloud is a shared cloud environment that is designed to meet the specific needs of a particular community of users. It is built and managed either by the community members themselves or by a third-party service provider. This model ensures that the cloud infrastructure is tailored to the unique requirements of the community, providing them with a secure and resource-rich environment to fulfill their objectives.

The key characteristics of a community cloud include:

- **Shared Infrastructure:** The underlying infrastructure is shared among the community members, enabling them to leverage common resources and reduce costs.

- **Common Interest:** The community members have shared interests, concerns, or regulatory requirements that make it beneficial for them to collaborate on a common cloud platform.

- **Customization:** The community cloud can be customized to meet the specific needs of the community, including security, compliance, and scalability requirements.

- **Control and Governance:** The community members have a say in the governance and management of the community cloud, ensuring that their collective needs are addressed.

- **Security and Privacy:** The community cloud provides enhanced security measures to protect the data and assets of the community members, as well as robust privacy controls.

Benefits of Community Cloud

Community cloud offers several advantages to its members, making it an attractive option for organizations with shared interests or requirements. Let's explore some of the key benefits:

Cost Sharing: By sharing the cloud infrastructure, community members can significantly reduce their individual costs. The expense of building and maintaining the infrastructure is distributed among the members, leading to cost efficiencies.

Customization and Control: Unlike public cloud services, where users have limited control, community cloud allows members to have a greater level of customization and control over the infrastructure. This enables them to adapt the cloud environment to their specific needs and requirements.

Collaboration and Knowledge Sharing: Community cloud fosters collaboration and knowledge sharing among its members. Organizations within the community can leverage each other's expertise and resources, leading to enhanced innovation and problem-solving.

Improved Security and Compliance: Community cloud providers often implement robust security measures to address the specific security and compliance requirements of the community. This ensures that sensitive data and assets are well-protected and that regulatory obligations are met.

Shared Expertise: Community cloud brings together organizations with similar interests or concerns, creating a pool of shared expertise. Members can benefit from the collective knowledge and experience of the community, leading to better decision-making and problem-solving.

Challenges of Community Cloud

While community cloud offers numerous benefits, it also poses certain challenges that need to be addressed. Let's discuss some of the challenges:

Trust and Collaboration: For a community cloud to be successful, there needs to be a high level of trust and collaboration among the participating organizations. They must be willing to work together, share resources, and align their objectives for the greater good of the community.

Governance and Decision-making: Establishing effective governance structures and decision-making processes can be a challenge in a community cloud. It's crucial to have a mechanism in place that allows all members to have a say in the management and operation of the cloud, while also ensuring that conflicts and disagreements are appropriately addressed.

Scalability and Resource Allocation: As the community of users grows, scalability and resource allocation become critical factors. The cloud infrastructure should be able to accommodate the increasing demands of the community members without compromising performance or availability.

Compliance and Regulatory Requirements: Each organization within the community may have specific compliance and regulatory obligations. The community cloud must be designed in a way that allows these requirements to be met effectively, ensuring that all members can operate within the legal boundaries.

Real-world Examples

Let's look at a couple of real-world examples to understand how community cloud is being utilized in different scenarios:

Healthcare Community Cloud: In the healthcare industry, various hospitals, clinics, and research institutions form a community cloud to securely store and share electronic health records, conduct collaborative research, and facilitate telemedicine services. The community cloud ensures that sensitive patient information is adequately protected, and it promotes collaboration among healthcare providers for better patient care.

Government Community Cloud: Governments at various levels, such as federal, state, and local, often collaborate to establish a community cloud platform for sharing resources, data, and applications. This enables more efficient service delivery, interagency collaboration, and cost savings by eliminating duplication of infrastructure and services.

Closing Thoughts

Community cloud offers a unique approach to cloud computing, bringing together organizations with shared interests or requirements. It provides a platform for collaboration, customization, and cost sharing, while also addressing the specific security and compliance needs of the community. By leveraging the collective expertise and resources, community cloud opens up new avenues for innovation and problem-solving. However, it's essential to overcome the challenges of trust, governance, and scalability to ensure the successful implementation and operation of the community cloud.

As cloud computing continues to evolve, the concept of community cloud is likely to gain more traction, enabling organizations to work together towards common goals and harness the power of shared resources. The next section will introduce the concept of multi-cloud orchestration, which takes cloud computing to a whole new level of scalability and flexibility. So buckle up and get ready for the fucking ride!

The Holy Grail: Multi-Cloud Orchestration

Multi-cloud orchestration is a game-changer in the world of cloud computing. It refers to the management and coordination of multiple cloud environments, combining different cloud service providers to create a unified and seamless infrastructure. In this section, we will delve into the intricacies of multi-cloud orchestration, its advantages, challenges, and how it can help organizations conquer the cloud.

Understanding Multi-Cloud Orchestration

Cloud computing has come a long way from a single provider offering all-in-one solutions. Organizations now have the luxury of choosing different cloud service providers based on their specific needs and preferences. Multi-cloud orchestration takes advantage of this choice and allows organizations to leverage the strengths of multiple providers.

At its core, multi-cloud orchestration is about managing heterogeneous cloud environments. It involves integrating various cloud services, APIs, and technologies to create a unified infrastructure. This orchestration layer sits on top of the individual cloud providers and enables centralized management, automation, and optimization of resources across different clouds.

With multi-cloud orchestration, organizations can enjoy the benefits of flexibility, scalability, and redundancy. They can distribute workloads across different cloud environments, reduce dependency on a single provider, and tailor their infrastructure to meet specific requirements. It also allows organizations to leverage the unique capabilities and offerings of different providers, maximizing their cloud investment.

Advantages of Multi-Cloud Orchestration

1. **Vendor Independence:** By adopting multi-cloud orchestration, organizations are not chained to a single cloud provider. They have the freedom to choose the best solutions from multiple providers, preventing vendor lock-in and ensuring competitive pricing.

2. **Enhanced Resilience:** Multi-cloud environments provide higher resilience and disaster recovery capabilities. Organizations can distribute their workloads

across different cloud providers, mitigating the risks associated with single-point failures.

3. **Optimized Performance:** With multi-cloud orchestration, organizations can harness the strengths of different providers to achieve optimal performance. They can utilize the geographic distribution of cloud resources, enabling reduced latency and improved user experience.

4. **Cost Optimization:** Multi-cloud orchestration allows organizations to strategically allocate workloads to providers offering the most cost-effective services. It also enables the utilization of spot instances or reserved instances from different providers, depending on cost and resource requirements.

5. **Innovation and Agility:** By leveraging multiple cloud environments, organizations can quickly adopt innovative services and technologies. They can experiment and integrate new features without disrupting their core infrastructure, fostering agility and encouraging innovation.

Challenges of Multi-Cloud Orchestration

While multi-cloud orchestration offers numerous advantages, it also brings forth several challenges that organizations need to address:

1. **Complexity and Integration:** Managing different cloud environments requires expertise in various platforms, tools, and APIs. Orchestrating these diverse resources and ensuring seamless integration can be complex and time-consuming.

2. **Security and Compliance:** Each cloud provider may have different security measures and compliance standards. Ensuring consistent security and compliance across multiple providers can be challenging and requires comprehensive planning and management.

3. **Interoperability and Data Portability:** Transferring data and workloads across different cloud environments must be done efficiently and without disruption. Organizations need to ensure they have the necessary tools and processes in place for seamless interoperability and data portability.

4. **Monitoring and Performance Optimization:** Monitoring and optimizing performance across multiple clouds can be demanding. Organizations must leverage appropriate tools and techniques to track resource utilization, detect bottlenecks, and ensure efficient resource allocation.

5. **Skill Set and Training:** Managing multi-cloud environments often requires a diverse skill set. Organizations need to invest in training and development to equip their IT teams with the knowledge and expertise needed to handle multiple cloud platforms effectively.

Strategies for Multi-Cloud Orchestration

To effectively orchestrate a multi-cloud environment, organizations can adopt the following strategies:

1. **Unified Management Platform:** Utilize a centralized management platform that allows organizations to monitor, provision, and manage resources across multiple cloud environments. This platform should provide a unified view of all resources, enabling seamless orchestration and simplifying management tasks.

2. **Automation and Orchestration Tools:** Leverage automation and orchestration tools to streamline deployment, configuration, and management of resources across different clouds. These tools should enable organizations to define policies, automate workflows, and optimize resource allocation.

3. **Interconnectivity and Integration:** Establish efficient and secure connectivity between cloud environments. Utilize technologies such as virtual private networks (VPNs), direct network interconnections, or software-defined wide-area networks (SD-WANs) to ensure seamless integration and data transfer.

4. **Containerization and Microservices:** Embrace containerization and microservices architecture to enhance portability and simplify deployment across multiple cloud providers. Container orchestration platforms like Kubernetes can facilitate the management of applications and services in a multi-cloud environment.

5. **Governance and Security Policies:** Implement consistent governance and security policies across different cloud providers. This includes defining access controls, encryption standards, and compliance requirements to ensure a unified and secure environment.

Real-World Example: Multi-Cloud E-commerce Platform

Let's consider a scenario where an e-commerce company wants to leverage multi-cloud orchestration for their online platform. They want to utilize the scalable infrastructure of one cloud provider, the advanced analytics services of another, and the content delivery capabilities of a third provider.

By adopting multi-cloud orchestration, the company can distribute their workload across these providers based on specific requirements. They can utilize the scalable compute resources of one provider during peak shopping seasons, leverage the advanced analytics services to gain customer insights, and use the content delivery network (CDN) of another provider for fast and reliable content delivery.

To ensure efficient orchestration, the company can use a centralized management platform that provides a unified view of all resources. They can automate deployment and management using tools like Ansible or Terraform, enabling seamless integration and efficient resource allocation.

The company must also address challenges such as data synchronization between different providers, security across multiple environments, and consistent application performance. By implementing appropriate strategies, including robust data replication techniques, consistent security policies, and performance monitoring tools, they can overcome these challenges and achieve a well-orchestrated multi-cloud solution.

Recommended Resources

To dive deeper into multi-cloud orchestration, explore the following resources:

- **Book:** "Multi-Cloud Orchestration: Automating Multi-Cloud Environments with AWS, Azure, and Google Cloud" by Stefan Lienhard.

- **Whitepaper:** "Multi-Cloud Strategy: Benefits, Challenges, and Recommendations" by Gartner.

- **Blog Post:** "Multi-Cloud Orchestration Made Easy: Strategies and Tools" by Cloud Academy.

- **Online Course:** "Multi-Cloud Management and Orchestration" on Pluralsight.

Remember, multi-cloud orchestration is the holy grail of cloud computing, enabling organizations to harness the power of multiple cloud providers while effectively managing and optimizing their infrastructure. Embrace the diverse capabilities of various clouds, conquer the cloud, and rise above the competition. The future of cloud computing lies in multi-cloud orchestration, so grab the reins and scale new heights!

Advantages and Challenges of Cloud Computing

Cost Reduction and Scalability

In the world of cloud computing, there are two major factors that make it a game-changer: cost reduction and scalability. These two factors are interconnected, and together, they have revolutionized the way businesses operate and expand their operations.

Cost Reduction

One of the primary reasons why organizations are flocking to the cloud is the potential cost reduction it offers. In the traditional on-premises model, businesses had to invest heavily in physical servers, storage, networking equipment, and data centers. These upfront costs can be exorbitant, especially for small and medium-sized enterprises (SMEs), and are often a major barrier to entry into the market.

Cloud computing, on the other hand, operates on a pay-as-you-go model. Instead of bearing the burden of upfront costs, organizations only pay for the resources and services they use. This shift in cost structure allows businesses to reduce their capital expenditure (CapEx) and shift to operational expenditure (OpEx) models. It also enables organizations to allocate their financial resources more efficiently, investing in innovation and growth rather than infrastructure.

Let's take an example to illustrate the cost reduction benefits of cloud computing. Consider a growing e-commerce startup that experiences seasonal fluctuations in demand. During peak shopping periods, the demand for computing resources spikes, requiring additional servers and storage. In a traditional on-premises model, the startup would have to invest in the infrastructure required to handle peak traffic, resulting in underutilized resources during off-peak periods. With cloud computing, the startup can leverage the scalability of the cloud to dynamically adjust resource allocation based on demand, eliminating the need for upfront investment in excess capacity. This not only reduces costs but also ensures optimal resource utilization.

Furthermore, cloud service providers offer numerous cost optimization tools and features that enable organizations to monitor and control their spending. These tools provide insights into resource consumption, identify areas of potential savings, and offer recommendations for cost reduction. For example, organizations can take advantage of auto-scaling capabilities to automatically adjust resource allocation based on predefined thresholds, ensuring efficient resource utilization and cost optimization.

Scalability

Scalability is another critical aspect of cloud computing that has transformed the way businesses operate. Scalability refers to the ability to quickly and easily adjust the size and capacity of computing resources to meet changing demands.

In the traditional on-premises model, scaling up or down requires significant upfront investments in additional hardware, software licenses, and infrastructure. This process can be time-consuming, costly, and often results in underutilization of resources during periods of low demand.

Cloud computing offers inherent scalability, allowing organizations to scale resources up or down on-demand. This capability is particularly valuable for businesses with fluctuating workloads or seasonal demand patterns. With the scalability of the cloud, organizations can ensure that they always have the optimal amount of resources available to meet the demands of their applications and services.

There are two types of scalability in the cloud: vertical and horizontal. Vertical scalability, also known as scaling up, involves adding more resources to an existing virtual machine or instance. For example, if a web application experiences increased traffic, the organization can vertically scale by adding more memory, processing power, or storage to the virtual machine.

Horizontal scalability, on the other hand, refers to scaling out by adding more instances or virtual machines. This approach allows organizations to distribute the workload across multiple instances, improving performance and availability. For instance, if a web application is struggling to handle increased user requests, the organization can horizontally scale by adding more instances to share the load.

Additionally, the cloud offers elasticity, which goes hand in hand with scalability. Elasticity refers to the ability to automatically and dynamically adjust the allocation of resources based on workload fluctuations. This ensures that organizations only pay for the resources they need at any given time, preventing overprovisioning and optimizing cost efficiency.

To illustrate the scalability benefits of cloud computing, let's consider a media streaming service that experiences significant spikes in demand during peak hours. During these peak periods, the service needs to handle a large number of concurrent users and deliver high-quality video content without buffering or interruptions. By leveraging the scalability of the cloud, the media streaming service can dynamically provision additional resources to handle the increased workload. This ensures a seamless user experience and eliminates the need to invest in and maintain an infrastructure that would remain underutilized during off-peak periods.

Scalability also enables businesses to quickly respond to market demands, adapt to changing customer needs, and scale their operations as they grow. Instead of being limited by the capacity of their own on-premises infrastructure, organizations can leverage the virtually unlimited resources of the cloud to scale their applications, services, and user base. This flexibility and agility provide businesses with a competitive edge in today's fast-paced digital landscape.

In conclusion, cost reduction and scalability are two fundamental advantages of cloud computing that have disrupted traditional IT paradigms. By shifting from upfront investments to pay-as-you-go models, organizations can reduce costs, optimize resource allocation, and focus on innovation and growth. The scalability of the cloud empowers businesses to meet changing demands, quickly adapt to market dynamics, and scale their operations to new heights. The combination of cost reduction and scalability has revolutionized the way businesses operate, enabling them to conquer new frontiers in the digital world.

Flexibility and Accessibility

Flexibility and accessibility are two key advantages of cloud computing that have revolutionized the way we access and use technology. In this section, we will explore how cloud computing provides flexibility and accessibility, enabling users to adapt and utilize resources based on their needs and preferences.

Flexibility in Cloud Computing

One of the most remarkable aspects of cloud computing is its inherent flexibility. Traditional computing models often required substantial upfront investments in hardware and software, limiting scalability and adaptability. However, with cloud computing, users can easily scale their resources up or down based on demand, paying only for what they use.

Dynamic Resource Allocation In cloud computing, the allocation of computing resources can be dynamically adjusted to meet the changing needs of an application or service. This allows organizations to optimize resource utilization, minimize costs, and enhance performance. Cloud service providers offer a variety of options for resource allocation, including virtual machines, containers, and serverless computing platforms.

For example, imagine a retail company experiencing a sudden surge in website traffic during a flash sale. With cloud computing, the company can quickly scale up its resources to handle the increased demand, ensuring that its website remains responsive and available to customers. Once the sale is over, the company can easily scale back down, avoiding unnecessary costs.

High Availability and Redundancy Cloud computing also provides high availability and redundancy, ensuring that applications and services remain accessible even in the event of hardware failures or other disruptions. By leveraging the distributed nature of cloud infrastructure, service providers can replicate data and distribute it across multiple locations.

For instance, consider a healthcare provider storing patient records in the cloud. By choosing a cloud service that offers geographic redundancy, the provider can ensure that the data is automatically replicated to multiple data centers in different regions. In the event of a disaster or outage in one location, the data remains accessible and operations can continue uninterrupted.

Accessibility in Cloud Computing

Accessibility is another vital aspect of cloud computing—enabling users to access their resources and applications anytime, anywhere, and from any device with an internet connection. This level of accessibility has transformed the way people work and collaborate, breaking down barriers and enabling seamless communication and collaboration.

Remote Access Cloud computing allows users to access their applications and data remotely, without being tied to a specific physical location. This remote access is particularly advantageous in situations where employees need to work from home, travel, or collaborate with colleagues in different locations.

For example, imagine a team of designers working on a project. With cloud-based design software, they can access and collaborate on their work from anywhere, using their preferred devices. This remote accessibility empowers teams to work together effectively, regardless of their physical locations.

Device Independence In addition to remote access, cloud computing provides device independence, allowing users to access their resources and applications from a variety of devices, such as desktops, laptops, tablets, and smartphones. This flexibility enables individuals to choose the device that best suits their needs or preferences, without being limited by specific hardware or software requirements.

Consider a student preparing for an exam. With cloud-based note-taking applications, they can access their study materials from different devices, such as a laptop during a study session, a tablet while commuting, or a smartphone during a quick review. The ability to seamlessly switch between devices ensures continuous access to resources, optimizing productivity and learning.

Challenges and Considerations

While flexibility and accessibility are significant advantages of cloud computing, it is crucial to address the challenges and considerations associated with these capabilities.

Dependence on Internet Connectivity Cloud computing heavily relies on internet connectivity. Users must have a stable and reliable internet connection to access their resources and applications. Any disruption in internet connectivity, such as network outages or slow connections, can hinder accessibility and productivity.

To mitigate this challenge, users can consider redundancy options, such as having backup internet connections or utilizing offline capabilities offered by certain applications. Additionally, cloud service providers often have multiple data centers distributed globally, improving accessibility by reducing the impact of localized internet outages.

Data Security and Privacy Accessibility and remote access raise concerns regarding the security and privacy of data stored and transmitted in the cloud. Organizations and individuals must ensure that appropriate security measures are in place to protect sensitive information and comply with data protection regulations.

Implementing encryption, multi-factor authentication, and regular security audits are essential practices to safeguard data. It is also crucial to choose reputable cloud service providers that prioritize security and provide robust privacy controls.

Vendor Lock-In Adopting cloud computing solutions may introduce a degree of vendor lock-in, limiting the ability to easily switch between different service providers or migrate to alternative solutions. This can become a concern if a service provider increases prices significantly, experiences a service outage, or fails to meet specific requirements.

To mitigate the risk of vendor lock-in, organizations can adopt a multi-cloud strategy, leveraging services from multiple providers. This approach allows for flexibility, redundancy, and the ability to select the most suitable services from various vendors based on specific needs and priorities.

ADVANTAGES AND CHALLENGES OF CLOUD COMPUTING

Summary

Flexibility and accessibility are fundamental advantages of cloud computing that have reshaped the way we utilize and access technology. The dynamic resource allocation, high availability, remote access, and device independence offered by cloud computing enable users to adapt to changing demands, work from anywhere, and leverage a wide range of devices. However, challenges such as internet dependence, data security, privacy concerns, and vendor lock-in must be addressed to maximize the benefits of flexibility and accessibility in the cloud.

In the next section, we will delve into the security and privacy concerns associated with cloud computing and discuss best practices for ensuring data protection in a cloud environment. Stay fucking tuned!

Security and Privacy Concerns

Whoa, wait a fucking minute! As much as we love cloud computing and all its benefits, we can't ignore the security and privacy concerns that come along with it. We've got to be aware of the risks and take necessary precautions to keep our data safe and private. So, let's dive deep into the murky waters of cloud security and privacy concerns.

The Cloud Conspiracy

Okay, I might be exaggerating a bit with the word "conspiracy," but bear with me. When you're dealing with cloud computing, you're essentially entrusting your data to a third-party provider. And that can sometimes make you feel like you're losing control over your precious information. But fear not, my friend! There are measures in place to address these concerns.

Data Protection

First and foremost, let's talk about data protection. When your data resides in the cloud, it's crucial to ensure that it is protected from unauthorized access, theft, or any other kind of malicious activity. This means implementing strong security measures, such as encryption and access controls.

Encryption is like armor for your data. It scrambles it up so that even if someone gets their hands on it, they won't be able to make any sense of it. It's like having your own secret code language. And the best part is that even if someone intercepts your data while it's traveling from your device to the cloud (yeah, those hackers can be sneaky bastards), they won't be able to read it without the decryption key.

Access controls, on the other hand, are like the bouncers at a club. They decide who gets in and who gets kicked out. In the cloud world, access controls ensure that only authorized users can access your data. You can set up granular permissions, so that even within your organization, only specific people have access to certain data. This helps minimize the risk of internal breaches and keeps the bad guys at bay.

Compliance and Regulations

Now, let's talk about compliance and regulations. Nobody likes rules, but in this case, they're necessary. Depending on the nature of your business or the type of data you're storing in the cloud, you might be subject to certain compliance requirements and regulations. And believe me, you don't want to mess with those.

For example, if you're dealing with sensitive information like health records or financial data, you need to comply with HIPAA (Health Insurance Portability and Accountability Act) or PCI DSS (Payment Card Industry Data Security Standard), respectively. These regulations set out specific security and privacy requirements that you must follow to avoid hefty fines and legal troubles. And let's be honest, nobody wants to deal with that shit.

So, make sure you do your homework and understand the compliance landscape. Choose a cloud service provider that complies with the necessary regulations and provides the necessary controls to help you stay on the right side of the law.

Vendor Lock-In and Data Portability

Now, let's talk about something that can be a real pain in the ass - vendor lock-in. When you choose a cloud service provider, you're essentially signing a contract (maybe not in blood, but close enough). And once you're locked in, it can be a real pain in the ass to switch providers.

So, what's the big deal with vendor lock-in? Well, let's say you're not happy with the services or pricing of your current provider (it happens, trust me). If you're locked in, it means you can't just pack your bags and move to another provider without a whole lot of hassle. It's like being trapped in a toxic relationship, but with technology.

That's why data portability is important. You need to have the ability to easily move your data from one provider to another, without losing any of it or going through a mind-numbing migration process. It's like having a universal translator for your data. With data portability, you can switch providers or even bring your data back in-house if you so desire. It gives you the freedom to choose and the power to say, "Fuck you, I'm taking my data elsewhere!"

Fears, Doubts, and Fucking Uncertainties

Let's face it, the cloud can be scary at times. It's like venturing into the unknown, where your data floats around in cyberspace, vulnerable to all kinds of threats. And that can give you a serious case of FUD (Fear, Uncertainty, and Doubt). But don't worry, my friend, you're not alone.

One of the biggest fears people have about the cloud is the fear of a security breach. What if someone hacks into the cloud and steals your sensitive data? It's a valid concern, considering that even big-name companies have fallen victim to such attacks. But here's the thing: cloud service providers have a lot at stake. Their entire business relies on keeping your data safe. So, you can bet your ass they're investing in top-notch security measures to protect their customers. But that doesn't mean you should be complacent. Always be vigilant and take your own security precautions as well.

Another fear that keeps people up at night is the fear of losing control over their data. When you store your data in the cloud, you're putting it in someone else's hands. And that can make you feel like you're no longer in control. But fear not, my friend! As long as you choose a reputable cloud service provider and take necessary precautions, you can maintain control over your data. Remember, encryption and access controls are your best friends.

Privacy is another big concern, especially in the age of data breaches and government surveillance. People worry that their data might be snooped on or used for nefarious purposes. And let me tell you, those concerns are not unfounded. However, most cloud service providers have robust privacy policies in place to protect your data. Just make sure you read the fine print and understand how your data will be handled. And don't forget that encryption I've been harping on about. It adds an extra layer of protection for your privacy.

Wrapping It Up

So, there you have it - the security and privacy concerns of cloud computing. It's not all rainbows and unicorns, but with proper precautions and a solid understanding of the risks, you can navigate the cloud with confidence.

Remember, encryption and access controls are your best defense against unauthorized access to your data. Be aware of compliance requirements and choose a provider that meets your specific needs. And keep an eye out for vendor lock-in, while ensuring you have the ability to move your data around. Finally, don't let fear paralyze you. The cloud may be a bit mysterious, but with the right knowledge, you can conquer any security and privacy concerns that come your way.

Now, get out there and conquer that cloud!

Vendor Lock-In and Data Portability

When it comes to cloud computing, one of the biggest concerns for businesses and individuals is the concept of vendor lock-in. Vendor lock-in refers to the situation where a customer becomes dependent on a particular cloud service provider and faces significant barriers to switching to another provider. In this section, we will explore the concept of vendor lock-in in cloud computing and discuss the importance of data portability.

Understanding Vendor Lock-In

In the world of cloud computing, different service providers offer a wide range of services, such as infrastructure as a service (IaaS), platform as a service (PaaS), and software as a service (SaaS). While the variety of services is beneficial, it also poses certain risks, particularly in terms of vendor lock-in.

Vendor lock-in occurs when a customer becomes heavily dependent on a particular cloud service provider's technology, proprietary formats, or APIs (Application Programming Interfaces). This dependency can make it incredibly challenging to switch to another provider or even migrate back to on-premises infrastructure. It essentially restricts the freedom of customers and can result in substantial costs, loss of control, and limited flexibility.

Impact of Vendor Lock-In

The impact of vendor lock-in can be severe, hindering innovation, and limiting business growth. Here are some consequences that organizations can face due to vendor lock-in:

- **Limited Flexibility**: Once an organization has invested heavily in a specific cloud provider's services, it becomes difficult to adapt to changing business needs or take advantage of new advancements in technology. The organization becomes bound by the capabilities and limitations of the chosen provider, inhibiting agility and competitiveness.

- **Increased Costs**: Switching cloud providers can be a complicated and costly process. Organizations may need to invest time, resources, and manpower in rearchitecting applications, retraining staff, and migrating data. Additionally, new providers may have different pricing models, resulting in higher costs for reestablishing infrastructure and services.

ADVANTAGES AND CHALLENGES OF CLOUD COMPUTING

- **Loss of Control:** With vendor lock-in, organizations may find themselves at the mercy of the service provider. Decisions about service updates, pricing changes, or even the termination of certain services are entirely in the hands of the provider. This lack of control can leave organizations vulnerable and dependent on the provider's actions.

Ensuring Data Portability

Data portability is closely tied to the issue of vendor lock-in. It refers to the ability to easily transfer data from one cloud provider to another, preserving its integrity, structure, and meaning. Data portability is crucial as it enables organizations to retain ownership and control over their data, mitigating the risks associated with vendor lock-in.

To ensure data portability, it is essential to follow certain best practices:

- **Data Interoperability:** Choosing cloud providers that support open standards and formats is crucial for data portability. Open standards enable data to be easily understood and processed by different systems, reducing the reliance on proprietary formats and making migration between providers more feasible.

- **Backup and Export Options:** Regularly backing up data and having the ability to export it in a neutral format is essential. This allows organizations to maintain a copy of their data and switch providers when necessary. It is important to verify that backup and export options are available and compatible with the organization's needs.

- **Avoiding Tight Integration:** Overly tight integration with a cloud provider's proprietary tools and services can increase the risk of lock-in. By using open-source or vendor-agnostic solutions, organizations can preserve data portability and remain flexible in their cloud strategy.

Fears, Doubts, and Fucking Uncertainties of the Cloud

Cloud computing offers numerous advantages and exciting possibilities for organizations and individuals alike. However, it also raises concerns that cannot be ignored. In this section, we will explore some of the fears, doubts, and fucking uncertainties associated with the cloud.

Security and Privacy Concerns

One of the main concerns when it comes to the cloud is the security and privacy of data. When you store your information in the cloud, there is always a risk of unauthorized access, data breaches, and cyber attacks. This is particularly worrying for sensitive data such as personal information, financial records, and proprietary business data.

Cloud service providers invest heavily in security measures to protect your data, including encryption, access controls, and intrusion detection systems. However, no system is completely foolproof, and vulnerabilities can exist. It is essential to choose reputable cloud providers that prioritize security and have a track record of successfully protecting data.

To mitigate security risks, organizations should implement strong encryption methods and regularly assess their security posture. Additionally, establishing proper access controls and employing multi-factor authentication can help prevent unauthorized access. Ultimately, a combination of strong security practices and a trusted cloud provider can help address these concerns.

Availability and Reliability

Another fear with the cloud is the possibility of service downtime, resulting in the unavailability of critical applications and data. While cloud service providers strive to offer high availability and reliability, occasional outages can occur due to technical glitches, maintenance, or even natural disasters.

To ensure business continuity, organizations can implement backup and disaster recovery plans. These plans involve replicating data across multiple cloud regions or even utilizing a hybrid cloud approach, combining both public and private clouds. By implementing redundancy measures, organizations can minimize the impact of cloud service disruptions and ensure continuous access to their data and applications.

Vendor Lock-In and Data Portability

Once organizations commit to a specific cloud service provider, they may face challenges if they decide to switch providers in the future. This concern is known as vendor lock-in. Vendor lock-in occurs when organizations become heavily dependent on a particular provider's services, making it difficult and costly to migrate to another platform.

To mitigate the risks associated with vendor lock-in, organizations should choose cloud providers that adhere to open standards and promote data portability. Open standards ensure that data and applications can be easily transferred between different cloud platforms without significant disruptions or reengineering.

Furthermore, organizations should develop strategies for data governance, establishing clear guidelines on data formats, storage locations, and management policies. By doing so, organizations retain control over their data and have the flexibility to switch providers if necessary.

Compliance and Legal Issues

Cloud computing involves the storage, processing, and transmission of data, which may be subject to various legal and regulatory requirements. Depending on the industry and the type of data being stored, organizations may be obligated to comply with privacy regulations, data protection laws, and industry-specific standards.

Compliance with these regulations in a cloud environment can be complicated, as organizations must ensure that the cloud provider meets the necessary requirements. It is crucial for organizations to assess the cloud provider's compliance certifications, such as ISO 27001, SOC 2, or HIPAA, depending on the specific requirements of the industry.

Additionally, organizations should establish clear agreements with cloud providers regarding data ownership, data handling, and legal responsibilities. These agreements should address issues such as data breach notification, data retention, and jurisdiction to avoid potential legal disputes.

Fucking Ethical Dilemmas of the Cloud

As cloud computing continues to advance, it raises ethical considerations that require careful examination. Artificial intelligence (AI) and machine learning algorithms used in the cloud can introduce biases, discrimination, and privacy risks. These technologies are often powered by vast amounts of data, which may contain inherent biases and perpetuate social inequalities when used to make decisions.

Organizations should incorporate ethical principles and responsible AI practices into their cloud deployments. This includes conducting regular audits to identify and address biases within algorithms, implementing transparency measures to ensure users understand how their data is being used, and obtaining informed consent for data collection and processing.

It is crucial for individuals, organizations, and policymakers to engage in ongoing discussions about the ethical impacts of cloud computing. By openly addressing these concerns, we can create a responsible and inclusive cloud environment that respects privacy, fairness, and human rights.

Summary

In this section, we have explored some of the fears, doubts, and fucking uncertainties associated with cloud computing. We discussed concerns related to security and privacy, availability and reliability, vendor lock-in and data portability, compliance and legal issues, as well as the ethical dilemmas posed by cloud technologies.

While these concerns are valid, it is important to note that cloud computing also offers numerous benefits and opportunities. By understanding and addressing these uncertainties, organizations and individuals can make informed decisions and leverage the power of the cloud while mitigating potential risks. Ultimately, the future of the cloud depends on our ability to navigate these challenges responsibly and ethically.

Cloud Infrastructure

Hardware and Data Centers

Servers and Storage

In this section, we will delve into the fascinating world of servers and storage in the context of cloud computing. Servers and storage are the backbone of the cloud infrastructure, providing the computational power and data storage capabilities needed to deliver services to users worldwide. We will explore the hardware components of servers, the different storage options available in the cloud, and the technologies that make it all possible.

Servers: The Workhorses of the Cloud

Servers are the heart and soul of any cloud infrastructure. They are the workhorses that handle all the computing tasks and provide the resources needed to run applications and store data in the cloud. In simple terms, a server is a powerful computer system that is connected to a network and provides services to other computers, devices, or users.

Hardware Components of Servers A typical server consists of several key hardware components that work together to enable its functionality. Let's take a closer look at each of these components:

- **Central Processing Unit (CPU):** Also known as the processor, the CPU is responsible for executing instructions and performing calculations. It is the brain of the server, handling tasks such as running applications, processing data, and managing system operations.
- **Random Access Memory (RAM):** RAM is the short-term memory of a server. It provides fast storage for data and instructions that the CPU needs

to access quickly. The amount of RAM in a server determines its ability to handle multiple tasks simultaneously and respond to user requests efficiently.

- **Hard Disk Drives (HDDs) and Solid State Drives (SSDs):** These are the primary storage devices in a server. HDDs use spinning magnetic disks to store and retrieve data, while SSDs use flash memory technology for faster performance. The choice between HDDs and SSDs depends on factors such as cost, capacity, and performance requirements.

- **Network Interface Cards (NICs):** NICs allow servers to communicate with other devices on the network. They provide the physical connection to the network and enable data transmission over Ethernet, Wi-Fi, or other networking protocols.

- **Power Supply Unit (PSU):** The PSU converts AC power from the electrical outlet into DC power that the server components can use. It provides a reliable and stable power source to ensure the server's continuous operation.

- **Cooling System:** Servers generate a significant amount of heat, so a cooling system is essential to prevent overheating. This typically involves fans, heatsinks, and airflow management to maintain optimal operating temperatures.

- **Motherboard:** The motherboard serves as the main circuit board that connects and integrates all the components of the server. It provides the infrastructure for communication between the CPU, RAM, storage devices, and other peripherals.

Server Virtualization Server virtualization is a critical technology that enables the efficient utilization of server resources in the cloud. It allows multiple virtual servers, or virtual machines (VMs), to run on a single physical server. Each VM operates as if it were a separate physical machine, with its own dedicated CPU, RAM, storage, and operating system.

By abstracting the underlying hardware, server virtualization provides several benefits, including:

- **Resource Optimization:** Virtualization allows for better utilization of server resources by consolidating multiple VMs on a single physical server. This leads to cost savings in terms of hardware, power, and cooling.

HARDWARE AND DATA CENTERS

- **Scalability and Flexibility:** Virtual servers can be easily created, scaled up or down, and migrated across physical hosts without disrupting the underlying infrastructure. This provides businesses with the agility to respond to changing demands quickly.

- **Isolation and Security:** Each VM operates in its own isolated environment, providing enhanced security and preventing one VM from interfering with or compromising the others.

- **Disaster Recovery:** VMs can be replicated and moved between physical servers to ensure high availability and facilitate disaster recovery in the event of hardware failures or system crashes.

Serverless Computing Serverless computing is a paradigm that takes the abstraction of servers to the next level. In serverless architecture, developers focus solely on writing and deploying code functions, without the need to manage servers or infrastructure. The cloud provider takes care of automatically scaling and managing the underlying server resources as needed.

Serverless computing offers several advantages, including:

- **Simplified Development:** Developers can focus on writing code without worrying about server management tasks, such as provisioning, scaling, and maintenance.

- **Automatic Scaling:** Serverless platforms automatically scale the resources allocated to code functions based on demand. This allows applications to handle varying workloads without manual intervention.

- **Pay-Per-Use Billing:** With serverless, you only pay for the actual compute resources consumed by your code functions, rather than paying for idle server time.

- **Event-Driven Architecture:** Serverless is well-suited for event-driven applications where code functions are triggered by events, such as data changes, user actions, or system events.

- **Rapid Time-to-Market:** Serverless enables faster development cycles and quicker deployment of new features, allowing businesses to innovate and iterate more rapidly.

Storage in the Cloud

In addition to servers, storage is a fundamental component of cloud computing. It provides the ability to store and access data over the network, enabling users to save and retrieve their files, documents, images, and other digital content. The cloud offers a variety of storage options, each with its own characteristics, performance, and cost considerations.

Object Storage Object storage is a popular storage model in the cloud, designed to handle the massive scale and flexibility required by modern applications. In this model, data is stored as objects, each with its unique identifier (often called a key). These objects can be files, images, videos, or any other type of unstructured data.

Key features of object storage include:

- **Scalability:** Object storage systems can store an enormous amount of data, ranging from terabytes to petabytes or more. It can handle the growing data demands of modern applications without the need for manual capacity management.

- **Durability and Redundancy:** Object storage stores data across multiple servers and data centers, providing built-in redundancy and fault tolerance. This ensures that data remains available even in the event of hardware failures or natural disasters.

- **Accessibility:** Objects in object storage can be accessed over the network using standard APIs. This makes it easy to integrate object storage into applications and enables seamless access from anywhere in the world.

- **Cost-Effectiveness:** Object storage is cost-effective for storing large amounts of data, as cloud providers typically offer low-cost storage options based on usage and data redundancy requirements.

- **Metadata and Tags:** Object storage allows users to add custom metadata and tags to objects, making it easier to organize and search for specific files or data sets.

Object storage is widely used for various cloud storage services, such as Amazon S3, Google Cloud Storage, and Azure Blob Storage.

HARDWARE AND DATA CENTERS

Block Storage   Block storage is a storage model that provides raw block-level storage to virtual machines and other cloud-based instances. Unlike object storage, which deals with unstructured data, block storage is used for structured data that requires direct interaction with the underlying storage blocks.

Key features of block storage include:

- **Performance:** Block storage offers high-performance storage capabilities, making it suitable for applications and workloads that require low latency and high I/O operations.

- **Data Integrity:** Block storage provides data integrity features, such as checksums and RAID configurations, to ensure that data is protected against corruption or loss.

- **Compatibility:** Block storage presents the storage devices to the operating system or application as if they were locally attached storage devices. This makes it compatible with existing applications and operating systems.

- **Flexibility:** Block storage allows for partitioning, formatting, and running file systems on top of the storage devices. This enables users to have fine-grained control over the storage and use it in a way that suits their specific needs.

Block storage is commonly used in cloud-based databases, virtual machine disk images, and other scenarios where low-level access to storage is required.

File Storage   File storage provides a shared file system that can be accessed over the network by multiple clients or instances. It offers a traditional file-based approach to storing and retrieving data, using familiar hierarchical file structures with directories and files.

Key features of file storage include:

- **Shared Access:** File storage allows multiple clients or instances to access and modify files concurrently. This makes it suitable for collaborative environments or scenarios where shared file access is required.

- **Consistency and Metadata:** File storage maintains file-level consistency and supports metadata such as permissions, timestamps, and extended attributes. This enables fine-grained control over file access and provides additional information about the stored data.

- **Compatibility:** File storage leverages standard file protocols such as NFS (Network File System) or SMB (Server Message Block), making it compatible with a wide range of applications and operating systems.

- **Scalability:** Cloud providers offer scalable file storage solutions that can handle large amounts of data and growing workloads. This scalability enables businesses to easily accommodate changing storage requirements.

File storage is commonly used for home directories, content management systems, file sharing, and other scenarios that require shared access to files.

Database Storage Database storage in the cloud refers to the storage solutions specifically designed for hosting and managing databases. Cloud providers offer managed database services, such as Amazon RDS, Azure SQL Database, and Google Cloud Spanner, that handle the complex tasks of database administration, replication, and backups.

Key features of database storage include:

- **High Availability and Durability:** Database storage is designed to provide high availability and durability guarantees for critical data. It leverages replication, failover mechanisms, and automated backups to ensure data is protected and accessible.

- **Performance and Scalability:** Database storage solutions are optimized for high-performance database workloads, offering features like caching, indexing, and query optimization. They are also scalable, allowing businesses to handle growing database demands.

- **Data Consistency:** Database storage ensures data consistency and integrity through transactional processing and ACID (Atomicity, Consistency, Isolation, Durability) properties. This makes it suitable for applications that require strong data consistency guarantees.

- **Security and Access Control:** Database storage provides built-in security features, such as encryption, authentication, and fine-grained access control. This helps protect sensitive data and ensures that only authorized users can access and modify the database.

Database storage is used for various types of databases, including relational databases (e.g., MySQL, PostgreSQL) and NoSQL databases (e.g., MongoDB, Apache Cassandra).

Use Cases and Best Practices

Now that we have explored the different aspects of servers and storage in the cloud, let's discuss some practical use cases and best practices for their effective utilization.

Use Case 1: Web Hosting Web hosting is one of the most popular use cases for servers and storage in the cloud. It involves hosting websites, web applications, and other online services accessible over the internet.

In this scenario, virtual servers are used to handle incoming web requests, process dynamic content, and serve static files. Object storage can be employed to store website assets, such as images and videos, while databases can hold the data necessary for the web application's functionality.

Best practices for web hosting in the cloud include:

- Utilizing Load Balancers: Load balancers distribute incoming web traffic across multiple servers, ensuring high availability and scalability.

- Employing Content Delivery Networks (CDNs): CDNs cache and serve static content from edge locations closer to end-users, reducing latency and improving website performance.

- Implementing Caching Solutions: Caching mechanisms, such as server-side caching or caching proxies, can improve the speed and responsiveness of web applications, reducing the load on servers.

- Monitoring and Scaling: Regular monitoring of server and storage resources is crucial to identify performance bottlenecks and scale resources as needed to handle increasing traffic or workload spikes.

- Regular Backups and Disaster Recovery: Implementing automated backup strategies and disaster recovery plans is essential to ensure data protection in case of hardware failures, data corruption, or other unforeseen events.

Use Case 2: Big Data Processing Big data processing involves the analysis of large volumes of data to extract valuable insights and patterns. Servers and storage in the cloud play a vital role in supporting big data frameworks and distributed computing systems.

In this use case, servers are used to run data processing frameworks, such as Apache Hadoop or Apache Spark, which distribute data across a cluster of machines for parallel processing. Block storage is commonly used to provide the required high-performance, low-latency storage infrastructure for data input, processing, and output.

Best practices for big data processing in the cloud include:

- Choosing Scalable Storage: Big data storage requirements can grow rapidly, so selecting scalable and durable storage solutions is crucial. Object storage, with its ability to handle massive data sets, is often an excellent choice.

- Optimizing Data Processing: Efficient data processing techniques, such as partitioning, indexing, and utilizing in-memory computing, can significantly improve the performance of big data analysis.

- Leveraging Managed Big Data Services: Cloud providers offer managed big data services, such as Amazon EMR, Azure HDInsight, and Google Cloud Dataproc, that simplify the deployment and management of big data frameworks.

- Ensuring Data Security and Governance: With the increasing volume and sensitivity of data, implementing adequate security measures, data encryption, and access controls is of utmost importance for protecting the privacy and integrity of the data.

- Considering Cost Optimization: Big data workloads can be resource-intensive, so optimizing resource usage and selecting cost-effective storage and compute options is essential to control costs.

Use Case 3: Data Backup and Archiving Data backup and archiving are critical for ensuring data resiliency, compliance, and business continuity. Cloud-based storage solutions offer a cost-effective and scalable approach to backup and archive large amounts of data.

In this use case, servers are responsible for handling data transfer, compression, encryption, and metadata management for backup and archival purposes. Object storage is commonly used due to its durability, scalability, and cost-effectiveness.

Best practices for data backup and archiving in the cloud include:

- Defining Backup and Retention Policies: Establishing clear policies around data retention, backup frequency, and backup versioning is essential for effective backup and archiving.

- Implementing Incremental and Differential Backups: To minimize storage and network bandwidth usage, incremental and differential backup strategies can be employed to back up only the changes since the last backup.

- Automating Backup Processes: Automating backup processes reduces the risk of human error and ensures that critical data is backed up regularly and consistently.

- Enforcing Data Encryption: To protect sensitive data during transit and storage, encrypting data at rest and in transit using industry-standard encryption algorithms is highly recommended.

- Periodic Testing and Recovery: Regularly testing backup and recovery processes, including data integrity checks, is crucial to ensure that backups are reliable and can be restored when needed.

Conclusion

Servers and storage are the foundation of cloud computing, providing the computational power and data storage capabilities that enable businesses and individuals to harness the power of the cloud. In this section, we explored the hardware components of servers, the concept of server virtualization, and the rise of serverless computing. We also discussed different storage options available in the cloud, including object storage, block storage, file storage, and database storage, along with their respective use cases and best practices.

As cloud computing continues to evolve, the demand for more powerful servers and scalable storage solutions will only increase. It is crucial for businesses and individuals to stay updated with the latest trends, technologies, and best practices in servers and storage to fully leverage the benefits of the cloud and conquer new frontiers of computing.

Now that we have covered servers and storage, let's move on to the exciting world of software-defined networking (SDN) and its impact on cloud infrastructure.

Networking Equipment

In the world of cloud computing, networking equipment plays a vital role in establishing and maintaining communication between various components of the cloud infrastructure. It forms the backbone of the network, enabling data transfer and ensuring seamless connectivity. In this section, we will explore the different types of networking equipment used in cloud computing and their significance in enabling efficient and reliable networking.

Routers

Routers are a fundamental component of any network, including cloud computing environments. They are responsible for routing data packets between networks, facilitating communication between different devices. Routers examine the destination address of a packet and determine the most optimal path for it to reach its intended destination. They possess a routing table, which contains information about the network topology and the paths to various destinations.

In cloud computing, routers are used in data centers to establish local area networks (LANs) and wide area networks (WANs). LAN routers connect devices within a data center while WAN routers connect different data centers or cloud regions. They ensure efficient data transfer and help in load balancing by directing traffic along the most suitable paths. Routers also provide security features like firewalls to protect the network from unauthorized access.

Let's consider an example. Suppose you are running a cloud-based gaming service where users from different geographical locations connect to your cloud servers. Routers play a crucial role here in ensuring that data packets are efficiently routed between the users and your servers. They examine the source and destination addresses of the packets and choose the best path to minimize latency and ensure a smooth gaming experience for your users.

Switches

Switches are another essential networking equipment used in cloud computing. They operate at the data link layer of the network and enable the efficient transfer of data packets within a local network. Unlike routers, switches do not examine the destination address of packets. Instead, they use MAC addresses to determine the destination device and establish a direct connection between the sender and the recipient.

In cloud computing environments, switches are used to connect various devices within a data center or a cluster of servers. They play a crucial role in ensuring high-speed and reliable communication between servers, storage systems, and other network devices. Switches have multiple ports, each capable of handling high data transfer rates. They use the MAC address table to determine the outgoing port for each packet, minimizing latency and optimizing network performance.

To illustrate the importance of switches, let's consider a scenario in which a company is running a cloud-based e-commerce platform. The platform consists of multiple servers that handle customer requests, process transactions, and manage inventory. Switches connect these servers, ensuring seamless communication

HARDWARE AND DATA CENTERS 75

among them. When a customer places an order, the switch directs the request to the appropriate server, enabling efficient order processing and ensuring a smooth shopping experience for the customers.

Firewalls

Firewalls are crucial networking equipment that provide security to cloud computing environments. They act as a barrier between internal networks, such as data centers, and external networks, such as the internet. Firewalls monitor incoming and outgoing network traffic, examining the data packets and enforcing security policies to block unauthorized access attempts.

In cloud computing, firewalls play a critical role in protecting sensitive data and preventing unauthorized access to cloud resources. They act as the first line of defense by filtering network traffic based on predefined rules. Firewalls can block malicious requests and prevent unauthorized users from accessing the cloud infrastructure. They also play a role in preventing Distributed Denial of Service (DDoS) attacks by identifying and blocking suspicious traffic patterns.

For example, imagine a cloud-based financial services application that handles sensitive customer data. To ensure the security of the data, firewalls are implemented to prevent unauthorized access attempts. The firewalls monitor network traffic, allowing only trusted sources to access the application and blocking any suspicious or potentially harmful requests.

Load Balancers

Load balancers are critical networking equipment used in cloud computing to distribute incoming network traffic across multiple servers or resources. They help optimize resource utilization, improve performance, and enhance availability. Load balancers use various algorithms to determine the most suitable server to handle each incoming request, ensuring that no single server is overloaded.

In cloud computing environments, load balancers are typically deployed in front of a pool of servers or resources. They receive incoming requests and distribute them evenly among the available servers based on factors such as server capacity, current load, and response time. Load balancers also monitor the health and availability of servers and can dynamically adjust the routing of traffic in case of server failures or performance degradation.

Let's consider a real-world example of load balancers in action. Suppose you are running a cloud-based video streaming service that experiences high traffic volumes during peak hours. Load balancers play a crucial role in evenly distributing the incoming video requests across multiple video servers. By distributing the load, load balancers ensure that each server can handle an optimal number of concurrent video streams, reducing buffering time and providing a seamless streaming experience for your users.

Virtual Private Network (VPN) Gateways

In cloud computing, Virtual Private Network (VPN) gateways are networking equipment that provide secure remote access to cloud resources. They enable users to establish encrypted connections to the cloud infrastructure, ensuring the privacy and integrity of data transmitted over public networks like the internet. VPN gateways create a secure tunnel through which data can pass between the user's device and the cloud resources.

VPN gateways play a crucial role in enabling remote access to cloud-based applications and resources. They ensure that data transmitted between the user's device and the cloud infrastructure remains confidential and protected from eavesdropping or unauthorized access. By encrypting the data traffic, VPN gateways provide a secure and private connection, even when accessing cloud resources from untrusted networks.

For example, imagine a company where employees work remotely and need access to cloud-based applications and data. VPN gateways allow these employees to establish secure connections to the company's cloud infrastructure, ensuring that sensitive data remains protected during transmission. This enables employees to work remotely without compromising the security of corporate resources.

Conclusion

Networking equipment forms the foundation of cloud computing, enabling the efficient transfer of data and ensuring seamless connectivity. Routers, switches, firewalls, load balancers, and VPN gateways are just a few examples of the critical equipment that powers cloud networks. Understanding these networking components is essential for building and maintaining robust and secure cloud infrastructure.

As the world of cloud computing continues to evolve, networking equipment will continue to play a vital role in enabling scalable and reliable cloud services. From managing network traffic to establishing secure connections, these equipment ensure efficient and secure communication within the cloud infrastructure.

In the next section, we will delve into the fascinating world of software-defined networking (SDN), which is revolutionizing how networks are designed and managed in cloud computing environments. Get ready to dive into the fucking magic behind SDN and explore its applications and benefits.

Virtualization and Hypervisors

In the world of cloud computing, virtualization plays a pivotal role in the efficient utilization of hardware resources. Virtualization allows multiple virtual machines (VMs) to run on a single physical server, enabling better resource allocation, scalability, and flexibility. At the heart of virtualization lies the concept of hypervisors, which serve as the foundation for creating and managing these virtualized environments.

Introduction to Virtualization

Virtualization is the process of creating a virtual version of a physical resource, such as a server, storage device, network, or operating system. By abstracting the underlying physical infrastructure, virtualization enables the efficient sharing of resources among multiple users or applications.

One of the key components of virtualization is the hypervisor, also known as a virtual machine monitor. A hypervisor is software that enables the creation and management of virtual machines. It sits between the physical hardware and the virtual machines, providing isolation and resource allocation among them.

Types of Hypervisors

There are two primary types of hypervisors: Type 1 and Type 2.

Type 1 hypervisors, also known as bare-metal hypervisors, are installed directly on the physical hardware. They have direct access to the underlying resources and manage the virtual machines independently. Examples of Type 1 hypervisors include Citrix XenServer, Microsoft Hyper-V, and VMware ESXi. These hypervisors offer high performance and are typically used in enterprise-level cloud infrastructure.

Type 2 hypervisors, on the other hand, are installed on top of an existing operating system. They rely on the host operating system to manage hardware resources and provide virtualization capabilities. Examples of Type 2 hypervisors include Oracle VirtualBox and VMware Workstation. While Type 2 hypervisors are convenient for desktop virtualization and testing, they are not as efficient as Type 1 hypervisors due to the additional layer of abstraction.

Virtualization Techniques

Hypervisors employ different virtualization techniques to create and manage virtual machines. Two commonly used techniques are full virtualization and para-virtualization.

In full virtualization, the hypervisor simulates the entire hardware environment for each virtual machine, allowing them to run unmodified operating systems. The guest operating systems are unaware that they are running within a virtualized environment. This technique provides a high level of compatibility but may introduce some performance overhead due to the need for hardware emulation.

Para-virtualization, on the other hand, requires modifications to the guest operating systems to be aware of the virtualization layer. The hypervisor provides a set of APIs that the guest operating systems can use to interact directly with the underlying hardware. This approach eliminates the need for hardware emulation, resulting in improved performance. However, it requires modifying the guest operating systems, making it less flexible than full virtualization.

Benefits of Virtualization

Virtualization offers numerous benefits in the context of cloud computing:

- **Resource utilization**: By running multiple virtual machines on a single physical server, virtualization enables better utilization of hardware resources.

- **Scalability**: Virtual machines can be easily provisioned or scaled down based on demand, allowing for efficient resource allocation.

- **Isolation**: Each virtual machine operates independently, providing isolation and security between different applications or users.

- **Flexibility**: Virtualization allows for the migration of virtual machines across physical servers without disrupting services, offering flexibility and reducing downtime.

- **Disaster recovery**: Virtualization simplifies the process of creating backups and restoring virtual machines, enhancing disaster recovery capabilities.

HARDWARE AND DATA CENTERS

Challenges and Considerations

While virtualization brings many benefits, there are also challenges and considerations to keep in mind:

- **Performance overhead:** Virtualization introduces a certain level of performance overhead due to the additional layer of abstraction and resource sharing.

- **Management complexity:** Managing a large number of virtual machines can be complex, requiring robust management tools and processes.

- **Security concerns:** The shared nature of hardware resources in virtualized environments introduces new security considerations. Proper isolation and security measures must be in place to mitigate risks.

- **Vendor lock-in:** Virtualization technologies and hypervisors may have proprietary features or dependencies, leading to vendor lock-in if not carefully considered.

Real-World Example: VMware vSphere

One of the most widely used virtualization platforms is VMware vSphere, which incorporates a Type 1 hypervisor called ESXi. vSphere provides a comprehensive suite of tools and features for creating, managing, and scaling virtualized environments.

Suppose a company wants to transition its on-premises infrastructure to the cloud using vSphere. They can utilize ESXi hypervisors to run multiple virtual machines on a cluster of physical servers. This consolidation enables them to maximize resource utilization while achieving high availability and scalability.

The company can also leverage vSphere's management tools, such as VMware vCenter Server, to simplify virtual machine provisioning, monitoring, and resource allocation. vSphere's robust security features, including network segmentation and access control, ensure the isolation and protection of virtualized workloads.

By adopting vSphere, the company can achieve cost savings, improved efficiency, and flexibility in managing their cloud infrastructure.

Further Resources

For further exploration of virtualization and hypervisors, consider the following resources:

1. *Virtualization Essentials* by Matthew Portnoy: This book provides a comprehensive guide to understanding virtualization concepts and technologies.

2. VMware Virtualization blog: The official blog of VMware offers insights, tutorials, and updates on virtualization and cloud technologies.

3. Virtualization Review: An online publication that covers the latest trends and technologies in the field of virtualization.

Summary

Virtualization, enabled by hypervisors, is a fundamental technology in cloud computing. It allows for the efficient utilization of hardware resources, scalability, and flexibility. By creating virtual machines that run on a single physical server, virtualization provides benefits such as improved resource utilization, isolation, and disaster recovery capabilities. However, it also introduces challenges, including performance overhead and security considerations. Understanding virtualization and choosing the right hypervisor are essential for building and managing cloud-based infrastructure effectively.

Data Center Architecture

In the world of cloud computing, data centers play a crucial role as the backbone of the infrastructure. These highly sophisticated facilities house thousands of servers, storage devices, networking equipment, and other components that enable the delivery of cloud services. Understanding the architecture of data centers is essential to comprehend how cloud computing works and how it can scale to meet the demands of modern applications.

Components of a Data Center

A typical data center comprises several key components that work together to provide a reliable and efficient computing environment. Let's dive into each of these components in detail:

1. Servers: Servers are the workhorses of a data center. They are responsible for running various applications and hosting virtual machines (VMs) that encapsulate the computing resources needed by cloud users. The servers are usually organized in racks, with each rack containing multiple server units. These units are designed to provide high-performance computing capabilities while minimizing energy consumption.

2. **Storage devices:** Data centers rely on multiple types of storage devices to meet the diverse needs of cloud users. These devices include hard disk drives (HDDs), solid-state drives (SSDs), and network-attached storage (NAS) devices. HDDs are commonly used for cost-effective bulk storage, while SSDs offer faster access speeds for applications that require high-performance storage. NAS devices provide shared storage accessible to multiple servers or VMs, enabling data sharing and collaboration.

3. **Networking equipment:** Networking is a critical component of data center architecture. It involves various devices, such as switches, routers, and firewalls, that enable communication between the servers, storage devices, and external networks. These devices ensure that data flows smoothly and securely within the data center and enable connectivity to the internet and other external networks.

4. **Power infrastructure:** Data centers consume a significant amount of electricity to power the servers and other equipment. To ensure uninterrupted operation, data centers incorporate redundant power systems, including backup generators and multiple power feeds from the utility grid. Uninterruptible power supply (UPS) systems are also used to provide temporary power during short outages or while the generators start up.

5. **Cooling systems:** Data centers generate a considerable amount of heat due to the high density of servers and other equipment. Therefore, efficient cooling systems are critical to maintain optimal operating conditions. These systems include chillers, air handlers, and computer room air conditioning (CRAC) units. They work together to remove heat from the data center and maintain a controlled environment to prevent equipment overheating.

6. **Physical security:** Data centers house valuable and sensitive data, making physical security a top priority. Access to data center facilities is tightly controlled, with security measures such as biometric authentication, video surveillance, and access control systems. Additionally, data centers often have redundant security systems and multiple layers of physical barriers to protect against unauthorized access.

7. **Monitoring and management:** Data centers employ comprehensive monitoring and management systems to ensure smooth operation and timely detection of any issues. These systems include environmental monitoring to track temperature and humidity levels, power monitoring to measure energy consumption, and performance monitoring to identify potential bottlenecks or anomalies. Additionally, management software and tools are used to automate tasks, allocate resources, and optimize the utilization of hardware.

Data Center Network Architecture

An efficient network architecture is crucial for data centers to ensure fast and reliable communication between servers, storage devices, and external networks. Let's explore the key elements of data center network architecture:

1. Top-of-Rack (ToR) Switches: ToR switches are located at the top of each server rack and act as the primary point of connection for servers within the rack. They provide high-speed connectivity and handle the traffic between servers and the rest of the data center network.

2. Aggregation Switches: Aggregation switches aggregate the traffic from multiple ToR switches and connect them to the core data center network. They ensure efficient communication between racks and facilitate load balancing and redundancy.

3. Core Switches: Core switches form the backbone of the data center network. They connect aggregation switches and provide high-bandwidth connectivity between different parts of the data center. Core switches are designed for low latency and high throughput to handle the massive amounts of data traffic within the data center.

4. Virtual Local Area Networks (VLANs): VLANs are used to logically group and isolate network devices within the data center. They provide separation, security, and flexibility by partitioning the network into multiple virtual networks within a single physical network infrastructure. VLANs enable efficient resource allocation and traffic management within the data center.

5. Network Load Balancers: Network load balancers distribute network traffic across multiple servers to ensure scalability, high availability, and optimal performance. They play a critical role in handling incoming requests and directing them to the appropriate servers within the data center.

6. Redundancy and Failover: Data centers implement redundancy and failover mechanisms to ensure uninterrupted service availability. Redundant components, such as switches, power supplies, and network connections, are deployed to eliminate single points of failure. Additionally, failover mechanisms are employed to automatically switch to backup systems or alternative paths in the event of a failure.

7. Software-Defined Networking (SDN): SDN is an emerging technology that brings programmability and automation to data center networks. It decouples the network control plane from the physical infrastructure, allowing administrators to manage and control network resources through software-based controllers. SDN simplifies network management, enables rapid provisioning of network services, and enhances overall network agility.

Data Center Scalability and Performance

Scalability and performance are key considerations in data center architecture to effectively handle the increasing demands of cloud computing. Here are some essential techniques and concepts related to scalability and performance:

1. Distributed Systems: Data centers often employ distributed systems to achieve scalability and fault tolerance. Distributed systems divide workloads across multiple servers, allowing parallel processing and efficient resource utilization. They enable horizontal scaling by adding more servers to handle increased workload demand.

2. Clustering: Clustering is a technique used to group multiple servers together to collectively provide a single service. It enhances reliability, scalability, and performance by balancing the workload across multiple servers and enabling redundancy. Clustering can be applied to various components in a data center, including servers, storage devices, and network switches.

3. Load Balancing: Load balancing distributes workload evenly across multiple servers to ensure optimal resource utilization and prevent any single server from becoming overloaded. This helps achieve higher performance, scalability, and availability. Load balancing can be performed at various levels, including application-level, network-level, and DNS-level.

4. **Caching:** Caching is a technique that stores frequently accessed data closer to the users or applications to reduce latency and improve performance. It helps alleviate the load on the primary storage systems by serving data from faster storage tiers, such as solid-state drives or in-memory caches. Caching can be implemented at different levels, including the application level, database level, or content delivery network (CDN) level.

5. **Content Delivery Networks (CDNs):** CDNs are a distributed network of servers deployed across multiple locations to deliver content to users with minimized latency and network congestion. CDNs store cached copies of web content, including images, videos, and static files, in data centers strategically positioned closer to end-users. By serving content from the nearest CDN edge server, latency is reduced, resulting in faster content delivery.

6. **Elasticity:** Elasticity is the ability of a data center to dynamically allocate computing resources based on demand. It allows for automatic scaling up or down of resources to accommodate workload fluctuations. Cloud providers implement elasticity through features such as auto-scaling groups, which automatically add or remove servers based on predefined scaling conditions.

7. **Latency Optimization:** Minimizing latency is crucial for delivering a responsive user experience. Data center architects employ various techniques, such as optimizing network routing, reducing packet processing time, and deploying edge computing systems, to reduce latency. Edge computing brings compute resources closer to the end-users, reducing the round-trip time for data transmission.

Data Center Architecture: Summary

Data center architecture is the foundation upon which cloud computing is built. Understanding the components, network architecture, and scalability techniques employed in data centers is essential for comprehending the complexities of cloud computing.

In this section, we explored the key components of a data center, including servers, storage devices, networking equipment, power infrastructure, cooling systems, physical security, and monitoring systems. We also delved into data center network architecture, discussing the roles of switches, VLANs, load balancers, and high availability mechanisms.

Furthermore, we examined important concepts related to scalability and performance, such as distributed systems, clustering, load balancing, caching, content delivery networks, elasticity, and latency optimization.

As cloud computing continues to evolve and transform various industries, a solid understanding of data center architecture is crucial for developers, administrators, and anyone interested in leveraging the power of cloud computing. By embracing the principles and techniques discussed in this section, organizations can build robust and efficient data centers that enable the deployment and scaling of cloud services to conquer the challenges of the digital era.

The Fucking Hardware That Powers the Cloud

In this section, we're going to take a deep dive into the fucking hardware that powers the cloud. You know, the physical stuff that makes all the virtual magic possible. We'll explore the servers, storage devices, networking equipment, and data center architecture that work together to keep the cloud running smoothly. So buckle up, because shit's about to get real.

Servers and Storage

At the heart of the cloud are the servers, those powerful machines that handle all the computing and storage tasks. These bad boys come in different shapes and sizes, but they all have the same mission: to process and store your data. Think of them as the workhorses of the cloud.

Servers are packed with processing power and memory, allowing them to handle multiple simultaneous tasks from different users. They're equipped with processors (CPUs), which are like the brains of the operation, and RAM (Random Access Memory), which is like the short-term memory that allows for quick and easy access to data.

Now, when it comes to storage in the cloud, there are two main types: object storage and block storage. Object storage is all about storing unstructured data, such as images, videos, and documents. It's like a giant warehouse where you can store a shit ton of stuff without worrying about organizing it too much. On the other hand, block storage is more structured and is used for storing data in fixed chunks called blocks. It's like storage units where you can access and modify individual blocks independently.

Networking Equipment

To make the cloud work, we need networking equipment to connect all the different parts together. This includes routers, switches, and firewalls. These devices ensure that your data gets from point A to point B in the blink of an eye.

Routers are like traffic managers. They direct data packets on the most efficient path to their destination. Switches, on the other hand, act like traffic controllers. They decide where to send the data within a local network. And firewalls? Well, they're like bouncers at a club. They filter out any unwanted or malicious data, keeping your shit safe and secure.

Virtualization and Hypervisors

Here comes the cool part: virtualization. This technology allows multiple virtual machines (VMs) to run on a single physical server. It's like having several mini-computers coexisting in harmony, each with its own operating system and applications.

The secret sauce behind virtualization is a piece of software called a hypervisor. This badass motherfucker sits between the physical server and the virtual machines, managing their resources and ensuring they play nice with each other. It's like the referee of the virtual world, keeping everything in check.

Data Center Architecture

Now, let's talk about data center architecture. Data centers are the physical locations where all the cloud hardware is housed. They're massive buildings filled with racks upon racks of servers, storage devices, and networking equipment.

Data centers are designed to be highly reliable and secure. They have redundant power supplies, backup generators, and cooling systems to ensure that the servers don't overheat. They also have fire suppression systems and physical security measures to protect against any catastrophic events or unauthorized access.

Furthermore, data centers are often spread out across different locations to provide geographical redundancy. This means that if one data center goes down, your data is still safe and accessible from another location. It's like having a backup plan for your backup plan.

The Fucking Hardware Ecosystem

So, to summarize, the hardware that powers the cloud is a fucking complex ecosystem of servers, storage devices, networking equipment, and data center architecture. It's a carefully orchestrated dance where each component plays a crucial role in delivering the cloud services we rely on.

But the hardware is just the beginning. In the next sections, we'll dive deeper into the software and technologies that make the cloud even more powerful and flexible. It's like adding a turbocharger to a race car. So buckle up, because there's a whole lot more fucking magic to explore. Let's go!

Key Takeaways:
- Servers are the workhorses of the cloud, handling processing and storage tasks. - Object storage is used for unstructured data, while block storage is used for structured data. - Networking equipment, such as routers, switches, and firewalls, connects the different parts of the cloud. - Virtualization allows multiple virtual machines to run on a single physical server, managed by a hypervisor. - Data centers are the physical locations where the cloud hardware is housed, designed to be reliable and secure.

Software-Defined Networking (SDN)

Network Virtualization

In this section, we will dive into the fascinating world of network virtualization, a key technology in cloud computing that allows for the creation of virtual networks on top of a physical network infrastructure. Network virtualization is instrumental in providing a flexible and efficient way to manage network resources, improve security, and enhance network performance.

Introduction to Network Virtualization

Traditionally, network devices like routers, switches, and firewalls have been physical hardware entities that are dedicated to specific functions and tasks. Each device operates independently, leading to a complex and static network infrastructure that is difficult to manage and scale. Network virtualization changes this by decoupling the network hardware from the software that controls it, enabling the creation of virtual networks that are isolated, scalable, and programmable.

At its core, network virtualization is about abstracting the physical network infrastructure and providing a logical representation of network resources. This logical representation, known as a virtual network, allows for the creation of multiple independent networks running on top of the same physical infrastructure. Each virtual network can have its own unique network topology, addressing scheme, security policies, and quality of service settings.

Principles of Network Virtualization

Network virtualization relies on a few key principles to provide its capabilities:

1. **Virtual Network Overlay:** Network virtualization overlays virtual networks on top of the existing physical network infrastructure. This overlay creates an abstraction layer that separates the virtual networks from the underlying hardware, allowing for flexibility and scalability.

2. **Network Hypervisor:** The network hypervisor is the software component that provides the virtualization functionality. It manages the creation, configuration, and termination of virtual networks. It also handles the mapping of virtual network traffic to the physical network infrastructure.

3. **Isolation and Segmentation:** One of the key advantages of network virtualization is the ability to isolate and segment virtual networks. Each virtual network operates in its own virtual environment, ensuring that the traffic and resources of one virtual network do not interfere with those of another.

4. **Resource Pooling:** Network virtualization allows for the pooling of network resources, such as bandwidth and ports, across multiple virtual networks. This pooling increases resource utilization and ensures efficient use of network resources.

5. **Programmability and Automation:** Network virtualization makes networks programmable and automatable. The virtual networks can be dynamically created, modified, and destroyed through software-defined networking (SDN) technologies. This programmability enables greater agility and responsiveness in network management and provisioning.

Network Virtualization Technologies

Network virtualization is enabled by various technologies and protocols. Let's explore some of the key ones:

1. **Virtual Local Area Networks (VLANs):** VLANs are a widely used technology that allows for the logical segmentation of a physical LAN into multiple virtual LANs. Each VLAN operates as a separate broadcast domain, enabling network isolation and improved security.

2. **Virtual Extensible LAN (VXLAN):** VXLAN is an overlay network technology that provides network virtualization at the layer 2 level. It enables the creation of virtual networks across different physical networks, extending the reach of a virtual network beyond a single data center.

3. **Network Virtualization using Generic Routing Encapsulation (NVGRE):** NVGRE is another overlay network technology similar to VXLAN. It encapsulates layer 2 and layer 3 network traffic within IP packets, allowing for the creation of virtual networks that span multiple physical networks.

4. **Software-Defined Networking (SDN):** SDN separates the network control plane from the data plane, centralizing network management and control. By leveraging SDN, network virtualization can be implemented through the use of network controllers that programmatically configure and manage virtual networks.

Use Cases and Benefits of Network Virtualization

Network virtualization offers numerous benefits and has a wide range of use cases in modern computing environments. Let's explore some of the key use cases and benefits:

Use Cases:

- **Data Center Networks:** Network virtualization is heavily utilized in data centers to create virtual networks for different tenants or applications. This allows for efficient resource allocation, isolation, and improved network management.

- **Multi-Tenancy:** Network virtualization enables service providers to create separate virtual networks for each tenant, offering them the illusion of a dedicated network infrastructure while sharing the underlying physical network.

- **Network Function Virtualization (NFV):** NFV leverages network virtualization to replace traditional dedicated network appliances with virtualized network functions. This allows for more flexible and scalable deployment of network services.

- **Disaster Recovery:** Network virtualization can help simplify and accelerate disaster recovery processes by allowing for the efficient replication of virtual networks and virtual machines between different data centers or cloud regions.

- **Cloud Computing:** Network virtualization is a fundamental component of cloud computing. It enables cloud service providers to create virtual networks for their customers, ensuring network isolation, security, and efficient resource utilization.

Benefits:

- **Efficient Resource Utilization:** Network virtualization allows for better resource utilization by pooling network resources across virtual networks. This leads to higher network efficiency and cost savings.

- **Improved Security:** Virtual networks provide isolation and segmentation, enhancing security by isolating traffic and preventing unauthorized access between virtual networks.

- **Scalability and Flexibility:** Virtual networks can be easily created, modified, or removed, providing scalability and flexibility in network management and provisioning.

- **Reduced Time to Deployment:** Network virtualization enables automation and programmability, reducing the time required to deploy and configure networks.

- **Simplified Network Management:** Network virtualization simplifies network management by centralizing configuration and control, allowing for easier monitoring and troubleshooting.

Challenges and Considerations

Despite its many benefits, network virtualization also comes with its own set of challenges and considerations. It is important to be aware of these factors when implementing network virtualization:

- **Performance Overhead:** Network virtualization introduces some performance overhead due to the need for packet encapsulation and decapsulation, as well as additional processing required by the network hypervisor.

- **Complexity**: Network virtualization adds another layer of complexity to the network infrastructure, requiring specialized knowledge and skills for its design, implementation, and management.

- **Interoperability**: Ensuring interoperability between different virtualization technologies and protocols can be challenging. Careful planning and coordination are required to integrate various virtualization solutions seamlessly.

- **Security Considerations**: While network virtualization can enhance network security, it can also introduce new security challenges. It is essential to implement proper security measures to protect against attacks and vulnerabilities specific to virtualized environments.

Case Study: Network Virtualization in Cloud Networking

To illustrate the practical applications of network virtualization, let's consider its implementation in cloud networking. In cloud environments, network virtualization plays a crucial role in enabling seamless connectivity, security, and scalability for virtual machines and applications.

Scenario:

A cloud service provider wants to offer its customers the ability to create virtual networks for their applications. The provider needs to ensure network isolation, efficient resource utilization, and simplified network management.

Solution:

By leveraging network virtualization, the cloud service provider can create virtual networks for each customer, allowing them to define their own network topology and security policies. The network hypervisor manages the virtual networks, mapping the customer's virtual traffic to the physical network infrastructure.

With network virtualization, the cloud service provider can achieve the following benefits:

- **Enhanced Security**: Each customer's virtual network is isolated from others, ensuring traffic separation and preventing unauthorized access.

- **Efficient Resource Utilization**: Network resources, such as bandwidth and ports, are shared across virtual networks, optimizing resource utilization and reducing costs.

- Scalability and Flexibility: Multiple virtual networks can be easily created, modified, or removed, providing scalability and flexibility to customers.

- Simplified Network Management: Network virtualization centralizes network management, simplifying configuration, monitoring, and troubleshooting.

In this case study, network virtualization enables the cloud service provider to offer a robust and secure network infrastructure to its customers, meeting their specific networking requirements while maximizing resource efficiency.

Conclusion

Network virtualization is a transformative technology that revolutionizes the way networks are designed, configured, and managed. It provides a flexible and scalable approach to network resource utilization, enhances security and isolation, and simplifies network management.

In this section, we explored the principles of network virtualization, the technologies that enable it, and its use cases and benefits. We also discussed the challenges and considerations associated with network virtualization, highlighting the importance of careful planning and implementation.

Network virtualization is a critical component of cloud computing and modern networking architectures. It empowers organizations to build agile and efficient networks that can keep pace with the ever-evolving demands of the digital world.

Now that we have a solid understanding of network virtualization, let's move on to the exciting world of containerization and orchestration in the next section!

SDN Controllers and Switches

SDN (Software-Defined Networking) is a revolutionary approach to network management that simplifies network configuration and control by separating the control plane from the data plane. In SDN, the network control logic is centralized in a software-based controller, while the data forwarding is performed by programmable switches. In this section, we will explore the key components of SDN, including SDN controllers and switches, and discuss their functionalities and advantages.

SDN Controllers

The SDN controller is the brain behind the SDN architecture. It is responsible for managing and controlling the network infrastructure by translating high-level network policies into low-level instructions for the switches. The controller acts as a central point of control, enabling network administrators to dynamically manage network resources, automate network provisioning, and enforce network policies.

There are several popular SDN controller platforms available today, each with its own features and capabilities. Some of the leading SDN controllers in the market include:

1. OpenDaylight: An open-source SDN controller platform supported by a vibrant community of users and developers. It provides a wide range of network services and supports multiple southbound protocols, making it highly flexible and interoperable.

2. ONOS (Open Network Operating System): Another open-source SDN controller that focuses on performance and scalability. It offers advanced features such as distributed control and high availability, making it suitable for large-scale networks.

3. Ryu: A lightweight open-source SDN controller written in Python. It is highly extensible and provides a simple framework for implementing custom network applications.

SDN controllers communicate with the switches using southbound protocols, such as OpenFlow, which is the most widely adopted protocol for SDN. OpenFlow enables the controller to directly program the forwarding behavior of the switches, allowing for centralized control and network virtualization.

SDN Switches

SDN switches, also known as OpenFlow switches, form the data plane of the SDN architecture. They are responsible for forwarding network traffic based on the instructions received from the SDN controller.

SDN switches are programmable devices that can be controlled and configured by the SDN controller. They provide fine-grained control over traffic flows, allowing network administrators to define traffic policies, set up quality-of-service (QoS) rules, and implement advanced network services.

OpenFlow, as mentioned earlier, is the most commonly used protocol for communication between the SDN controller and the switches. It enables the controller to specify the flow entries in the switch's flow table, which determine how incoming packets are processed and forwarded.

SDN switches are designed to be flexible and modular, supporting various hardware and software capabilities. They can be implemented using commodity hardware or purpose-built hardware, depending on the specific requirements of the network. Additionally, some switches support OpenFlow in hybrid mode, allowing for both traditional networking and SDN capabilities on the same device.

Benefits of SDN Controllers and Switches

SDN controllers and switches offer numerous benefits over traditional networking approaches. Here are some of the key advantages:

1. Network programmability: SDN allows network administrators to program and automate network tasks using software, reducing manual configuration efforts and enabling rapid service deployment.

2. Centralized management: With SDN, network management is centralized in the controller, providing a holistic view of the network. This allows for easier troubleshooting, policy enforcement, and network optimization.

3. Flexibility and scalability: SDN switches are highly programmable and can adapt to changing network requirements. They enable dynamic reconfiguration of network resources, making it easier to scale the network and accommodate new services or applications.

4. Network agility: SDN facilitates the creation of virtual networks and network slices, allowing different tenants or applications to share the same physical infrastructure while maintaining isolation and security.

5. Enhanced security: SDN provides granular control over network traffic, making it easier to detect and mitigate security threats. By centralizing security policies and enforcement, SDN can help prevent unauthorized access and protect against network attacks.

SDN Controllers and Switches in Action

To better understand the role of SDN controllers and switches, let's consider an example scenario.

Suppose you are a network administrator responsible for managing a large enterprise network. With traditional networking, configuring network switches and implementing new services can be a time-consuming and error-prone process. However, with SDN, you can leverage an SDN controller to streamline network management tasks.

Using the SDN controller, you can define network policies and service requirements in a centralized manner. The controller then communicates with the SDN switches, instructing them on how to process network traffic.

For example, let's say you want to prioritize video conferencing traffic over other types of traffic in your network. With the SDN controller, you can define a QoS policy that assigns a higher priority to video conferencing packets.

The controller will then program the SDN switches to prioritize the video conferencing traffic based on the defined policy. The switches will inspect incoming packets, classify them as video conferencing traffic, and forward them accordingly.

This level of granular control and automation is made possible by the separation of the control plane and data plane in SDN. By centralizing network control in the SDN controller and programmable switches, network administrators can achieve greater flexibility, scalability, and manageability.

Wrap Up

In this section, we explored SDN controllers and switches in the context of software-defined networking. We learned that SDN controllers act as the central control point, translating network policies into low-level instructions for the switches. On the other hand, SDN switches are programmable devices responsible for forwarding network traffic based on the controller's instructions.

SDN controllers and switches offer significant advantages over traditional networking approaches, including network programmability, centralized management, flexibility, scalability, network agility, and enhanced security. By leveraging these technologies, network administrators can simplify network management, automate tasks, and achieve greater control and efficiency in their networks.

SDN is a rapidly evolving field with ongoing research and development. As the demand for agile and efficient network infrastructure grows, SDN is expected to play a crucial role in shaping the future of networking. Stay tuned for new advancements and applications in SDN as the technology continues to mature.

Now that we have covered SDN controllers and switches, let's move on to the next section, where we will explore containerization and orchestration in the context of cloud infrastructure.

SDN Applications and Use Cases

SDN, or Software-Defined Networking, is an innovative approach to network management and control that allows network administrators to programmatically control and configure network devices. In this section, we will explore some of the specific applications and use cases of SDN in various industries and scenarios.

Data Centers and Virtualization

One of the primary areas where SDN has gained significant traction is in data centers. Data centers are the backbone of cloud computing and other internet-based services, and they require robust and scalable networking infrastructure. SDN offers several benefits in this domain:

- **Network Virtualization:** SDN allows for the creation of virtual networks, which are separate and isolated logical networks running on the same physical infrastructure. This enables efficient sharing of network resources and better utilization of hardware resources.

- **Automated Network Provisioning:** With SDN, network administrators can quickly and easily provision and configure network resources. It eliminates the need for manual configuration and reduces the time required for deploying and managing network services within a data center.

- **Dynamic Load Balancing:** SDN enables dynamic load balancing within a data center by intelligently distributing network traffic across multiple servers. This ensures optimal resource utilization and improves overall network performance.

- **Scalability and Elasticity:** SDN provides a scalable and elastic network infrastructure that can easily adapt to changing workloads and demands. It offers the ability to dynamically allocate and deallocate network resources based on application requirements, leading to better resource utilization and cost savings.

Wide Area Networks and Traffic Engineering

In addition to data centers, SDN can also be used to optimize and manage Wide Area Networks (WANs) and perform traffic engineering tasks. WANs connect geographically dispersed locations and often face challenges such as high latency and limited bandwidth. SDN brings several advantages in this context:

- **Traffic Optimization:** SDN enables network administrators to optimize the flow of network traffic across geographically dispersed locations. It allows for traffic engineering techniques such as traffic rerouting, congestion control, and quality of service (QoS) prioritization, leading to improved network performance and reduced latency.

- **Improved Network Security:** SDN provides better network security by allowing administrators to implement centrally controlled security policies across the entire network. It enables rapid threat response, real-time traffic monitoring, and automated security enforcement, enhancing network security and reducing vulnerabilities.

- **Bandwidth Management:** SDN facilitates efficient bandwidth management by dynamically allocating bandwidth based on application requirements. It allows for dynamic adjustment of network capacity, ensuring optimal bandwidth utilization and minimizing network congestion.

- **Multi-Tenant Networks:** SDN enables the creation of multi-tenant networks, where multiple organizations or entities share the same network infrastructure. It provides network isolation and segmentation, ensuring the privacy and security of each tenant while reducing infrastructure costs.

Internet of Things (IoT) and Smart Cities

The Internet of Things (IoT) is a rapidly growing field that encompasses interconnected devices and sensors. SDN can play a crucial role in managing and orchestrating IoT infrastructure and applications, particularly in the context of smart cities:

- **Network Management and Control:** SDN allows for centralized management and control of IoT devices and sensors. It provides a unified view of the entire IoT infrastructure, making it easier to monitor and manage connected devices, and enabling automated troubleshooting and fault detection.

- **Secure and Resilient IoT Networks:** SDN enables secure communication and data exchange between IoT devices by implementing encryption, access control, and traffic segmentation. It also enhances network resilience by offering redundancy and failover mechanisms, ensuring uninterrupted connectivity.

- **Traffic Optimization and Energy Efficiency:** SDN can optimize traffic flows in IoT networks, reducing congestion and improving overall network performance. Additionally, it helps in achieving energy efficiency by dynamically controlling the connectivity of IoT devices based on their usage patterns, thus minimizing energy consumption.

- **Smart City Services:** SDN can be leveraged to build a comprehensive network infrastructure for smart cities. It allows for efficient management of various city services such as transportation systems, energy grids, waste management, and public safety, leading to improved quality of life for citizens.

Education and Research Networks

SDN has the potential to revolutionize education and research networks by providing flexibility, scalability, and control. Here are some notable applications in this domain:

- **Virtual Laboratories:** SDN enables the creation of virtual network laboratories in educational institutions, allowing students to gain hands-on experience with complex network configurations and experiments. It provides a cost-effective and scalable solution for creating realistic network environments.

- **Traffic Engineering and QoS:** SDN can optimize network traffic in educational institutions by implementing traffic engineering techniques like load balancing, congestion control, and QoS prioritization. This ensures efficient utilization of network resources and enhances the overall user experience.

SOFTWARE-DEFINED NETWORKING (SDN)

- **Network Monitoring and Management:** SDN simplifies network monitoring and management in educational institutions by providing centralized control and visibility into network activity. Network administrators can easily detect and resolve network issues, ensuring smooth and uninterrupted network access for students and faculty.

- **Research Experimentation:** SDN offers a programmable and customizable network infrastructure, ideal for research experimentation. Researchers can simulate various network scenarios, test new protocols, and study the impacts of different network configurations, leading to advancements in networking technologies.

SDN applications and use cases are diverse and span across various industries and domains. The evolution of SDN continues to unlock new possibilities, enabling organizations to build more efficient, scalable, and secure network infrastructures. As technology advances and new challenges emerge, SDN will continue to play a vital role in shaping the future of networking.

The Fucking Magic Behind SDN

SDN, or Software-Defined Networking, is the magic that makes modern networks flexible, scalable, and dynamic. In this section, we will delve into the fucking fascinating world of SDN and understand how it revolutionizes traditional networking.

The Need for SDN

Traditional networks, with their complex and static architectures, can be a real pain in the ass to manage and maintain. Making changes to the network requires manual configuration and troubleshooting, leading to time-consuming and error-prone processes. Moreover, these networks are not designed to handle the ever-increasing demand for bandwidth and scalability in modern applications.

This is where SDN comes into play. It is a new approach to networking that separates the control plane from the data plane, allowing for centralized control and programmability. In essence, SDN decouples the network control and forwarding functions, making the network more agile, intelligent, and fucking manageable.

SDN Architecture

At the heart of SDN is its architecture, which consists of three main components:

1. **Application Layer:** This layer comprises the network applications and services that utilize SDN capabilities. These applications can leverage the centralized control plane to dynamically control the network behavior based on application requirements.

2. **Control Layer:** This layer is responsible for maintaining a global view of the network and making decisions about how network traffic should be forwarded. It includes the SDN controller, which is where the magic of SDN really happens.

3. **Infrastructure Layer:** This layer consists of the physical and virtual network devices, such as switches, routers, and access points. These devices, also known as SDN switches, are responsible for forwarding network traffic based on the instructions received from the SDN controller.

The Fucking Workings of SDN

Now, let's get to the core of the fucking magic behind SDN. At the control layer, the SDN controller plays a crucial role in orchestrating the network. It communicates with the infrastructure layer to gather information about the network topology, link capacities, and traffic patterns. This information is often collected through protocols like OpenFlow.

Based on the gathered information, the controller can make intelligent decisions about how the network traffic should be forwarded. It can program the SDN switches to enforce certain policies, such as forwarding traffic based on specific criteria, implementing quality of service (QoS) rules, or applying security measures.

The SDN switches, unlike traditional switches, are no longer responsible for making forwarding decisions. Instead, they rely on the instructions received from the SDN controller. When a packet arrives at an SDN switch, it is sent to the controller, which examines the packet header and decides where the packet should be forwarded. Then, the controller programs the appropriate SDN switch to perform the forwarding action.

This separation of the control plane and data plane allows for centralized control and management of the network. It enables network administrators to define policies and make changes to the network dynamically, without having to manually configure each individual network device.

SOFTWARE-DEFINED NETWORKING (SDN)

Benefits and Use Cases

The fucking magic of SDN brings numerous benefits and opens up exciting possibilities in networking. Let's explore some of these benefits and the fucking use cases where SDN shines:

- **Network Agility**: SDN allows for rapid deployment and reconfiguration of networks, making it perfect for dynamic environments where network requirements change frequently.

- **Centralized Control**: With SDN, network administrators have a centralized view and control over the entire network, simplifying management and troubleshooting.

- **Programmability**: SDN enables network customization and programmability, providing the flexibility to tailor network behavior to specific application requirements.

- **Traffic Optimization**: By analyzing network traffic patterns, SDN controllers can optimize traffic flow, leading to improved performance, reduced congestion, and better resource utilization.

- **Virtualization and Multitenancy**: SDN makes it easier to create virtual networks and support multiple tenants, allowing for efficient and isolated network sharing.

Some popular use cases of SDN include data center networking, wide area networks (WAN), network slicing in 5G, and IoT networks. SDN brings increased efficiency, scalability, and flexibility to these domains.

Fucking Challenges and Limitations

While SDN is revolutionary and fucking awesome, it does come with its fair share of challenges and limitations. Let's take a look at some of them:

- **Security**: Centralized control and programmability introduce new security risks and attack vectors. Proper security measures must be implemented to protect SDN infrastructure and prevent unauthorized access.

- **Interoperability**: SDN involves different vendors and technologies, which can lead to interoperability issues. Standards such as OpenFlow help address this challenge, but full interoperability is still a work in progress.

- **Scalability**: Scalability remains a concern, especially when dealing with large-scale networks. As the network grows, the SDN controller may face challenges in handling the increased load and maintaining real-time responsiveness.

- **Dependency on Controller**: The centralized control provided by the SDN controller means that the controller becomes a single point of failure. Redundancy and failover mechanisms must be in place to ensure high availability.

Overcoming these challenges is essential for the widespread adoption of SDN and its full realization of its fucking potential.

Exploring Further

If you're interested in diving deeper into the world of SDN, here are some resources that you can explore:

- **Books**: "Software-Defined Networks: A Comprehensive Approach" by Paul Goransson and Chuck Black provides a comprehensive overview of SDN concepts and technologies.

- **Online Courses**: Platforms like Coursera, edX, and Udemy offer online courses on SDN and network virtualization. Look for courses by reputable institutions such as Stanford University and the University of Washington.

- **Open Source Projects**: Open source projects like OpenDaylight and ONOS provide platforms for experimenting with SDN technologies and building scalable SDN solutions.

- **Industry Conferences and Events**: Attending industry conferences and events such as the Open Networking Summit (ONS) can provide valuable insights into the current trends and advancements in the field of SDN.

Remember, understanding the fucking magic behind SDN is just the beginning. The world of networking is evolving rapidly, and embracing new technologies like SDN is essential for staying at the fucking forefront. So keep exploring, experimenting, and fucking conquering the world of SDN!

Containerization and Orchestration

Introduction to Containers

In this section, we will delve into the fascinating world of containers and explore how they have revolutionized software development and deployment. Containers are lightweight, portable, and self-contained units that package applications and their dependencies, allowing them to run consistently across different computing environments. This section will cover the definition and characteristics of containers, the benefits and use cases, and the popular tools and frameworks used for container deployment and management.

Definition and Characteristics

A container is an isolated and independent execution environment that encapsulates an application with its runtime dependencies. It allows applications to run smoothly across different operating systems and infrastructure without requiring modifications or configuration changes. Containers achieve this by leveraging operating system-level virtualization, which enables multiple containers to run on a single host machine.

Containers have some key characteristics that differentiate them from traditional virtual machines (VMs). First, containers share the host operating system kernel, which makes them lightweight and fast to start up compared to VMs. Additionally, containers provide consistent and predictable behavior, as they encapsulate not only the application but also its runtime libraries, dependencies, and configuration settings. This consistency eliminates the "it works on my machine" problem and ensures that applications behave the same way across different environments.

Benefits and Use Cases

The adoption of containers has skyrocketed in recent years due to the numerous benefits they offer to developers, IT operations teams, and organizations as a whole. Let's explore some of these benefits and discuss how containers are being used in various scenarios.

1. **Simplified Application Deployment:** Containers provide a standardized and repeatable deployment model, making it easier to package and distribute applications. Developers can build an application once and run it anywhere, eliminating compatibility issues and reducing time spent on troubleshooting environment-related problems.

2. **Scalability and Resource Efficiency:** Containers enable efficient utilization of resources and allow applications to scale horizontally. With containers, it is simple to spin up multiple instances of an application to handle increased traffic or demand. This flexibility and scalability make containers well-suited for cloud-native and microservices architectures.

3. **Isolation and Security:** Containers offer strong isolation between applications and the underlying host system. Each container has its own file system, process space, and network stack, which helps prevent interference and improves security. Isolation also enables different versions of software libraries to coexist peacefully, avoiding conflicts between application dependencies.

4. **Continuous Integration and Delivery (CI/CD):** Containers play a crucial role in modern CI/CD pipelines. By packaging an application into a container image, developers can ensure consistent testing and deployment environments throughout the software development lifecycle. Containers can be easily integrated into automation tools to streamline build, test, and deployment processes.

5. **Hybrid and Multi-Cloud Environments:** Containers are highly portable, making them an ideal choice for hybrid and multi-cloud deployments. Applications packaged in containers can be easily moved between different cloud providers or on-premises environments without requiring significant modifications. This portability enables organizations to embrace a multi-cloud strategy and avoid vendor lock-in.

6. **Rapid Development and Experimentation:** Containers provide an isolated and reproducible environment for rapid prototyping and experimentation. Developers can quickly spin up containers with specific configurations, test new features, and iterate on their code without affecting production environments. This flexibility encourages innovation and accelerates the development process.

Popular Tools and Frameworks

To leverage the power of containers, developers and organizations rely on a variety of tools and frameworks that simplify the deployment and management of containerized applications. Let's explore some of the most popular ones:

1. **Docker:** Docker is the de facto standard for container technology. It provides an easy-to-use command-line interface and a powerful container runtime that manages the lifecycle of containers. Docker also offers a registry to store and distribute container images, making it convenient for sharing and collaborating with others.

2. **Kubernetes:** Kubernetes is an open-source container orchestration platform developed by Google. It automates the deployment, scaling, and management of

containerized applications. Kubernetes provides advanced features like container load balancing, service discovery, and self-healing capabilities, making it ideal for managing complex containerized environments.

3. Red Hat OpenShift: OpenShift is a popular container platform built on top of Kubernetes. It provides additional features and tools for streamlined development, deployment, and management of containerized applications. OpenShift simplifies the adoption of containers by offering an integrated and user-friendly experience for developers and operations teams.

4. AWS Elastic Container Service (ECS): ECS is a fully managed container orchestration service provided by Amazon Web Services (AWS). It simplifies the deployment of containers on AWS and integrates seamlessly with other AWS services. ECS allows developers to run containers without managing the underlying infrastructure, making it an attractive option for organizations already utilizing AWS.

5. Azure Kubernetes Service (AKS): AKS is a managed container orchestration service offered by Microsoft Azure. It provides an enterprise-grade Kubernetes environment without the complexity of managing the underlying infrastructure. AKS integrates with other Azure services, making it easy to build and deploy cloud-native applications.

6. Google Kubernetes Engine (GKE): GKE is a managed Kubernetes service provided by Google Cloud Platform (GCP). It offers a highly available and scalable Kubernetes environment with integrated monitoring, logging, and identity and access management capabilities. GKE is well-suited for organizations leveraging GCP for their cloud infrastructure.

These are just a few examples of the tools and frameworks available for container deployment and management. The choice of the right tool depends on specific requirements, existing infrastructure, and the level of control desired.

In the next section, we will explore Docker and Kubernetes in more detail, as they are two of the most widely used container technologies. We will delve into their architecture, key concepts, and how to use them effectively for containerizing and deploying applications.

Summary

In this section, we explored the fascinating world of containers, understanding their definition, characteristics, and benefits. We discussed how containers revolutionize application deployment, enabling simplified processes, scalability, isolation, and security. We also examined popular tools and frameworks like

Docker, Kubernetes, OpenShift, AWS ECS, Azure AKS, and GCP GKE, which make container deployment and management more accessible and efficient.

Containers have become a game-changer in the software development industry. Their ability to encapsulate applications and dependencies into portable and lightweight units has simplified the deployment process and improved scalability, resource efficiency, and security. With the rise of cloud computing and modern development practices, containers have become an essential tool in the toolkit of every developer and IT professional.

In the next section, we will dive deeper into Docker, one of the most widely adopted container technologies. We will explore its architecture, core concepts, and demonstrate how to use Docker to build, package, and run applications in containers. The journey into the world of containers continues, so buckle up and get ready to explore the power of Docker!

Docker and Kubernetes

When it comes to modern cloud computing, two names have been making waves in the industry: Docker and Kubernetes. These tools have revolutionized the way applications are deployed, managed, and scaled in the cloud. In this section, we will take a deep dive into Docker and Kubernetes, exploring their concepts, functionalities, and how they work together to empower developers and system administrators. So put on your seatbelts, because we're about to embark on an adrenaline-pumping journey into the world of containerization and orchestration.

Containerization with Docker

Traditionally, applications were run on physical or virtual machines, each with its own operating system and dependencies. This approach had its fair share of challenges and limitations. That's where Docker steps in, offering a lightweight and flexible solution to package applications into containers.

What is Docker?

Docker is an open-source platform that enables developers to create and run applications in isolated environments called containers. These containers are self-contained, meaning they include everything the application needs to run seamlessly, from libraries to dependencies. By using Docker, you can be sure that your application will run the same way on any machine, regardless of the underlying infrastructure.

How does Docker work?

At the heart of Docker is the Docker engine, which is responsible for building, running, and distributing containers. Docker uses a client-server architecture, where the Docker client communicates with the Docker daemon, which in turn manages the containers.

Docker Images and Containers

To understand Docker, we need to grasp the concepts of images and containers. An image is a lightweight, standalone, and executable package that includes everything needed to run a piece of software, including the code, runtime, libraries, and dependencies. Think of it as a snapshot of an application at a specific point in time.

A container, on the other hand, is an instance of an image. It is a running process that is isolated from the host system and other containers. Multiple containers can be created from a single image, each having its own isolated environment. Containers are lightweight, and they start quickly, making them ideal for deploying and scaling applications.

Benefits of Using Docker

Docker brings a wide range of benefits to the table.

- **Portability:** Docker containers can run on any system that has the Docker engine installed, making them portable and eliminating the "it works on my machine" problem.

- **Scalability:** Docker makes it easy to scale applications by running multiple containers simultaneously and distributing the workload.

- **Isolation:** Each container runs in its own isolated environment, ensuring that applications remain separate and don't interfere with each other.

- **Resource Efficiency:** Containers are lightweight and share the host system's operating system, resulting in efficient resource utilization.

Orchestration with Kubernetes

Now that we have a good understanding of Docker and containerization, let's take a look at Kubernetes, the king of container orchestration. Kubernetes, often referred to as K8s (pronounced "Kates"), is an open-source platform that automates the deployment, scaling, and management of containerized applications.

What is Kubernetes?

Originally developed by Google, Kubernetes is a container orchestration platform that provides a robust framework for managing containerized applications. It offers a declarative approach to application deployment and scaling, where you describe the desired state of your application, and Kubernetes takes care of making it happen.

Key Concepts in Kubernetes

To understand Kubernetes, we need to familiarize ourselves with some key concepts.

- **Pods:** A pod is the basic building block in Kubernetes. It represents a single instance of a running process or a set of tightly coupled processes that share the same resources.

- **ReplicaSets:** ReplicaSets ensure that a specified number of identical pods are running at all times. If a pod fails or gets terminated, the ReplicaSet replaces it with a new one to maintain the desired state.

- **Services:** Services provide stable network connectivity to pods and enable load balancing across multiple instances of an application.

- **Deployments:** Deployments are higher-level abstractions that define the desired state of an application, including the number of replicas, container images, and upgrade strategies.

Why Use Kubernetes?

Kubernetes offers numerous benefits for managing containerized applications.

- **Efficient Resource Utilization:** Kubernetes optimizes resource allocation by intelligently scheduling containers across the cluster based on available resources and constraints.

- **Horizontal Scaling:** Kubernetes allows you to scale your application horizontally by automatically adding or removing pods based on demand.

- **Self-Healing:** In case of pod failures or crashes, Kubernetes automatically restarts or replaces them, ensuring the application is always available and stable.

- **Rolling Updates and Rollbacks:** Kubernetes simplifies the process of updating applications by enabling rolling updates, where new versions are gradually deployed while monitoring the application's health. If something goes wrong, it can easily roll back to the previous version.

Docker and Kubernetes in Harmony

Docker and Kubernetes complement each other seamlessly, with Docker providing an efficient containerization solution and Kubernetes handling the orchestration aspect. When used together, they form a powerful duo that simplifies the deployment, management, and scaling of applications in the cloud.

Containerization with Docker, Orchestration with Kubernetes

Organizations often use Docker as a tool for building containers and packaging applications, while Kubernetes takes care of deploying and managing those containers in a cluster. Docker images are created and pushed to a container registry, which Kubernetes then uses to pull the images and create the necessary pods and services.

Using Docker and Kubernetes Locally

Both Docker and Kubernetes can be used locally for development and testing purposes. Docker Desktop provides an easy way to run Docker containers on your local machine, while tools like Minikube and Kind allow you to create a lightweight Kubernetes cluster on a single node.

Public Cloud and Managed Kubernetes Services

Public cloud providers, such as Amazon Web Services (AWS), Microsoft Azure, and Google Cloud Platform (GCP), offer managed Kubernetes services that simplify the deployment and management of Kubernetes clusters. They handle the underlying infrastructure, allowing you to focus on developing and running your applications.

Continuous Integration/Continuous Deployment (CI/CD) with Docker and Kubernetes

Docker and Kubernetes play a crucial role in modern CI/CD pipelines. Developers package their applications into Docker images, which are then tested and deployed to Kubernetes clusters. Continuous integration tools like Jenkins or GitLab CI/CD automate this process, ensuring a smooth and efficient delivery pipeline.

Conclusion

In conclusion, Docker and Kubernetes have transformed the way applications are deployed and managed in the cloud. Docker's containerization technology provides lightweight and portable containers, while Kubernetes takes care of orchestrating and scaling those containers. Together, they offer a powerful solution for building, deploying, and managing applications in modern cloud environments.

So, strap in and get ready for the exciting journey ahead as you dive into the world of Docker and Kubernetes. These tools will empower you to conquer the challenges of deploying and scaling applications, and give you the freedom to unleash your creativity in the cloud. Remember, the sky's the limit when it comes to cloud computing, so go forth and conquer!

Deploying and Managing Containers

In this section, we will delve into the fascinating world of deploying and managing containers. Containers have quickly gained popularity in the world of cloud computing due to their lightweight and portable nature. They offer a consistent environment for applications to run, making them ideal for building, deploying, and scaling applications in the cloud. In this section, we will explore the key concepts and best practices for deploying and managing containers effectively.

Container Orchestration

Deploying and managing containers at scale requires a robust orchestration system. Container orchestration platforms enable the automation of tasks such as deployment, scaling, and management of containers. Kubernetes, one of the most popular container orchestration platforms, is widely used in the industry. It provides a rich set of features for managing containerized applications, including service discovery, load balancing, and automatic scaling.

Container Registry

Before deploying containers, it is crucial to store container images in a container registry. A container registry is a repository that stores and manages container images. Docker Hub, Google Container Registry, and Amazon Elastic Container Registry (ECR) are examples of popular container registry services. These services allow you to securely store and distribute container images to various environments, making it easier to deploy containers across different cloud providers.

Defining Containers

To deploy containers, you need to define the desired state of your application using container manifest files. These files, typically written in YAML or JSON format, describe the container images, resources, networking, and other dependencies required for your application. Kubernetes uses manifest files known as "Pod" files to specify the desired state of a group of containers. These manifest files serve as a blueprint for orchestrating and managing containers effectively.

Container Deployment Strategies

When deploying containers, you have several strategies to choose from based on your application requirements. Let's explore some common deployment strategies:

- **Single Container Deployment:** In this strategy, each container runs a single instance of an application. This approach is suitable for simple applications that do not require high scalability or fault tolerance.

- **Multi-Container Deployment:** In more complex scenarios, multiple containers work together to form a cohesive application. Each container handles a specific task, such as a web server, application server, or database. Docker Compose is a tool commonly used to define and manage multi-container deployments.

- **Microservices Architecture:** In a microservices architecture, an application is divided into small, loosely coupled services that can be independently developed, deployed, and scaled. Each service runs in its own container, and inter-service communication is typically handled through APIs. Container orchestration platforms like Kubernetes excel at managing microservices deployments.

Container Networking

Containers within a cluster need to communicate with each other to form a functional application. Container orchestration platforms provide networking capabilities to facilitate this communication. Kubernetes, for example, uses a virtual network overlay to establish connectivity between containers across different hosts. Additionally, Kubernetes supports the definition of Services, which expose containers to other components within or outside the cluster.

Container Scaling

One of the advantages of containerization is the ability to scale applications quickly based on demand. Container orchestrators offer mechanisms for scaling containers automatically. Horizontal Pod Autoscaling (HPA) is a feature in Kubernetes that scales the number of container replicas based on metrics such as CPU utilization or request throughput. This dynamic scaling ensures optimal resource utilization without manual intervention.

Health Checks and Self-Healing

To maintain the availability and reliability of containerized applications, it is essential to implement health checks and self-healing mechanisms. Container orchestrators continuously monitor the health of containers and automatically restart or replace failed containers. By defining health checks in the container manifest files, you can ensure that unhealthy containers are detected and remediated promptly.

Rolling Updates and Rollbacks

Updating containerized applications without disrupting the user experience requires careful management. Container orchestration platforms provide rolling update mechanisms to update containers gradually, reducing downtime. In case an update introduces issues, rollback mechanisms allow you to revert to the previous working version. These features enable seamless updates and minimize the impact on your users.

Container Logging and Monitoring

Logging and monitoring are crucial aspects of container management. Container orchestrators provide tools for aggregating log data from containers and making it accessible for analysis. Additionally, metrics and monitoring data can be collected, enabling proactive monitoring and troubleshooting of containerized applications. Popular logging tools include Elastic Stack and Fluentd, while Prometheus and Grafana are commonly used for monitoring containerized workloads.

Container Security

Ensuring the security of containerized applications is paramount. Containers should be built from trusted base images and regularly updated to address vulnerabilities. Container runtime security tools, like Docker Security Scanning and Kubernetes Security Contexts, can be used to enforce security policies. Additionally, network segmentation, access control, and encryption mechanisms should be implemented to protect sensitive data and prevent unauthorized access.

Container Storage

Containers often require data storage for persistent application state. Container orchestration platforms offer various storage options, including Persistent Volumes (PVs) and Persistent Volume Claims (PVCs). These mechanisms enable the provisioning and management of storage volumes for containers. Additionally, cloud-native storage solutions, such as Amazon Elastic Block Store (EBS) or Google Persistent Disk, can be utilized for container storage in the cloud.

Best Practices and Tips

To effectively deploy and manage containers, consider the following best practices:

- Use a container registry to store and distribute container images securely.
- Leverage container orchestration platforms like Kubernetes for effective container management.
- Define resource limits and requests for containers to ensure optimal resource utilization.
- Implement health checks and self-healing mechanisms to maintain application availability.
- Regularly update container images to address security vulnerabilities.
- Monitor containerized applications for performance issues and use log aggregation tools for centralized visibility.
- Backup and store critical data outside the container environment to prevent data loss.
- Follow the principle of least privilege to enforce appropriate access controls for containers.

Summary

In this section, we explored the important concepts and practices related to deploying and managing containers. We discussed the role of container orchestration platforms, container registries, deployment strategies, networking, scaling, health checking, rolling updates, logging and monitoring, security, and storage. By following best practices and utilizing container orchestration tools effectively, you can unlock the full potential of containerization for building scalable and resilient applications in the cloud.

Exercises

1. Describe the role and benefits of container orchestration platforms in managing containerized applications.

2. Compare and contrast single container deployment, multi-container deployment, and microservices architecture. Provide examples of scenarios where each approach is suitable.

3. Explain the concept of health checks in the context of containerized applications. How can they contribute to the overall reliability of the application?

4. Discuss the importance of logging and monitoring in managing containerized workloads. What are some popular tools used for these tasks?

5. How can you ensure the security of containerized applications? Outline some best practices and tools for implementing container security.

Additional Resources

- Kubernetes Documentation: `https://kubernetes.io/docs/home/`
- Docker Documentation: `https://docs.docker.com/`
- "The DevOps Handbook: How to Create World-Class Agility, Reliability, and Security in Technology Organizations" by Gene Kim, Jez Humble, Patrick Debois, and John Willis
- "The Docker Book: Containerization is the New Virtualization" by James Turnbull

Take your time to complete the exercises and explore the additional resources. Once you feel confident in deploying and managing containers, you are ready to conquer the cloud with your scalable and resilient applications!

The Fucking Container Revolution

In this section, we will dive into the exciting world of containerization and explore how it has revolutionized the way applications are deployed and managed in the cloud. Get ready to have your mind blown, because containers are fucking awesome!

Introduction to Containers

Traditional application deployment involves running an application on a dedicated server or virtual machine (VM). However, this approach has its limitations. Each VM requires its own operating system and resources, which can lead to inefficiencies and increased costs. This is where containers come in and turn the game upside down.

A container is a lightweight, standalone package that includes everything needed to run an application, including the code, dependencies, and system tools. Containers provide an isolated and consistent environment for applications, making them portable and easy to deploy across different computing environments.

Docker and Kubernetes: The Dynamic Duo

When it comes to containers, two names stand out: Docker and Kubernetes. Docker is an open-source platform that simplifies the creation and management of containers. It provides a simple and elegant way to package applications and their dependencies into a container image.

Kubernetes, on the other hand, is an open-source container orchestration platform. It automates the deployment, scaling, and management of containers across clusters of hosts. Kubernetes allows you to declaratively define the desired state of your application and handles all the complexities of scheduling, networking, and scaling.

Together, Docker and Kubernetes form a powerful combination that enables efficient container-based deployment, scaling, and management of applications in the cloud.

Deploying and Managing Containers

Now that you understand the fundamentals of containers, let's explore the process of deploying and managing them in the cloud. Buckle up, because we're about to go on a wild ride!

1. **Building container images:** The first step in deploying a container is to build an image. This involves creating a Dockerfile, which specifies the necessary dependencies and configuration for your application. Once the Dockerfile is ready, you can build the image using the Docker CLI.

2. **Pushing and pulling images:** After you have built a container image, you need to push it to a container registry like Docker Hub or a private registry. This allows you to share the image with others and use it for deployment. To deploy a

container, you simply pull the image from the registry onto the host where you want to run it.

3. **Running containers**: Running a container is as simple as executing a single command: `docker run`. This command launches a new container based on a specified image. You can specify various options and parameters to customize the container's behavior and resource allocation.

4. **Managing container lifecycles**: Containers have a lifecycle that includes creation, running, pausing, stopping, and restarting. Docker provides a set of commands for managing containers at each stage of their lifecycle. With Kubernetes, you can use its API or CLI to manage and control container lifecycles, including scaling the number of replicas, rolling out updates, and more.

5. **Networking and storage**: Containers can be connected to networks to establish communication with other containers or external systems. Docker and Kubernetes provide mechanisms to manage networking and storage, allowing containers to interact with each other and access external resources.

6. **Monitoring and logging**: It's crucial to monitor the health and performance of containers to ensure they are running smoothly. Docker and Kubernetes offer built-in features for collecting metrics, monitoring resource utilization, and aggregating logs. Additionally, you can integrate popular monitoring and logging tools like Prometheus and ELK stack for more advanced monitoring and analysis.

7. **Deployment strategies**: When deploying containers, you have several strategies to choose from. Blue-green deployment, canary deployment, and rolling updates are some of the popular strategies that minimize downtime and allow for seamless updates and rollbacks.

8. **Security and compliance**: Container security is a key consideration when deploying applications in the cloud. Docker and Kubernetes provide security features like image scanning, role-based access control (RBAC), and network policies to protect containers from attacks and ensure compliance with regulations.

The Fucking Benefits of Containerization

Now that you've got a good grasp on containerization, let's talk about the fucking benefits it brings to the table:

1. **Portability**: Containers encapsulate all the dependencies and configuration needed to run an application, making them highly portable across different environments. You can develop and test applications locally, and then deploy them reliably in any cloud environment.

2. **Consistency**: Containers provide a consistent application environment, regardless of the underlying infrastructure. This eliminates the dreaded "works on

my machine" problem and ensures that your application behaves the same way everywhere it runs.

3. **Scalability**: Containers are lightweight and can be quickly scaled up or down to handle varying workloads. With Kubernetes, you can easily scale your application horizontally by adding or removing container instances based on demand.

4. **Resource efficiency**: Containers share the host system's operating system kernel, which results in significant resource savings compared to running multiple VMs. This allows you to maximize resource utilization and reduce costs.

5. **Faster deployment and rollbacks**: Containers enable fast and reliable deployment of applications. With Docker and Kubernetes, you can deploy updates seamlessly, roll back to a previous version if issues arise, and minimize downtime during updates.

6. **Isolation and security**: Containers provide isolation between applications, ensuring that they do not interfere with each other. Additionally, Docker and Kubernetes offer various security features to protect containers from external threats and vulnerabilities.

7. **Ecosystem and community support**: The container ecosystem is vibrant and thriving, with a rich set of tools and services built around Docker and Kubernetes. There is a wealth of community support, documentation, and best practices to help you get up and running quickly.

Real-World Examples: Containers in Action

Let's take a look at a few real-world examples that showcase the power and versatility of containers:

1. **Netflix**: Netflix uses containers extensively to power its video streaming platform. Containers allow them to rapidly scale their services, deploy updates without disrupting user experience, and ensure consistent performance across different regions.

2. **Spotify**: Spotify leverages containers to improve the scalability and reliability of its music streaming service. With Kubernetes, they can handle millions of concurrent users, perform rolling updates seamlessly, and meet the demands of a rapidly growing user base.

3. **NASA**: NASA uses containers to process and analyze large amounts of satellite data. By containerizing their scientific workflows, they can achieve higher efficiency and scalability, allowing researchers to focus on data analysis rather than infrastructure management.

These examples highlight how containers have become a game-changer for organizations of all sizes, enabling them to scale their applications, reduce costs, and innovate at a faster pace.

Resources and Further Reading

Here are some recommended resources and further reading to deepen your knowledge of containers:

- **Docker Documentation:** Official documentation for Docker, which provides detailed guides, tutorials, and examples: https://docs.docker.com/

- **Kubernetes Documentation:** Official documentation for Kubernetes, featuring comprehensive guides, concepts, and examples: https://kubernetes.io/docs/

- **The Docker Book:** A comprehensive guide to Docker by James Turnbull, covering both basic and advanced topics: http://www.dockerbook.com/

- **Kubernetes Up and Running:** A practical guide to Kubernetes by Kelsey Hightower, Brendan Burns, and Joe Beda, offering hands-on tutorials and best practices: http://shop.oreilly.com/product/0636920158038.do

Explore these resources to become a fucking container expert and conquer the world of cloud computing!

Exercises

1. **Containerizing an application:** Choose an application of your choice and containerize it using Docker. Write a Dockerfile, build the image, and push it to a container registry. Deploy the application on a local machine or a cloud environment.

2. **Scaling with Kubernetes:** Set up a Kubernetes cluster using a cloud provider of your choice. Deploy a containerized application on the cluster and configure autoscaling to handle increased traffic. Test the scaling capabilities by generating a high load on the application.

3. **Container security analysis:** Research popular container security tools like Clair and Falco. Choose one tool, install it, and analyze the security vulnerabilities of a container image. Implement measures to mitigate the identified vulnerabilities.

4. **Container deployment strategies:** Research different deployment strategies like blue-green deployment, canary deployment, and rolling updates. Choose an application, deploy it using each strategy, and compare the advantages and disadvantages of each approach.

5. **Container networking exploration:** Explore different container networking models like bridge, host, and overlay networks. Set up a simple application with multiple containers and experiment with different networking configurations.

These exercises will give you hands-on experience with containers and help solidify your understanding of the container revolution. Get your hands dirty, embrace the fucking containers, and conquer the cloud!

Edge Computing and IoT

Overview of Edge Computing

Alright, buckle up, folks! We're about to take a deep dive into the exciting world of edge computing. This is the shit that will blow your mind and revolutionize the way we think about cloud computing. So, let's get started!

What the Hell is Edge Computing?

Edge computing is like the cool kid on the block. It brings the power of the cloud closer to the users, right at the fringes of the network. Instead of storing and processing data in some distant data center, edge computing does its magic at the edge devices themselves. We're talking about your smartphones, IoT devices, network gateways, and even cars. Yeah, you heard me right, cars!

The idea behind edge computing is to reduce latency and bandwidth usage by performing computations closer to where the data is generated. Imagine you're streaming a live video or playing some intense multiplayer game. You don't want to wait for your commands to travel all the way to a data center and back. That would be a freaking disaster! Edge computing swoops in to save the day by bringing that processing power and data storage right to your device. Now that's what I call convenience, my friends.

Why the Fuck Do We Need Edge Computing?

Alright, let's break it down. Edge computing offers a bunch of advantages that make it oh-so-bloody important. First up, we have reduced latency. You know how frustrating it is when you have to wait for ages for your data to travel back and forth to the cloud? Well, edge computing cuts that shit down by reducing the distance between where the data is generated and where it's processed. Boom! Instantaneous results, baby!

Next up, we have improved reliability. Imagine you're in the middle of a tornado, and you need help ASAP. You don't want to rely on a cloud-based system that could go down if the server farm gets wiped out. With edge computing, your devices can continue to function even if the network connection to the cloud goes kaput. It's like having a Plan B for when shit hits the fan.

Now, let's talk about bandwidth. We all know that our home internet connections can be a bit flaky at times, right? Well, with edge computing, we don't have to depend on a stable and strong network connection to the cloud. Our devices handle most of the processing and storage locally, minimizing the need to constantly transfer data back and forth. It's a win-win situation, my friends!

Examples of Edge Computing in Action

Now, let me hit you with some real-world examples to make this shit more tangible. Picture this: you're driving your fancy Tesla (because you're a baller like that), and suddenly there's a pedestrian in your way. You don't have time to wait for the data to travel to the cloud and back to make a split-second decision. Nah, that would be some deadly shit right there. With edge computing, the sensors in your car process the data and make a quick decision to avoid turning that pedestrian into roadkill. Talk about saving lives with some badass technology!

Here's another example for you. Imagine you're at a music festival, grooving to the beats like there's no tomorrow. You want to share your sick dance moves with your friends on social media, but damn, the network connection is as slow as a turtle on a Sunday stroll. Fear not, my friend, because edge computing has got your back. Local edge servers near the festival grounds can process and store data, so you can upload those dance videos at lightning speed. That's what I call instant fame, baby!

Challenges and Limitations of Edge Computing

Now, let's not pretend edge computing is all rainbows and unicorns. It does come with its fair share of challenges and limitations. One major challenge is the need for robust security measures. Since edge devices are more vulnerable to physical attacks and breaches, we need to beef up security like nobody's business. We're talking about strong encryption, authentication mechanisms, and constant monitoring to keep the bad guys at bay.

Another challenge is the management and coordination of edge devices. With tons of devices spread across the edge of the network, keeping track of them and ensuring they work together seamlessly can be a freaking nightmare. We need proper management tools and protocols to orchestrate these devices and make sure they play nicely with each other.

The Future of Edge Computing

Alright, folks, hold onto your seats because the future of edge computing is looking damn exciting. We're talking about edge AI and fog computing. Edge AI brings artificial intelligence algorithms to the edge devices themselves, allowing them to make intelligent decisions without relying on the cloud. It's like giving your devices a brain of their own! And fog computing? Well, that's like the big brother of edge computing. It's all about creating a decentralized network of edge devices and cloud resources to tackle complex tasks. It's a freaking powerhouse of computing!

We're also exploring the possibilities of quantum computing in the realm of edge computing. Quantum computers offer mind-boggling computational power, and if we can bring that power to the edge devices, we'll enter a whole new dimension of possibilities. Just imagine the kind of mind-blowing applications we can build!

And let's not forget about the ethical considerations. As edge computing becomes more prevalent, we need to address privacy concerns, fairness in AI algorithms, and responsible development and use. We don't want to unleash a Frankenstein's monster of a technology, do we?

Wrap it Up, Baby!

Alright, my lovely readers, that's a solid overview of edge computing. We've covered the basics, explored its advantages and challenges, witnessed some kickass real-world examples, and peeked into the future. Edge computing is all about bringing the power of the cloud to the fringes of the network, reducing latency, improving reliability, and giving your devices some serious computational muscle. So, embrace the edge, my friends, and get ready to ride the wave of this mind-blowing technology!

Internet of Things (IoT)

The Internet of Things (IoT) is an emerging field that has gained significant attention in recent years. It refers to the network of physical objects, devices, and machines that are connected to the internet and can collect and exchange data. These objects can be anything from smart home appliances and wearable devices to industrial equipment and vehicles. The IoT has the potential to revolutionize various sectors, including healthcare, agriculture, transportation, and manufacturing.

Principles of IoT

The principles underlying the IoT are based on the concept of connectivity and communication between devices. These devices are equipped with sensors and actuators that enable them to gather and transmit data over the internet. The data collected from these devices can be analyzed and used to gain insights, automate processes, and improve decision-making.

One of the key principles of the IoT is interoperability, which refers to the ability of devices from different manufacturers to communicate and work together seamlessly. This is essential in ensuring that the IoT ecosystem is open and adaptable, allowing for the integration of various devices and systems.

Another important principle is scalability. The IoT infrastructure should be able to accommodate a large number of connected devices and handle the massive amount of data generated by these devices. Scalability ensures that the IoT can support the growing demand for connectivity and data processing.

Challenges in IoT

While the IoT holds tremendous potential, it also presents significant challenges that need to be addressed. One of the major challenges is security and privacy. With a large number of devices connected to the internet, there is an increased risk of cyber attacks and unauthorized access to sensitive data. Ensuring the security of IoT devices and the data they collect is crucial to prevent breaches and protect user privacy.

Another challenge is the management and analysis of the vast amount of data generated by IoT devices. The sheer volume, velocity, and variety of data require robust storage, processing, and analytics capabilities. This necessitates the use of scalable and efficient technologies to handle the data deluge and derive meaningful insights from it.

Furthermore, the heterogeneity of IoT devices, protocols, and standards poses interoperability challenges. Different devices may use different communication protocols and data formats, making it difficult to integrate and exchange data seamlessly. Standardization efforts are crucial in establishing common frameworks and protocols that enable interoperability across various IoT devices and platforms.

Use Cases of IoT

The applications of IoT are diverse and wide-ranging, with potential use cases in almost every industry. Here are some examples:

- **Smart Homes:** IoT-enabled devices, such as thermostats, lighting systems, and security cameras, can be controlled and monitored remotely using smartphones or voice assistants. These devices can also learn from user behavior to optimize energy consumption and enhance comfort.

- **Healthcare:** IoT devices can assist in remote patient monitoring, allowing healthcare providers to track vital signs, medication adherence, and other health indicators. This enables personalized care and early detection of potential health issues.

- **Transportation:** IoT technology can be used in smart traffic management systems to reduce congestion and improve traffic flow. Connected vehicles can communicate with each other and with infrastructure to optimize routes, reduce accidents, and enhance overall transportation efficiency.

- **Industrial Automation:** IoT devices can be integrated into manufacturing processes to monitor equipment performance, detect faults, and optimize production. This leads to improved operational efficiency, reduced downtime, and cost savings.

- **Agriculture:** IoT sensors can be used in precision farming to monitor soil moisture, temperature, and other environmental factors. This data can help farmers optimize irrigation, apply fertilizers effectively, and improve crop yield.

Real-World Example: Smart Cities

One of the most ambitious applications of IoT is in the creation of smart cities. A smart city leverages IoT technology to improve the quality of life for residents and enhance the efficiency of urban operations. Here's a real-world example:

In Singapore, the government has implemented various IoT initiatives to transform the city-state into a smart city. These initiatives include the deployment of smart sensors and cameras throughout the city to monitor factors such as traffic flow, air quality, and waste management. The data collected from these sensors is analyzed in real-time to optimize transportation systems, reduce pollution, and improve overall urban planning.

Additionally, the Singapore government has launched a Smart Nation Platform, which serves as a centralized digital infrastructure to collect and analyze data from various sources. This platform allows for better coordination and decision-making across different government agencies, leading to more efficient public services and a better living environment for residents.

Resources and Further Reading

If you're interested in learning more about the Internet of Things, here are some recommended resources:

- *The Fourth Industrial Revolution* by Klaus Schwab: This book explores the impact of IoT and other technologies on the global economy and society.

- *Architecting the Internet of Things* by Dieter Uckelmann, Mark Harrison, and Florian Michahelles: This book provides an in-depth guide to designing and implementing IoT architectures.

- Online platforms such as *IoT World* and *IoT Agenda* offer news, articles, and insights into the latest trends and advancements in the IoT space.

Key Takeaways

- The Internet of Things (IoT) refers to the network of connected physical objects and devices that can collect and exchange data.

- Interoperability and scalability are key principles of the IoT, enabling seamless communication and adaptability to a large number of devices.

- Challenges in the IoT include security, data management, and interoperability.

- IoT has diverse applications, including smart homes, healthcare, transportation, industrial automation, and agriculture.

- Real-world examples, such as smart cities, demonstrate the potential of IoT in improving urban living and efficiency.

In this section, we've explored the principles, challenges, and applications of the Internet of Things. The IoT has the power to connect our physical world like never before, enabling us to create smarter, more efficient, and sustainable environments. As the technology continues to evolve, it's important to stay updated on the latest advancements and best practices in this rapidly expanding field. So buckle up, because the IoT revolution is just beginning, and the future is going to be fucking connected.

Combining Cloud and Edge Computing

Cloud computing and edge computing are two powerful paradigms that have revolutionized the way we process and store data. But what if we could harness the best of both worlds? That's where the concept of combining cloud and edge computing comes into play. In this section, we will explore the benefits, challenges, and potential applications of this hybrid approach.

Understanding Cloud Computing

Before we dive into the world of combining cloud and edge computing, let's quickly recap what cloud computing is all about. In simple terms, cloud computing involves the delivery of on-demand computing services over the internet. This includes storage, servers, databases, networking, software, and more.

Cloud computing offers several advantages. It enables businesses and individuals to access resources without the need for physical infrastructure. It provides scalability, flexibility, and cost-efficiency. Users can pay for what they use, and they have the freedom to scale up or down based on their needs.

Exploring Edge Computing

On the other hand, edge computing brings processing power closer to the source of data. Instead of relying on a centralized cloud infrastructure, edge devices perform data processing and analysis locally, at the edge of the network. This minimizes latency, reduces bandwidth usage, and enhances real-time capabilities.

Edge computing is a critical component in enabling the Internet of Things (IoT). With the rapid growth of connected devices, edge computing helps process the vast amounts of data generated by these devices efficiently. Industries such as healthcare, manufacturing, and transportation benefit greatly from the reduced latency and improved reliability offered by edge computing.

The Benefits of Combining Cloud and Edge Computing

Now, let's discuss the advantages of combining cloud and edge computing. By leveraging the strengths of both paradigms, organizations can achieve a more holistic and optimized approach to data processing and storage.

One key benefit is improved latency. With edge computing, data is processed locally, eliminating the need to transmit it to a distant cloud server. This results in faster response times and better user experiences, particularly for applications that require real-time processing, such as autonomous vehicles or live video streaming.

Another advantage is enhanced bandwidth efficiency. By offloading certain processing tasks to edge devices, organizations can reduce the volume of data that needs to be transmitted to the cloud. This is especially valuable in scenarios where network connectivity is limited or unreliable.

Combining cloud and edge computing also improves reliability. Since edge devices operate independently, they can continue processing and storing data even if the connection to the cloud is disrupted. This ensures continuous operation and enables critical applications to function reliably in the face of network outages.

Challenges and Considerations

While the benefits of combining cloud and edge computing are evident, several challenges need to be addressed. One major challenge is data integrity and synchronization. With distributed processing across multiple edge devices and the cloud, ensuring consistent and up-to-date data becomes more complex. Organizations must implement robust synchronization mechanisms to avoid data inconsistencies.

Security is another important consideration. With data being processed at multiple locations, ensuring the confidentiality and integrity of sensitive information becomes paramount. Encryption, access controls, and secure communication protocols must be implemented to maintain data security throughout the hybrid environment.

Furthermore, managing and orchestrating the deployment of applications across diverse cloud and edge resources can be challenging. Organizations need to have a comprehensive strategy in place to effectively distribute, monitor, and manage their computing workloads in a hybrid environment.

Real-World Applications

Combining cloud and edge computing opens up various exciting applications across industries. Let's explore a few examples:

- Autonomous Vehicles: By combining cloud-based AI for complex decision-making tasks with edge computing for real-time sensor data processing, autonomous vehicles can operate safely and efficiently.

- Smart Cities: Edge devices deployed throughout a city can monitor and analyze data related to traffic, energy usage, waste management, and more. This data can be processed locally and sent to the cloud for further analysis and decision-making.

- Telemedicine: Edge computing can enable real-time analysis of patient vitals, reducing the need for constant cloud connectivity. Critical alerts can be generated locally, improving response times and patient care.

- Retail: Real-time inventory management and personalized shopping experiences can be facilitated through edge devices in physical stores. Cloud-based analytics can provide insights and recommendations to improve customer satisfaction and optimize operations.

Conclusion

Combining cloud and edge computing represents a promising approach to achieve the best of both worlds. By leveraging the localized processing capabilities of edge computing and the scalability and flexibility of cloud computing, organizations can enhance latency, bandwidth efficiency, reliability, and security.

While challenges such as data synchronization, security, and orchestration need to be addressed, the potential applications in various industries are vast and exciting. As cloud and edge technologies continue to evolve, the possibilities for combining them will only grow, empowering organizations to harness the full potential of their data-driven initiatives.

Key Takeaways:

- Cloud computing delivers on-demand computing services over the internet, providing scalability, flexibility, and cost-efficiency.

- Edge computing brings processing power closer to the data source, minimizing latency and enabling real-time capabilities.

- Combining cloud and edge computing offers benefits such as improved latency, enhanced bandwidth efficiency, and increased reliability.

- Challenges include data synchronization, security, and management of distributed resources.

- Real-world applications include autonomous vehicles, smart cities, telemedicine, and retail.

The Fucking Edge of the Cloud

In the fast-paced world of cloud computing, staying on the edge is the key to success. In this section, we will explore the concept of edge computing, its relationship with the cloud, and its growing importance in the modern digital landscape.

Overview of Edge Computing

Edge computing is a paradigm that brings computation and data storage closer to the devices that generate and consume them. Rather than relying solely on central cloud servers located in data centers, edge computing distributes these capabilities to the network's edge, which can include devices such as routers, gateways, and even smart devices.

The goal of edge computing is to reduce latency and improve performance by processing data at or near the source, minimizing the need for data to travel long distances to reach a centralized cloud server. By doing so, edge computing enables real-time data processing, decision-making, and response, which is crucial for time-sensitive applications like autonomous vehicles, industrial automation, and remote healthcare.

The Relationship Between Edge Computing and the Cloud

Edge computing and cloud computing are not mutually exclusive; in fact, they work hand in hand to provide a comprehensive and efficient solution for modern computing needs.

The cloud provides the scalability, flexibility, and vast resources required to process and store massive amounts of data. It acts as the backbone, handling tasks that are not time-sensitive and can benefit from centralized processing, such as big data analytics, machine learning, and resource-intensive simulations.

On the other hand, edge computing complements the cloud by extending its capabilities to the network's edge. By processing data closer to the source, it reduces network congestion, minimizes latency, and improves overall system performance. Edge computing also enhances data privacy and security, as sensitive information can be processed locally instead of being transmitted to the cloud.

Use Cases and Benefits of Edge Computing

Edge computing has a wide range of applications across various industries. Let's take a look at some popular use cases that highlight the benefits of edge computing:

1. **Autonomous Vehicles:** In the realm of self-driving cars, real-time decision-making is critical to ensuring safety. Edge computing enables vehicles to process sensor data locally, allowing them to respond quickly to changing road conditions and make split-second decisions.

2. **Smart Grids:** Edge computing plays a vital role in modernizing power grids. By deploying edge devices at different points in the grid, utilities can monitor power usage, detect faults, and perform predictive maintenance in real-time.

3. **Healthcare:** Edge computing enables remote patient monitoring, bringing healthcare services directly to patients' homes. With edge devices collecting and analyzing vital signs, doctors can provide timely interventions and save lives, especially in emergencies.

4. **Industrial Automation:** In factories and manufacturing plants, edge computing powers real-time monitoring and control systems. By processing data at the edge, industrial IoT devices can quickly adjust parameters, detect anomalies, and prevent costly downtime.

The benefits of edge computing go beyond improved performance and latency reduction. Edge computing also reduces data transmission and storage costs by filtering and aggregating data at the source, sending only relevant information to the cloud. It also enhances data privacy and compliance with regulations by keeping sensitive information within the local network.

Challenges and Considerations

While edge computing offers significant advantages, it also presents challenges and considerations that need to be addressed:

1. **Hardware Limitations:** Edge devices typically have limited computational power, storage capacity, and energy resources. Optimizing algorithms and designing efficient edge infrastructure becomes crucial to make the most of these constraints.

2. **Data Synchronization:** In scenarios where both edge and cloud systems are involved, ensuring data consistency and synchronization can be challenging. Managing data integrity and maintaining a coherent view of the system require careful design and synchronization protocols.

3. **Security Risks:** Distributing computation and storage to the network's edge introduces additional security concerns. Edge devices become potential attack vectors, and protecting them from unauthorized access and securing local data becomes paramount.

4. **Reliability and Redundancy:** Edge computing heavily relies on network connectivity. Ensuring reliable and consistent network connections, as well as

implementing redundancy mechanisms, is crucial to avoid disruptions in critical applications.

The Fucking Edge of Innovation

Edge computing continues to push the boundaries of innovation and technology. As the proliferation of IoT devices and the demand for real-time applications grows, edge computing becomes an essential part of the modern digital infrastructure.

To stay on the fucking edge of the cloud, businesses and individuals must embrace the possibilities of edge computing and the cloud. By understanding its capabilities, addressing its challenges, and exploring its potential applications, we can unlock a new era of computing that is faster, more efficient, and more connected than ever before.

So, buckle up, fellow tech enthusiasts. The fucking edge of the cloud is where the action is, and by embracing edge computing, we're going to revolutionize the way we live, work, and connect in this increasingly digital world.

Serverless Computing

Function as a Service (FaaS) Architecture

Function as a Service (FaaS) is a cloud computing model that allows developers to deploy and execute small, discrete pieces of code, known as functions, without the need to manage the underlying infrastructure. FaaS provides a serverless architecture where developers can focus solely on writing and deploying their code, while the cloud provider takes care of provisioning and scaling the necessary resources.

In FaaS, functions are event-driven, meaning they are triggered by specific events or requests. When an event occurs, such as an HTTP request or a change in a database, the associated function is invoked to perform a specific task. This event-driven approach allows for a highly scalable and efficient execution environment, where functions are only invoked when needed, reducing costs and improving resource utilization.

The architecture of FaaS involves several components, including the function execution environment, event sources, and the FaaS platform itself. Let's explore each of these components in more detail:

Function Execution Environment

The function execution environment is the runtime environment in which the function code is executed. It provides the necessary resources and dependencies for the code to run, such as the operating system, programming language runtime, and any libraries or frameworks required by the function.

In FaaS, each function has its own isolated execution environment, allowing for greater security and scalability. When a function is invoked, the FaaS platform spins up an instance of the execution environment, loads the function code into it, and executes the code. Once the function has completed its execution, the instance is disposed of, freeing up resources for other functions.

Event Sources

Event sources are the triggers that invoke functions in FaaS. They can be a variety of events, such as HTTP requests, database changes, file uploads, or time-based intervals. Event sources provide the context and data needed for the function to perform its task.

FaaS platforms typically provide integrations with various event sources, allowing developers to easily connect their functions to these events. For example, an HTTP endpoint can be used as an event source to trigger a function when a specific URL is requested. Similarly, a database change event can invoke a function to process and update data in real-time.

FaaS Platform

The FaaS platform is the cloud infrastructure that manages the deployment, execution, and scaling of functions. It provides a set of services and tools for developers to create, deploy, monitor, and manage their functions.

One of the key features of a FaaS platform is automatic scaling. As the number of events or requests increases, the platform automatically provisions additional resources to handle the load. This dynamic scaling eliminates the need for manual capacity planning and ensures that functions can handle sudden spikes in traffic or workload.

Additionally, FaaS platforms often provide monitoring and logging capabilities, allowing developers to gain insights into the performance and behavior of their functions. They can track metrics such as execution time, resource usage, and error rates to optimize their functions and identify potential issues.

Example: Image Processing on the Fly

To better understand the concept of FaaS, let's consider an example of image processing on the fly. Imagine a website where users can upload images and apply various filters or transformations to them.

With FaaS, developers can implement functions that perform specific image processing tasks, such as resizing, cropping, or applying filters. These functions can be triggered by an event source, such as a file upload to a storage service like Amazon S3.

When a user uploads an image, the event source triggers the corresponding function, which then retrieves the image from the storage, applies the desired transformations, and returns the processed image. The user gets the transformed image without the need for any manual intervention or complex infrastructure management. The FaaS platform automatically handles the execution and scaling of the functions based on the incoming requests.

This example illustrates the power and simplicity of FaaS. Developers can focus on writing the code for the image processing functions without worrying about the underlying infrastructure. The event-driven nature of FaaS ensures that the functions are executed only when needed, providing cost-efficiency and scalability.

Caveats and Considerations

While FaaS offers significant benefits, there are some caveats and considerations to keep in mind when adopting this architecture:

- **Function Execution Time:** FaaS platforms often impose time limits on function execution to ensure efficient resource allocation. Long-running or computationally intensive functions may need to be divided into smaller, more manageable tasks or consider alternative architectures.

- **Cold Start Overhead:** When a function is invoked for the first time or after a period of inactivity, there may be a slight delay known as a "cold start" as the execution environment is provisioned. This overhead can impact the overall responsiveness of the system, especially for functions with strict latency requirements.

- **Stateless Functions:** FaaS functions are typically stateless, meaning they do not retain any data or state between invocations. Any required data must be provided as input, and outputs must be stored externally, such as in a database or object storage. Stateful operations can be challenging to implement in a serverless environment and may require additional architectural considerations.

- **Vendor Lock-In:** While FaaS has gained popularity across cloud providers, each platform has its own APIs and deployment configurations. Switching between different FaaS platforms may require significant code modifications, leading to potential vendor lock-in. It's essential to consider the long-term implications and evaluate vendor-specific features and capabilities.

In summary, Function as a Service (FaaS) architecture in cloud computing provides developers with a serverless environment to deploy and execute small code functions triggered by events. FaaS platforms handle the provisioning, scaling, and management of the underlying infrastructure, allowing developers to focus on writing code. While FaaS offers scalability and cost-efficiency, it is essential to consider factors such as function execution time, cold start overhead, statelessness, and vendor lock-in when adopting this architecture.

Now that we have explored the concept of FaaS, let's delve into other fascinating aspects of cloud computing in the subsequent sections. Stay tuned for an exploration of storage and database services, compute and container services, networking and content delivery services, security and identity services, and the exciting world of AI and machine learning in the cloud. Remember, the fucking possibilities are endless in the cloud!

Benefits and Use Cases of Serverless Computing

Serverless computing, also known as Function as a Service (FaaS), is a cloud computing model that eliminates the need for the user to manage servers or infrastructure. Instead, developers can focus solely on writing and deploying code in the form of individual functions or microservices that are executed in a serverless environment. This approach offers several benefits and opens up a wide range of use cases that can revolutionize the way applications are built and deployed.

Benefits of Serverless Computing

1. Cost Efficiency: One of the primary advantages of serverless computing is the cost savings it offers. Traditional server-based models require the provisioning of infrastructure to handle peak loads, which often leads to over-provisioning and wasted resources. With serverless, you only pay for the actual time your code is executed, which makes it highly cost-efficient, especially for applications with unpredictable or variable workloads.

Example: Imagine a ride-sharing application that experiences high demand during peak hours. With serverless computing, the application can dynamically scale up and down based on the number of requests, ensuring optimal resource utilization and cost savings.

2. Scalability and Elasticity: Serverless platforms can automatically scale your application up or down based on the incoming workload. The infrastructure can handle an increasing number of requests without the need for manual intervention, allowing your application to seamlessly handle spikes in traffic or scale down during periods of low activity.

Example: A social media platform might experience a sudden surge in user activity due to a viral post. Serverless computing allows the platform to scale up instantly, ensuring every user can access and interact with the post without any performance degradation.

3. Reduced Operational Overhead: With serverless, the cloud provider manages the underlying infrastructure, including server provisioning, maintenance, and security updates. This eliminates the need for dedicated IT teams to manage and monitor servers, enabling developers to focus on writing code and delivering value to end-users.

Example: A small startup can leverage serverless computing to streamline their development process. Instead of spending valuable time and resources on infrastructure management, they can focus on building their core application features and delivering an exceptional user experience.

4. **Rapid Development and Deployment:** Serverless platforms enable developers to quickly deploy code changes without worrying about infrastructure setup or configuration. This faster development cycle can lead to quicker time-to-market and more frequent iterations, allowing businesses to iterate and adapt their applications at a rapid pace.

Example: A mobile app developer can make instant updates to the serverless backend of their application, introducing new features or fixing bugs, without the need for complex deployment processes or downtime.

5. **High Availability and Fault Tolerance:** Serverless computing platforms inherently provide high availability and fault tolerance. They replicate your functions across multiple data centers, ensuring that your application remains available even in the event of hardware failures or network disruptions. Additionally, serverless platforms handle automatic load balancing, making sure that the incoming requests are evenly distributed across available resources.

Example: An e-commerce website using serverless computing can guarantee that its product catalogue and order processing functions are always available, even if individual servers or data centers experience failures.

Use Cases of Serverless Computing

1. **Web and Mobile Applications:** Serverless is an excellent choice for building web and mobile applications that have varying or unpredictable workloads. It allows developers to focus on writing code for specific functions or features without getting bogged down by infrastructure management. Additionally, serverless computing can handle the scaling and load balancing required by these applications, ensuring a seamless user experience.

Example: A food delivery application can utilize serverless computing to handle incoming orders, process payments, and send real-time notifications to both customers and delivery partners.

2. **Real-time Data Processing:** Serverless computing enables the processing of real-time data streams or events, making it a preferred choice for applications that require near-instantaneous data analysis or reactions. Serverless platforms can efficiently handle and process high volumes of data, allowing businesses to gain valuable insights and make intelligent decisions in real-time.

Example: An e-commerce platform can utilize serverless computing to analyze customer behavior in real-time, personalize recommendations, and trigger targeted marketing campaigns based on user interactions.

3. **Chatbots and Voice Assistants:** Serverless computing is ideal for building chatbots and voice assistants that can handle natural language processing and respond to user queries. It enables developers to leverage the power of AI and machine learning without worrying about the underlying infrastructure, allowing them to focus on delivering conversational experiences.

Example: A customer support chatbot can be built using serverless computing to provide instant responses to frequently asked questions, handle customer interactions, and escalate complex queries to human agents when needed.

4. **Internet of Things (IoT) Applications:** Serverless computing is a natural fit for IoT applications that generate a vast amount of data from sensors or devices. It enables efficient data processing, analysis, and decision-making at the edge without the need for complex infrastructure management.

Example: A connected smart home system can utilize serverless computing to process sensor data, trigger automated responses based on predefined rules, and provide real-time notifications to homeowners on their mobile devices.

5. **Data and Media Processing:** Serverless computing can handle compute-intensive tasks such as data processing, image or video transcoding, and data transformation. It provides the flexibility to process large volumes of data or media files, ensuring efficient and cost-effective data processing pipelines.

Example: A media streaming platform can leverage serverless computing to convert video files to various formats and resolutions on-demand, ensuring compatibility with different devices and network conditions.

Conclusion

Serverless computing offers significant benefits such as cost efficiency, scalability, reduced operational overhead, rapid development, and high availability. It is suitable for a wide range of use cases, including web and mobile applications, real-time data processing, chatbots and voice assistants, IoT applications, and data and media processing. By eliminating the need for infrastructure management and providing automatic scaling and fault tolerance, serverless computing empowers developers to focus on building innovative applications that can scale seamlessly with user demand. Whether you're a startup or an enterprise, exploring the potential of serverless computing can accelerate your development process and drive digital transformation. So embrace the serverless paradigm and unleash the full power of the cloud!

Serverless Tools and Frameworks

Serverless computing, also known as Function as a Service (FaaS), has gained significant popularity in recent years. It allows developers to focus on writing code to implement specific functionalities without worrying about server management or infrastructure setup. In this section, we will explore various serverless tools and frameworks that simplify the development and deployment process.

AWS Lambda

AWS Lambda, provided by Amazon Web Services (AWS), is one of the leading serverless computing platforms. It allows you to run code without provisioning or managing servers. Lambda supports multiple programming languages, including Python, Node.js, Java, and C#. It offers various integrations with other AWS services, such as Amazon S3, Amazon DynamoDB, and Amazon Kinesis.

Lambda provides event-driven computing, where your code is executed in response to specific events, such as changes to data in an Amazon S3 bucket or updates in an Amazon DynamoDB table. You can define functions as Lambda handlers that process these events. Lambda automatically scales the execution environment to handle incoming requests, ensuring high availability and scalability.

Example:
Let's say you are building a web application that requires image processing. You can use AWS Lambda to create a function that automatically resizes images uploaded to your application. Whenever a new image is uploaded, Lambda will trigger the function, which will resize the image and save it to a specific location. This eliminates the need for setting up and managing servers for image processing.

Azure Functions

Azure Functions, offered by Microsoft Azure, is another popular serverless computing platform. It allows you to build and deploy applications using various programming languages, including C#, JavaScript, Python, and PowerShell. Azure Functions integrates seamlessly with other Azure services, such as Azure Storage, Azure Cosmos DB, and Azure Event Grid.

Similar to AWS Lambda, Azure Functions provides event-driven computing. You can define functions that respond to specific triggers, such as changes in Azure Storage or incoming messages in a message queue. Azure Functions automatically manages the underlying infrastructure, ensuring scalability and fault tolerance.

Example:

Suppose you are developing a chat application that requires real-time notifications. You can use Azure Functions to create a function that triggers whenever a new message is sent. The function can send push notifications to connected clients, providing instant message updates. With Azure Functions, you can focus on writing the logic for handling events, while the serverless platform handles the scalability and infrastructure concerns.

Google Cloud Functions

Google Cloud Functions is a serverless computing platform offered by Google Cloud. It enables you to build and deploy applications using languages such as Node.js, Python, and Go. Cloud Functions integrates well with other Google Cloud services, such as Google Cloud Storage, Google Cloud Pub/Sub, and Firebase.

Cloud Functions follows the event-driven model, where functions are triggered by events occurring in other Google Cloud services. For example, you can create a function that processes new files uploaded to Cloud Storage or reacts to events from Firebase. Google Cloud Functions automatically manages the underlying infrastructure, allowing you to focus on writing code for your application's specific functionalities.

Example:

Consider a scenario where you are developing a data analytics platform that requires processing data from multiple sources. With Google Cloud Functions, you can create functions that process and analyze data whenever new events occur. For instance, when new data is added to a database or when a new message is published to a topic, Cloud Functions can trigger the corresponding functions to perform data processing and generate insights.

Serverless Framework

The Serverless Framework is an open-source framework that simplifies the deployment and management of serverless applications across different cloud providers. It provides a unified way to define and deploy functions, manage event triggers, and handle dependencies.

With the Serverless Framework, you can write serverless applications using familiar programming languages and define your application's infrastructure as code. It offers a plugin architecture that allows you to extend its functionality and integrate with different services. The framework supports various cloud providers, including AWS, Azure, and Google Cloud.

SERVERLESS COMPUTING

Example:

Suppose you are developing a multi-cloud serverless application, where different functionality is implemented in different cloud providers. Using the Serverless Framework, you can define your functions, event triggers, and dependencies in a single configuration file. The framework will then deploy and manage your application across the selected cloud providers, abstracting away the provider-specific details.

Benefits of Serverless Tools and Frameworks

Serverless tools and frameworks provide several benefits for application development and deployment:

- **Simplified Development:** Serverless tools abstract away the underlying infrastructure, allowing developers to focus solely on writing code to implement specific functionalities. This reduces the development effort and accelerates time-to-market.

- **Automatic Scalability:** Serverless platforms automatically scale your functions based on the incoming request load. You don't have to worry about configuring and managing servers to handle peak loads. This ensures high availability and cost-effective scalability.

- **Cost Optimization:** Serverless computing follows a pay-per-use model, where you are only charged for the actual execution time and resources consumed by your functions. This can lead to significant cost savings compared to traditional server-based architectures.

- **Integration with Cloud Services:** Serverless tools seamlessly integrate with other cloud services, enabling you to leverage functionalities such as storage, messaging, and databases. This allows you to build complex applications by combining multiple cloud services.

- **Event-Driven Architecture:** Serverless platforms follow an event-driven model, where functions are triggered in response to specific events. This allows you to build real-time applications that respond to changes in data, user interactions, or system events.

Caveats and Considerations

While serverless tools and frameworks offer numerous benefits, there are some caveats and considerations to keep in mind:

- **Cold Start Latency:** Serverless platforms may experience a cold start latency when executing a function that has not been recently invoked. This can introduce a slight delay in the response time for the first request. However, subsequent requests to the same function will benefit from the warm execution environment.

- **Execution Time Limits:** Serverless platforms impose execution time limits on functions. If your function exceeds the time limit, it will be terminated. It's essential to design your functions to be within the execution time limits, or consider splitting complex operations into smaller functions.

- **Vendor Lock-In:** Using a specific serverless platform may result in vendor lock-in, as each platform has its own proprietary features and integrations. It's important to consider the long-term implications and choose a platform that aligns with your application requirements and vendor strategy.

- **Monitoring and Debugging:** Serverless architectures may introduce additional challenges when it comes to monitoring and debugging. Monitoring the performance and error handling of functions distributed across different cloud providers can be complex. It's crucial to have robust monitoring and logging solutions in place.

Resources

Here are some resources to further explore serverless tools and frameworks:

1. **AWS Lambda Documentation:** The official AWS Lambda documentation provides detailed information on how to get started with Lambda, various programming languages supported, and integration with other AWS services. You can access it at `https://aws.amazon.com/documentation/lambda/`.

2. **Azure Functions Documentation:** The official Azure Functions documentation offers comprehensive guides on creating, deploying, and managing functions on the Azure platform. It covers different programming languages, triggers, and integrations. You can access it at `https://docs.microsoft.com/en-us/azure/azure-functions/`.

3. **Google Cloud Functions Documentation:** The official Google Cloud Functions documentation provides in-depth resources on building and deploying functions using different programming languages, event triggers,

and service integrations. You can access it at `https://cloud.google.com/functions/docs`.

4. **Serverless Framework Documentation:** The Serverless Framework documentation offers extensive guidance on using the framework to develop and deploy serverless applications. It provides examples, best practices, and plugin references. You can access it at `https://www.serverless.com/framework/docs`.

Summary

Serverless tools and frameworks, such as AWS Lambda, Azure Functions, Google Cloud Functions, and the Serverless Framework, simplify the development and deployment of serverless applications. They provide automatic scalability, cost optimization, and integration with cloud services. However, it's important to consider caveats like cold start latency, execution time limits, vendor lock-in, and monitoring challenges. Exploring the available documentation and resources will enable you to leverage the power of serverless computing effectively in your applications.

The Fucking Freedom of Serverless

Serverless computing, also known as Function as a Service (FaaS), is a revolutionary concept in cloud computing that allows developers to focus solely on writing and deploying code without worrying about infrastructure management. This section will explore the concepts, benefits, and challenges of serverless computing, and delve into real-world examples to help you understand the fucking freedom it brings.

Introduction to Serverless Computing

Traditionally, when building applications, developers had to provision and manage servers, configure networking, and maintain the underlying infrastructure. This tedious and time-consuming process often took away valuable time from developers, delaying the deployment of features and updates.

Serverless computing eliminates this headache by abstracting away the infrastructure. With serverless, developers write their code as individual functions that perform specific tasks or operations. These functions are event-driven and only execute in response to specific triggers or events, such as an HTTP request or changes in a database.

The Benefits of Serverless Computing

The fucking freedom of serverless computing comes with a variety of benefits that make it an attractive choice for modern application development. Let's dive into some of these benefits:

1. **Scalability:** Serverless platforms automatically handle the scaling of functions based on demand. This means that your application can seamlessly handle a few requests per minute or thousands of requests per second without any manual intervention.

2. **Cost Efficiency:** With serverless, you only pay for the execution time of your functions. Since there are no idle servers to maintain, you don't pay for unused resources. This makes serverless a cost-effective solution, especially for applications with varying workloads.

3. **Reduced Administrative Tasks:** Without the need to provision or manage servers, developers can focus solely on writing code and delivering value. This eliminates administrative tasks and allows teams to operate at a higher velocity.

4. **Faster Time to Market:** With serverless, you can rapidly develop and deploy features. The simplified development process and reduced architectural complexity enable faster time to market, empowering you to iterate and experiment more efficiently.

5. **Automatic High Availability:** Serverless platforms provide built-in high availability and fault tolerance. Functions are automatically distributed and replicated across multiple data centers, ensuring your application remains resilient in the face of failures.

Challenges of Serverless Computing

While serverless computing offers numerous benefits, it's not without its challenges. Let's explore some of these challenges to get a comprehensive view:

1. **Vendor Lock-In:** Serverless platforms are provided by cloud service providers, such as AWS Lambda, Azure Functions, and Google Cloud Functions. This creates a level of vendor lock-in, as moving serverless functions to another provider may require rewriting and refactoring code.

2. **Cold Start Latency:** The first invocation of a serverless function may experience a cold start latency, where the platform provisions the necessary resources to execute the function. This can introduce a slight delay in the response time, which might not be desirable for latency-sensitive applications.

3. **Limited Execution Time:** Serverless functions have a maximum execution time limit enforced by the platform. This means that long-running tasks or batch processing might not be suitable for serverless architectures, and other approaches might be necessary for such use cases.

4. **Debugging and Testing:** Debugging and testing serverless functions can be challenging compared to traditional development. Tools and techniques specific to serverless architectures need to be adopted to effectively identify and fix issues.

5. **Security Concerns:** Serverless functions rely on proper configuration and security best practices to ensure the protection of data and prevent unauthorized access. Proper authentication, authorization, and input validation are crucial to maintaining a secure serverless environment.

Real-World Examples

To fully grasp the fucking freedom of serverless computing, let's explore a couple of real-world use cases where serverless shines:

1. **Web Applications:** Serverless is an excellent choice for handling HTTP requests in web applications. Functions can be triggered by HTTP events, allowing you to build API endpoints or handle specific routes with ease. This approach reduces the operational overhead of managing web servers and allows you to abstract away the infrastructure layer.

2. **Data Processing and ETL:** Serverless is ideal for processing data in real-time or batch scenarios. Functions can be triggered by events like file uploads or changes in data streams, enabling you to perform data transformations, aggregations, or analytics without the need for dedicated servers.

3. **Microservices Architecture:** Serverless functions provide a microservices-friendly approach to building applications. Each function can perform a specific task, and you can combine them to compose complex

workflows. This reduces code complexity, improves maintainability, and allows for rapid development and deployment of microservices.

4. **Internet of Things (IoT):** Serverless computing is a natural fit for IoT applications. Functions can be triggered by sensor data or device events, allowing you to process, analyze, and respond to data from IoT devices in real-time. This enables you to build scalable and event-driven IoT architectures while reducing operational overhead.

Conclusion

Serverless computing brings the fucking freedom to developers, allowing them to focus on writing code and delivering value without worrying about the underlying infrastructure. With benefits like scalability, cost efficiency, reduced administrative tasks, faster time to market, and automatic high availability, serverless is shaping the future of cloud computing.

However, it's important to be mindful of the challenges it presents, such as vendor lock-in, cold start latency, limited execution time, debugging complexities, and security concerns. By understanding these challenges and leveraging serverless for the right use cases, you can fully embrace the fucking freedom of serverless computing and unlock its full potential for your applications.

Cloud Services

Storage and Database Services

Object Storage

In this section, we will dive into the fascinating world of object storage in cloud computing. Object storage is a popular data storage solution that is designed to handle massive amounts of unstructured data. Unlike traditional file systems, which organize data into a hierarchical structure, object storage organizes data as discrete objects, each with a unique identifier. This unique identifier allows for easy retrieval and management of the data.

Background

Before we delve deeper into object storage, let's quickly recap the basic principles of cloud computing. Cloud computing is a model for delivering computing resources over the internet, providing on-demand access to a shared pool of configurable computing resources. These resources can include networks, servers, storage, applications, and services.

One of the key advantages of cloud computing is scalability. Cloud providers offer the ability to scale resources up or down based on demand, allowing businesses to allocate resources efficiently and pay only for what they use. Object storage is a fundamental component of cloud computing, providing a reliable and scalable solution for storing large amounts of data.

Principles of Object Storage

Object storage is built upon a few key principles that differentiate it from traditional file systems:

- **Flat Namespace**: In object storage, data is organized in a flat namespace, meaning there are no hierarchical directories or folders. Each object is assigned a unique key that serves as its identifier, allowing for fast and direct access to the data. This architecture eliminates the limitations of directory-based structures and allows for easy scaling and management of data.

- **Metadata**: Objects in object storage are accompanied by metadata, which provides additional information about the object. Metadata can include attributes such as the creation timestamp, last modified timestamp, file size, and user-defined tags. This metadata makes it easier to organize, search, and retrieve objects.

- **Durability and Redundancy**: Object storage systems are designed to be highly durable and redundant. Data is typically stored across multiple physical locations, ensuring that even if one or more storage nodes fail, the data remains available. Redundancy and data replication mechanisms guarantee the durability of objects stored in the cloud.

Use Cases and Examples

Object storage is suitable for a wide range of use cases, including:

- **Archiving and Backup**: Object storage provides a cost-effective solution for long-term data retention. Its durability and redundancy features make it an ideal choice for storing backups and archives that need to be preserved for extended periods.

- **Content Distribution**: Object storage is commonly used for distributing large media files, such as videos or images, across different geographical regions. Content Delivery Networks (CDNs) leverage object storage to cache and deliver content efficiently to end-users, ensuring a smooth and fast user experience.

- **Data Analytics**: Many organizations leverage object storage for storing massive datasets used in data analytics and machine learning. The scalability and flexibility of object storage allow businesses to store, process, and analyze vast amounts of unstructured data.

- **Internet of Things (IoT)**: Object storage is also used in IoT applications, where sensors and devices generate a tremendous amount of data. Object storage provides a reliable and scalable storage solution for storing and analyzing IoT data in real-time.

Let's take a look at a real-world example to understand how object storage is used in practice.

Example: Image Storage and Delivery

Imagine you are building a photo-sharing application that allows users to upload and share their pictures. With a traditional file-based storage system, you would face challenges in terms of scalability, performance, and management. However, by leveraging object storage, you can overcome these challenges.

When a user uploads an image, it is treated as an object and stored in the object storage system. The object is given a unique identifier, such as a hash of the image contents. This identifier can be used to retrieve the image quickly. Additionally, metadata can be attached to the object, such as the user's name, creation date, and tags.

To deliver the image to a user, the object is retrieved based on its identifier and served directly from the object storage system. CDNs can be used to cache the images across different regions, ensuring fast and efficient delivery to users.

Resources

To learn more about object storage and its implementation in various cloud platforms, here are some recommended resources:

- "Cloud Storage for Dummies" by Linda Koontz and Sigalit Narcisio: This book provides a comprehensive introduction to cloud storage, including object storage, and covers various concepts, architectures, and best practices.

- Amazon Simple Storage Service (S3) Documentation: Amazon S3 is a popular object storage service provided by Amazon Web Services (AWS). The official documentation offers detailed guidance on using S3, including APIs, security, and pricing.

- Google Cloud Storage Documentation: Google Cloud Storage is another prominent object storage solution offered by Google Cloud Platform (GCP). The documentation provides in-depth information on using Google Cloud Storage, including storage classes, lifecycle management, and access control.

Conclusion

Object storage is a critical component of cloud computing, providing a scalable and reliable solution for storing unstructured data. Its unique architecture, metadata capabilities, and durability features make it suitable for a variety of use cases, ranging from data archiving to content distribution. By understanding the principles and advantages of object storage, you can leverage this technology to optimize your cloud-based applications and services.

Remember, in this increasingly data-driven world, mastering object storage will give you a powerful toolset to conquer the cloud and scale your applications to new heights. So dive in, explore the limits, and embrace the possibilities of object storage in the modern era of computing. The cloud is your playground, so conquer it!

Block Storage

Block storage is a fundamental component of cloud computing that provides persistent and high-performance storage for virtual machines (VMs) and other applications. In this section, we will explore the concept of block storage, its characteristics, and its benefits. We will also delve into the different types of block storage available in cloud computing and discuss their use cases.

Understanding Block Storage

In the context of cloud computing, block storage refers to the storage of data in fixed-sized blocks or chunks, typically ranging from a few kilobytes to several megabytes in size. These blocks are organized in a hierarchical manner to form a logical storage volume that can be accessed and manipulated by applications.

Unlike file storage, which deals with files and directories, block storage operates at a lower level and presents storage devices as a series of blocks that can be read from or written to. This low-level access allows for efficient data management and precise control over storage resources.

One of the key characteristics of block storage is its ability to provide direct and fast access to data. Since data is stored in fixed-sized blocks, it can be accessed randomly without the need to retrieve or read the entire volume. This makes block storage ideal for applications that require low-latency and high-performance storage, such as databases, transactional systems, and virtual machines.

Types of Block Storage

In cloud computing, there are primarily two types of block storage: *Elastic Block Store (EBS)* in Amazon Web Services (AWS) and *Managed Disks* in Microsoft Azure. Let's explore each type in more detail:

Elastic Block Store (EBS): EBS is a block storage service provided by AWS. It allows you to create, attach, and detach storage volumes to EC2 instances. EBS volumes are network-attached and can be accessed by a single EC2 instance at a time. These volumes provide low-latency, durable, and persistent block-level storage.

EBS volumes offer different performance options, including *General Purpose (SSD)*, *Provisioned IOPS (SSD)*, and *Throughput Optimized Hard Disk Drive (HDD)*. General Purpose SSD volumes are suitable for a wide range of workloads, while Provisioned IOPS SSD volumes are designed for applications that require high I/O performance. Throughput Optimized HDD volumes are ideal for large, sequential workloads that require high throughput.

Managed Disks: Managed Disks is the block storage offering of Microsoft Azure. It provides scalable and durable storage for Azure virtual machines. Managed Disks abstracts the underlying storage infrastructure, making it easy to create and manage storage volumes. These volumes are automatically replicated to ensure data durability and availability.

Similar to EBS, Managed Disks offer different performance tiers, including *Standard* and *Premium*. Standard disks are suitable for most workloads, while Premium disks provide high-performance storage for I/O-intensive applications.

Use Cases and Benefits

Block storage offers several benefits and is well-suited for a variety of use cases in cloud computing. Let's explore some of the use cases and benefits below:

Use Cases:

- *Database Storage*: Block storage provides a reliable and high-performance storage solution for databases. It allows for efficient data retrieval and supports the transactional requirements of database systems.

- *Virtual Machine Storage*: Block storage is commonly used to store the operating system, applications, and user data in virtual machines. It enables quick and direct access to data, ensuring optimal performance for VMs.

- *Big Data and Analytics*: Block storage is well-suited for storing and processing large volumes of data in big data and analytics workloads. Its low-latency and high-IOPS characteristics enable faster data processing and analysis.

Benefits:

- *Scalability*: Block storage allows for flexible scaling of storage capacity as per the needs of the application. You can easily increase or decrease the storage capacity based on demand.

- *Durability*: Data stored in block storage is typically replicated across multiple devices, ensuring high data durability and availability.

- *Performance*: Block storage offers high-performance storage with low latency and high IOPS, making it ideal for applications with demanding performance requirements.

Block Storage Pricing

As with any cloud service, it's essential to understand the pricing models associated with block storage. Both AWS EBS and Azure Managed Disks have different pricing structures based on factors such as storage capacity, performance tiers, and data transfer.

In AWS, the pricing for EBS volumes is based on the volume type, the amount of provisioned storage, and the number of I/O requests. You can refer to the AWS documentation for detailed pricing information and examples.

In Azure, the pricing for Managed Disks is determined by the disk type (Standard or Premium), the provisioned storage capacity, and any additional features or services. The Azure pricing documentation provides comprehensive details on the cost structure.

To optimize costs, it's crucial to analyze your workload requirements and choose the appropriate storage type and performance tier that aligns with your application needs.

Summary

In this section, we explored the concept of block storage in cloud computing. We learned about its characteristics, the types of block storage available in Amazon Web Services (AWS) and Microsoft Azure, and their respective use cases and benefits. We explored how block storage is well-suited for databases, virtual machines, and big data analytics workloads. Additionally, we discussed the pricing models associated with block storage and the importance of optimizing costs based on workload requirements.

Remember, block storage is a powerful tool in your cloud computing arsenal, providing efficient and high-performance storage for your applications.

STORAGE AND DATABASE SERVICES 151

Understanding its nuances and choosing the right type of block storage will go a long way in building robust and scalable cloud solutions. So, don't underestimate the power of block storage, and harness its capabilities to scale and conquer the cloud!

Relational Databases

Relational databases are a fundamental component of cloud computing, providing a structured and efficient way to store and organize data. In this section, we will explore the principles of relational databases, their components, and their role in cloud computing.

Introduction to Relational Databases

Relational databases are based on the concept of relational models, which were first introduced by Edgar F. Codd in the 1970s. These databases organize data into tables, where each table represents a specific entity or concept. Each row in a table, known as a record or tuple, represents an individual instance of that entity, while each column represents a specific attribute or characteristic.

The relationship between tables is established through the use of keys. A primary key is a unique identifier for each record in a table, while a foreign key establishes a link between two tables. This link allows for the creation of relationships and referential integrity, ensuring consistency and accuracy in the data.

Relational Database Management System (RDBMS)

A Relational Database Management System (RDBMS) is software that allows for the creation, management, and querying of relational databases. RDBMS provide tools and functionalities to handle the storage, retrieval, and manipulation of data efficiently.

Examples of popular RDBMS include MySQL, PostgreSQL, Oracle Database, and Microsoft SQL Server. These systems offer a wide range of features, such as transaction management, concurrency control, and data manipulation capabilities.

SQL: The Language of Relational Databases

Structured Query Language (SQL) is a powerful language used to interact with relational databases. SQL allows users to define the structure of the database, manipulate the data, and retrieve information through the execution of queries.

There are several types of SQL statements, including:

- **Data Definition Language (DDL)**: Used to define and modify the structure of the database, including creating tables, indexes, and constraints.

- **Data Manipulation Language (DML)**: Used to insert, update, and delete data from the database.

- **Data Control Language (DCL)**: Used to control access and permissions to the database, including granting or revoking privileges.

- **Transaction Control Language (TCL)**: Used to manage transactions, including committing or rolling back changes.

SQL provides a flexible and intuitive way to interact with relational databases, making it an essential skill for working with cloud-based infrastructure.

Database Normalization

Database normalization is the process of organizing data within a relational database to eliminate redundancy and improve data integrity. The normalization process involves decomposing a table into multiple tables, each focusing on a single entity or concept.

Normalization follows a set of rules, known as normal forms, to ensure that the resulting database is efficient and free from data anomalies. The most common normal forms are the First Normal Form (1NF), Second Normal Form (2NF), and Third Normal Form (3NF).

By applying normalization techniques, we can reduce data redundancy, improve the efficiency of queries, and minimize update anomalies. However, it is important to strike a balance between normalization and performance, as excessive normalization can lead to complex queries and reduced performance.

Relational Database Modeling

Relational database modeling is the process of designing the structure and relationships of a relational database. It involves identifying the entities, attributes, and relationships within a domain and representing them as tables in a database.

Entity-Relationship (ER) modeling is a widely used technique for database modeling. It allows for the visual representation of entities, attributes, and relationships using diagrams. In ER diagrams, entities are represented as rectangles, attributes as ovals, and relationships as lines connecting entities.

The process of database modeling involves analyzing the requirements of the system, identifying entities and their attributes, determining relationships and constraints, and translating them into a database schema. This schema serves as a blueprint for creating tables and establishing relationships within a database.

Relational Databases in the Cloud

Cloud computing has revolutionized the way we store and manage data, and relational databases are no exception. Cloud service providers offer managed relational database services, allowing users to focus on their applications without the need for infrastructure management.

These managed database services provide features such as automatic backups, scalability, high availability, and security. In addition to traditional relational databases, cloud providers also offer specialized database services, such as Amazon RDS, Azure SQL Database, and Google Cloud SQL.

By leveraging the power of cloud computing, organizations can benefit from the scalability, reliability, and cost-effectiveness of relational databases. Furthermore, the cloud provides the flexibility to deploy, manage, and scale databases based on demand, making it an essential component in modern database architecture.

Example: Online Shopping Database

To illustrate the principles of relational databases, let's consider the example of an online shopping database. The database needs to store information about customers, products, orders, and shipping details.

We can start by creating separate tables for each entity, such as the customers, products, orders, and shipping information. Each table will have a primary key, such as customer ID, product ID, order ID, and shipping ID.

The relationship between tables can be established through foreign keys. For example, the order table can have a foreign key referencing the customer ID and the product ID, linking the order to the customer and the purchased product.

With this relational database schema, we can easily query and retrieve information. For instance, we can retrieve all orders made by a specific customer, or all customers who have purchased a particular product.

By utilizing the power of relational databases, we can efficiently store and retrieve data for various applications, making it an essential component in modern cloud computing.

Exercises

1. Consider a relational database for a university. Identify the entities, attributes, and relationships that would be relevant for this domain. Create an ER diagram to represent the database schema.

2. Research and compare different cloud-based relational database services, such as Amazon RDS, Azure SQL Database, and Google Cloud SQL. Identify their features, pricing models, and benefits.

3. Discuss the concept of referential integrity in relational databases. Why is it important, and how does it ensure data consistency?

4. Suppose you have a table called "Employees" with the following attributes: EmployeeID, FirstName, LastName, DepartmentID, and ManagerID. Write an SQL query to retrieve the employees' first names and last names along with their corresponding manager's first name and last name.

5. Explore the concept of denormalization in relational databases. When and why would denormalization be used? What are the trade-offs? Provide real-world examples.

6. Investigate the impact of cloud computing on relational databases. How has cloud computing changed the way we design, deploy, and manage relational databases?

7. Research NoSQL databases, such as MongoDB and Cassandra. Compare and contrast the differences between relational databases and NoSQL databases. In which scenarios would you choose one over the other?

8. Discuss the challenges of scaling relational databases in the cloud. How does cloud computing allow for horizontal and vertical scaling? What are the considerations and trade-offs involved?

9. Explore the concept of ACID in relational databases. What does ACID stand for, and why is it important in maintaining data integrity? Provide examples of ACID transactions in real-world scenarios.

10. Investigate the role of indexes in relational databases. How do indexes improve query performance? What are the different types of indexes, and when should they be used?

Remember, practice makes perfect! Work on these exercises to strengthen your understanding of relational databases and their role in the cloud.

Additional Resources

- Connolly, T. M., & Begg, C. E. (2014). *Database Systems: A Practical Approach to Design, Implementation, and Management.* Pearson.

- Ramakrishnan, R., & Gehrke, J. (2003). *Database Management Systems*. Tata McGraw-Hill Education.
- Silberschatz, A., Korth, H. F., & Sudarshan, S. (2010). *Database System Concepts*. McGraw-Hill Education.
- "Relational Databases" - Oracle Documentation: https://docs.oracle.com/cd/E11882_01/server.112/e40540/intro.htm
- "SQL Tutorial" - W3Schools: https://www.w3schools.com/sql/
- "Introduction to Relational Databases" - Coursera: https://www.coursera.org/learn/intro-db/

NoSQL Databases

NoSQL databases are a revolutionary alternative to traditional relational databases, offering increased scalability, flexibility, and performance for modern applications. In this section, we will explore the definition, characteristics, and various types of NoSQL databases, as well as their advantages, challenges, and real-world examples.

Definition and Characteristics

NoSQL, which stands for "not only SQL," is a broad term used to describe a class of database management systems that deviate from the traditional table-based relational model. Instead of using structured query language (SQL), NoSQL databases employ various data models to store and retrieve data. These databases are designed to handle large volumes of unstructured, semi-structured, and structured data in a distributed fashion.

The characteristics of NoSQL databases can be summarized as follows:

- **Schema-less:** Unlike relational databases that enforce a predefined schema, NoSQL databases allow for dynamic and flexible data modeling. This means you can store data without defining its structure in advance, making it easier to iterate and adapt as your application evolves.

- **Horizontal scalability:** NoSQL databases are designed to scale horizontally, meaning they can handle massive amounts of data and traffic by distributing the load across multiple servers or nodes. This scalable architecture allows for high-performance and high availability.

- **High performance:** By eliminating the need for complex joins and enforcing a flexible schema, NoSQL databases can achieve high write and read throughput. This makes them well-suited for use cases requiring real-time data processing, such as streaming analytics and content management.

- **Data model diversity:** NoSQL databases provide a range of data models, including key-value pairs, document-oriented, columnar, and graph-based. This versatility allows developers to choose the most appropriate data model for their specific use case, optimizing performance and query efficiency.

- **Fault tolerance:** NoSQL databases are designed to handle failures gracefully. They employ replication, sharding, and distributed consensus protocols to ensure data durability and high availability, even in the presence of hardware or network failures.

Types of NoSQL Databases

NoSQL databases can be broadly classified into four main types based on their data models:

1. **Key-Value Stores:** Key-value stores are the simplest form of NoSQL databases, where data is stored as a collection of key-value pairs. The keys are unique identifiers used to access the corresponding values. This data model is highly efficient for simple read and write operations. Examples of key-value stores include Redis, Riak, and Amazon DynamoDB.

2. **Document Databases:** Document databases are designed to store, retrieve, and manage semi-structured or unstructured data in the form of JSON or XML documents. Each document can have its own structure, and the database system indexes them for efficient querying. MongoDB, CouchDB, and Apache Cassandra are popular document databases.

3. **Columnar Databases:** Columnar databases store data in columns rather than rows, allowing for efficient data compression and query performance. This data model is particularly suited for analytical workloads that involve aggregations and complex queries. Apache Cassandra, Apache HBase, and Apache Druid are examples of columnar databases.

4. **Graph Databases:** Graph databases are specialized NoSQL databases designed to store and query highly interconnected data, such as social networks, recommendation engines, and fraud detection. They represent data as nodes (entities) and edges (relationships), allowing for efficient traversal and analysis of complex relationships. Neo4j, Amazon Neptune, and ArangoDB are examples of graph databases.

Each type of NoSQL database has its own strengths and weaknesses, and the choice of database depends on the specific requirements of your application.

Advantages of NoSQL Databases

NoSQL databases offer several advantages over traditional relational databases, making them a popular choice for modern applications:

- **Scalability:** NoSQL databases are designed to scale horizontally, allowing them to handle massive amounts of data and traffic. They can easily accommodate growing workloads by adding more servers or nodes to the cluster.

- **Flexibility:** With a schema-less design, NoSQL databases provide the flexibility to store and query data without the need to define a fixed schema in advance. This makes it easier to adapt to changing business requirements and iterate quickly.

- **Performance:** NoSQL databases excel at handling large volumes of data and supporting high throughput and low latency workloads. They eliminate the need for complex joins, enabling fast and efficient data retrieval.

- **Horizontal Scaling:** By distributing data across multiple nodes, NoSQL databases can achieve high availability and fault tolerance. They can automatically replicate data and handle failures without downtime.

- **Designed for the Cloud:** NoSQL databases are built from the ground up with distributed architectures, making them well-suited for cloud environments. They can take advantage of cloud-native features and services, such as auto-scaling and automated backups.

Challenges of NoSQL Databases

While NoSQL databases offer many benefits, they also present certain challenges that need to be considered:

- **Data Consistency:** NoSQL databases prioritize scalability and performance over strong data consistency. In some cases, data consistency guarantees may be relaxed, leading to eventual consistency or the need for manual conflict resolution.

- **Limited Query Capabilities:** NoSQL databases may lack the rich querying capabilities provided by SQL in relational databases. Ad-hoc queries and complex aggregations may require additional data processing frameworks or approaches.

- **Data Modeling Complexity:** The flexible schema of NoSQL databases can make data modeling more complex. Designing efficient data models for specific use cases requires careful consideration of query patterns and access patterns.

- **Skill Set and Learning Curve:** NoSQL databases often require developers to learn new programming interfaces and query languages. This may involve a learning curve for developers accustomed to SQL and relational database concepts.

- **Maturity and Ecosystem:** Some NoSQL databases may have a less mature ecosystem compared to traditional relational databases. This can result in a smaller community, limited tools, and less comprehensive documentation.

Despite these challenges, NoSQL databases have gained significant popularity and have become the go-to choice for many modern applications.

Real-World Examples

NoSQL databases have been widely adopted by companies across various industries for a range of use cases. Here are a few real-world examples:

- **MongoDB at The New York Times:** The New York Times leverages MongoDB as their primary content management system, storing articles, images, and metadata. MongoDB's flexible document model allows for efficient content delivery and easy content updates.

- **Amazon DynamoDB at Airbnb:** Airbnb uses Amazon DynamoDB, a key-value store, to store user profiles, property data, and availability information. DynamoDB's scalability and low-latency performance enable Airbnb to handle millions of users and property listings.

- **Cassandra at Netflix:** Netflix utilizes Apache Cassandra, a columnar database, for various purposes, including user account information, viewing history, and recommendations. Cassandra's ability to handle high write and read workloads at scale makes it a suitable choice for Netflix's data-intensive applications.

- **Neo4j at LinkedIn:** LinkedIn employs Neo4j, a graph database, to power their "People You May Know" feature. Neo4j's ability to efficiently traverse complex relationships allows LinkedIn to suggest relevant connections based on shared connections and interests.

These real-world examples demonstrate the versatility and scalability of NoSQL databases in addressing various data management challenges.

Summary

In this section, we delved into the world of NoSQL databases and explored their definition, characteristics, types, advantages, challenges, and real-world examples. NoSQL databases offer a flexible and scalable alternative to traditional relational databases, allowing developers to optimize performance and handle massive amounts of data. Understanding the strengths and weaknesses of different NoSQL database types is crucial for choosing the right database for your specific use case. Whether it's a key-value store, document database, columnar database, or graph database, NoSQL databases continue to shape the modern landscape of data management and cloud computing.

The Fucking Databases in the Cloud

Databases, my dear readers, are the backbone of any fucking modern application. Whether you're browsing through your favorite social media feed, ordering food on a delivery app, or streaming your favorite show, chances are that a database in the cloud is working its magic behind the scenes to provide you with the information you need. In this section, we're going to dive into the world of databases in the cloud and explore the different types and services that are available. Buckle up, because we're about to take a deep fucking dive!

Types of Databases

In the realm of cloud computing, there are two main types of databases that reign supreme: relational databases and NoSQL databases. Let's take a closer look at each of them, shall we?

Relational Databases Relational databases, my friends, are like the traditionalists of the database world. They follow a structured and organized approach to storing and managing data. In a relational database, data is stored in tables with rows and columns, similar to a spreadsheet. Each row represents a record, and each column represents a specific piece of information about that record. Relational databases use a language called SQL (Structured Query Language) to manipulate and retrieve data.

One of the most popular relational databases in the cloud is Amazon Relational Database Service (RDS), offered by our friends at Amazon Web

Services (AWS). RDS supports a wide range of popular relational database engines, including MySQL, PostgreSQL, Oracle, and Microsoft SQL Server. It's a fully managed service, which means that AWS takes care of all the underlying infrastructure, backups, and software updates, so you can focus on building your awesome applications.

NoSQL Databases Now, my curious readers, let's talk about NoSQL databases. NoSQL stands for "not only SQL," and these databases take a more flexible and dynamic approach to data storage. Unlike relational databases, which store data in tables, NoSQL databases store data in a variety of formats, such as key-value pairs, documents, or graphs. This flexibility allows for faster and more scalable data processing, making NoSQL databases ideal for modern applications with massive amounts of data.

One popular NoSQL database in the cloud is MongoDB Atlas, provided by MongoDB. This fully managed database service offers a document-based data model, which allows you to store and retrieve complex data structures with ease. MongoDB Atlas is known for its scalability, reliability, and automatic scaling features, making it a top choice for developers building modern, data-intensive applications.

Database as a Service (DBaaS)

Now that we understand the different types of databases, let's talk about the convenience of using a Database as a Service (DBaaS) in the cloud. DBaaS, my wonderful readers, is a cloud-based service that allows you to provision, manage, and scale databases without the need to worry about the underlying infrastructure. It's like having a personal database administrator that takes care of all the technical shit for you!

DBaaS providers, such as Amazon RDS, Google Cloud Spanner, and Microsoft Azure Cosmos DB, offer a range of features that make managing databases in the cloud a breeze. These services handle tasks like database installation, patching, backups, and failover, so you can focus on creating amazing applications.

Database Scaling

Scalability, my ambitious readers, is a key aspect of cloud databases. The ability to handle increasing amounts of data and growing user demands is what sets cloud databases apart from their on-premises counterparts. In the cloud, you can scale your databases vertically or horizontally, depending on your specific needs.

Vertical Scaling   Vertical scaling, also known as scaling up, involves increasing the resources of a single database instance. This can be done by upgrading to a more powerful server with more CPU, memory, or storage capacity. Vertical scaling is a good option when you need to handle increased load or performance demands for a single database.

For example, let's say you have an e-commerce website that experiences a sudden surge in traffic during a flash sale. By vertically scaling your database, you can ensure that it has enough resources to handle the increased number of transactions without slowing down.

Horizontal Scaling   On the other hand, my resourceful readers, we have horizontal scaling, also known as scaling out. This involves adding more database instances to distribute the workload and increase the overall capacity. Horizontal scaling is the way to go when you need to handle a massive amount of data or accommodate a rapidly growing user base.

Imagine you're working on a popular streaming service that needs to handle millions of concurrent users streaming their favorite shows. By horizontally scaling your database, you can add more instances and distribute the data across them, ensuring smooth and uninterrupted streaming for all your users.

Database Security

Security, my cautious readers, is always a top concern when it comes to databases, especially in the cloud. Cloud service providers have a variety of security measures in place to protect your precious data. Let's take a look at some of the important security features offered by cloud database services.

Encryption   Encryption, my security-conscious friends, is a fundamental aspect of protecting data. Cloud database services often provide encryption at rest and in transit. Encryption at rest ensures that your data is stored securely on disk, while encryption in transit ensures that data is encrypted as it travels between the database and your application.

For example, Amazon RDS supports encryption at rest using AWS Key Management Service (KMS) to manage encryption keys. It also provides the option to enable SSL/TLS encryption for connections to the database, ensuring that data is protected during transmission.

Access Control Access control, my vigilant readers, is another crucial aspect of database security. Cloud database services allow you to define fine-grained access controls to ensure that only authorized users can access and manipulate the data. This typically involves managing user roles, permissions, and authentication mechanisms.

For instance, MongoDB Atlas offers Role-Based Access Control (RBAC), which allows you to assign specific roles to users and control their access privileges. You can define roles such as read-only, read-write, or administrative access, depending on the needs of your application.

Auditing and Monitoring Auditing and monitoring, my watchful readers, are essential for detecting and responding to any suspicious activities or security breaches. Cloud database services offer built-in auditing and monitoring features that allow you to track database activities, monitor performance metrics, and set up alerts for any unusual behavior.

Microsoft Azure Cosmos DB, for example, provides Azure Monitor, a comprehensive monitoring solution that collects and analyzes performance and usage data. It offers features like metrics, logs, and alerts, giving you full visibility into the health and security of your database.

Real-World Examples

Now that we've covered the fundamentals of databases in the cloud, let's explore a couple of real-world examples to illustrate their importance and impact.

Example 1: Netflix Netflix, the beloved streaming giant, relies heavily on cloud databases to deliver a seamless and personalized experience to millions of users worldwide. They use a combination of traditional relational databases and scalable NoSQL databases to store and manage customer profiles, movie recommendations, and streaming data.

By leveraging the power of cloud databases, Netflix can handle the massive amount of data generated by its users and use it to provide personalized recommendations based on their viewing history. This is just one example of how cloud databases enable companies to deliver a superior user experience.

Example 2: Airbnb Another prime example, my adventurous readers, is Airbnb. The popular online marketplace for rental accommodations uses cloud databases to power its platform and ensure that hosts and guests can connect seamlessly.

STORAGE AND DATABASE SERVICES

Airbnb's database stores and manages property listings, user profiles, and booking information. By utilizing the scalability and flexibility of cloud databases, Airbnb can handle the constant influx of new listings, user registrations, and booking requests, providing a smooth and reliable experience for its users.

Further Resources

If you're interested in delving deeper into the world of databases in the cloud, I've got a couple of recommendations for you:

- **Read:** "Seven Databases in Seven Weeks" by Eric Redmond and Jim R. Wilson. This book provides a comprehensive overview of various database types, including both relational and NoSQL databases, and explores their strengths and weaknesses.

- **Explore:** The documentation and tutorials provided by cloud service providers like Amazon Web Services, Microsoft Azure, and Google Cloud Platform. They offer detailed resources and hands-on examples to help you get started with databases in the cloud.

Exercises

To reinforce your understanding of databases in the cloud, my devoted readers, here are a couple of exercises for you to tackle:

1. Identify a modern application that heavily relies on a database in the cloud. Discuss the specific challenges that this application might face in terms of scalability, security, and data modeling.

2. Compare and contrast the features and scalability options of a relational database and a NoSQL database in the cloud. Discuss the scenarios in which one type might be more suitable than the other.

3. Research and analyze a recent security breach or data leak involving a cloud database. Discuss the potential causes and consequences of the incident, as well as the lessons that can be learned from it.

Note: The exercises provided are just a starting point. Feel free to explore additional topics and challenges related to databases in the cloud, and share your insights with your fellow learners.

Conclusion

And there you have it, my inquisitive readers! We've covered the fundamentals of databases in the cloud, including the different types of databases, the convenience of Database as a Service (DBaaS), scaling options, security measures, real-world examples, and further resources for you to explore. Databases in the cloud play a crucial role in powering our modern applications, and understanding how to leverage their power can set you on the path to cloud computing mastery. Keep learning, keep exploring, and keep conquering the cloud!

Compute and Container Services

Virtual Machines (VMs)

Virtual Machines (VMs) are a fundamental building block of cloud computing. They provide a way to run multiple operating systems and applications on a single physical server. In this section, we will dive into the nitty-gritty of VMs, exploring their architecture, advantages, and real-world use cases. So buckle up and get ready to explore the virtual world of VMs!

Understanding Virtualization

At the heart of virtual machines lies the concept of virtualization. Virtualization is the technique of creating multiple virtual instances of a physical resource, such as a server or an operating system, to maximize resource utilization and improve efficiency. Virtualization allows for the abstraction of physical hardware, enabling the creation of software-defined virtual resources.

In the context of cloud computing, virtualization is used to create and manage virtual machines. Each virtual machine acts as a separate and independent computing environment with its own operating system and applications. It is isolated from other virtual machines running on the same physical server, providing a secure and dedicated environment.

Virtual Machine Architecture

Virtual machines are built upon the concept of software emulation of hardware resources. They consist of three primary components: the host machine, the hypervisor, and the guest machine.

The host machine, also known as the physical machine, is the underlying hardware that runs the virtualization software. It provides the necessary

COMPUTE AND CONTAINER SERVICES 165

computing resources, such as the CPU, memory, and storage, to support the execution of multiple virtual machines.

The hypervisor, also known as the virtual machine monitor (VMM), is the software layer that enables the creation and management of virtual machines. It sits between the host machine and the guest machines, intercepting and managing hardware requests from the guest machines.

The guest machine, also known as the virtual machine instance, is the virtual representation of a physical computer system. It runs its own operating system and applications, isolated from other guest machines and the host machine. The guest machine interacts with the hypervisor to access hardware resources, which are abstracted by the hypervisor.

Advantages of Virtual Machines

Virtual machines offer several advantages that make them a powerful tool in cloud computing:

1. **Resource Isolation:** Each virtual machine operates in an isolated environment, providing a high degree of security and stability. Applications running on one virtual machine are isolated from those on other virtual machines, preventing potential conflicts and ensuring reliable performance.

2. **Hardware Abstraction:** Virtual machines abstract the underlying hardware, allowing applications to run on different operating systems and hardware configurations. This flexibility enables businesses to migrate legacy applications to the cloud without having to rewrite or modify the code.

3. **Scalability:** Virtual machines are highly scalable, as additional virtual machines can be easily provisioned on demand. This allows businesses to quickly scale up or down their computing resources based on fluctuating workloads and demand spikes.

4. **Fault Isolation:** If a virtual machine encounters an issue or crashes, it doesn't affect the other virtual machines running on the same physical server. This fault isolation ensures that failures are contained within the virtual machine, minimizing the impact on the overall system.

5. **Hardware Consolidation:** By running multiple virtual machines on a single physical server, hardware resources can be efficiently utilized. This reduces the cost of hardware procurement and maintenance, as well as the power consumption and physical footprint of the data center.

6. **Live Migration:** Virtual machines can be migrated between physical servers without interrupting the running applications. Live migration enables load balancing, maintenance, and disaster recovery scenarios, providing high availability and seamless user experience.

Real-World Use Cases

Virtual machines find applications in various industries and scenarios. Here are some real-world use cases highlighting the versatility of VMs:

1. **Software Testing and Development:** Virtual machines provide a sandboxed environment for developers to test and deploy applications. They allow developers to quickly spin up multiple instances of different operating systems and software configurations for thorough testing, without the need for dedicated physical hardware.

2. **Legacy Application Migration:** Virtual machines enable the migration of legacy applications to modern cloud infrastructure without the need for significant code changes. By encapsulating the application and its dependencies within a virtual machine, businesses can modernize their IT infrastructure and take advantage of cloud-based services.

3. **Disaster Recovery:** Virtual machines play a vital role in disaster recovery strategies. By replicating virtual machine instances across geographically dispersed data centers, businesses can ensure data redundancy and quickly recover from system failures or natural disasters.

4. **Multi-Tenancy:** Virtual machines enable service providers to offer Infrastructure as a Service (IaaS) to multiple customers simultaneously. Each customer is allocated their own isolated virtual machine, providing them with a secure and dedicated computing environment within a shared physical infrastructure.

5. **Desktop Virtualization:** Virtual machines can be used to provide virtual desktop infrastructure (VDI) solutions. Users can access their desktop environment remotely from any device, while the virtual machine handles the processing and storage requirements centrally.

Conclusion

Virtual machines are the workhorses of cloud computing, offering a powerful and flexible way to deploy applications and manage computing resources. Through virtualization, businesses can achieve higher resource utilization, improved flexibility, and enhanced security. Whether it's for software development, legacy application migration, or disaster recovery, virtual machines provide the foundation for building scalable and efficient cloud-based solutions.

Now that you've gained a solid understanding of virtual machines, it's time to explore other exciting topics in cloud computing. So keep reading, keep learning, and get ready to conquer the cloud!

Container Instances

In this section, we will delve into the concept of container instances in cloud computing. Containers have revolutionized the way applications are deployed and managed in the cloud. They provide a lightweight and portable solution for packaging an application along with all its dependencies and running it consistently across different environments.

Introduction to Containers

Before we jump into container instances, let's briefly discuss the concept of containers. In traditional computing, applications are typically installed directly onto a host operating system. This approach can lead to compatibility issues, as different applications may require different versions of libraries or software frameworks.

Containers solve this problem by encapsulating an application and all its dependencies within a self-contained unit. Each container runs in isolation from other containers and the underlying host system. This isolation ensures that the application operates consistently, regardless of the environment it is deployed on.

Docker

Docker is a widely used containerization platform that simplifies the process of creating, deploying, and managing containers. It provides a standardized format for packaging applications and their dependencies, known as Docker images. These images are portable and can be easily deployed across different cloud providers or on-premises infrastructure.

To run a container, you need a Docker engine installed on the host system. The Docker engine reads the instructions in a Docker image and creates an instance of the container based on those instructions. This instance is what we refer to as a container instance.

Characteristics of Container Instances

Container instances have several key characteristics that make them an attractive choice for deploying and running applications in the cloud:

- **Speed and Efficiency:** Container instances have minimal overhead compared to traditional virtual machines. They can be created and started within seconds, allowing for rapid scaling and deployment of applications. Additionally, containers share the operating system kernel of the host system, resulting in efficient resource utilization.

- **Portability:** Containers are highly portable, thanks to their standardized format. You can create a container image once and run it on various platforms without modification. This portability makes it easier to move applications between development, testing, and production environments.

- **Isolation:** Each container instance runs in isolation from other containers and the underlying host system. This isolation provides security and prevents applications from interfering with each other.

- **Resource Control:** Container instances offer fine-grained control over the allocation of resources such as CPU, memory, and disk space. This control allows for efficient utilization of resources and ensures that containers receive the required amount of resources to operate effectively.

Container Orchestration

When dealing with a large number of containers spread across multiple hosts, manual management becomes impractical. Container orchestration tools help automate the deployment, scaling, and management of containerized applications.

Kubernetes is the leading container orchestration platform, providing a robust set of features for managing container instances. It allows you to define how containers should be deployed, how they should scale based on workload, and how they should interact with each other. Kubernetes ensures high availability and fault tolerance by automatically restarting failed containers and distributing the workload across available resources.

Benefits of Container Instances

Container instances offer several benefits for cloud computing:

- **Consistency**: Containers encapsulate applications and their dependencies, ensuring consistent behavior across different environments. This consistency simplifies the development, testing, and deployment processes.

- **Scalability**: Container instances can be easily scaled up or down based on workload demands. Containers are designed to be lightweight, making it efficient to deploy multiple instances in parallel to handle increased traffic.

- **Resource Efficiency**: Containers maximize resource utilization by sharing the host system's operating system kernel. This efficient use of resources allows for running more applications on the same infrastructure.

- **Flexibility**: Containers provide flexibility in terms of choosing the programming language, frameworks, and libraries for developing applications. Developers can package an application with all its dependencies and deploy it on any platform that supports containers.

Real-World Example: Media Streaming

Let's take a real-world example to illustrate the power of container instances. Consider a media streaming service that needs to handle a sudden surge in user traffic due to a popular live event. By leveraging container instances, the service can quickly scale up its infrastructure by deploying additional containers to handle the increased load. Once the event is over, the service can scale back down by terminating the unnecessary containers.

Container instances also allow for easy deployment of application updates without causing downtime. By rolling out new containers with updated application code and configurations, the service can seamlessly switch traffic to the new containers without interrupting the user experience.

Conclusion

Container instances have revolutionized the way applications are deployed and managed in the cloud. They offer speed, efficiency, portability, and isolation, making them an attractive choice for modern cloud computing environments. By leveraging container orchestration platforms like Kubernetes, organizations can automate the deployment and scaling of container instances, ensuring high availability and fault tolerance. With their benefits of consistency, scalability, resource efficiency, and flexibility, container instances are a valuable tool in the cloud computing arsenal. So hop on the container train and ride it to cloud success!

Auto Scaling

Auto Scaling, my friends, is a powerful feature provided by cloud service providers that allows you to automatically adjust the number of compute resources in your application based on real-time demand. Think of it as the brain of your cloud infrastructure, always working behind the scenes to optimize resource allocation and ensure your applications are running smoothly.

Why Auto Scaling Matters

Imagine this scenario: you have a popular e-commerce website. During the holiday season, your website experiences a huge surge in traffic as people shop for gifts and discounts. Now, if you have a fixed number of servers running your website, they might struggle to handle this sudden spike in traffic. This can lead to slower response times, unresponsive pages, and worst of all, angry customers. Yikes!

But fear not, my fellow cloud enthusiasts! This is where auto scaling comes to the rescue. Auto Scaling allows you to automatically add more servers when the demand for your application increases, and scale down when the demand decreases. This ensures that you always have just the right amount of resources to handle the load, which means happier customers and a healthier bottom line.

How Auto Scaling Works

Now that we understand the importance of auto scaling, let's delve into how it actually works, shall we?

Auto Scaling operates based on certain predefined policies or rules, which you can configure according to your specific needs. These policies take into account various metrics such as CPU utilization, network traffic, and application response time to determine whether to scale up or scale down.

When the auto scaling system determines that additional resources are needed, it spins up new instances or virtual machines (VMs) to handle the increased workload. These instances are exact replicas of your original server, complete with the same software stack and configurations. This ensures consistent performance and eliminates any compatibility issues.

On the other hand, when the demand decreases, the auto scaling system removes excess instances, saving you money by reducing costs. This dynamic adjustment of resources based on demand not only maximizes the efficiency of your application but also optimizes costs, as you only pay for what you use.

COMPUTE AND CONTAINER SERVICES

Auto Scaling Policies

Now that we know the basics, let's explore some common auto scaling policies that you can use to control the behavior of your auto scaling group.

1. **Target Tracking Scaling:** This policy allows you to set a specific target value for a predefined metric, such as average CPU utilization or network throughput. The auto scaling system will then automatically adjust the number of instances to maintain this target value. For example, if you set a target of 70% CPU utilization, the system will add or remove instances as needed to keep the CPU utilization close to that value.

2. **Step Scaling:** This policy is more flexible and allows you to define scaling adjustments based on predefined steps. For example, you can increase the number of instances by 2 if CPU utilization exceeds 80%, and decrease the number of instances by 1 if CPU utilization falls below 30%. This policy is great for handling sudden traffic spikes or specific workload patterns.

3. **Scheduled Scaling:** As the name suggests, this policy allows you to define a specific schedule for scaling your application. For example, if you know that every Monday at 9 AM you have a spike in traffic due to a weekly sale, you can schedule the auto scaling group to add more instances before the sale starts and remove them afterwards. This helps you proactively handle predictable changes in demand.

4. **Predictive Scaling:** Now we're entering the realm of the future, my friends. Predictive scaling uses machine learning algorithms and historical data to forecast future demand for your application. It can automatically adjust the number of instances based on these predictions, ensuring you have just the right amount of resources before the demand actually hits. Talk about being ahead of the game!

Considerations and Best Practices

Auto Scaling is a powerful tool, but like any tool, it requires some careful planning and consideration to make the most of it. Let's go over some best practices and considerations when working with auto scaling:

1. **Health Checks:** Make sure your application and auto scaling group have health checks in place to detect any issues with your instances. This way, if an instance fails the health check, it can be replaced automatically, ensuring the stability and availability of your application.

2. **Monitoring and Alerting:** Use cloud monitoring services to keep an eye on key metrics such as CPU utilization, network traffic, and response time. Set up alerts to notify you when these metrics reach certain thresholds, so you can take proactive action if needed.

3. **Graceful Scaling:** When scaling down, it's important to ensure a smooth transition by draining connections and finishing any ongoing tasks before terminating instances. This prevents any disruption or data loss.

4. **Load Testing:** Test, test, and test some more! Before deploying your application to production, conduct load testing to ensure your auto scaling policies are properly configured and your application can handle the expected load.

5. **Networking Considerations:** When using auto scaling, keep in mind that the IP addresses of your instances may change as instances are added or removed. Use elastic load balancers or DNS-based load balancing to distribute incoming traffic across your instances.

6. **Cost Optimization:** While auto scaling can provide cost savings, it's important to optimize your infrastructure and make good use of resources. Use tools provided by your cloud service provider to analyze and optimize costs, such as spot instances or reserved instances.

Remember, auto scaling allows your application to dynamically respond to changes in demand, ensuring optimal performance and cost efficiency. So embrace the power of auto scaling and let your application scale gracefully in the cloud!

In a Nutshell

Auto Scaling is the brain of your cloud infrastructure, adjusting the number of compute resources based on real-time demand. It ensures your application can handle surges in traffic without breaking a sweat or angering your customers. With policies like target tracking, step scaling, scheduled scaling, and even predictive scaling, you can fine-tune the behavior of your auto scaling group to meet your specific needs. Just remember to plan ahead, test rigorously, and monitor your application to make the most of this powerful feature. Happy scaling!

Serverless Computing Platforms

Serverless computing, also known as Function as a Service (FaaS), is a cloud computing model that allows developers to build and run applications without the need to manage and provision servers. In serverless computing, developers focus solely on writing code for their application's functions, which are triggered by specific events or requests.

Serverless computing platforms provide a convenient and scalable way of deploying applications by abstracting away the underlying infrastructure. The platforms automatically manage the allocation and deallocation of computing resources based on the demand of the application. As a result, developers can focus

COMPUTE AND CONTAINER SERVICES   173

on writing code and delivering functionality rather than worrying about the operational aspects of their application.

Key components of serverless computing platforms

To understand serverless computing platforms, it is important to grasp the key components that make them work efficiently. These components include:

- **Functions:** In serverless computing, functions are the centerpiece. Developers write code for individual functions that perform specific tasks. Functions are event-driven, which means they are triggered by specific events such as a new file upload or an HTTP request.

- **Event sources:** Event sources are responsible for triggering functions. They can be external services like databases, message queues, or HTTP requests. Whenever an event occurs, the event source notifies the serverless platform to invoke the respective function.

- **Runtime environment:** The runtime environment is where the function code is executed. Serverless platforms provide the necessary execution environments for different programming languages such as JavaScript, Python, or Java. These environments take care of loading the function code, managing the runtime, and handling inputs and outputs.

- **Execution context:** When a function is triggered, the serverless platform creates an execution context. This context includes all the information needed for the function to execute, such as request parameters, environment variables, and authentication details. The execution context is created and torn down for each function invocation.

Benefits of serverless computing platforms

Serverless computing platforms offer several benefits that make them attractive to developers and organizations. Some of the key benefits include:

- **Scalability:** Serverless platforms automatically scale the computing resources based on the demand of the application. Functions are invoked only when triggered, and the platform handles the allocation and deallocation of resources. This makes serverless platforms highly scalable, allowing applications to handle sudden spikes in traffic without manual intervention or worrying about provisioning additional servers.

- **Cost efficiency:** Since serverless platforms allocate resources only when functions are triggered, developers do not have to pay for idle resources. This pay-per-use model ensures cost efficiency, as you are only billed for the actual execution time of your functions. Additionally, the automatic scaling of resources prevents overprovisioning, further reducing costs.

- **Developer productivity:** Serverless computing platforms greatly simplify the development and deployment process. Developers can focus on writing code for their application's functions without worrying about managing servers or dealing with infrastructure. The platforms provide tools and frameworks to streamline the development workflow, allowing developers to iterate quickly and deliver functionality faster.

- **Maintenance and operations:** With serverless platforms, much of the operational overhead is abstracted away. The platforms handle server management, operating system patching, and resource allocation, allowing developers to focus on building applications. This reduces the maintenance burden and frees up valuable time and resources.

- **High availability and fault tolerance:** Serverless platforms inherently provide high availability and fault tolerance. Functions are automatically replicated and distributed across multiple servers and availability zones. If one server or data center fails, the platform seamlessly redirects the execution to another available instance. This ensures that applications remain robust and available even in the face of infrastructure failures.

Use cases for serverless computing platforms

Serverless computing platforms are versatile and can be applied to a wide range of use cases. Some of the common use cases include:

- **Web applications:** Serverless platforms are well-suited for building web applications where certain tasks, such as image processing or user authentication, can be offloaded to functions. This helps in keeping the web servers lightweight and scalable, offloading the heavy lifting to serverless functions.

- **Data processing and analytics:** Serverless platforms are increasingly used for data processing and analytics tasks. Functions can be triggered by data events and perform real-time transformations, filtering, or aggregation. Serverless platforms integrate well with data storage and streaming services, allowing for seamless data processing pipelines.

- **Event-driven applications:** Applications that rely heavily on event-driven architecture can benefit from serverless platforms. Functions can be triggered by various events such as database updates, message queue records, or IoT sensor readings. Serverless platforms enable real-time processing and reaction to events, making them suitable for event-driven use cases.

- **Chatbots and voice assistants:** Serverless functions can power chatbots and voice assistants. Functions can handle natural language processing, intent recognition, and interaction with external services. Serverless platforms provide the necessary scalability and flexibility to handle the dynamic nature of chatbot and voice assistant applications.

- **Microservices architectures:** Serverless computing fits well within a microservices architecture, where applications are composed of small, independent services. Each microservice can be implemented as a function, allowing for granular scaling and independent deployment. Serverless platforms provide the infrastructure for managing and orchestrating microservices at scale.

Challenges and limitations of serverless computing platforms

While serverless computing platforms offer numerous benefits, they also come with certain challenges and limitations. Some of the common ones include:

- **Cold start latency:** Serverless platforms allocate computing resources on demand, which means that there may be a slight delay when a function is invoked for the first time. This delay, known as the cold start latency, occurs as the platform spins up the necessary resources to execute the function. While the cold start latency is usually negligible, it can become a concern for latency-sensitive applications.

- **Vendor lock-in:** Serverless platforms are provided by different cloud service providers, and each platform has its own set of features and APIs. Migrating a serverless application from one platform to another can be challenging due to vendor-specific dependencies and differences in implementation. This can result in vendor lock-in, limiting the flexibility to switch between platforms.

- **Execution and resource limits**: Serverless platforms impose certain execution and resource limits on functions. For example, there may be limits on the maximum execution time, maximum memory allocation, or maximum concurrency of functions. These limits can impact the design and implementation of applications, especially if they require long-running or memory-intensive operations.

- **Debugging and observability**: Debugging serverless functions can be more challenging compared to traditional applications. Since functions are executed in a managed environment, it can be difficult to reproduce and diagnose issues. Observability into function execution, performance, and logs is crucial for troubleshooting, but it may require additional configuration and tooling to achieve comprehensive observability.

- **State management**: Serverless functions are typically stateless, which means they do not maintain any state between invocations. While this stateless nature simplifies scaling and reduces complexity, it can pose challenges for certain applications that require state persistence. Managing and persisting application state may require external storage or database services, adding complexity to the application architecture.

Despite these challenges, serverless computing platforms continue to evolve, and new tools and frameworks are emerging to address some of these limitations. Developers need to carefully evaluate the trade-offs and considerations when adopting serverless platforms for their applications.

Conclusion

Serverless computing platforms provide a powerful and efficient way of deploying applications without the need to manage infrastructure. By abstracting away the operational complexities, serverless platforms empower developers to focus on building functionality, increasing developer productivity, and reducing time-to-market. They also offer benefits such as scalability, cost efficiency, and high availability.

However, serverless computing platforms come with their own set of challenges and limitations, including cold start latency, vendor lock-in, execution limits, and state management. Understanding these challenges and making informed architectural decisions is important when leveraging the capabilities of serverless platforms.

As serverless computing continues to grow in popularity, it is essential for developers to stay up-to-date with advancements and best practices in order to harness its full potential and conquer the cloud.

So, go forth, my fellow cloud conquerors, and embrace the power of serverless computing platforms. Harness their scalability, cost efficiency, and increased productivity to build amazing applications that will shape the future of technology. The cloud is yours to conquer!

The Fucking Compute Power of the Cloud

In this section, we will dive into the thrilling world of cloud computing and explore the compute power it offers. The compute power of the cloud is the backbone of any cloud service and it enables the delivery of scalable, on-demand computational resources to users.

Virtual Machines (VMs)

One of the fundamental components of the compute power in the cloud is the concept of virtual machines (VMs). Just like in the physical world, a VM is a software emulation of a physical computer that runs an operating system and applications. However, in the cloud, multiple VMs can coexist on a single physical server, enabling efficient utilization of resources. The deployment and management of VMs are handled by the cloud service providers, allowing users to focus on their applications rather than worrying about the underlying infrastructure.

Container Instances

Another element of compute power in the cloud revolves around containerization. Containers are lightweight, isolated environments that package applications along with their dependencies, enabling them to run consistently across different computing environments. In the cloud, container instances provide a faster and more resource-efficient alternative to VMs. With containers, you can effectively isolate applications, scale them independently, and achieve faster startup times. Docker and Kubernetes are popular tools for deploying and managing containers in the cloud.

Auto Scaling

Auto Scaling is a vital feature of cloud compute power that allows your applications to automatically adjust their capacity based on demand. With this capability, you don't need to manually provision or de-provision resources to match varying workloads. Instead, the cloud service providers monitor resource utilization and traffic patterns, and automatically scale your applications up or down accordingly. This ensures optimal performance and cost-efficiency, as you only pay for the resources you actually need.

Serverless Computing Platforms

Serverless computing is a paradigm that further simplifies application development and deployment by abstracting away servers and infrastructure management. With serverless computing platforms like AWS Lambda, Google Cloud Functions, and Azure Functions, you can run your code in a function-as-a-service (FaaS) model, where the underlying infrastructure is completely hidden from you. This allows you to focus solely on writing and deploying code as functions in response to events or triggers. Serverless computing offers granular scalability, high availability, and reduces operational complexities.

The Fucking Compute Power Unleashed

Thanks to the compute power of the cloud, businesses and developers can now harness the enormous scalability and processing capabilities that were once only available to large enterprises. The cloud provides virtually limitless compute resources, enabling you to run massive data processing tasks, train machine learning models with vast datasets, and handle high-traffic websites and applications. Whether you're a startup, a small business, or a large corporation, the compute power of the cloud empowers you to scale your operations without the need for massive upfront investments in physical infrastructure.

Real-World Example: Netflix

To illustrate the immense compute power of the cloud, let's take a look at the streaming giant Netflix. With over 200 million subscribers worldwide, Netflix relies heavily on cloud computing to deliver its vast library of content. When a user streams a movie or show on Netflix, the video files are split into small chunks and distributed across multiple servers in the cloud. This distributed architecture allows Netflix to handle millions of concurrent streams seamlessly. Additionally, by leveraging the auto-scaling capabilities of the cloud, Netflix can quickly add or remove servers based on demand, ensuring a smooth streaming experience for its users.

Further Reading and Resources

If you're interested in exploring more about the compute power of the cloud, here are some recommended resources:

- *Cloud Computing Concepts, Technology & Architecture* by Thomas Erl, Ricardo Puttini, and Zaigham Mahmood.
- *AWS Documentation on EC2 Instances* - Get a detailed understanding of Amazon EC2 instances and their compute power capabilities.
- *Google Cloud Computing Services* - Explore the compute options offered by Google Cloud Platform.
- *Azure Compute Documentation* - Learn about the compute services provided by Microsoft Azure.

Summary

In this section, we explored the compute power of the cloud, which is at the heart of cloud computing services. We discussed the importance of virtual machines, container instances, auto scaling, and serverless computing platforms. We also looked at a real-world example of Netflix, showcasing how cloud compute power enables smooth streaming for millions of users. The compute power of the cloud provides immense scalability, flexibility, and cost-efficiency, unlocking a world of possibilities for businesses and developers.

Networking and Content Delivery Services

Virtual Private Cloud (VPC)

In the realm of cloud computing, a Virtual Private Cloud (VPC) is like your own personal slice of the cloud. It allows you to create a virtual network within the cloud environment, giving you control over your own private space in the vastness of the internet. Think of it as your own secret hideout within the cloud, where you can securely deploy and manage your applications and resources.

Understanding VPC

A VPC provides an isolated and secure environment for your cloud workloads. It allows you to define a logically isolated network, complete with its own IP address range, subnets, route tables, and security groups. You have the freedom to customize and configure your VPC to suit your specific needs, just like decorating your own room.

A VPC operates as a software-defined network within a public cloud provider's infrastructure. It allows you to abstract away the underlying physical network infrastructure and focus on your applications and services. This means you don't have to worry about the nitty-gritty details of setting up and managing physical network hardware - leave that to the cloud provider.

Getting Started with VPC

To begin your journey into the world of VPC, you first need to create one in your chosen cloud provider's console. You'll typically be asked to define the IP address range for your VPC, which determines the maximum number of IP addresses you can assign to your resources within the VPC.

Once your VPC is up and running, you can start partitioning it into smaller subnets. Subnets are like rooms within your VPC, where you can place specific resources and control their network access. For example, you might have one subnet for your web servers and another for your database servers, ensuring a clear separation of concerns.

Networking within VPC

Within your VPC, you can define and configure routing tables to control the flow of network traffic. Routing tables determine how packets are forwarded between different subnets within your VPC and to the outside world. It's like setting up the road signs and traffic lights within your private neighborhood.

To connect your VPC to the internet, you can allocate an internet gateway. This allows resources within your VPC to communicate with the internet, enabling access to external services and resources. You can also set up network address translation (NAT) gateways to allow your private subnets to access the internet while keeping them secure and shielded from direct exposure.

Security in VPC

In the ever-changing landscape of cybersecurity, security should always be a top priority. Thankfully, VPC provides a range of security features to help you protect your resources and data. One such feature is security groups, which act as virtual firewalls for your instances. You can define inbound and outbound traffic rules at the instance level, allowing you to control what traffic is allowed in and out.

Another powerful security feature within VPC is network access control lists (ACLs). ACLs are like security guards at the entrances of your subnets, allowing you to define granular rules for inbound and outbound traffic at the subnet level. This adds an extra layer of protection to your network, complementing the security groups.

Hybrid Connectivity

Sometimes you may want to extend your VPC to your on-premises data center or connect it to another cloud provider's network. This is where hybrid connectivity comes into play. With the right configuration, you can establish a secure and private connection between your VPC and your on-premises network using technologies like Virtual Private Network (VPN) or Direct Connect.

Hybrid connectivity offers the flexibility to leverage resources from multiple environments. It allows you to take advantage of the scalability and cost-effectiveness of the cloud while keeping sensitive data and critical workloads on-premises or in a different cloud environment.

Real-world Example: Secure E-commerce Application

Let's consider a real-world example to understand how VPC can be utilized. Imagine you're building an e-commerce application that handles sensitive customer data and online transactions. Security is paramount, as any breach could lead to loss of customer trust and financial damage.

By leveraging VPC, you can create a secure and isolated environment for your e-commerce application. You can define separate subnets for your front-end servers, database servers, and administrative tools. Each subnet can have its own security groups and ACLs to control traffic flow and restrict access.

You can further enhance the security of your application by deploying Web Application Firewall (WAF) services within your VPC. These services can provide protection against common web attacks and ensure the integrity and availability of your e-commerce platform.

Resources for Further Learning

To continue your journey into the world of VPC, here are a few resources you can explore:

- Cloud provider documentation: Each major cloud provider offers comprehensive documentation on VPC, including tutorials, best practices, and API references. Check out the documentation from providers like Amazon Web Services (AWS), Microsoft Azure, and Google Cloud Platform (GCP).

- Online courses: Platforms like Coursera, Udemy, and Pluralsight offer courses on cloud networking and VPC specifically. These courses provide in-depth knowledge and practical hands-on exercises to sharpen your skills.

- Community forums: Engage with the community on platforms like Stack Overflow and Reddit. These forums are filled with experts and enthusiasts who are always ready to help and discuss cloud-related topics, including VPC.

Remember, VPC provides you with the foundation to build secure, scalable, and highly available applications in the cloud. So go ahead, launch your VPC, and conquer the cloud!

Ethical Considerations: Privacy and Data Protection in VPCs

As we delve deeper into the realm of cloud computing, we must also consider the ethical implications and responsibilities that come with handling sensitive customer data within VPCs. These considerations include privacy and data protection.

When designing and managing your VPC, it is crucial to implement strong security measures to protect customer data, such as using encrypted communication protocols (e.g., HTTPS) and properly configuring access controls. You must also follow industry best practices and comply with relevant data protection regulations, such as the General Data Protection Regulation (GDPR) in the European Union.

Transparency and accountability are paramount in ensuring customer trust. Clearly communicate your data handling practices to your users and obtain their consent for data collection and processing. Regularly review and update your privacy policy to reflect any changes in how you handle customer data within your VPC.

By prioritizing privacy and data protection in your VPC, you can build a reputation of trust and ensure that your customers' information remains secure. Always strive to go above and beyond the legal requirements to protect the privacy of your users.

Unconventional Tip: Networking Parties in Your VPC

Networking can be intimidating, both in the digital world and the real world. But fear not, for we have an unconventional tip to help you grasp networking concepts in VPC: throw a virtual networking party!

Imagine each subnet in your VPC as a different room at a party, and the instances within each subnet as the guests. You can define different rules for each guest (instance) on how they interact with others. By visualizing your VPC as a networked party, you can understand how different traffic, security rules, and configurations apply to your instances (guests) within each subnet (room).

So grab a virtual drink, put on some virtual tunes, and let your VPC party begin! Remember, learning can be fun, even in the world of cloud computing.

Load Balancing

In the world of cloud computing, load balancing plays a crucial role in ensuring efficient resource allocation, optimal performance, and high availability of applications and services. Simply put, load balancing is the process of distributing incoming network traffic across multiple servers or resources to prevent any single resource from becoming overwhelmed or overloaded. It acts as a traffic cop, directing requests to the most suitable server based on various factors such as server capacity, response time, and current workload.

Load balancing can be achieved through various methods, each with its own advantages and considerations. Let's take a closer look at some of the popular load balancing techniques used in cloud environments:

Round Robin

One of the simplest and most widely used load balancing algorithms is the Round Robin approach. In Round Robin load balancing, incoming requests are sequentially distributed across the available servers in a cyclic manner. Each server in the pool takes turns handling the requests, ensuring an equal distribution of the workload.

For example, let's say we have three servers: Server A, Server B, and Server C. When a request comes in, it is directed to Server A. The next request goes to Server B, followed by Server C, and then back to Server A. This cycle continues as new requests arrive. Round Robin load balancing is easy to implement and requires little overhead. However, it assumes that all servers in the pool have similar computing power and responsiveness, which may not always be the case.

Weighted Round Robin

In a real-world scenario, not all servers are created equal. Some may have more processing power or better hardware specifications than others. This is where the Weighted Round Robin algorithm comes into play. Instead of a simple cyclic distribution, this approach assigns different weights or priorities to each server, reflecting their capabilities.

Servers with higher weights receive a larger portion of the incoming traffic, while servers with lower weights handle a smaller portion. This load balancing technique ensures that more powerful servers are utilized to their full potential, while still allowing lesser-powered servers to contribute to the workload. For example, if Server A has a weight of 3, Server B a weight of 2, and Server C a weight of 1, then Server A would handle three times the requests of Server C.

Least Connection

The Least Connection algorithm takes a different approach to load balancing. Instead of considering the computing power or weight of each server, it distributes new requests to the server with the fewest active connections at that moment. This technique aims to evenly balance the current workload among available servers, regardless of their capabilities.

This approach ensures that no single server gets burdened with more connections than others, preventing potential performance degradation or overload. The Least Connection algorithm dynamically adjusts to changes in traffic patterns, allowing it to adapt and maintain optimal resource utilization. However, it may not consider server response time or other performance-related factors, so it may not always be the most efficient load balancing method.

Layer 4 and Layer 7 Load Balancing

In addition to the aforementioned algorithms, load balancers can be categorized based on the network layer at which they operate: Layer 4 and Layer 7 load balancing.

Layer 4 load balancers work at the transport layer of the networking stack and make decisions based on IP addresses and port numbers. They are primarily concerned with routing traffic between client requests and server responses, considering factors such as server availability, response time, and number of connections.

On the other hand, Layer 7 load balancers operate at the application layer, enabling them to make more intelligent routing decisions based on application-specific information. These load balancers can inspect HTTP headers, cookies, and other application-layer attributes to distribute traffic based on more fine-grained criteria, such as URL patterns or user sessions.

Layer 7 load balancing is often used in scenarios where advanced application-level handling is required, such as session persistence, content-based routing, or SSL offloading. However, Layer 7 load balancers are generally more resource-intensive and may introduce additional latency compared to Layer 4 load balancers.

Load Balancer Configuration and High Availability

Load balancers can be implemented using dedicated hardware appliances or as software-based solutions running on virtual machines or containers. They often operate as a middle tier between the clients and the underlying application servers, intercepting and redirecting incoming requests.

To ensure high availability and avoid single points of failure, load balancer configurations commonly involve the use of multiple instances working in parallel. These instances can be deployed across different availability zones or regions to distribute the load and provide redundancy. By combining load balancing techniques with fault-tolerant architectures, cloud providers can maintain continuous service availability even in the event of hardware or software failures.

It's important to note that load balancing is not a one-size-fits-all solution. The optimal load balancing strategy depends on various factors, such as the specific requirements of the applications or services being load balanced, the characteristics of the underlying infrastructure, and the anticipated traffic patterns. Therefore, it is essential to carefully analyze the workload and consider multiple load balancing techniques to achieve the desired performance and availability goals.

Load Balancing in Action: A Real-World Example

Let's dive into a real-world example to illustrate how load balancing works in practice. Consider an e-commerce website that experiences heavy traffic during peak shopping periods. To ensure smooth and uninterrupted user experience, the website employs load balancers to distribute incoming requests among multiple web servers.

When a user visits the website and makes a request, the load balancer receives the request and examines various criteria, such as server load, response time, and session persistence requirements. Based on this analysis, the load balancer selects an available web server from a pool and forwards the request to that server.

As more users visit the website and make requests, the load balancer continues to distribute the load evenly across the available web servers. This prevents any single server from becoming overwhelmed, ensuring that the website remains responsive and accessible to all users.

Now, let's say one of the web servers in the pool unexpectedly goes offline due to a hardware failure. The load balancer detects this failure and automatically removes the affected server from the pool, redirecting incoming requests to the remaining servers. This automatic failover mechanism ensures that the website remains operational, even in the presence of failures.

Additionally, load balancers can provide various health checks and monitoring capabilities to continually assess the status and availability of the web servers. These health checks can include regular HTTP responses, checking for valid application responses, or even monitoring server resource utilization. If a server fails the health check, it is temporarily removed from the pool until it returns to a healthy state.

Load balancing, in combination with redundancy and fault tolerance measures, not only improves performance and responsiveness but also enhances the overall reliability and availability of cloud-based applications and services.

Further Resources and Caveats

Load balancing is a vast topic with deep technical intricacies. This section has provided a high-level overview of load balancing techniques, highlighting some of the commonly used algorithms and concepts. However, there are numerous other load balancing algorithms and strategies available, each with its own advantages and considerations.

For those interested in diving deeper into load balancing, the following resources provide more in-depth information and practical guidance:

- **Book:** "Load Balancing in the Cloud: An In-depth Guide to the Fundamentals, Tools, and Techniques" by Shane Cook

- **Documentation:** Vendor-specific documentation and user guides for load balancer solutions provided by cloud service providers like Amazon Web Services, Microsoft Azure, and Google Cloud Platform

- **Tutorials and Blogs:** Online tutorials and blog posts by technology experts and cloud enthusiasts that cover load balancing implementation details, best practices, and real-world deployment scenarios

While load balancing greatly enhances the performance and availability of cloud-based applications, it's important to recognize that it is not a panacea for all scalability and performance issues. Factors such as database bottlenecks, application design, and network latency can still impact overall system performance, even with effective load balancing in place.

As such, load balancing should be considered as part of a comprehensive architecture and performance testing strategy. Assessing the complete system architecture and identifying potential performance bottlenecks is crucial for building scalable and high-performing cloud-based solutions.

Now that we have explored load balancing in depth, let's move on to other essential components and services that make up the cloud computing landscape.

Content Delivery Networks (CDNs)

In today's digital world, where users expect fast and seamless access to online content, Content Delivery Networks (CDNs) play a crucial role in delivering content efficiently and effectively. CDNs have revolutionized the way we access websites and consume online media by optimizing and accelerating content delivery. In this section, we will delve into the inner workings of CDNs, explore their benefits, and understand how they are reshaping the digital landscape.

Introduction to CDNs

A Content Delivery Network (CDN) is a distributed network of servers strategically placed around the world to deliver web content to users. Instead of relying on a single central server, CDNs distribute content across multiple servers, known as edge servers or points of presence (PoPs), located in close proximity to end users. When a user requests content, the CDN delivers it from the edge server that is geographically closest to the user, ensuring faster load times and reduced latency.

CDNs are employed by various types of content providers, including websites, streaming platforms, e-commerce sites, and online gaming platforms. They are designed to handle high traffic volumes and effectively manage content distribution, enabling smooth and reliable user experiences.

How CDNs Work

CDNs employ several key techniques to optimize content delivery:

- **Caching:** CDNs use caching to store copies of content in edge servers. When a user requests content that is already cached, the CDN can deliver it directly from the edge server, eliminating the need to retrieve it from the origin server. This significantly reduces latency and improves the overall performance of content delivery.

- **Load Balancing:** CDNs balance the load across multiple edge servers by intelligently directing user requests to the server that can deliver the content most efficiently. Load balancing ensures that no single server is overwhelmed with traffic, improving overall scalability and preventing performance bottlenecks.

- **Route Optimization:** CDNs optimize content delivery by dynamically choosing the most optimal network path between the edge server and the user. By minimizing the number of network hops and choosing paths with low latency and high bandwidth, CDNs ensure faster and more reliable content delivery.

- **Request Prioritization:** Not all content is equally important or time-sensitive. CDNs allow content providers to prioritize certain types of content, such as critical website assets or streaming media, to ensure that they are delivered with minimal delay. This prioritization improves user experience and enables efficient resource utilization.

Benefits of CDNs

CDNs offer several benefits for content providers and end users alike:

Improved Performance: By distributing content to edge servers located closer to end users, CDNs significantly reduce latency and improve load times. Faster content delivery leads to enhanced user experiences, increased engagement, and higher conversion rates for e-commerce websites.

Scalability and Reliability: CDNs are designed to handle high volumes of traffic without compromising performance. They can dynamically scale their infrastructure to meet peak demand, ensuring that content delivery remains smooth and uninterrupted even during traffic spikes or flash crowds.

Global Reach: CDNs operate a geographically distributed network of edge servers, allowing content providers to reach users across the globe with minimal latency. This enables seamless content delivery to users regardless of their location, fostering a global and inclusive online experience.

Bandwidth Optimization: CDNs are able to optimize bandwidth usage by offloading traffic from the origin servers. By caching and delivering content from edge servers, CDNs reduce the strain on origin servers, leading to lower bandwidth costs and improved overall cost-efficiency.

Enhanced Security: Many CDNs offer additional security features, such as Distributed Denial of Service (DDoS) protection and web application firewalls, to protect content providers and end users from malicious attacks. CDNs act as a buffer between the origin server and potential attackers, absorbing and mitigating malicious traffic.

Analytics and Insights: CDNs provide content providers with valuable analytics and insights into content usage, user behavior, and performance metrics. These insights help content providers make data-driven decisions, optimize content delivery, and enhance overall user experiences.

Real-World Example: Netflix and CDNs

To illustrate the importance and effectiveness of CDNs, let's take a look at how Netflix, the popular streaming platform, leverages CDNs to deliver their vast library of movies and TV shows to millions of viewers worldwide.

Netflix operates its own CDN, Open Connect, which consists of thousands of edge servers deployed in Internet Service Provider (ISP) data centers around the world. When a Netflix user requests a movie or TV show, the CDN identifies the user's location and delivers the content from the edge server that is closest to the user. This ensures that the content is delivered with minimal delay and buffering, providing a seamless streaming experience.

By leveraging CDNs, Netflix not only achieves faster content delivery but also reduces strain on their origin servers. By storing and serving popular content directly from the edge servers, Netflix offloads traffic from their central servers, enabling them to handle a larger user base and scale their streaming infrastructure more efficiently.

Conclusion

Content Delivery Networks (CDNs) have revolutionized the way we access online content by optimizing and accelerating content delivery to end users. CDNs employ caching, load balancing, route optimization, and request prioritization to ensure faster, more reliable, and scalable content delivery. They offer numerous benefits, including improved performance, scalability, global reach, bandwidth optimization, enhanced security, and valuable analytics.

CDNs have become an integral part of the digital landscape, enabling content providers to deliver rich and engaging user experiences while managing large volumes of traffic effectively. As the demand for online content continues to grow, CDNs will continue to play a vital role in shaping the future of cloud computing and content delivery.

DNS Management

Domain Name System (DNS) management is a crucial aspect of cloud computing and plays a vital role in ensuring the smooth functioning of web applications and services. In this section, we will dive into the principles of DNS, its role in the cloud, and the various tools and techniques used for DNS management.

Understanding DNS

DNS is like the phone book of the internet. It translates human-readable domain names (e.g., www.example.com) into machine-readable IP addresses (e.g., 192.0.2.1) that computers use to communicate with each other. Without DNS, we would have to remember and type in IP addresses for every website we visit, which would be a total nightmare.

DNS operates through a distributed network of servers that work together to provide prompt and reliable name resolution. When a user enters a domain name in a web browser, the browser sends a DNS query to the DNS resolver (usually provided by the Internet Service Provider). The resolver then contacts the authoritative DNS server responsible for that domain and retrieves the corresponding IP address. Finally, the resolver returns the IP address to the browser, allowing it to establish a connection with the desired web server.

DNS in the Cloud

In the context of cloud computing, DNS plays a critical role in managing the infrastructure and services deployed on cloud platforms. Cloud providers often offer DNS services as part of their infrastructure stack, allowing users to manage domain names and map them to their cloud resources effortlessly.

DNS in the cloud offers several advantages. First, it enables elastic scaling of applications and services. By using DNS load balancing, traffic can be distributed across multiple instances of a service to ensure high availability and improved performance. Moreover, DNS allows for easy migration and management of resources, as changes in IP addresses or resource locations can be easily accommodated through DNS records.

DNS Management Tools and Techniques

Various tools and techniques are available for effective DNS management in the cloud environment. Let's take a look at some of them:

1. **DNS Providers:** Cloud service providers like Amazon Web Services (AWS), Microsoft Azure, and Google Cloud Platform offer DNS management services as part of their offerings. These services provide user-friendly interfaces and APIs to manage DNS records, set up routing policies, and configure advanced features.

2. **DNS Zones:** DNS zones allow organizing domain names and their associated records into logical groups. For example, you might have a zone for your primary domain and separate zones for subdomains or different regions. This hierarchical structure simplifies management and enhances scalability.

3. **Traffic Management:** DNS-based traffic management techniques like round-robin, weighted routing, and geolocation routing help distribute traffic across multiple servers or regions based on predefined rules. This allows you to optimize resource utilization, improve response times, and provide fault tolerance.

4. **DNSSEC:** DNS Security Extensions (DNSSEC) provides a mechanism for securing DNS responses and preventing attacks such as DNS cache poisoning. It uses digital signatures to verify the authenticity and integrity of DNS data, ensuring that users are connecting to the correct server.

5. **Monitoring and Alerting:** Monitoring DNS health is crucial for identifying and resolving issues promptly. DNS management tools often provide monitoring capabilities to track the performance and availability of DNS servers, detect anomalies, and send alerts in case of failures.

Example: DNS Load Balancing

Let's consider an example to illustrate the concept of DNS load balancing in a cloud environment. Imagine you have deployed a web application that experiences high traffic and wants to distribute the load across multiple instances for scalability and fault tolerance.

To achieve DNS load balancing, you can create multiple DNS records with the same domain name but different IP addresses corresponding to your application instances. When a user sends a DNS query, the DNS resolver randomly selects one of the IP addresses from the pool and returns it as the result. Subsequent requests from the same user might receive a different IP address, ensuring that the load is distributed evenly.

For instance, if you have three instances of your web application with IP addresses 192.0.2.1, 192.0.2.2, and 192.0.2.3, the DNS resolver might respond with 192.0.2.2 for the first request, 192.0.2.3 for the second request, and so on. This way, your application instances share the load, providing better performance and availability.

Resources and Best Practices

Here are some additional resources and best practices to enhance your DNS management skills:

- **AWS DNS Best Practices**: Check out the AWS documentation on DNS best practices, which provides guidelines for configuring DNS in AWS environments.

- **Cloudflare DNS**: Explore Cloudflare's DNS service, which offers additional performance and security features, including DDoS protection and traffic optimization.

- **Automation with Infrastructure as Code (IaC)**: Consider using tools like Terraform or AWS CloudFormation to automate DNS management tasks and ensure consistency across different environments.

- **Caveat: TTL and Caching**: Keep in mind that DNS updates might take time to propagate due to Time-to-Live (TTL) values set in DNS records and caching mechanisms. Adjust the TTL wisely to balance between responsiveness and update time.

Summary

In this section, we explored DNS management in the context of cloud computing. We learned about the principles of DNS, its role in the cloud, and the importance of effective DNS management for scalable and reliable services. We also discussed various tools and techniques for DNS management, including DNS providers, traffic management, DNSSEC, and monitoring. Finally, we explored an example of DNS load balancing and highlighted additional resources and best practices for DNS management. With this knowledge, you are well-equipped to conquer the world of DNS management in the cloud!

NETWORKING AND CONTENT DELIVERY SERVICES

Exercise: Imagine you are designing a cloud-based e-commerce platform. How would you utilize DNS management techniques to ensure high availability and improved performance for your platform? Consider the use of DNS load balancing, failover strategies, and multi-region deployment.

Alright, let's dive into the exciting world of cloud networking and explore the fucking network backbone of the cloud. In this section, we will discuss the critical components and principles that enable the smooth operation and connectivity within cloud computing environments.

The Fucking Network Backbone of the Cloud

The network backbone of the cloud refers to the underlying infrastructure and technology that supports the communication and data transfer between various components of a cloud computing system. It is the invisible force that connects all the dots and ensures seamless interaction within the cloud.

Networking Principles

To understand the network backbone of the cloud, we need to grasp some fundamental networking principles. Here are a few key concepts that will help us navigate this fascinating domain:

- **Protocols:** In the cloud, communication between different components relies on protocols, which are standardized rules that specify how data is transmitted and received. Some common cloud networking protocols include TCP/IP, UDP, HTTP, and HTTPS.

- **IP Addressing:** Every device connected to a network, including those in the cloud, has a unique IP address. IP addressing is crucial for identifying and locating devices, allowing them to send and receive data over the network.

- **Routing:** Routing is the process of determining the optimal path for data packets to travel from a source to a destination. In cloud networks, routers play a vital role in forwarding packets across different segments of the network, ensuring efficient and reliable data transfer.

- **Switching:** Switching is the process of forwarding network traffic from one device to another within a local network. Switches are responsible for creating dedicated communication channels between devices, improving network performance and reducing collisions.

- **Firewalls:** Firewalls act as a security barrier between a cloud network and external threats. They monitor and control incoming and outgoing network traffic based on predefined security policies, protecting the cloud infrastructure from unauthorized access or malicious activities.

Now that we have a basic understanding of networking principles, let's explore the various components that form the backbone of the cloud network.

Cloud Network Infrastructure

The cloud network infrastructure consists of a combination of physical and virtual components that work together to provide connectivity and deliver cloud services. Let's take a closer look at each of these components:

- **Data Centers:** Data centers are the backbone of the cloud. They house the servers, storage devices, and networking equipment necessary to operate cloud services. Data centers are designed to provide high availability, scalability, and redundancy to ensure uninterrupted operation of cloud resources.

- **Servers and Storage:** Servers are powerful computers that process and store data in the cloud. They provide the computational resources needed to run applications and services. Storage devices, on the other hand, store the vast amounts of data required by cloud applications and services.

- **Networking Equipment:** Networking equipment, such as routers, switches, and load balancers, form the connectivity fabric within the cloud. They enable data packets to flow between different components of the cloud infrastructure, ensuring efficient and reliable communication.

- **Virtualization and SDN:** Virtualization is a key technology that allows the creation of virtual resources from physical hardware. In the cloud, virtualization enables the efficient utilization of hardware resources by running multiple virtual machines or containers on a single physical server. Software-Defined Networking (SDN) further enhances network agility and flexibility by separating the control plane from the data plane, making it easier to manage and control network traffic.

Cloud Network Services

In addition to the underlying infrastructure, the cloud provides a variety of network services that further enhance the functionality and capabilities of cloud applications. Here are some essential cloud network services:

- **Virtual Private Cloud (VPC)**: A VPC provides a logically isolated virtual network within the cloud environment. It allows you to define your own IP addressing scheme, subnets, and network access control policies, enabling secure communication and control over your cloud resources.

- **Load Balancing**: Load balancers distribute incoming network traffic across multiple servers or instances to improve performance, scalability, and availability. They help prevent any single server from becoming overloaded and ensure that the cloud services can handle increased traffic demands.

- **Content Delivery Networks (CDNs)**: CDNs are geographically distributed networks of servers that cache and deliver content closer to end users. By storing content in multiple locations worldwide, CDNs reduce latency and improve the delivery speed of cloud services, resulting in a better user experience.

- **Domain Name System (DNS) Management**: DNS is responsible for translating domain names into IP addresses. In the cloud, DNS management services provide the ability to configure and manage domain names, allowing users to access cloud services using user-friendly names rather than complex IP addresses.

Real-World Examples

To solidify our understanding, let's look at a couple of real-world examples that demonstrate the importance of the network backbone in the cloud:

- **Video Streaming**: When you stream a video on platforms like YouTube or Netflix, the network backbone of the cloud comes into play. The video content is delivered from servers located in multiple data centers to your device. Load balancers distribute the traffic, CDNs cache the video content to reduce buffering, and the underlying network infrastructure ensures a seamless streaming experience.

- **Online Gaming:** Online gaming heavily relies on the cloud network backbone to ensure smooth gameplay. The cloud infrastructure handles real-time communication between gamers, minimizes latency, and provides scalable computing resources to support multiplayer gaming experiences. Without the robust network backbone, online gaming would suffer from laggy connections and poor performance.

Troubleshooting and Caveats

While the cloud network backbone is designed to be resilient and highly available, issues can still arise. Here are some common troubleshooting steps and caveats to keep in mind when dealing with cloud network problems:

- **Troubleshooting Steps:** When experiencing network connectivity issues in the cloud, start by checking the network configuration, security group settings, and firewall rules. Ensure that the relevant ports and protocols are allowed, and verify the health of the underlying network infrastructure. Logs and monitoring tools can provide valuable insights into the root cause of network problems.

- **Network Performance:** Remember that network performance may vary depending on your cloud service provider, the geographic location of your resources, and the overall network architecture. Factors like latency, bandwidth limitations, and network congestion can affect the performance of your cloud applications, especially if you have globally distributed users.

- **Scaling Challenges:** As cloud applications scale, network challenges may arise due to increased traffic and data transfer requirements. It's important to design your applications and network architecture with scalability in mind, ensuring that the network backbone can handle the anticipated growth.

Summary

In this section, we dove deep into the network backbone of the cloud, exploring the critical components, principles, and services that enable seamless connectivity and data transfer within cloud computing environments. We learned about networking principles, cloud network infrastructure, network services, and real-world examples that illustrate the importance of a robust network backbone in the cloud. Troubleshooting steps and caveats were discussed to assist in addressing potential network issues. Now, armed with this knowledge, you are ready to conquer the fucking network challenges in the vast realm of cloud computing.

Security and Identity Services

Before I dive into the exciting world of Identity and Access Management (IAM), let me give you a quick rundown of what IAM is all about. In the realm of cloud computing, IAM refers to the policies, technologies, and processes that enable organizations to manage and control access to their resources, applications, and data in a secure and efficient manner.

Identity and Access Management (IAM)

IAM forms the foundation of any robust security framework in cloud computing. It involves identifying and authenticating users, authorizing access to resources based on roles and permissions, and ensuring the confidentiality, integrity, and availability of those resources. In a nutshell, IAM allows you to manage who can do what in your cloud environment.

Authentication and Authorization

Authentication is the process of verifying the identity of a user or entity, ensuring that they are who they claim to be. This can be done using various factors, such as passwords, biometrics, or multi-factor authentication (MFA), which combines two or more authentication methods.

Once a user is authenticated, authorization comes into play. Authorization determines what actions a user can perform within a system or application. It is based on the roles and permissions assigned to each user, controlling access to specific resources and functionalities.

Roles and Permissions

Roles and permissions are two essential concepts in IAM. A role is a collection of permissions that define what actions a user can take. It is an organized way to manage access control and simplify permission management. For example, you can have roles like "admin," "developer," or "customer support," each with its own set of permissions.

Permissions, on the other hand, are granular actions that can be applied to resources. For example, a permission might allow a user to read, write, or delete data. By assigning roles to users, you can easily manage access at scale without having to individually assign permissions to each user.

Access Control Policies

Access control policies are the rules and regulations that govern access to resources. These policies define who can access what resources and under what conditions. They provide a centralized way to manage permissions across multiple users, groups, and resources.

Access control policies are typically defined using a policy language that allows you to specify conditions, such as time of day, IP address, or geographic location, under which access is granted or denied. By implementing access control policies, you can enforce the principle of least privilege, ensuring that users have only the necessary permissions to perform their tasks.

Single Sign-On (SSO)

Single Sign-On (SSO) is a convenient way to manage access across multiple systems and applications. It allows users to authenticate themselves once and gain access to multiple resources without having to authenticate again. SSO improves user experience, reduces the risk of password-related issues, and simplifies access management.

In an SSO scenario, a user logs in to an identity provider (IdP), which then authenticates the user and generates a token. This token can be used to access various applications and services without the need for additional authentication. SSO is typically implemented using industry-standard protocols like SAML (Security Assertion Markup Language) or OpenID Connect.

Auditing and Monitoring

IAM also involves monitoring and auditing user activities to detect and respond to security threats. By keeping track of access logs and monitoring user behavior, organizations can detect suspicious activities, such as unauthorized access attempts or data breaches. Auditing helps in compliance with regulatory requirements and allows for post-incident analysis and investigation.

To effectively audit and monitor IAM, organizations can leverage various tools and technologies that provide real-time alerts, log analysis, and anomaly detection. These tools help in identifying and mitigating security risks, ensuring that the cloud environment remains secure and compliant.

Final Words

Identity and Access Management (IAM) is a critical component of any cloud computing environment. It provides the foundation for secure access control, authentication, and authorization. Implementing IAM best practices allows organizations to protect their cloud resources, data, and applications from unauthorized access, ensuring the confidentiality, integrity, and availability of their digital assets.

So, my dear readers, now you have a solid understanding of IAM in cloud computing. Remember, IAM is the gatekeeper of your cloud kingdom. So, embrace it, master it, and conquer the cloud with the power of secure access control!

Encryption and Key Management

In the vast universe of cloud computing, encryption plays a vital role in securing sensitive data and maintaining privacy. Encryption is the process of converting plaintext into ciphertext, making it unreadable to unauthorized individuals. In this section, we will dive deep into encryption and explore the various aspects of key management in the context of cloud computing.

The Basics of Encryption

Before we embark on our journey into the world of key management, let's first understand the fundamental concepts of encryption. At its core, encryption relies on two main components: an encryption algorithm and a key. The encryption algorithm is the mathematical formula used to transform plaintext into ciphertext, and the key is the secret element that unlocks the encrypted data.

There are two main types of encryption: symmetric and asymmetric.

Symmetric encryption, also known as private-key encryption, employs a single key for both encryption and decryption. This means that the same key is used to both scramble and unscramble the data. It's like using the same secret language to write and decipher messages. Examples of symmetric encryption algorithms include Advanced Encryption Standard (AES) and Data Encryption Standard (DES).

Asymmetric encryption, also referred to as public-key encryption, uses a pair of keys: a public key for encryption and a private key for decryption. The public key can be freely shared with anyone, while the private key must be kept secret. This approach allows for secure communication between two parties without needing a shared secret key. The most widely used asymmetric encryption algorithms are RSA and Elliptic Curve Cryptography (ECC).

Encryption in Cloud Computing

Cloud computing brings unique challenges when it comes to encryption. Unlike traditional computing environments, where data is stored and processed locally, cloud computing involves outsourcing computational resources to remote servers operated by cloud service providers (CSPs).

When data is stored or transmitted in the cloud, it is crucial to ensure the confidentiality, integrity, and availability of that data. Encryption provides a robust security measure to achieve these goals. By encrypting data before it leaves the user's premises and remains encrypted while in the cloud, the sensitive information is protected from unauthorized access.

There are several considerations to keep in mind when implementing encryption in the cloud:

- **Data Encryption at Rest:** Encrypting data at rest refers to encrypting the data when it is stored in persistent storage, such as hard drives or databases. This protects the data from unauthorized access in case the storage media is stolen or compromised. Cloud service providers often offer native encryption capabilities to encrypt data at rest, such as AWS S3 Server-Side Encryption and Azure Storage Service Encryption.

- **Data Encryption in Transit:** Encrypting data in transit ensures that the information remains secure while being transmitted over the network. Protocols such as Transport Layer Security (TLS) and Secure Sockets Layer (SSL) are commonly used to establish secure communication channels between clients and servers. It is essential to verify that the cloud service provider supports encryption for data in transit to protect against eavesdropping and man-in-the-middle attacks.

- **Bring Your Own Key (BYOK):** While cloud service providers offer encryption services, some organizations may prefer to have full control over their encryption keys. BYOK allows customers to generate and manage their encryption keys on-premises, encrypt their data using these keys, and then securely transfer the encrypted data to the cloud provider for storage or processing. This approach provides an additional layer of security and mitigates the risk of unauthorized access to the data.

- **Key Rotation:** Key rotation is a security best practice that involves periodically changing encryption keys. Regularly rotating keys reduces the risk of a compromised key being used to decrypt sensitive data. Key rotation should be seamless and transparent to applications and users to ensure uninterrupted access to the encrypted data. Cloud service providers often offer built-in key rotation mechanisms to simplify the process and enhance security.

- **Granular Access Control:** Key management is not just about the encryption keys themselves but also about who has access to those keys. It is crucial to enforce strict access control policies to ensure that only authorized individuals or applications can manage and use the encryption keys. This is typically achieved through role-based access control (RBAC) mechanisms and strong authentication measures.

- **Compliance Requirements:** Organizations operating in certain industries, such as healthcare or finance, may have specific regulatory compliance requirements regarding data encryption and key management. It is essential to ensure that the cloud service provider complies with industry-specific regulations and standards to meet these requirements. Examples of such standards include the Health Insurance Portability and Accountability Act (HIPAA) and the Payment Card Industry Data Security Standard (PCI DSS).

Key Management

As we've seen, encryption relies heavily on the management of cryptographic keys. Key management involves the entire lifecycle of cryptographic keys, including key generation, distribution, storage, rotation, and revocation.

In a cloud computing environment, effective key management is essential to maintain the security and integrity of encrypted data. Let's explore some key management principles and practices:

- **Key Generation:** Keys should be generated using cryptographically secure pseudo-random number generators (CSPRNGs) to ensure that they are truly random and unpredictable. Keys of sufficient length should be used to resist brute-force attacks. Both symmetric and asymmetric keys need to be generated securely and stored in a way that protects their confidentiality and integrity.

- **Key Distribution:** Distributing keys securely to authorized users or systems is a critical step in key management. It requires establishing secure channels for key exchange, such as using secure protocols like Diffie-Hellman key exchange or transporting keys via physical media in a secure manner. Secure key distribution prevents unauthorized individuals from obtaining access to the keys.

- **Key Storage:** Safely storing encryption keys is crucial to prevent unauthorized access. Cloud service providers often offer secure key storage options, such as Hardware Security Modules (HSMs) or Key Management Services (KMS), which provide a high level of protection for encryption keys. These storage options employ physical and logical controls to prevent unauthorized access and protect keys from theft or tampering.

- **Key Rotation and Revocation:** Regularly rotating encryption keys is a security best practice that helps mitigate the risk of compromised keys. When rotating keys, it is essential to ensure that the new key is securely distributed and any data encrypted with the old key is re-encrypted with the new key. In case of a suspected key compromise or a lost key, revocation procedures should be in place to prevent unauthorized access to encrypted data.

- **Auditing and Logging:** Maintaining comprehensive audit logs of key management activities is vital for security and compliance purposes. Auditing and logging key operations help detect any unauthorized access attempts or suspicious activities related to encryption keys. Cloud service providers often offer built-in logging and monitoring capabilities that can be leveraged to track key management activities.

- **Disaster Recovery:** Key management should consider disaster recovery scenarios to ensure the availability and resilience of encryption keys. Backup and recovery procedures should be in place to prevent permanent loss of keys in case of hardware failures or natural disasters. Additionally, organizations should have contingency plans to ensure uninterrupted access to encrypted data even in the event of key management system failures.

Real-World Examples and Resources

To illustrate the importance of encryption and key management in cloud computing, let's explore some real-world examples:

- **Example 1: Cloud Storage Encryption**

  Imagine a small business that utilizes cloud storage services to store sensitive customer data. To protect this data from unauthorized access, the business implements client-side encryption, encrypting the data before it leaves their premises. They generate a unique encryption key for each customer and store the keys securely in their on-premises key management system. This approach ensures that even if the cloud service provider experiences a security breach, the encrypted data remains inaccessible without the corresponding encryption keys.

- **Example 2: BYOK in Practice**

    A large financial institution with strict compliance requirements decides to adopt cloud computing while maintaining control over their encryption keys. They choose a cloud service provider that supports Bring Your Own Key (BYOK) capabilities. The institution generates and manages their cryptographic keys on-premises using a hardware security module (HSM). These keys remain in the institution's possession and are used to encrypt sensitive data before transferring it to the cloud provider's storage. This approach allows the institution to retain full control over their keys and provide an additional layer of security for their data.

Here are some valuable resources to further explore encryption and key management in the context of cloud computing:

- **NIST Special Publication 800-57:** NIST provides comprehensive guidance on key management principles and best practices. The publication covers various aspects of key management, including key generation, distribution, storage, and destruction.

- **Cloud Security Alliance (CSA):** The CSA offers several resources and best practice documents related to encryption and key management in cloud computing. Their guidance helps organizations understand the unique challenges and best practices for securing data in the cloud.

- **Cloud Service Provider Documentation:** Cloud service providers like Amazon Web Services (AWS), Microsoft Azure, and Google Cloud Platform (GCP) provide extensive documentation on encryption and key management capabilities offered within their platforms. These resources offer detailed insights into the native encryption and key management services available from each provider.

Final Thoughts

Encryption and key management are critical components of securing data in the cloud. By employing robust encryption algorithms and implementing sound key management practices, organizations can ensure the confidentiality, integrity, and availability of their sensitive information. Understanding the principles and best practices of encryption and key management is essential for anyone working in the field of cloud computing.

In the next section, we will delve into the exciting realm of AI and Machine Learning services offered in the cloud. So, strap in and get ready for some fucking mind-blowing AI advancements!

Security Groups and Firewalls

In the vast and ever-expanding realm of cloud computing, security is of paramount importance. With the proliferation of interconnected devices and the constant threat of cyber attacks, it is crucial to establish robust security measures to protect our valuable data and ensure the integrity and confidentiality of our systems. One of the fundamental tools in this regard are security groups and firewalls.

Understanding Security Groups

A security group is a virtual firewall that acts as a barrier between your cloud resources and the outside world. It defines a set of rules that control inbound and outbound traffic, allowing you to specify which types of connections are permitted or denied. Essentially, security groups serve as the gatekeepers of your cloud environment, monitoring and filtering incoming and outgoing network traffic based on a defined set of rules.

Security groups are associated with specific instances or virtual machines within your cloud infrastructure, and each instance can be assigned one or more security groups. These groups function at the instance level, meaning that all inbound and outbound traffic to and from the instance is subject to the rules defined in its associated security groups.

The Anatomy of a Security Group

To effectively configure a security group, you need to understand its basic components. Each security group consists of multiple rules, which are essentially access control lists (ACLs) that guide the behavior of network traffic. These rules enable you to specify various parameters, such as the type of traffic allowed, the

SECURITY AND IDENTITY SERVICES

source and destination IP addresses, and the protocols and ports that can be accessed.

Let's consider an example. Suppose you have a web server hosted in the cloud, and you want to allow inbound traffic on port 80 (HTTP) and port 443 (HTTPS) while blocking all other types of connections. You would create a rule in your security group that permits incoming traffic on these specific ports and deny any other incoming connections.

Furthermore, security groups provide the ability to specify security group rules and network ACLs that define the traffic flow between different instances within a virtual private cloud (VPC). This enables the creation of security groups that allow communication only between trusted instances, while blocking traffic from untrusted sources.

Benefits of Security Groups

Why should we bother with security groups when we already have firewalls? Well, security groups offer several distinct advantages over traditional firewalls:

- **Simplicity:** Security groups are simple to set up and configure. They operate at the instance level, allowing you to manage and control traffic flow at a granular level. This ease of use facilitates quick and efficient deployment of robust security measures.

- **Dynamic Scaling:** As cloud environments are known for their scalability, security groups can adapt and scale automatically as instances are added or removed. This ensures that security measures remain consistent and comprehensive even in highly dynamic environments.

- **Stateful Filtering:** Security groups maintain state information about network connections, keeping track of the traffic flow. This means that if a request is allowed based on a particular rule, the response is automatically permitted as well. Stateful filtering significantly simplifies network security management and reduces the risk of misconfigurations.

- **Built-in Network Segmentation:** By leveraging security groups, you can easily establish segregated network segments within your cloud infrastructure. This enables you to create secure isolated environments for different applications, protecting sensitive data and providing an extra layer of defense against potential threats.

Firewalls in Cloud Computing

In addition to security groups, many cloud service providers also offer firewall services that can be used to augment network security. These firewalls often provide advanced features and additional layers of protection beyond what can be achieved with security groups alone.

Cloud firewalls operate at the network level, filtering traffic based on predefined rules and policies. They are positioned outside the instances themselves, acting as a dedicated layer of defense. These firewalls can be configured to filter traffic based on IP addresses, ports, protocols, and other parameters, giving you fine-grained control over network access.

One notable advantage of cloud firewalls is their ability to protect multiple instances simultaneously, ensuring consistent security policies across an entire virtual network. They can also be deployed in conjunction with security groups, providing a comprehensive security framework.

Best Practices and Considerations

When configuring security groups and firewalls, it is essential to follow best practices to maximize the effectiveness of your security measures. Consider the following guidelines:

- **Principle of Least Privilege**: Only allow access to the network resources that are strictly necessary. Adopting the principle of least privilege minimizes the potential attack surface and reduces the risk of unauthorized access.

- **Regular Audit and Review**: Perform regular audits and reviews of your security group rules and firewall configuration. This helps to identify and address any vulnerabilities or misconfigurations that may have arisen as your cloud environment evolves.

- **Secure Communication Channels**: Utilize encryption protocols, such as Secure Sockets Layer/Transport Layer Security (SSL/TLS), to establish secure communication channels between your cloud resources and the users or clients accessing them. This protects data during transmission and mitigates the risk of eavesdropping or data interception.

- **Logging and Monitoring**: Implement logging and monitoring systems to track network traffic and detect any suspicious activities or potential threats. By monitoring your security groups and firewalls, you can gain insights into the network behavior and take proactive measures to prevent security breaches.

Real-World Example

To illustrate the importance of security groups and firewalls, let's consider a real-world example. Imagine that you are a developer working for a technology company that provides software as a service (SaaS) to customers. You have set up a cloud-based infrastructure to host your application and customer data.

To ensure the security of your customers' data, you configure security groups to allow inbound traffic only from trusted sources, such as your company's internal network and specific IP addresses known to belong to your customers. You also set up firewall rules to block all other incoming connections.

Additionally, you implement logging and monitoring solutions to track network activity and detect any suspicious behavior. Using these tools, you can identify any unauthorized attempts to access your system and take immediate action to mitigate the risk.

By leveraging security groups and firewalls, you establish a strong defense against potential threats, safeguarding your customers' data and fostering trust in your services.

Conclusion

In the ever-advancing landscape of cloud computing, the security of our systems and data is a critical aspect that cannot be overlooked. Security groups and firewalls play a vital role in enforcing access control and protecting our cloud resources from unauthorized access and malicious activities. By understanding the principles and best practices associated with these tools, we can establish robust security measures and confidently embrace the power and potential of the cloud.

So, don't overlook the importance of security groups and firewalls in your cloud infrastructure. They might just be the knights in shining armor protecting your valuable assets from the ever-looming threats.

Threat Detection and Incident Response

In the world of cloud computing, the security of data and systems is of utmost importance. As the saying goes, "With great power comes great responsibility." Cloud service providers (CSPs), such as Amazon Web Services (AWS), Microsoft Azure, Google Cloud Platform (GCP), and IBM Cloud, have an obligation to ensure the safety of their customers' assets. However, threats and incidents in the cloud environment are inevitable. Therefore, threat detection and incident response play a vital role in maintaining a secure cloud infrastructure.

Threat detection involves identifying and assessing potential security risks. It aims to detect any suspicious activities, vulnerabilities, or breaches that may compromise the confidentiality, integrity, and availability of resources in the cloud. Incident response, on the other hand, focuses on responding to and mitigating the impact of security incidents promptly and efficiently. Let's dive deeper into these two crucial aspects: threat detection and incident response.

Threat Detection

Threat detection begins with understanding the threat landscape and adopting a proactive approach to identify potential risks. It involves leveraging various security technologies and practices to detect threats in the cloud environment. Here are some key components and strategies involved in effective threat detection:

1. Log Analysis: Logs contain valuable information about system activities, user actions, and network traffic. Analyzing logs can help detect any unusual or suspicious behavior. Employing security information and event management (SIEM) systems, which aggregate and correlate log data from various sources, can enhance threat detection capabilities.

2. Intrusion Detection Systems (IDS) and Intrusion Prevention Systems (IPS): IDS and IPS are security systems that monitor network traffic and identify potential security breaches. IDS detects and alerts administrators about suspicious activities, while IPS takes immediate action to prevent or block malicious actions. These systems use rule-based, signature-based, and anomaly-based approaches to identify threats.

3. Security Information Sharing and Collaboration: Sharing information about known threats and attacks across organizations can help improve threat detection. Organizations can join threat intelligence platforms that provide real-time threat updates and promote data sharing to stay ahead of emerging threats.

4. Threat Hunting: Threat hunting is a proactive approach to discovering threats that may have bypassed traditional security defenses. It involves analyzing historical data, searching for indicators of compromise, and performing targeted investigations to identify potential threats.

SECURITY AND IDENTITY SERVICES

5. **Machine Learning and Artificial Intelligence (AI):** Machine learning and AI techniques can be employed to analyze large amounts of data and identify patterns indicative of potential threats. These technologies can improve the accuracy of threat detection and reduce false positives, allowing security teams to focus on genuine threats.

6. **Vulnerability Scanning:** Regularly scanning systems and applications for vulnerabilities is crucial in detecting potential entry points for attackers. Vulnerability scanning tools identify weaknesses and provide recommendations for remediation.

7. **Security Audits and Penetration Testing:** Conducting security audits and penetration tests helps identify vulnerabilities or misconfigurations that may be exploited by attackers. These proactive testing methodologies provide insights into the effectiveness of existing security controls.

By leveraging these techniques and best practices, organizations can improve their ability to detect and respond to threats effectively.

Incident Response

Incident response is a coordinated approach to managing and resolving security incidents promptly and effectively. It aims to minimize the impact, recover compromised systems, and prevent similar incidents in the future. Here are the key steps involved in incident response:

1. **Incident Identification and Categorization:** The first step in incident response is identifying and categorizing the incident based on its severity and potential impact. Promptly detecting and reporting incidents is crucial to initiate the response process.

2. **Incident Triage:** Once an incident is identified, it needs to be triaged to determine its scope, impact, and potential escalation. This involves assessing the affected systems, the type of attack or compromise, and the criticality of the assets involved.

3. **Containment and Mitigation:** After triaging the incident, the focus shifts to containing the incident to prevent further damage or spread. This may involve isolating affected systems, disabling compromised accounts, or blocking malicious IP addresses. Mitigation strategies are implemented to reduce the immediate impact of the incident.

4. **Investigation and Root Cause Analysis:** A thorough investigation is conducted to understand the cause, extent, and impact of the incident. It involves analyzing log files, system memory, and other relevant data sources to identify the root cause of the incident. The findings are documented for future reference and remediation efforts.

5. **Recovery and Restoration:** Once the incident is contained and the root cause is identified, the focus shifts to recovering affected systems and restoring normal operations. This may involve rebuilding compromised servers, restoring from backups, or patching vulnerabilities.

6. **Lessons Learned and Documentation:** After resolving the incident, it is essential to conduct a post-incident review to identify areas for improvement. Lessons learned from the incident can help refine incident response plans, update security controls, or provide additional training to personnel.

7. **Continuous Improvement:** Incident response is an iterative process. Organizations should continuously improve their incident response capabilities by incorporating feedback, refining processes, and staying up to date with industry best practices.

It's important to note that organizations should have a well-defined incident response plan in place before an incident occurs. This plan should outline roles and responsibilities, communication procedures, and steps to be followed in the event of an incident.

Real-World Example

Let's consider a real-world example of threat detection and incident response in the cloud. Imagine a company that uses a cloud service provider for hosting its e-commerce website. One day, the company's security team receives alerts from the IDS system indicating potential unauthorized access attempts to customer databases.

The incident response process begins with incident identification and categorization. The security team quickly triages the incident, finding that an attacker may have exploited a vulnerability in one of the website's plugins to gain unauthorized access to customer data. The team immediately takes action to contain the incident by blocking the attacker's IP address, isolating affected systems, and disabling compromised accounts.

An investigation is initiated to determine the root cause of the incident. The security team analyzes log files and system memory to understand the attack vector and identify any signs of data exfiltration. It is discovered that the vulnerable plugin had an unpatched security flaw, which allowed the attacker to gain access.

To mitigate the impact of the incident, the security team works on recovering affected systems by applying patches and updates to prevent further exploitation. They also restore customer data from backups to ensure business continuity.

After resolving the incident, a post-incident review is conducted to identify areas for improvement. The security team updates incident response procedures, patches known vulnerabilities, and provides additional training to developers and system administrators to prevent similar incidents in the future.

Resources and Best Practices

To further explore threat detection and incident response in the context of cloud computing, consider the following resources and best practices:

- The Cloud Security Alliance (CSA) offers guidance on incident response in the cloud environment, including recommendations, frameworks, and best practices.

- The National Institute of Standards and Technology (NIST) provides a comprehensive Computer Security Incident Handling Guide that offers a detailed step-by-step approach to incident response.

- The Sans Institute offers various incident response training courses and resources, including incident handling methodologies and incident response planning templates.

- Cloud service providers, such as AWS, Azure, GCP, and IBM Cloud, provide documentation and guidance on their respective incident response procedures and best practices within their cloud environments.

By exploring these resources and adopting best practices, organizations can enhance their threat detection and incident response capabilities, ensuring a secure and resilient cloud environment.

Exercises

1. Discuss the importance of log analysis in threat detection within the cloud environment. Provide an example of how log analysis can help identify a security incident.

2. Explain how machine learning and AI techniques can be utilized to enhance threat detection in the cloud. Provide examples of how these technologies can help identify and prevent potential security threats.

3. Develop an incident response plan for a fictitious organization that heavily relies on cloud services. Include the key steps involved in incident response, roles and responsibilities, and communication procedures.

4. Conduct research on a recent cloud security incident and analyze its impact on the affected organization. Discuss the lessons learned and propose improvements to the incident response approach implemented by the organization.

Remember to challenge yourself and think critically while completing these exercises. The more you practice, the better equipped you will be to handle threats and incidents in the cloud environment.

The Fucking Security Blanket of the Cloud

In today's interconnected world, where data is the new gold, ensuring the security and protection of information has become a paramount concern. The rise of cloud computing has revolutionized the way we store, process, and access data, but it has also introduced new challenges and vulnerabilities. In this section, we will explore the security measures and best practices that form the "fucking security blanket" of the cloud.

Understanding Cloud Security

Before we dive into the specifics of cloud security, let's first understand the basic principles and concepts that underpin it. Cloud security is the discipline of protecting data, applications, and infrastructure in cloud environments from unauthorized access, data breaches, and other cyber threats.

At the heart of cloud security lies the concept of shared responsibility. While cloud service providers (CSPs) are responsible for securing the underlying infrastructure, customers are responsible for securing their own data and applications within the cloud. This shared responsibility model means that both parties must work together to ensure a secure computing environment.

SECURITY AND IDENTITY SERVICES 213

Security Controls and Countermeasures

To protect data and applications in the cloud, various security controls and countermeasures are employed. Let's take a closer look at some of the key components of the cloud security infrastructure:

1. **Identity and Access Management (IAM):** IAM is a fundamental aspect of cloud security that enables organizations to manage user identities, roles, and permissions. It ensures that only authorized individuals can access resources and perform specific actions within the cloud environment.

2. **Encryption and Key Management:** Encryption is a critical security measure that protects data by converting it into an unreadable format, thereby rendering it useless to unauthorized parties. Encryption keys are used to encrypt and decrypt data, and effective key management ensures the security and accessibility of these keys.

3. **Security Groups and Firewalls:** Security groups and firewalls act as the first line of defense by controlling network traffic in and out of the cloud environment. They enforce access control policies, filter malicious traffic, and prevent unauthorized access to resources.

4. **Threat Detection and Incident Response:** Cloud environments must have robust mechanisms in place to detect and respond to security threats. This includes the use of intrusion detection systems, security information and event management (SIEM) tools, and incident response processes to quickly identify and mitigate security incidents.

5. **Secure Network Communications:** The secure transmission of data between cloud resources and users is vital. This is achieved through the use of secure network protocols such as SSL/TLS for encrypted communication, virtual private networks (VPNs) for secure remote access, and secure gateways for data exchange.

6. **Physical Security Measures:** Cloud service providers employ stringent physical security measures to protect their data centers. These measures include strict access controls, video surveillance, biometric authentication, and round-the-clock security personnel.

Challenges and Risks

While the cloud offers numerous advantages, it also presents its fair share of challenges and risks. Let's explore some of the key challenges in cloud security:

1. **Data Breaches:** Data breaches can have severe consequences, ranging from financial losses to reputational damage. Cloud service providers are a prime target for cybercriminals, making it crucial to implement robust security measures to protect sensitive data.

2. **Compliance and Regulatory Requirements:** Organizations operating in specific industries, such as healthcare or finance, must comply with stringent regulations regarding data privacy and security. Moving data to the cloud requires careful consideration of legal and regulatory requirements to ensure compliance.

3. **Data Loss:** The potential for data loss, whether due to accidental deletion, hardware failure, or natural disasters, is a real concern. Cloud users must implement backup and disaster recovery strategies to mitigate the risk of data loss and ensure business continuity.

4. **Insider Threats:** While external threats often grab headlines, internal threats can be just as damaging. Organizations need to implement access controls, monitoring systems, and employee education programs to protect against insider threats.

5. **Shared Environment Vulnerabilities:** Cloud environments are shared among multiple tenants, making them potentially vulnerable to attacks targeting weaknesses in the underlying infrastructure. Security measures such as isolation, virtual private clouds, and regular vulnerability assessments are essential.

Best Practices for Cloud Security

To strengthen the "fucking security blanket" of the cloud, organizations should adhere to best practices that minimize risk and enhance the overall security posture. Here are some recommended practices:

1. **Strong Authentication and Access Controls:** Implement multi-factor authentication (MFA) and least privilege access controls to ensure that only authorized users can access sensitive resources.

2. **Encryption Everywhere:** Encrypt data at rest and in transit within the cloud environment. Utilize encryption mechanisms provided by the cloud service provider or consider client-side encryption for added security.

3. **Regular Security Audits and Assessments:** Conduct regular audits and assessments to identify vulnerabilities, weaknesses, and misconfigurations within the cloud environment. This includes penetration testing, vulnerability scanning, and security code reviews.

4. **Continuous Monitoring and Alerting:** Implement robust monitoring and alerting systems to detect suspicious activities, unauthorized access attempts, or security breaches. Use security information and event management (SIEM) tools to aggregate and analyze security logs.

5. **Employee Education and Awareness:** Train employees on cloud security best practices, including password hygiene, social engineering awareness, and safe browsing habits. Educate them on the potential risks and consequences of security breaches.

6. **Incident Response and Disaster Recovery:** Develop and test comprehensive incident response and disaster recovery plans to ensure timely and effective responses to security incidents. Regularly back up critical data and test recovery procedures to minimize downtime.

Real-World Example

Let's consider a real-world example to illustrate the importance of cloud security. Imagine a company that stores sensitive customer data in the cloud. Without proper security measures in place, such as encryption, strong access controls, and regular security audits, the company is at high risk of a data breach. If hackers gain access to the customer data, it could lead to financial losses, legal liabilities, and irreparable damage to the company's reputation.

By implementing robust security controls, conducting regular security assessments, and educating employees about cyber threats, the company can effectively protect its customer data and minimize the risk of a security breach.

Recommended Resources

To further expand your knowledge of cloud security, here are some recommended resources:

- Books:

    - "Cloud Security and Privacy" by Tim Mather, Subra Kumaraswamy, and Shahed Latif
    - "Cloud Computing Security: Foundations and Challenges" by John Vacca

- Online Courses:

    - Coursera - "Cloud Computing Security" by University of Colorado System
    - edX - "Cloud Computing for Enterprises" by Cloud Security Alliance

- Websites:

    - Cloud Security Alliance (cloudsecurityalliance.org)
    - National Institute of Standards and Technology (NIST) Cloud Computing Security Publications (nist.gov)

Summary

In this section, we explored the "fucking security blanket" of the cloud, focusing on the principles, security controls, challenges, best practices, and real-world examples. Cloud security is a dynamic and ever-evolving field that requires a proactive and multi-layered approach to protect information assets. By implementing the recommended practices and staying up to date with the latest security trends, organizations can harness the full potential of the cloud while mitigating the associated risks. Remember, in the world of cloud computing, security should not be an afterthought but a fundamental consideration from the very beginning.

AI and Machine Learning Services

Overview of AI and Machine Learning

Artificial Intelligence (AI) and Machine Learning (ML) have become buzzwords in recent years, captivating the imagination of both tech enthusiasts and everyday users. But what exactly do these terms mean? In this section, we will delve into the fundamentals of AI and ML, exploring their purpose, principles, and potential.

AI AND MACHINE LEARNING SERVICES

What is Artificial Intelligence?

Artificial Intelligence, in simple terms, refers to the ability of a machine or computer system to mimic and simulate human intelligence. It involves the development of intelligent algorithms and models that can understand, learn, reason, and make decisions. AI encompasses a wide range of techniques, including machine learning, natural language processing, computer vision, and robotics.

At its core, AI seeks to replicate human cognitive abilities, such as problem-solving, pattern recognition, and decision-making. It aims to build machines that can perform complex tasks autonomously, without explicit programming or human intervention. AI-powered systems can analyze vast amounts of data, extract insights, and predict future outcomes, bringing a new level of efficiency and intelligence to various domains.

What is Machine Learning?

Machine Learning is a subfield of AI that focuses on developing algorithms and models that enable computers to learn and improve from experience, without being explicitly programmed. Instead of relying on specific instructions, ML algorithms learn patterns and relationships in the data and use them to make predictions or take actions.

The ML process revolves around training models using training data, evaluating their performance, and refining them iteratively. These models can then be used to make predictions or perform tasks on new, unseen data. The ability to learn from data and adapt to changing circumstances is what sets ML apart from traditional rule-based programming.

Principles of Machine Learning

To better grasp the principles underlying ML, let's examine some key concepts:

- **Data:** ML algorithms rely on data to learn patterns and make predictions. The quality and quantity of the data directly influence the performance and accuracy of the models.

- **Features:** Features are the measurable characteristics or attributes of the data that ML algorithms use to make predictions. Selecting relevant features is crucial for the success of the model.

- **Supervised Learning:** In supervised learning, the algorithm learns from labeled examples where the correct answers are known. It maps input data to output labels by finding patterns and relationships in the data.

- **Unsupervised Learning:** Unsupervised learning involves training a model on unlabeled data, where the algorithm discovers patterns or hidden structures in the data. It is mainly used for exploratory analysis and clustering.

- **Reinforcement Learning:** Reinforcement learning involves training an agent to interact with an environment and learn from the feedback it receives. The agent learns to take actions that maximize a cumulative reward signal.

- **Neural Networks:** Neural networks are a fundamental component of many ML models. They consist of interconnected layers of artificial neurons that mimic the structure of the human brain. Deep Learning, a subset of ML, leverages neural networks with multiple hidden layers to learn complex representations.

- **Evaluation Metrics:** Evaluation metrics are used to assess the performance of ML models. Common metrics include accuracy, precision, recall, and F1 score, which measure different aspects of predictive accuracy.

Real-World Applications

AI and ML have found numerous applications across various industries, revolutionizing sectors such as healthcare, finance, marketing, and transportation. Let's explore a few examples:

- **Healthcare:** ML algorithms can analyze medical records and imaging data to aid in the diagnosis of diseases, predict patient outcomes, and recommend personalized treatment plans.

- **Finance:** ML is used in fraud detection, credit scoring, portfolio management, and algorithmic trading. It can detect anomalies, identify patterns, and make predictions based on market trends.

- **Marketing:** ML helps businesses optimize marketing campaigns, personalize user experiences, and improve customer segmentation. It can also analyze social media data to gauge customer sentiment and predict consumer behavior.

- **Transportation:** ML powers self-driving cars, enabling them to perceive their surroundings, make decisions, and navigate safely. It also aids in predicting traffic patterns, optimizing routes, and managing logistics.

Ethical Considerations and Challenges

While AI and ML offer tremendous potential, they also present ethical challenges and concerns. It is crucial to explore these aspects to ensure responsible and ethical use of these technologies. Some key considerations include:

- **Privacy and Data Protection:** ML models require access to vast amounts of data, raising concerns about privacy, data ownership, and the potential misuse of personal information.

- **Fairness and Bias:** ML models can inadvertently perpetuate biases present in the training data, leading to unfair or discriminatory outcomes. It is essential to address these biases and ensure fairness in the decision-making process.

- **Transparency and Explainability:** ML models often operate as black boxes, making it challenging to understand how they arrive at their decisions. Ensuring transparency and interpretability is crucial for trust and accountability.

- **Job Displacement:** AI and ML technologies have the potential to automate tasks traditionally performed by humans, leading to concerns about job displacement and the need for upskilling and retraining.

Resources for Further Learning

Here are some resources to deepen your understanding of AI and ML:

- **Books:** "Hands-On Machine Learning with Scikit-Learn, Keras, and TensorFlow" by Aurélien Géron, "Deep Learning" by Ian Goodfellow, Yoshua Bengio, and Aaron Courville, "Artificial Intelligence: A Modern Approach" by Stuart Russell and Peter Norvig.

- **Online Courses:** Coursera's "Machine Learning" by Andrew Ng, edX's "Deep Learning" by Deeplearning.ai, Fast.ai's Practical Deep Learning for Coders.

- **Blogs and Websites:** Towards Data Science (towardsdatascience.com), Kaggle (kaggle.com), Medium (medium.com) - featuring a wide range of AI and ML articles, tutorials, and discussions.

Remember, AI and ML are rapidly evolving fields, so it's essential to stay curious, embrace continuous learning, and explore the cutting-edge developments shaping our technological landscape.

Caveat Emptor: Just because you're armed with AI and ML knowledge doesn't mean you're destined to create the next Skynet. Remember to apply these tools ethically and responsibly, and always prioritize the well-being of humans. So go forth, my tech-savvy friend, and conquer the world with your newfound knowledge of AI and ML!

Training and Inference

When it comes to harnessing the power of Artificial Intelligence (AI) and Machine Learning (ML), the processes of training and inference play a crucial role. These two activities are integral to developing and deploying AI models that can perform complex tasks and make intelligent decisions. In this section, we will delve into the concepts of training and inference, their importance, and how they are carried out in the cloud.

Training

Training is the process of teaching an AI model to recognize patterns, make predictions, or perform specific tasks. Think of training as the boot camp for the model, where it is exposed to vast amounts of labeled data and learns to generate accurate outputs based on the inputs it receives. The goal is to train the model to generalize from the training data and make accurate predictions on new, unseen data.

In the cloud, training AI models is typically done by leveraging the computational power and scalability of cloud infrastructure. The training process involves several steps, such as data preprocessing, model selection, hyperparameter tuning, and optimization. Let's take a closer look at each of these steps:

1. **Data preprocessing:** Before feeding the data into the model, it needs to be cleaned, normalized, and transformed into a suitable format. This step ensures that the data is in a consistent and understandable form for the model to learn from.

2. **Model selection:** Choosing the right model architecture is crucial for achieving optimal performance. The model architecture determines the network structure, the number of layers, and the connections between them. Different types of models, such as convolutional neural networks (CNNs) for image data or recurrent neural networks (RNNs) for sequential data, are used for different types of tasks.

3. **Hyperparameter tuning:** Hyperparameters are settings that control the learning process of the model. These parameters are not learned from the data but are set by the developer. Tuning hyperparameters involves finding the best combination of values that optimize the model's performance. Hyperparameters can include learning rate, batch size, regularization strength, and activation functions.

4. **Optimization:** During training, the model adjusts its internal parameters to minimize the difference between predicted outputs and the actual labels in the training data. This is done through an optimization algorithm, typically gradient descent, which fine-tunes the weights and biases of the model.

Training AI models can be computationally demanding, especially for large datasets and complex models. Cloud providers offer scalable computing resources, such as Graphics Processing Units (GPUs) or Tensor Processing Units (TPUs), to accelerate the training process. By leveraging distributed processing and parallel computing, cloud platforms allow for faster and more efficient training, speeding up the development and refinement of AI models.

Inference

Once an AI model has been trained, it is ready to be put into action. This is where inference comes into play. Inference is the process of using a trained model to make predictions or generate outputs based on new, unseen data. It is the real-world application of the knowledge acquired during the training phase.

In the cloud, performing inference involves feeding new data into the trained model and obtaining predictions or outputs. The inference process is different from training in the sense that it focuses on efficiency, speed, and low-latency processing. Whereas training can be a time-consuming process, inference needs to be fast and responsive to meet real-time or near-real-time requirements.

To accelerate inference and handle high volumes of requests, cloud providers offer specialized services and hardware, such as AWS DeepLens or Google Edge TPU, that are optimized for AI workloads. These services offload the computational burden from the application and provide pre-trained models or inference APIs that can be easily integrated into applications.

Training vs. Inference Cost Considerations

When deploying AI models in the cloud, it is important to consider the cost implications of both training and inference. Training typically requires substantial computational resources, especially for large-scale models or complex tasks. Cloud providers offer various pricing models, including pay-as-you-go or spot instances, which can help optimize costs based on usage patterns and budget constraints.

On the other hand, inference is generally less resource-intensive and more cost-effective compared to training. However, the number of inference requests and the required response time can impact the overall cost. Cloud providers often charge based on the number of inference API calls or the size of the deployed model.

To optimize costs, it is important to carefully plan the resource allocation for both training and inference stages. Techniques such as model compression, quantization, or transferring learned knowledge from pre-trained models can be used to reduce the computational requirements and save on costs without sacrificing performance.

Real-World Example: Image Classification

Let's consider a real-world example to illustrate the training and inference processes in action. Suppose you want to develop an AI model that can classify images into different categories, such as cats, dogs, and birds. Here's how training and inference would work for this scenario:

- **Training**: To train the model, you would collect a large dataset of labeled images, where each image is associated with the correct category. You would preprocess the images, normalize the pixel values, and convert them into a suitable format for the model. Then, you would select a suitable model architecture, such as a convolutional neural network (CNN), and train it using the labeled dataset. The model would learn to recognize patterns and features that distinguish cats, dogs, and birds. Through an iterative process of adjusting hyperparameters and optimizing the model's performance, you would refine the model until it achieves satisfactory accuracy.

- **Inference**: Once the model is trained, you can deploy it to the cloud for inference. Let's say you have a mobile application where users can take

AI AND MACHINE LEARNING SERVICES

pictures of animals and get the predicted category in real-time. When a user captures an image, the image is sent to the cloud, processed, and fed into the deployed model. The model generates predictions based on the learned patterns, and the predicted category is returned to the application. The entire process should be fast and responsive to provide a seamless user experience.

By leveraging the computational power, scalability, and specialized services offered by cloud providers, the training and inference processes can be streamlined and optimized, enabling the development of intelligent AI applications on a large scale.

Summary

In this section, we explored the concepts of training and inference in the context of cloud computing and AI. We learned that training refers to the process of teaching an AI model to recognize patterns and make accurate predictions based on labeled data. In contrast, inference involves using a trained model to generate predictions or outputs on new, unseen data.

Training an AI model involves several steps, including data preprocessing, model selection, hyperparameter tuning, and optimization. Cloud platforms provide scalable computing resources, such as GPUs or TPUs, to accelerate the training process and enable the development of complex models.

Inference, on the other hand, focuses on efficiently generating predictions in real-time or near-real-time. Cloud providers offer specialized services and hardware optimized for AI workloads to handle high volumes of inference requests.

When deploying AI models in the cloud, it is essential to consider the cost implications of both training and inference. Cloud providers offer different pricing models and optimization techniques, such as model compression or knowledge transfer, to help optimize costs without sacrificing performance.

Overall, training and inference are critical components in the development and deployment of AI applications, and the cloud provides the necessary infrastructure and tools to support these processes. It's time to unleash the power of AI and conquer new frontiers in technology!

Natural Language Processing (NLP)

In this section, we will delve into the fascinating field of Natural Language Processing (NLP) and its applications in cloud computing. NLP is a subfield of artificial intelligence (AI) that focuses on the interaction between computers and human language. It enables machines to understand, interpret, and generate human language, allowing us to communicate with computers in a more natural and intuitive way.

Introduction to NLP

NLP encompasses a wide range of tasks, including but not limited to:

- **Language Understanding:** This involves tasks like sentiment analysis, entity recognition, topic modeling, and intent recognition. For example, NLP can analyze customer reviews to determine whether they are positive or negative, classify emails based on their content, or extract named entities like people, places, and organizations from a document.

- **Language Generation:** This includes machine translation, text summarization, speech synthesis, and dialogue systems. NLP can automatically translate text from one language to another, summarize lengthy documents into concise paragraphs, convert text into spoken words, and create conversational agents that can engage in meaningful dialogues with users.

- **Language Retrieval:** This involves tasks such as information retrieval, question answering, and document classification. NLP can search through vast amounts of text to retrieve relevant documents, answer specific questions based on text passages, and classify documents into predefined categories.

Principles of NLP

At the heart of NLP lies a set of underlying principles and techniques. Let's explore some of these key concepts:

- **Tokenization:** Tokenization is the process of breaking down a text into smaller units called tokens. Tokens can be words, sentences, or even subword units. This step is essential for further analysis as it allows the computer to understand the structure of the text.

- **Part-of-Speech (POS) Tagging:** POS tagging assigns grammatical information (such as noun, verb, adjective) to each token in a sentence. This helps in understanding the syntactic structure of sentences, which is crucial for many NLP tasks.

- **Named Entity Recognition (NER):** NER identifies and classifies named entities (e.g., persons, organizations, locations) in a text. This is important for tasks like information extraction and conversational agents that need to understand and refer to specific entities.

- **Word Embeddings:** Word embeddings are vector representations of words in a high-dimensional space. They capture semantic relationships between words and enable machines to understand the context and meaning of words. Popular methods for generating word embeddings include Word2Vec, GloVe, and FastText.

- **Sequence Labeling:** Sequence labeling is the task of assigning a label to each token in a sequence. It is commonly used for tasks like named entity recognition, part-of-speech tagging, and sentiment analysis.

- **Machine Learning Algorithms:** Many NLP tasks rely on machine learning algorithms to learn patterns from data and make predictions. Popular algorithms include decision trees, hidden Markov models, support vector machines, and deep learning models like recurrent neural networks (RNNs) and transformers.

Applications of NLP in the Cloud

NLP has numerous applications in the cloud computing domain, empowering developers and businesses to build intelligent applications and services. Let's explore some of these applications:

- **Chatbots and Virtual Assistants:** NLP enables the development of chatbots and virtual assistants that can understand and respond to user queries in natural language. These conversational agents can assist users with tasks, provide customer support, or even engage in small talk.

- **Sentiment Analysis:** NLP can analyze social media data, customer reviews, and feedback to determine the sentiment expressed by users. This information is valuable for businesses to understand customer satisfaction, identify trends, and make data-driven decisions.

- **Machine Translation:** With advances in NLP, machine translation has improved significantly. Cloud-based NLP services provide powerful translation capabilities, allowing users to translate text from one language to another with reasonable accuracy.

- **Text Summarization:** NLP techniques can automatically generate summaries of lengthy documents, making it easier for users to grasp the main points without going through the entire content. This has applications in news articles, research papers, and legal documents.

- **Voice Assistants:** NLP is at the core of voice assistants like Amazon Alexa, Google Assistant, and Apple Siri. These assistants use speech recognition and natural language understanding to perform tasks such as setting reminders, playing music, or answering questions.

- **Information Extraction:** NLP can extract structured information from unstructured text, such as extracting key entities from news articles or extracting structured data from invoices or receipts.

- **Spam Detection:** NLP techniques can be employed to analyze emails and messages for spam detection, improving the overall security and usability of communication platforms.

- **Search and Recommendations:** NLP enables more accurate and personalized search results and recommendations based on user preferences and historical data. This enhances user experience and drives user engagement.

Challenges and Limitations of NLP

While NLP has made tremendous progress in recent years, there are still several challenges and limitations that researchers and developers face:

- **Ambiguity and Polysemy:** Natural language is inherently ambiguous, with words and phrases having multiple meanings depending on the context. Resolving this ambiguity accurately remains a challenge in NLP.

- **Out-of-Distribution Data:** NLP models often struggle when encountering data that they have not been trained on. Generalizing the learned patterns to new and unseen examples is an ongoing challenge.

- **Lack of Contextual Understanding:** While NLP models have improved in understanding words, they still struggle with deeper contextual understanding. Truly comprehending language requires knowledge of the world, reasoning abilities, and common sense, which are difficult for machines to acquire.

- **Data Bias and Fairness:** NLP models are sensitive to the biases present in the training data, which can result in biased or unfair outcomes. Ensuring fairness and mitigating biases in NLP models is an important area of research.

- **Privacy and Ethical Concerns:** NLP deals with sensitive user data, raising concerns about privacy, security, and ethical use of the technology. Protecting user privacy and ensuring ethical guidelines are followed is of utmost importance.

Resources and Tools

Getting started with NLP can be daunting, but fortunately, there are abundant resources and tools available for developers and researchers:

- **NLTK (Natural Language Toolkit):** NLTK is a popular Python library for NLP that provides a wide range of tools and resources, including tokenization, POS tagging, NER, and much more. It's a great starting point for learning NLP concepts and experimenting with various techniques.

- **spaCy:** spaCy is another powerful Python library for NLP that focuses on high-performance and ease-of-use. It provides efficient implementations of various NLP tasks and supports multiple languages.

- **Transformers:** The transformers library, built on the PyTorch framework, provides a simple API for using state-of-the-art transformer models such as BERT, GPT-2, and RoBERTa. These models have revolutionized many NLP tasks and achieved state-of-the-art performance.

- **Cloud NLP Services:** Cloud providers like Amazon Web Services (AWS), Microsoft Azure, and Google Cloud Platform (GCP) offer NLP services that encompass a wide range of tasks. These services provide pre-trained models and APIs, making it easier to integrate NLP into your applications.

- **Research Papers and Conferences:** The field of NLP is dynamic, with new research papers and conferences emerging regularly. Keeping up with the latest advancements in the field can provide valuable insights and inspiration for your own projects.

An Unconventional Application: NLP for Emotion Recognition

One unconventional application of NLP is emotion recognition from text. By analyzing the text of a person's written or spoken words, NLP models can identify the underlying emotions expressed. This has applications in sentiment analysis, mental health support, and social media analysis.

For example, imagine a social media platform that uses NLP to detect if a user's posts show signs of distress or indicate a need for help. This could trigger an intervention or provide resources to the user. Similarly, NLP can be used to detect hate speech or cyberbullying, facilitating a safer and more inclusive online environment.

Emotion recognition from text can also be used in market research to gauge consumer sentiments towards products or services. By analyzing customer feedback, companies can gain valuable insights into how people feel about their offerings, allowing them to make data-driven decisions and improve customer satisfaction.

While emotion recognition from text is a challenging task due to the subjective nature of emotions and the need to understand subtle linguistic cues, advances in NLP and machine learning are making significant progress in this area.

Summary

In this section, we explored the exciting field of Natural Language Processing (NLP) and its applications in cloud computing. NLP empowers machines to understand, interpret, and generate human language, enabling a wide range of tasks like sentiment analysis, machine translation, and chatbot development. We discussed the underlying principles of NLP, including tokenization, word embeddings, and machine learning algorithms. We also examined the challenges and limitations faced by NLP researchers and developers and highlighted available resources and tools. Finally, we explored an unconventional application of NLP: emotion recognition from text. NLP continues to advance, opening up new possibilities for intelligent interaction with computers and enhancing various aspects of our lives.

Computer Vision

Computer Vision is a fascinating field of study that focuses on enabling computers to gain a high-level understanding from digital images or videos. It involves the development of algorithms and techniques that allow machines to perceive, interpret, and analyze visual data to extract meaningful information. This area of research has contributed to numerous real-world applications that impact various industries such as healthcare, autonomous vehicles, surveillance, and entertainment.

Introduction to Computer Vision

The goal of computer vision is to replicate the extraordinary capability of human vision by enabling machines to interpret visual data. Human vision is a complex process that involves the eyes capturing light, the brain interpreting the received information, and finally, the brain forming a perception of the visual scene. Computer vision attempts to mimic this process by using mathematical models and computer algorithms.

Key Concepts in Computer Vision

To understand computer vision, it is essential to grasp some fundamental concepts that form the building blocks of this field. Let's explore a few key concepts:

Image Formation Images are the primary source of data in computer vision. They are represented as a grid of pixels, where each pixel corresponds to a specific location in the image. The colors or intensities of these pixels encode the visual information. Understanding how images are formed, including the principles of light capture, sensor capabilities, and image formation process, is crucial for computer vision.

Image Processing Image processing refers to the manipulation of images to improve their quality or extract useful information. It involves a wide range of techniques such as filtering, edge detection, and noise removal. These techniques are applied to preprocess images before further analysis or feature extraction.

Feature Extraction Feature extraction is one of the fundamental tasks in computer vision. It involves identifying and extracting meaningful patterns or features from images. These features can be edges, corners, colors, textures, or any other distinctive characteristics that aid in distinguishing objects or regions of interest within an image.

Object Detection Object detection aims to locate and identify specific objects within an image or video. It involves two main steps: localization and classification. Localization determines the position and size of the objects, while classification assigns a label or category to each detected object. Object detection algorithms use various techniques, including machine learning algorithms and deep learning models.

Computer Vision Algorithms

Computer vision algorithms are the heart of computer vision applications. They are responsible for analyzing and interpreting visual data to perform specific tasks. Let's explore some prominent computer vision algorithms:

Image Classification Image classification is a fundamental task in computer vision that involves assigning labels or categories to images. It enables machines to recognize and categorize objects or scenes based on their visual content. This task has seen remarkable advancements with the advent of deep learning models such as Convolutional Neural Networks (CNNs).

Object Tracking Object tracking algorithms enable machines to follow the motion of objects across consecutive frames in a video. These algorithms are vital in applications such as video surveillance, autonomous vehicles, and human-computer interaction. Various approaches, including feature-based tracking and deep learning-based tracking, have been developed to achieve accurate and robust object tracking.

Semantic Segmentation Semantic segmentation refers to the task of labeling each pixel in an image with its corresponding category. It provides a detailed understanding of the image by segmenting it into different regions based on object boundaries. Deep learning techniques, particularly Fully Convolutional Networks (FCNs), have revolutionized semantic segmentation by achieving highly accurate and efficient results.

Object Recognition and Detection Object recognition and detection algorithms aim to identify and locate objects within images or videos. They allow machines to identify specific objects of interest, whether they are present as standalone instances or in a cluttered scene. Popular object recognition and detection frameworks include R-CNN, Fast R-CNN, and You Only Look Once (YOLO).

Applications of Computer Vision

Computer vision has countless applications across a wide range of industries. Let's explore a few notable applications:

Autonomous Vehicles Computer vision plays a crucial role in enabling autonomous vehicles to perceive and navigate their surroundings. It helps in detecting and tracking other vehicles, pedestrians, traffic signs, and traffic lights. Computer vision algorithms provide crucial information to the autonomous vehicle system, allowing it to make informed decisions in real-time.

Medical Imaging Computer vision is extensively used in medical imaging to analyze images from X-rays, MRIs, CT scans, and other imaging modalities. It assists in the detection and diagnosis of diseases, the identification of tumors and abnormalities, and surgical planning. Computer vision also aids in the development of advanced medical imaging techniques such as 3D reconstruction and image-guided interventions.

Augmented Reality Augmented reality (AR) overlays virtual elements on the real world to enhance the user's perception and interaction. Computer vision algorithms play a key role in AR by tracking the user's position and orientation, recognizing objects and scenes, and rendering virtual objects in real-time.

Surveillance and Security Computer vision is widely used in surveillance and security systems to detect and track suspicious activities, monitor crowds, and identify individuals. It enables real-time monitoring and alerting, enhancing the effectiveness of security personnel and improving public safety.

Virtual Reality and Gaming Computer vision contributes to virtual reality (VR) and gaming experiences by capturing and tracking the movement of the user's body and hands. It enables realistic interaction with virtual environments, creating immersive and engaging experiences.

Challenges and Future Directions

While computer vision has witnessed tremendous advancements, several challenges and future directions remain to be addressed. Some key challenges include:

Robustness to Variations Computer vision algorithms often struggle with variations in lighting conditions, viewpoint, scale, occlusions, and image quality. Developing algorithms that are robust to these variations is an ongoing challenge.

Data Annotation and Labeling Training computer vision algorithms often requires large amounts of labeled data. The process of annotating and labeling these datasets is time-consuming and labor-intensive. Developing efficient annotation tools and techniques is crucial to overcome this challenge.

Ethical Considerations As computer vision technology becomes more powerful and pervasive, ethical considerations regarding privacy, bias, fairness, and accountability become paramount. It is essential to ensure that computer vision systems are designed with responsible and ethical practices in mind.

Conclusion

Computer vision is an exciting and rapidly evolving field that has the potential to revolutionize various industries. It encompasses a wide range of algorithms and techniques designed to enable machines to interpret and understand visual data. As technology progresses, computer vision will continue to advance, leading to innovative applications and solutions that benefit society. By understanding the principles and concepts of computer vision, you will be well-equipped to explore this captivating field and contribute to its ongoing development.

Exercises

1. Discuss a real-world application where computer vision plays a critical role. Explain how computer vision technology is used in that application and the challenges it faces.

2. Research and explore recent advancements in computer vision algorithms and techniques. Discuss one breakthrough that has had a significant impact on the field.

3. Consider the ethical implications of computer vision technology. Discuss the potential risks and benefits of widespread adoption and identify strategies to address ethical concerns.

4. Choose an object recognition or detection framework (e.g., R-CNN, Fast R-CNN, YOLO) and explain its underlying principles and advantages over other approaches.

Resources

1. Szeliski, R. (2010). Computer Vision: Algorithms and Applications. Springer.
2. Forsyth, D., & Ponce, J. (2019). Computer Vision: A Modern Approach. Pearson.

AI AND MACHINE LEARNING SERVICES 233

3. OpenCV: Open Source Computer Vision Library. Retrieved from https://opencv.org/

4. PyTorch Computer Vision Cookbook. Retrieved from https://pytorchcv.readthedocs.io/

The Fucking Rise of Artificial Intelligence

Artificial Intelligence (AI) has been making waves in recent years, and its impact on cloud computing cannot be ignored. This section will delve into the fucking rise of AI, exploring its concepts, applications, and future potential.

Understanding Artificial Intelligence

AI refers to the simulation of human intelligence in machines that are programmed to think and learn like humans. It encompasses a broad range of technologies, including machine learning, natural language processing, and computer vision. These technologies enable computers to perform tasks that typically require human intelligence, such as problem-solving, decision making, and pattern recognition.

At the heart of AI lies machine learning, a subfield that focuses on algorithms and statistical models that enable machines to learn from and make predictions or decisions based on data. Machine learning algorithms are trained on vast amounts of data, allowing them to identify patterns, make accurate predictions, and continuously improve their performance over time.

Applications of Artificial Intelligence

AI has been integrated into various aspects of cloud computing, and its applications are widespread. Let's take a look at some major areas where AI is making a fucking significant impact:

1. **Data Analysis and Insights** AI-powered data analytics tools are revolutionizing how businesses extract insights from vast amounts of data stored in the cloud. By leveraging machine learning algorithms, these tools can analyze and interpret complex datasets to identify trends, detect anomalies, and make data-driven recommendations. This enables organizations to make informed decisions, optimize processes, and gain a competitive edge.

2. **Personalization and Recommendation Systems** AI algorithms are driving personalized user experiences by analyzing user behavior, preferences, and

historical data. These algorithms power recommendation systems that offer tailored product recommendations, content suggestions, and personalized marketing campaigns. By understanding user preferences and predicting user needs, businesses can deliver more relevant and engaging experiences, leading to increased customer satisfaction and loyalty.

3. **Natural Language Processing (NLP)** NLP, a branch of AI, focuses on the interaction between computers and human language. NLP algorithms enable machines to understand, interpret, and generate human language, enabling applications such as voice assistants, chatbots, and language translation services. These AI-powered tools enhance communication, streamline customer support, and automate repetitive tasks, making interactions with digital systems more natural and intuitive.

4. **Computer Vision** Computer vision combines AI algorithms with image processing techniques to enable machines to understand and interpret visual data. Applications of computer vision in cloud computing include facial recognition systems, object detection, and image classification. These technologies are transforming industries such as healthcare, retail, and manufacturing by automating processes, enhancing security, and improving overall efficiency.

5. **Predictive Maintenance and Optimization** AI-powered predictive analytics is aiding in the proactive maintenance of cloud infrastructure. By analyzing real-time data from sensors and monitoring systems, AI algorithms can predict asset failures, identify potential bottlenecks, and optimize resource allocation. This helps improve system performance, reduce downtime, and enhance overall operational efficiency.

Ethical Considerations and Challenges

While the rise of AI brings immense potential, it also raises ethical concerns and presents challenges. It is crucial to address these issues to ensure the responsible development and deployment of AI technologies.

1. **Privacy and Data Protection** AI relies on vast amounts of data for training and decision-making, raising concerns about data privacy and security. Organizations must implement robust data protection measures to safeguard sensitive data and ensure compliance with relevant regulations. Additionally, transparency in data collection and usage should be maintained to build trust with users.

AI AND MACHINE LEARNING SERVICES

2. Fairness and Bias in AI AI algorithms can be influenced by biases present in the datasets used for training. This can lead to unfair outcomes or perpetuate existing societal biases. It is essential to identify and mitigate biases in AI systems through careful dataset selection, bias-aware algorithms, and ongoing monitoring. Ensuring fairness and impartiality in AI decision-making is crucial for building trust and avoiding potential harm.

3. Responsible AI Development and Use As AI becomes more powerful and autonomous, responsible development and use are paramount. Developers and organizations must prioritize ethical considerations, accountability, and transparency throughout the AI lifecycle. Adhering to ethical frameworks, conducting proper impact assessments, and enabling human oversight can mitigate the potential risks associated with AI deployment.

4. Workforce Displacement and Skill Gap The rise of AI has raised concerns about the displacement of human workers due to automation. As AI technologies continue to advance, certain jobs may become obsolete while new ones emerge. Addressing the skill gap through reskilling and upskilling programs is crucial to ensure individuals are equipped with the necessary skills to adapt to the changing job market.

Looking Ahead: Future Opportunities

The rise of AI presents a vast array of opportunities for cloud computing. As technology continues to evolve, the following areas hold immense potential:

1. Explainable AI Advancements in explainable AI aim to enhance transparency and interpretability of AI systems. This will enable users to understand how algorithms make decisions and provide explanations for their outputs. Explainable AI is crucial for building trust, ensuring accountability, and addressing legal and ethical concerns associated with AI adoption.

2. AI-Enhanced Cybersecurity AI can play a vital role in combating cybersecurity threats by detecting anomalies, predicting attacks, and automating incident response. AI-powered cybersecurity systems can continuously monitor networks, detect vulnerabilities, and respond rapidly to mitigate risks. As cyber threats become more sophisticated, leveraging AI in cybersecurity will become fucking crucial.

3. Hybrid AI-Edge Architectures   The combination of AI and edge computing allows for real-time processing and analysis of data at the network edge, reducing latency and enhancing performance. This opens up opportunities for AI models to be deployed closer to the data source, enabling faster decision-making and reducing reliance on cloud resources. Hybrid AI-edge architectures will be instrumental in supporting applications that require low latency and offline capabilities.

4. AI-Driven Personalized Medicine   AI and cloud computing have the potential to revolutionize the healthcare industry, especially in personalized medicine. By analyzing large-scale patient data, genetic information, and medical records, AI algorithms can assist in accurate diagnosis, treatment selection, and drug discovery. The integration of AI in healthcare has the potential to significantly improve patient outcomes and reduce healthcare costs.

Conclusion

The fucking rise of artificial intelligence in cloud computing is reshaping industries, revolutionizing processes, and opening up new possibilities. AI-powered technologies are providing businesses with tools to extract valuable insights, enhance customer experiences, and drive innovation. However, it is crucial to address ethical considerations and challenges associated with AI deployment to ensure responsible and beneficial use. As technology continues to advance, the future of AI will bring even more opportunities for growth and transformation across various sectors.

Exercises

1. Discuss the differences between narrow and general artificial intelligence. Provide examples of each.

2. What are the potential benefits and challenges of integrating AI with cloud computing in the healthcare industry? Provide examples to support your answer.

3. Explain the concept of bias in AI systems. Why is it important to address bias in the development and deployment of AI technologies? Provide strategies that can help mitigate bias.

4. How can organizations ensure the responsible and ethical use of AI in their operations? Discuss the importance of transparency, accountability, and human oversight in AI development and deployment.

5. Research and discuss a recent case where AI technology has been used for social good or to address a pressing global issue. Explain the impact of AI in addressing the problem and the potential challenges associated with its implementation.

Additional Resources

1. Book: "Artificial Intelligence: A Modern Approach" by Stuart Russell and Peter Norvig.

2. Online Course: "AI for Everyone" offered by deeplearning.ai on Coursera.

3. Article: "The Ethics of Artificial Intelligence" by Nick Bostrom and Eliezer Yudkowsky.

4. Website: OpenAI (https://www.openai.com/) - A research organization advancing AI in a safe and ethical manner.

5. Podcast: "AI in Business" by Dan Faggella - Provides insights into AI applications across various industries.

Cloud Deployment and Operations

Cloud Service Providers

Amazon Web Services (AWS)

Welcome to the exciting world of Amazon Web Services (AWS), the titan of cloud computing! In this section, we'll dive into the ins and outs of AWS, exploring its key services, benefits, and real-world applications. Strap in, because we're about to embark on a cloud journey like no other!

Introducing Amazon Web Services

Amazon Web Services (AWS) is a comprehensive and highly scalable cloud computing platform offered by Amazon.com. Launched in 2006, AWS has rapidly grown to become the industry leader in cloud services, providing a wide range of solutions to individuals, startups, and enterprises alike.

AWS offers over 175 fully featured services across various domains, including computing power, storage, databases, networking, analytics, machine learning, and more. With its pay-as-you-go pricing model, customers can easily scale their resources up or down to meet changing demands, paying only for what they use.

Foundations of AWS

To fully understand AWS, it's crucial to grasp the foundations on which the platform is built. AWS operates on a global infrastructure comprising a vast network of data centers distributed across different regions and availability zones. This decentralized approach ensures high availability, fault tolerance, and reduced latency for applications hosted on AWS.

One of the key components of AWS infrastructure is Elastic Compute Cloud (EC2). EC2 provides virtual servers known as instances, allowing users to quickly deploy and scale computing resources as needed. These instances come in various types optimized for different workloads, such as general-purpose, memory-intensive, or GPU-enabled instances for high-performance computing.

Another fundamental service is Simple Storage Service (S3), which offers scalable object storage for any type of data. S3 provides a highly durable and available storage solution, allowing users to store and retrieve massive amounts of data with low latency. It's widely used for backup and restore, data archiving, content distribution, and serving static websites.

AWS Services in Action

Let's explore some popular AWS services in action, and how they empower businesses to achieve their goals more efficiently.

1. Amazon Elastic Beanstalk: Amazon Elastic Beanstalk allows developers to easily deploy and manage applications in various programming languages without having to worry about the underlying infrastructure. It automates the deployment process, handles capacity provisioning, load balancing, and application health monitoring. This allows developers to focus on writing code and speeding up the development cycle.

2. Amazon Relational Database Service (RDS): Amazon RDS makes it effortless to set up, operate, and scale relational databases in the cloud. With RDS, you can choose from various database engines, such as MySQL, PostgreSQL, Oracle, and SQL Server, and benefit from automated backups, software patching, and database scaling. This service eliminates the administrative overhead of managing databases, freeing up valuable time for developing robust applications.

3. Amazon DynamoDB: Amazon DynamoDB is a fully managed NoSQL database service that boasts single-digit millisecond latency at scale. It provides seamless scalability, with the ability to handle millions of requests per second, making it ideal for high-scale applications. DynamoDB's flexible data model allows you to store and retrieve any amount of data, adapt to changing workloads, and integrate seamlessly with other AWS services.

4. Amazon Aurora: Amazon Aurora is a highly performant and MySQL-compatible relational database engine. It combines the scalability and reliability of traditional databases with the cost-effectiveness and flexibility of cloud computing. Aurora is designed to provide excellent performance even with thousands of concurrent connections, making it a perfect choice for applications that require high throughput and low latency.

Real-World Examples

To understand the true power of AWS, let's take a look at some real-world examples of how organizations have harnessed its services to revolutionize their operations.

1. **Airbnb:** Airbnb, the world's largest online marketplace for lodging and hospitality, relies on AWS to handle its enormous scale of data and global operations. With over 150 million users and an extensive network of hosts and guests, Airbnb leverages various AWS services, including Amazon S3 for storing listing photos, Amazon EC2 for hosting its website, and Amazon Redshift for data analytics.

2. **Netflix:** Netflix, the popular streaming service, shifted its entire infrastructure to AWS in 2012. By leveraging AWS's scalability and reliability, Netflix transformed its business model, allowing subscribers to access content on-demand across a wide range of devices. This move enabled Netflix to expand globally and deliver high-quality streaming experiences to millions of users simultaneously.

3. **NASA:** NASA relies on AWS to process and store vast amounts of space exploration data. AWS provides the computing power and storage capabilities necessary for NASA's missions and research, such as satellite data analysis, climate modeling, and computational simulations. By utilizing AWS, NASA significantly reduces costs and gains the flexibility to scale resources based on project requirements.

Resources and Further Reading

As you dive deeper into the world of AWS, here are some valuable resources and references to expand your knowledge:

- **AWS documentation:** The official documentation on AWS's website is a goldmine of information, from getting started guides to in-depth technical documentation for each service.

- **AWS re:Invent:** AWS re:Invent is an annual conference where AWS experts and community members share insights, best practices, and the latest developments. Keep an eye out for sessions and videos from past conferences.

- **AWS Training and Certification:** AWS offers a comprehensive training program and certification exams to validate your skills and expertise in various AWS technologies. Take advantage of this opportunity to enhance your credentials.

- **AWS Blogs and Case Studies:** The AWS blogs and case studies section provides real-world experiences, success stories, and insights from customers and AWS experts, giving you a deeper understanding of how AWS is transforming industries.

Conclusion

Amazon Web Services (AWS) has revolutionized the way we build, deploy, and scale applications in the cloud. With its vast array of services, global infrastructure, and strong customer base, AWS remains at the forefront of innovation in cloud computing.

In this section, we explored the foundations of AWS, its key services, real-world examples, and resources for further learning. But remember, AWS is just one piece of the cloud computing puzzle. In the next section, we'll explore another major player in the cloud realm: Microsoft Azure. So buckle up, because there's much more to uncover on our cloud computing adventure!

Microsoft Azure

Microsoft Azure is one of the major players in the cloud computing industry, offering a wide range of services to cater to the diverse needs of businesses and individuals. In this section, we will dive into the world of Microsoft Azure and explore what makes it a strong contender in the cloud market.

Introduction to Microsoft Azure

Microsoft Azure is a cloud computing platform and infrastructure offered by Microsoft. It provides a variety of cloud services, including computing power, storage, and networking capabilities. Azure aims to empower businesses and organizations by providing them with tools and resources to build, deploy, and manage applications and services on a global scale.

Azure Services

Microsoft Azure offers a comprehensive suite of cloud services that can be classified into different categories based on their functionalities. Let's take a closer look at some of the key services provided by Azure.

Compute Services Azure provides a range of compute services to meet different workload requirements. The following are some of the compute services offered by Azure:

- **Virtual Machines (VMs):** Azure VMs give you the flexibility to create and manage virtual machines in the cloud. With VMs, you can run your choice of operating system and applications, providing a virtualized environment for your workloads.

- **App Service:** Azure App Service enables you to build, deploy, and scale web and mobile apps quickly. It supports popular programming languages like .NET, Java, Python, and Node.js, allowing developers to focus on building their applications without worrying about the underlying infrastructure.

- **Azure Functions:** Azure Functions is a serverless compute service that enables you to run event-driven code in the cloud. With Functions, you can execute small pieces of code (functions) in response to various triggers, such as HTTP requests, database changes, or timer-based schedules.

- **Azure Kubernetes Service (AKS):** AKS simplifies the deployment and management of containerized applications. It provides a fully managed Kubernetes service, allowing you to scale, monitor, and upgrade your applications seamlessly.

Storage Services Azure offers a range of storage services that cater to different storage needs. These services include:

- **Azure Blob Storage:** Blob Storage is designed for storing massive amounts of unstructured data, such as images, videos, and backups. It provides a simple and scalable storage solution with high availability and durability.

- **Azure Files:** Azure Files offers fully managed file shares in the cloud, accessible via the standard SMB (Server Message Block) protocol. It allows you to easily migrate existing applications that depend on file shares to the cloud.

- **Azure Disk Storage:** Disk Storage provides persistent and high-performance block storage for Azure VMs. It offers different disk types to meet various workload requirements, including Standard HDD, Standard SSD, and Premium SSD.

- **Azure Data Lake Storage:** Data Lake Storage is a scalable and secure repository for big data analytics workloads. It can store structured, semi-structured, and unstructured data, making it suitable for data exploration, analysis, and machine learning scenarios.

Networking Services Azure provides a robust set of networking services to build secure and scalable network architectures. Some of the key networking services offered by Azure include:

- **Azure Virtual Network (VNet):** VNet allows you to create isolated network environments in Azure, providing control over IP address ranges, subnets, and network gateways. It enables you to connect Azure resources and on-premises networks securely.

- **Azure Load Balancer:** Load Balancer distributes incoming network traffic across multiple virtual machines or services to ensure high availability and scalability. It supports both Internet-facing and internal load balancing scenarios.

- **Azure VPN Gateway:** VPN Gateway enables you to establish secure cross-premises connectivity between your on-premises network and Azure. It provides site-to-site and point-to-site VPN connections, allowing you to extend your network to the cloud.

- **Azure DNS:** Azure DNS is a hosting service for domain names, offering reliable and scalable domain name resolution. It allows you to manage DNS records for your domain names hosted on Azure or elsewhere.

Database Services Azure provides a wide range of database services to store, manage, and analyze data efficiently. These services include:

- **Azure Cosmos DB:** Cosmos DB is a globally distributed, multi-model database service. It supports various NoSQL APIs, including MongoDB, Cassandra, Gremlin, and SQL (DocumentDB), providing flexibility to choose the right data model for your applications.

- **Azure SQL Database:** SQL Database is a fully managed relational database service based on Microsoft SQL Server. It offers high performance, scalability, and security, making it an ideal choice for modern application development.

- **Azure Database for MySQL and Azure Database for PostgreSQL:** These services provide fully managed, enterprise-ready MySQL and PostgreSQL databases in the cloud. They offer built-in high availability, scalability, and security features.

- **Azure Synapse Analytics:** Synapse Analytics (formerly SQL Data Warehouse) is an analytics service that brings together big data and data warehousing into a single unified platform. It enables you to query and analyze large volumes of data with high performance and scalability.

Why Choose Microsoft Azure?

Now that we've covered some of the key services offered by Microsoft Azure, let's explore why you might choose Azure as your preferred cloud platform.

Integration with Microsoft Ecosystem One of the key advantages of Azure is its seamless integration with other Microsoft products and services. If you're already using tools like Microsoft Office 365, Active Directory, or Windows Server, Azure provides a natural extension to your existing infrastructure. It allows for smooth interoperability and synergy between your on-premises and cloud environments.

Scalability and Flexibility Azure offers a highly scalable and flexible platform that can meet the needs of businesses of any size. Whether you're a small startup or a large enterprise, Azure's pay-as-you-go pricing model enables you to scale your resources up or down as needed, without any upfront costs or long-term commitments. This flexibility allows you to adapt quickly to changing business demands and optimize costs.

Global Presence Azure has a vast global footprint, with data centers located in regions around the world. This global presence enables you to deploy your applications closer to your users, reducing latency and providing a better user experience. Additionally, Azure's global infrastructure ensures high availability and disaster recovery options to keep your applications running smoothly.

Security and Compliance Microsoft Azure takes security and compliance seriously. It provides a wide range of built-in security features, such as network security groups, Azure Firewall, and Azure DDoS Protection, to safeguard your applications and data. Furthermore, Azure complies with a comprehensive set of industry standards and regulations, including ISO 27001, SOC 2, HIPAA, and GDPR, ensuring that your data is protected and meets regulatory requirements.

Enterprise-Grade Support Azure offers enterprise-grade support to help you navigate the complexities of cloud computing. Microsoft provides 24/7 technical support, proactive monitoring, and service-level agreements (SLAs) for many Azure services. With Azure's support options, you can confidently deploy and manage your applications with peace of mind.

Conclusion

In this section, we explored Microsoft Azure, a powerful cloud computing platform that provides a wide range of services to meet the needs of businesses and organizations. We examined key services offered by Azure, including compute, storage, networking, and database services. We also discussed some compelling reasons why you might choose Azure for your cloud computing needs, such as integration with the Microsoft ecosystem, scalability and flexibility, global presence, security and compliance, and enterprise-grade support.

Whether you're a developer, an IT professional, or a business owner, Microsoft Azure offers the tools, resources, and support to help you leverage the power of the cloud and drive innovation. With Azure, you can unlock the full potential of your applications and services, enabling you to scale, conquer new markets, and stay ahead of the competition. So, why wait? Embrace the power of Azure and embark on your cloud journey today.

Resources:
- Microsoft Azure documentation: *docs.microsoft.com/en-us/azure/*
- Microsoft Azure YouTube channel: *youtube.com/c/Azure*
- Stack Overflow (Azure tag): *stackoverflow.com/questions/tagged/azure*
- Official Microsoft Azure Blog: *azure.microsoft.com/blog/*

Google Cloud Platform (GCP)

In this section, we will delve into the incredible world of Google Cloud Platform (GCP), one of the industry leaders in cloud computing. GCP offers a wide range of services and products that enable organizations to build, deploy, and scale their applications and infrastructure in a secure and reliable manner. So, buckle up and let's take a deep dive into the fascinating realm of GCP.

Overview of Google Cloud Platform

Google Cloud Platform, often referred to as GCP, is a suite of cloud computing services provided by Google, which includes computing power, storage resources, and scalable data analytics. GCP offers a rich set of tools and services, catering to a diverse range of needs, from small startups to large enterprises.

GCP's infrastructure spans across a global network of data centers, enabling users to deploy their applications in regions strategically located around the world. This global footprint provides low-latency access and redundancy, ensuring high availability and reliability for GCP customers.

GCP Services

GCP provides a wide array of services that can be broadly categorized into the following categories:

1. Computing Services: GCP offers a variety of computing services to cater to different application needs. These services include:

- **Compute Engine:** GCP's virtual machines (VMs) allow users to provision and manage virtual servers easily. Users can choose from predefined machine types or customize them based on their requirements.

- **Kubernetes Engine:** GCP provides a managed Kubernetes service that allows users to deploy, scale, and manage containerized applications on a cluster of VMs.

2. Storage and Database Services: GCP offers a range of storage and database services to meet various data storage and management needs. Some of these services include:

- **Cloud Storage:** GCP's object storage service provides unlimited scalability, durability, and low-latency access to data. It is suitable for storing and serving static content, backups, and archival data.

- **Cloud Datastore:** GCP's NoSQL document database allows users to store, retrieve, and query semi-structured data with ease.

- **Cloud SQL:** GCP's fully managed relational database service supports popular database engines like MySQL, PostgreSQL, and SQL Server.

3. **Networking Services:** GCP's networking services enable users to build secure and scalable network architectures. Key networking services include:

- **Virtual Private Cloud (VPC):** GCP's VPC allows users to create their virtual network, complete with subnets, firewall rules, and load balancers.

- **Cloud Load Balancing:** GCP's load balancing service automatically distributes incoming traffic across multiple instances to ensure higher availability and scalability.

4. **Big Data and Machine Learning Services:** GCP provides a powerful suite of tools for processing and analyzing large datasets and building machine learning models. Notable services in this category include:

- **BigQuery:** GCP's fully managed data warehouse allows users to run lightning-fast SQL queries on massive datasets.

- **Cloud Pub/Sub:** GCP's messaging service enables real-time data streaming and event-driven architectures.

- **Cloud ML Engine:** GCP's managed service for training and deploying machine learning models at scale.

Google Kubernetes Engine (GKE)

Google Kubernetes Engine (GKE) is a fully managed Kubernetes service provided by GCP. Kubernetes, also known as K8s, is an open-source container orchestration platform that automates the deployment, scaling, and management of containerized applications. GKE simplifies the management of Kubernetes clusters, making it easier for developers to build and deploy applications.

With GKE, users can leverage Kubernetes' powerful features, such as automated scaling, self-healing, and service discovery, to deploy and manage their applications. GKE also integrates seamlessly with other GCP services, allowing users to take advantage of the full suite of GCP offerings.

Example Scenario: Let's say you have developed a microservices-based application and want to deploy it on GCP using Kubernetes. With GKE, you can create a cluster with a few simple commands and define your application's deployment and service configurations using YAML files. GKE will then take care of provisioning the necessary resources, scheduling the containers, and managing the application's lifecycle.

GCP Marketplace

GCP Marketplace is a digital catalog of pre-configured software solutions that run on GCP. It allows users to easily discover, deploy, and manage popular software packages, ranging from open-source databases to AI-powered applications. GCP Marketplace provides a one-click deployment experience, streamlining the process of setting up complex software stacks.

By using GCP Marketplace, developers and businesses can save valuable time and effort by leveraging pre-configured solutions and integrating them seamlessly into their GCP environment.

Important Considerations

When considering Google Cloud Platform for your cloud computing needs, it's essential to keep the following factors in mind:

1. **Cost Management:** While GCP offers flexible pricing models, it's crucial to understand the cost implications of various services and features. GCP provides tools and resources for monitoring and optimizing costs, such as budgeting and usage tracking tools.

2. **Security and Compliance:** GCP ensures robust security measures to protect customer data. It provides identity and access management tools, encryption at rest and in transit, and compliance certifications to meet industry regulatory requirements.

3. **Support and Documentation:** GCP offers comprehensive documentation, tutorials, and best practices to guide users in utilizing its services effectively. Additionally, GCP provides technical support options to address customer queries and issues.

Resources and Further Reading

To dive deeper into Google Cloud Platform (GCP) and explore its vast offerings, you can check out the following resources:

- Official GCP documentation: `https://cloud.google.com/docs`

- GCP YouTube channel: `https://youtube.com/GoogleCloudPlatform`

+ Qwiklabs GCP labs: `https://www.qwiklabs.com/catalog?keywords=Google%20Cloud%20Platform`

Remember, GCP is just one of the many choices available in the cloud computing landscape, but it certainly stands tall with its extensive range of services and global infrastructure. So, go ahead and explore GCP to unleash the full potential of cloud computing for your projects and endeavors.

IBM Cloud

In this section, we will delve into the world of IBM Cloud and explore its features, services, and advantages. IBM Cloud is the cloud computing platform provided by IBM, one of the "fucking titans" of cloud computing. It offers a wide range of services and solutions to meet the diverse needs of businesses and developers.

Overview of IBM Cloud

IBM Cloud is built on a highly secure and scalable infrastructure that spans across a global network of data centers. It provides a comprehensive set of cloud services, including infrastructure as a service (IaaS), platform as a service (PaaS), and software as a service (SaaS) offerings. With IBM Cloud, users can deploy and manage applications, store and analyze data, and access advanced technologies such as AI and blockchain.

Key Features and Services

IBM Cloud offers a plethora of features and services that cater to various business requirements. Let's explore some of the key offerings in more detail:

IBM Watson - IBM Cloud provides access to IBM Watson, a powerful suite of AI-powered services and tools. From natural language processing to computer vision, Watson enables developers to build intelligent applications that understand, reason, and learn from data. For example, Watson Language Translator can be used to develop language translation applications, while Watson Visual Recognition can be utilized to build image recognition systems.

IBM Blockchain - Another standout service offered by IBM Cloud is IBM Blockchain. With this service, businesses can leverage the power of decentralized ledger technology (DLT) to create secure, transparent, and tamper-proof networks. IBM Blockchain provides a platform for developing and deploying

CLOUD SERVICE PROVIDERS

blockchain applications, enabling businesses to reshape industries and streamline their processes. For instance, supply chain management systems can be built on IBM Blockchain to enable end-to-end traceability and accountability.

IBM Cloud Functions - IBM Cloud Functions is IBM's serverless computing platform, also known as Function as a Service (FaaS). It allows developers to focus on writing code without worrying about infrastructure management. With Cloud Functions, developers can create individual functions that automatically scale in response to events or triggers. This provides flexibility and cost optimization, as resources are allocated only when needed. For example, developers can create a serverless function to process incoming data from IoT devices and trigger an alert based on specific conditions.

IBM Cloud Object Storage - IBM Cloud Object Storage offers scalable and durable storage for unstructured data. It provides a cost-effective solution for storing and accessing large volumes of data. With its built-in security features and integration capabilities, businesses can securely store and retrieve data from anywhere in the world. For example, media companies can use IBM Cloud Object Storage to store and deliver video content to their users, ensuring high availability and fast streaming.

IBM Cloud Pak for Applications - IBM Cloud Pak for Applications is a comprehensive solution for modernizing and developing cloud-native applications. It includes a set of tools, frameworks, and services that accelerate application development and deployment on IBM Cloud. Cloud Pak for Applications enables developers to build microservices-based architectures, utilize containerization technologies like Docker and Kubernetes, and automate the deployment and scaling of applications. This assists businesses in quickly adapting to changing market demands and reducing time-to-market for their applications.

Customer Success Stories

Let's take a look at some real-world examples of businesses that have leveraged IBM Cloud to achieve their goals:

Macy's - Macy's, the well-known American department store chain, utilized IBM Cloud to transform its customer experience. By implementing a cloud-based microservices architecture, Macy's was able to enhance its website performance, accommodate peak traffic, and provide a seamless shopping experience. Through the integration of AI capabilities from IBM Watson, Macy's also developed a virtual shopping assistant that assists customers in finding the products they desire.

Coca-Cola European Partners - Coca-Cola European Partners (CCEP) collaborated with IBM Cloud to modernize its IT infrastructure and streamline its operations. By migrating its SAP applications to IBM Cloud, CCEP achieved improved scalability, agility, and cost optimization. The company now benefits from reduced infrastructure complexity and increased flexibility, enabling it to respond more effectively to market changes.

Resources and Training

IBM provides extensive resources and training materials to help users get started with IBM Cloud. Here are a few noteworthy resources:

IBM Cloud Docs - The IBM Cloud Docs provide comprehensive documentation for all IBM Cloud services. It offers detailed guidance, tutorials, and best practices to assist users in understanding and utilizing the available services effectively.

IBM Developer - IBM Developer is a platform that offers a wealth of resources, including tutorials, code patterns, and sample applications related to IBM Cloud. It provides hands-on learning experiences and encourages collaboration among developers.

IBM Cloud Garage - The IBM Cloud Garage is a consultancy service that helps businesses accelerate their journey to the cloud. It provides expertise and guidance in application modernization, cloud adoption, and agile development practices.

Caveats and Considerations

While IBM Cloud offers a robust set of services, there are a few caveats and considerations to keep in mind:

Complexity - IBM Cloud's extensive range of offerings can sometimes lead to complexity, especially for beginners. It is important to carefully plan and understand the requirements before embarking on a project using IBM Cloud.

Pricing - Like other cloud service providers, IBM Cloud has a pricing structure that can be daunting to navigate. It is essential to thoroughly analyze the pricing details and choose the most cost-effective options for your specific needs.

Integration Challenges - Integrating IBM Cloud services with existing on-premises systems or other cloud platforms can present challenges. Proper planning and understanding of integration mechanisms are crucial to ensure a seamless integration experience.

Summary

IBM Cloud provides a comprehensive and innovative platform for businesses and developers to harness the power of cloud computing. With its versatile services, including AI, blockchain, serverless computing, and more, IBM Cloud empowers organizations to drive digital transformation and accelerate innovation. However, it is essential to consider the complexity, pricing, and integration challenges associated with IBM Cloud. By leveraging the provided resources and training, businesses can unlock the potential of IBM Cloud and stay ahead in the ever-evolving technological landscape.

The Fucking Titans of Cloud Computing

In the realm of cloud computing, there are a few major players who dominate the industry and have established themselves as the fucking titans of cloud computing. These companies have not only revolutionized the way we use and interact with technology, but they have also shaped the very landscape of cloud computing itself. In this section, we will take a closer look at four key cloud service providers: Amazon Web Services (AWS), Microsoft Azure, Google Cloud Platform (GCP), and IBM Cloud.

Amazon Web Services (AWS)

When it comes to cloud computing, Amazon Web Services (AWS) is undeniably the biggest badass on the block. Launched in 2006, AWS has grown to become the industry leader and the go-to platform for cloud services. With a comprehensive suite of over 200 services, AWS offers everything from computing power and storage to machine learning and analytics.

One of the reasons why AWS is such a fucking force to be reckoned with is its massive global infrastructure. AWS has a network of over 80 availability zones across 25 regions worldwide, allowing customers to deploy their applications closer to their end users and ensure high availability and low latency.

AWS offers a wide range of services, including Amazon Elastic Compute Cloud (EC2) for scalable virtual servers, Amazon Simple Storage Service (S3) for object storage, Amazon Relational Database Service (RDS) for managed relational databases, and Amazon Lambda for serverless computing.

Fucking remarkable, right? But here's something even cooler: AWS also has some truly innovative services in its arsenal. For example, Amazon Polly provides text-to-speech capabilities, Rekognition offers image and video analysis, and SageMaker allows you to build, train, and deploy machine learning models. AWS truly sets the bar high for cloud computing.

Microsoft Azure

Next up, we have Microsoft Azure, the cloud computing platform by the tech giant Microsoft. Azure may not have been the first to the game, but it has made significant strides to catch up with and challenge AWS.

With Azure, Microsoft brings its extensive experience in enterprise software and services to the cloud. Azure offers a robust set of services that spans computing, storage, databases, networking, and analytics. It also provides a seamless integration with other Microsoft products, such as Office 365 and Dynamics 365.

One of the key differentiators for Azure is its hybrid cloud capability. Azure allows you to seamlessly integrate your on-premises infrastructure with the cloud, providing the flexibility and scalability required by many organizations. This hybrid approach sets Azure apart from its competitors.

Azure offers services such as Azure Virtual Machines, Azure Blob Storage, Azure SQL Database, and Azure Functions for serverless computing. It also has its own AI and machine learning suite, including Azure Machine Learning and Azure Cognitive Services.

Overall, Azure is a fucking heavyweight contender in the cloud computing space, offering a robust set of services, hybrid capabilities, and seamless integration with the Microsoft ecosystem.

Google Cloud Platform (GCP)

When it comes to innovation and pushing the fucking boundaries of technology, Google Cloud Platform (GCP) is a true trailblazer. GCP leverages Google's extensive infrastructure and expertise in search, artificial intelligence, and data analytics to deliver a powerful cloud computing platform.

GCP provides a wide range of services, including virtual machines, storage, databases, networking, and big data analytics. What sets GCP apart is its focus on data and AI. GCP offers BigQuery, a fully managed, serverless data warehouse for analyzing massive datasets. It also provides Machine Learning Engine for training and deploying machine learning models, as well as an extensive suite of AI and natural language processing services.

But GCP doesn't stop there. It also boasts some interesting products like Google Kubernetes Engine for container orchestration, and Cloud Spanner, a globally distributed relational database service with strong consistency guarantees.

What really makes GCP shine is its dedication to sustainability. Google has been a leader in renewable energy investments, and GCP is committed to carbon neutrality. So not only can you harness the power of the cloud with GCP, but you can do it while fucking saving the planet. How cool is that?

IBM Cloud

Last but not least, we have IBM Cloud. While the aforementioned cloud service providers have dominated the market, IBM brings its own unique strengths and expertise to the cloud computing game.

IBM Cloud offers a wide array of services, including virtual servers, storage, databases, network solutions, and AI capabilities. One area where IBM differentiates itself is in its focus on security and compliance. IBM Cloud has achieved industry-leading certifications and provides robust security features to protect your data.

In addition to its standard cloud services, IBM cloud also offers some specialized services tailored to specific industries. For example, IBM Watson Health provides AI-driven solutions for healthcare, and IBM Blockchain Platform allows businesses to build and deploy blockchain networks.

IBM Cloud is also known for its strong support for open source technologies. It has actively contributed to projects such as Kubernetes and OpenStack, and provides a range of open source tools and frameworks for developers.

In summary, the fucking titans of cloud computing, AWS, Azure, GCP, and IBM Cloud, have established their dominance in the industry with their comprehensive suite of services, global infrastructure, and commitment to innovation. Each of these cloud service providers offers unique features and strengths, ensuring that customers have a wide range of options to choose from when it comes to deploying their applications in the cloud. So, pick your favorite fucking titan and conquer the world of cloud computing!

Cloud Migration Strategies

Lift and Shift

In the world of cloud computing, there are multiple strategies to migrate applications and workloads from on-premises infrastructure to the cloud. One of the most common strategies is known as "lift and shift." This approach involves moving existing applications, with minimal modifications, from a traditional on-premises environment to the cloud.

Understanding Lift and Shift

Lift and shift, also known as "rehosting," refers to the process of replicating the entire application stack, including the underlying infrastructure, onto a cloud platform. This strategy aims to achieve the migration quickly and with minimal changes to the existing application architecture. The goal is to take advantage of the scalability, flexibility, and cost-efficiency of the cloud without significant re-architecting or rewriting of the application.

In this approach, the application is lifted from its current environment and shifted or transplanted to the cloud. The underlying infrastructure, including servers, storage, and networking, is recreated in a cloud environment that best suits the organization's needs. This migration can be achieved using Infrastructure as a Service (IaaS) offerings provided by cloud service providers.

Benefits and Challenges

Benefits The lift and shift strategy offers several benefits, making it a popular choice for organizations looking to migrate their applications to the cloud:

- **Speed and simplicity**: Lift and shift migrations can be executed quickly, allowing organizations to take advantage of cloud benefits sooner rather than later. The process involves replicating the existing infrastructure and applications as-is, reducing the need for extensive modifications or rewrites.

- **Minimal disruption and risk**: With the lift and shift approach, the application's functionality remains largely unchanged. This minimizes the potential disruptions to business operations and reduces the risk of introducing new bugs or issues caused by major code changes.

- **Cost-effective scalability**: By migrating to the cloud, organizations can leverage the scalability and elasticity offered by cloud service providers. They can easily scale resources up or down based on demand, without the need to overprovision or manage on-premises infrastructure.

- **Access to cloud services:** By moving to the cloud, organizations gain access to a wide range of cloud services and capabilities offered by the cloud service provider. These services can help enhance application functionality, improve performance, and enable additional features that were not available in the on-premises environment.

Challenges While lift and shift offers numerous advantages, there are also challenges and considerations that organizations must address:

- **Compatibility and portability:** Not all applications are suitable for a lift and shift approach, especially if they have strong dependencies on the underlying infrastructure. Applications that are tightly coupled to physical servers or specific operating systems may require additional modifications or re-architecting.

- **Performance optimization:** Moving an application as-is to the cloud does not automatically guarantee optimal performance. Organizations may need to optimize the application, adjust resource allocations, or utilize cloud-native services to achieve desired performance levels.

- **Cost management:** While scalability is a significant advantage of the cloud, it can also lead to unexpected costs if not managed properly. Organizations must carefully monitor and manage resource usage to avoid unnecessary expenses.

- **Security and compliance:** Organizations need to assess the security and compliance implications of moving their applications to the cloud. They must ensure that appropriate security measures and compliance requirements are in place to protect data and meet regulatory obligations.

Real-World Example

Let's consider a real-world example of a retail organization that wants to migrate its on-premises e-commerce application to the cloud using the lift and shift strategy. The application includes a web server, a database server, and a storage server.

In this case, the organization would replicate the entire infrastructure stack onto a cloud platform, such as Amazon Web Services (AWS), including the virtual machines for the web server, the database server, and the storage server. The organization would also configure the necessary networking components to establish connectivity between these servers.

Once the infrastructure is set up, the organization would migrate the application code, configurations, and data onto the respective servers in the cloud environment. The final step would involve validating and testing the application to ensure that it functions correctly in the new cloud environment.

Resources and Best Practices

To successfully execute a lift and shift migration, organizations should consider the following best practices:

- **Thorough assessment and planning:** Before initiating the migration, organizations should conduct a comprehensive assessment of their existing applications to determine their suitability for lift and shift. This assessment should also include an evaluation of the cloud service provider's offerings, capabilities, and costs.

- **Dependency analysis:** Organizations should identify and document any dependencies between applications and underlying infrastructure elements. This analysis helps ensure that all necessary components are migrated together and that the application functions properly in the cloud environment.

- **Capacity planning:** Organizations should carefully analyze resource requirements to ensure that the cloud environment provides sufficient capacity for the migrated application. This involves considering factors such as compute, storage, and network requirements.

- **Testing and validation:** Before fully transitioning to the cloud, organizations should thoroughly test the migrated application to ensure that it operates as expected. This testing phase allows organizations to identify and address any compatibility issues or performance bottlenecks.

- **Ongoing management and optimization:** Once the application is successfully migrated, organizations should regularly monitor and optimize the cloud environment to ensure cost-effectiveness, performance, and security.

CLOUD MIGRATION STRATEGIES

Several resources can assist organizations in planning and executing a lift and shift migration:

- Cloud service provider documentation: Cloud service providers, such as AWS, Microsoft Azure, and Google Cloud Platform, offer comprehensive documentation, guides, and tutorials to help organizations understand and implement lift and shift migrations.

- Community forums and online communities: Online platforms provide opportunities to connect with experts and peers, allowing organizations to seek guidance, share experiences, and learn from others who have implemented lift and shift migrations.

- Consulting and professional services: Organizations can also seek the help of consulting firms or cloud service provider partners who specialize in cloud migrations. These experts can provide valuable insights, assistance, and guidance throughout the migration process.

Unconventional Tip

An unconventional tip for a successful lift and shift migration is to consider using automated tools and scripts to streamline the migration process. These tools can help identify dependencies, automate the provisioning of cloud resources, and ensure consistency throughout the migration. By leveraging automation, organizations can save time, reduce the risk of human errors, and achieve a smoother migration to the cloud.

Summary

Lift and shift, or rehosting, is a common migration strategy in cloud computing where organizations move their applications from on-premises infrastructure to the cloud without significant modifications. This approach allows organizations to quickly take advantage of the scalability, flexibility, and cost-efficiency offered by cloud service providers. While lift and shift offers numerous benefits, such as speed, simplicity, and cost-effective scalability, organizations must also consider challenges related to compatibility, performance optimization, cost management, and security. Thorough assessment, planning, and testing are essential for a successful lift and shift migration. By following best practices, utilizing available resources, and considering automated tools, organizations can navigate the lift and shift strategy to migrate their applications to the cloud effectively.

Replatforming

Replatforming is a strategy used in cloud migration that involves moving an application or system from one cloud platform to another. It is often chosen when the current platform no longer meets the needs of the organization or when there are better options available.

Understanding Replatforming

Replatforming differs from a lift and shift migration, where the focus is on simply moving the application to the cloud without significant changes. With replatforming, the goal is to optimize the application for the new cloud environment, taking advantage of the platform's features and capabilities.

The replatforming process typically involves making modifications to the application to align it with the new platform's requirements and best practices. This may include making changes to the architecture, infrastructure components, and application code.

Benefits of Replatforming

Replatforming offers several benefits over a lift and shift migration. By optimizing the application for the new platform, organizations can leverage the platform's native features and services, leading to improved performance, scalability, and cost-efficiency.

One of the key advantages of replatforming is the ability to take advantage of platform-specific services. For example, if an organization is moving from an on-premises environment to a cloud platform like AWS, they can leverage services like Amazon RDS for managed database instances or Amazon S3 for scalable object storage.

Replatforming also provides an opportunity to modernize the application's architecture and design. Organizations can adopt modern cloud-native patterns and approaches such as microservices, serverless computing, and event-driven architectures. This can result in improved flexibility, agility, and innovation.

Challenges of Replatforming

While replatforming offers many benefits, it is not without its challenges. One of the main challenges is the complexity involved in modifying the application to be compatible with the new platform. This may require significant development effort and expertise in the target platform.

Another challenge is ensuring a seamless transition during the replatforming process. Organizations must carefully plan and execute the migration to avoid any disruption to the business. This may involve testing the application in the new environment, ensuring data compatibility, and addressing any dependencies or integrations with other systems.

Replatforming Strategies

There are different strategies organizations can employ when replatforming their applications. The choice of strategy depends on factors such as the complexity of the application, the extent of modifications required, and the timeline for the migration.

One common replatforming strategy is a gradual migration, where the application is moved to the new platform in stages. This allows for a step-by-step approach, reducing the risk of disruption and enabling organizations to address any issues as they arise.

Another strategy is to use a hybrid approach, where certain components of the application are moved to the new platform while others remain in the existing environment. This can be useful when there are dependencies or integrations that need to be maintained with on-premises systems.

Example: Replatforming a Web Application

Let's consider an example of replatforming a web application that is currently hosted on a traditional server infrastructure. The organization wants to take advantage of the scalability and flexibility offered by a cloud platform like Google Cloud Platform (GCP).

In this case, the replatforming process would involve analyzing the application's architecture and infrastructure requirements. The organization would then modify the application to be compatible with GCP, making any necessary changes to the code and configuring the application to leverage GCP's services.

For example, the organization may choose to replatform the application using containers and deploy it on Google Kubernetes Engine (GKE). This would involve containerizing the application, creating Kubernetes manifests, and configuring GKE to auto-scale the application based on demand.

During the migration, the organization would test the application in the GCP environment to ensure it functions correctly and meets performance requirements. They would also consider data migration, making sure that any persistent data is properly transferred to GCP's storage services.

Throughout the replatforming process, the organization would closely monitor the application's performance and make any necessary adjustments or optimizations. This iterative approach allows for continuous improvement and fine-tuning of the application on the new platform.

Further Resources

Replatforming can be a complex process, but with proper planning and execution, organizations can reap the benefits of a modern and optimized cloud platform. For further reading on replatforming and cloud migration strategies, the following resources are recommended:

- "Cloud Migration Best Practices: A Guide to Successful Cloud Transition" by Amazon Web Services

- "Replatform: Moving the Organization to a Modern Architecture" by Adrian Cockcroft

- "Google Cloud Platform for Architects: Replatforming on Google Cloud Platform" by Vitthal Srinivasan

Key Takeaways

- Replatforming involves moving an application from one cloud platform to another with the goal of optimizing it for the new platform.

- Replatforming offers benefits such as leveraging native platform features, improving performance and scalability, and enabling modernization.

- Challenges of replatforming include the complexity of modifying the application and ensuring a seamless transition.

- Organizations can employ strategies like gradual migration or hybrid approaches when replatforming their applications.

- A real-world example of replatforming involves moving a web application from traditional server infrastructure to a cloud platform like GCP.

And that's replatforming, my friends! Now you have the knowledge to tackle the migration challenges and conquer the cloud with style. So go out there and replatform like a goddamn pro!

Refactoring

In the world of cloud computing, refactoring refers to a process of restructuring existing software applications or systems to optimize their performance and take advantage of the capabilities offered by cloud platforms. It involves making changes to the code, architecture, and design of an application to make it more efficient, scalable, and cost-effective in a cloud environment.

Why Refactor?

Refactoring is essential in cloud computing because it allows organizations to leverage the full potential of the cloud and adapt their applications to the changing needs of their business. By refactoring, developers can eliminate technical debt, reduce complexity, improve maintainability, and enhance the overall performance of their applications.

When applications are moved to the cloud without any modifications, they may not fully utilize the cloud platform's features, resulting in suboptimal performance and increased costs. Refactoring helps address these issues by redesigning the applications to take advantage of cloud-native services, auto-scaling capabilities, and other cloud-specific features.

Principles of Refactoring

Refactoring follows a set of principles aimed at improving the quality, efficiency, and reliability of an application. These principles include:

1. Identify Bottlenecks: Evaluate the performance bottlenecks and limitations of the existing system that can be addressed through refactoring. This could include inefficient code, database queries, or resource utilization.

2. Define Goals: Clearly outline the goals of the refactoring process, such as improving scalability, optimizing resource utilization, or reducing latency.

3. Break Down Monolithic Structures: Refactor monolithic applications into microservices or smaller components, making them more modular and easier to manage.

4. Leverage Cloud Services: Identify cloud-native services that can replace or enhance existing functionalities. For example, replacing in-house databases with managed database services or using serverless functions for specific tasks.

5. Enhance Scalability: Design applications to be scalable by incorporating auto-scaling capabilities and dynamically allocating resources as needed.

6. Optimize Resource Utilization: Analyze resource usage patterns and optimize the allocation of cloud resources to minimize costs while ensuring optimal performance.

7. Ensure Data Consistency and Availability: Implement appropriate strategies to ensure data consistency and availability in distributed environments, such as using distributed caches or data replication mechanisms.

Refactoring Strategies

There are several strategies and techniques that can be employed during the refactoring process. Here are a few commonly used ones:

1. Database Refactoring: Migrate from a relational database to a NoSQL database or leverage cloud-native database services such as Amazon RDS or Azure SQL Database for improved scalability and performance.

2. Application Restructuring: Break down monolithic applications into smaller microservices that can be independently deployed, scaled, and managed.

3. Caching Optimization: Implement caching mechanisms to reduce database queries and improve response times. Use distributed caching systems like Redis or Memcached to improve performance in a distributed environment.

4. Use of Serverless Functions: Identify specific functions or tasks within an application that can be separated and transformed into serverless functions, reducing the need for managing infrastructure and allowing for more efficient resource utilization.

5. Code Optimization: Analyze and optimize code for performance, eliminating unnecessary computations, improving algorithms, and reducing resource consumption.

Refactoring Example: E-Commerce Application

To illustrate the process of refactoring, let's consider an example of an e-commerce application that wants to migrate to a cloud platform.

The application currently runs on a traditional server infrastructure and consists of a monolithic architecture. It experiences occasional performance issues during peak periods and lacks the flexibility to scale dynamically.

During the refactoring process, the following steps could be taken:

1. Decoupling Modules: Identify different functionalities of the application and break them down into separate microservices. For example, create separate microservices for inventory management, order processing, and payment processing.

2. Database Migration: Migrate the central database to a cloud-native database service like Amazon Aurora or Google Cloud Spanner, providing scalability and performance improvements.

3. Caching Optimization: Implement a distributed caching mechanism using Redis or a cloud-native caching service to improve response times and reduce database load.

4. Serverless Functions: Identify non-core functions in the application, such as image processing or email notifications, and convert them into serverless functions to improve resource utilization and reduce costs.

5. Auto-Scaling: Design the application to auto-scale based on demand to handle peak loads efficiently. Utilize cloud provider's auto-scaling capabilities to add or remove resources dynamically.

By refactoring the e-commerce application, businesses can realize benefits such as improved scalability, better performance, reduced costs, and increased flexibility in managing resources.

Caveats and Considerations

While refactoring offers numerous benefits, it is important to consider some caveats and challenges:

1. Time and Effort: Refactoring an application requires time, effort, and careful planning. It is essential to allocate sufficient resources for a successful refactoring process.

2. Impact on Production Systems: Refactoring can have an impact on the production environment, requiring proper testing and validation to ensure a smooth transition.

3. Compatibility Issues: Compatibility issues may arise when integrating with cloud-native services or third-party APIs. Ensure thorough testing and consider backward compatibility when making changes.

4. Cost Optimization: While refactoring can lead to cost savings, it is important to avoid over-optimizing and analyze the trade-offs between performance improvements and associated costs.

Overall, refactoring is a crucial step in the migration to the cloud. By applying the principles and strategies mentioned above, organizations can unlock the full potential of cloud computing and build applications that are optimized for scalability, performance, and cost-efficiency.

Resources

- Fowler, M. (1999). Refactoring: Improving the Design of Existing Code. Addison-Wesley Professional.
- Newman, S. (2015). Building Microservices: Designing Fine-Grained Systems. O'Reilly Media.
- "Refactoring to Microservices." Martin Fowler. Available at: https://martinfowler.com/articles/refactoring-microservice-architectures.html
- "Refactoring Databases: Evolutionary Database Design." Scott W. Ambler and Pramod Sadalage. Available at: https://www.amazon.com/Refactoring-Databases-Evolutionary-paperback-Addison-Wesl
- YouTube: "Microservices Refactoring Patterns" - Microsoft Azure. Available at: https://www.youtube.com/watch?v=244M9nzA8Os
- "Best Practices for Optimizing Refactoring" - Amazon Web Services. Available at: https://aws.amazon.com/whitepapers/best-practices-for-optimizing-refactoring/

Exercise

Consider a legacy web application that is currently hosted on a dedicated server. The application experiences high traffic and occasional downtime during peak periods.

Design a refactoring plan for migrating the application to a cloud environment. Consider the following aspects:
- Identify the monolithic components that can be separated into microservices.
- Choose appropriate cloud-native services for database management, caching, and scaling.
- Outline the steps to optimize the application code and improve performance.
- Consider strategies for cost optimization and resource utilization.

Present your refactoring plan with associated diagrams, explaining each step and justifying your choices.

Retiring

Retiring is one of the strategies involved in cloud migration where an organization decides to completely eliminate a particular application or service from their IT infrastructure. It's like the final farewell party for an application that has served its purpose or is no longer relevant in the ever-changing technology landscape. You retire an application when it is no longer needed or when there are better alternatives available.

The retirement process involves a series of steps to ensure a smooth transition and minimize any impact on the business operations. Let's take a closer look at each step and understand the considerations involved:

Step 1: Identify the Application or Service to Retire

The first step in the retirement process is to identify the specific application or service that will be retired. This requires a thorough assessment of the organization's IT landscape and consultation with relevant stakeholders. It is important to evaluate the usage, functionality, and dependencies of the application to determine its retirement feasibility.

Step 2: Communication and Stakeholder Engagement

Once the application or service to be retired has been identified, it is crucial to communicate this decision to all relevant stakeholders. This includes users, IT teams, management, and any other parties involved in the application's lifecycle. Clear communication helps manage expectations and ensures everyone is aware of the retirement plan and its implications.

Step 3: Data Backup and Archiving

Before retiring an application, it is essential to securely backup and archive any data associated with the application. This step ensures the preservation of valuable information and supports compliance requirements. The data backup and archiving process should adhere to industry best practices and include proper encryption and access controls.

Step 4: Terminating Dependencies and Integrations

Applications often have dependencies and integrations with other systems or services. Therefore, it is necessary to identify and terminate these dependencies before retiring the application. Failure to address dependencies properly can lead to issues like broken business processes and data inconsistency. Organizations should carefully review all integrations to determine their impact on other systems and plan alternatives if necessary.

Step 5: Avoiding Orphaned Data and Resources

During the retirement process, organizations must ensure that no data or resources are left stranded or forgotten. Orphaned data and resources can pose security risks and consume unnecessary storage or computing resources. It is crucial to conduct thorough audits and verify that all associated data and resources have been properly migrated, archived, or deleted.

Step 6: Evaluate Financial and Legal Considerations

Retiring an application may have financial and legal implications, depending on the contractual agreements or regulatory requirements. It is essential to review any legal obligations, such as data privacy or vendor contracts, to ensure compliance. Additionally, organizations should assess the financial impact of retiring the application, considering factors like cost savings or the need for alternative solutions.

Step 7: Monitor and Evaluate the Retirement Process

Even after the retirement process is completed, it is crucial to monitor and evaluate the impact of the decision. This includes assessing user feedback, monitoring key performance indicators, and verifying if any unforeseen issues arise from the retirement. This feedback loop enables organizations to continuously improve their retirement strategies and learn from the process.

Example Scenario: Retirement of Legacy Email System

Let's consider an example scenario of retiring a legacy email system in favor of a cloud-based email service. The organization has decided to retire the old system due to its outdated technology, limited features, and high maintenance costs.

In this case, the first step involves identifying the legacy email system as the application to retire. The IT team communicates this decision to all stakeholders, including employees who rely on email for communication.

To ensure data preservation, the IT team performs a backup of all email accounts and archives historical emails securely. They also terminate any dependencies or integrations with other systems, such as calendar synchronization or data connections with CRM software.

To avoid orphaned data, the team conducts a thorough audit of the legacy email system and ensures all accounts and associated data are either migrated to the new cloud-based email service or archived for long-term retention.

During the retirement process, the organization reviews any legal requirements, such as data privacy regulations, and ensures compliance with all applicable laws.

Once the retirement process is completed, the IT team monitors user feedback and evaluates key performance indicators, such as user satisfaction and system reliability. This feedback helps identify areas for improvement and validates the successful retirement of the legacy email system.

Final Thoughts

Retiring an application or service is a significant decision that requires careful planning and execution. It allows organizations to streamline their IT infrastructure, reduce costs, and embrace modern technologies. However, it is essential to consider the impact on stakeholders, data preservation, and compliance requirements throughout the retirement process. By following a well-defined retirement strategy, organizations can ensure a smooth transition and pave the way for future innovations.

Now that we understand the retirement process, let's explore another strategy in cloud migration: refactoring.

The Fucking Journey to the Cloud

The journey to the cloud is an adventure that many organizations embark on to modernize their IT infrastructure and reap the benefits of cloud computing. It involves careful planning, strategic decision-making, and a whole lot of fucking hard work. In this section, we will explore the different strategies and considerations involved in this journey, along with some real-world examples to help you understand the process.

Assessing Readiness

Before you begin your journey to the cloud, it's important to assess your organization's readiness for this transformation. This involves evaluating your current IT infrastructure, applications, and data to determine what can be migrated to the cloud and what needs to be updated or restructured.

One approach to assessing readiness is the Cloud Readiness Assessment Framework (CRAF), which helps organizations evaluate their readiness across various dimensions, including technology, people, processes, and governance. The CRAF provides a structured methodology for identifying gaps and prioritizing areas for improvement.

For example, let's consider a fictional company called TechCo, which is looking to migrate its existing on-premises infrastructure to the cloud. As part of their readiness assessment, TechCo conducts a thorough inventory of their hardware, software, and applications. They also assess their team's skill sets and identify any gaps in cloud expertise. By doing so, TechCo gains a clear understanding of their current state and can develop a roadmap for their cloud journey.

Defining the Cloud Strategy

Once you've assessed your organization's readiness, it's time to define your cloud strategy. This involves setting clear goals, determining the scope of your cloud adoption, and selecting the most suitable cloud service model and deployment model for your needs.

Goals of cloud adoption can vary depending on the organization. Some common goals include cost reduction, scalability, agility, and improved customer experience. For example, a retail company may adopt the cloud to scale their e-commerce platform during peak shopping seasons or to provide a personalized and seamless customer experience across channels.

When selecting a cloud service model, you have three options to choose from: Infrastructure as a Service (IaaS), Platform as a Service (PaaS), and Software as a Service (SaaS). The choice depends on the level of control and responsibility you want to have over your IT infrastructure and applications.

For example, let's say TechCo wants to focus on developing their own applications without worrying about the underlying infrastructure. In this case, they would opt for PaaS, which provides a ready-to-use platform for application development and deployment.

Additionally, you need to consider the most suitable cloud deployment model for your organization. The options include public cloud, private cloud, hybrid cloud, and community cloud. Each model has its own advantages and considerations related to security, compliance, and control.

For instance, a healthcare organization may choose a hybrid cloud approach to securely store patient data on a private cloud while leveraging the scalability and cost-efficiency of a public cloud for non-sensitive applications.

Building a Cloud Migration Plan

Once you have defined your cloud strategy, it's time to create a detailed migration plan. This plan outlines the steps involved in migrating your applications, databases, and infrastructure to the cloud while minimizing disruption and ensuring data integrity.

A key consideration in building a migration plan is selecting the right migration approach. The approach can vary based on factors such as application complexity, dependencies, and criticality. Common migration approaches include lift and shift, replatforming, refactoring, and retiring.

For example, TechCo decides to start with a lift and shift approach for their initial cloud migration. They replicate their existing on-premises infrastructure in the cloud without making any significant changes to the applications. This allows them to quickly migrate to the cloud and benefit from increased scalability and flexibility.

During the migration process, it's important to conduct thorough testing to identify and mitigate any issues. This includes testing the performance, functionality, and security of your applications in the cloud environment. Additionally, you need to establish clear communication channels with your stakeholders to manage expectations and address any concerns.

Managing Change and Adoption

The journey to the cloud is not just about technical implementation. It also involves managing change and fostering a culture of cloud adoption within your organization. This requires effective communication, training, and support for your teams.

One approach to managing change is the ADKAR model, which stands for Awareness, Desire, Knowledge, Ability, and Reinforcement. This model provides a framework to understand and address the psychological and behavioral aspects of change.

For example, TechCo conducts training sessions and workshops to raise awareness about the benefits of cloud computing and to create a desire for cloud adoption among their employees. They also provide ongoing support and resources to help their teams acquire the knowledge and skills needed to work effectively in the cloud.

Additionally, it's important to establish governance and monitoring mechanisms to ensure compliance, security, and cost optimization in the cloud. This includes defining policies, implementing access controls, and leveraging monitoring and analytics tools to track usage, performance, and costs.

Real-World Examples

To illustrate the journey to the cloud, let's look at a couple of real-world examples:

- **Netflix:** Netflix, a popular streaming service, migrated its infrastructure to the cloud to support its massive user base and to enable global content delivery. By leveraging the scalability and elasticity of the cloud, Netflix can handle the fluctuating demand for streaming content and ensure a seamless viewing experience for its subscribers.

- **Capital One:** Capital One, a financial services company, embarked on a cloud journey to modernize its IT infrastructure and accelerate innovation. By adopting a hybrid cloud approach, Capital One achieved cost savings, enhanced agility, and improved customer experiences. They migrated critical applications and data to the cloud while leveraging on-premises infrastructure for sensitive and regulated workloads.

These examples highlight the diverse range of organizations and industries that can benefit from the journey to the cloud.

Key Takeaways

In this section, we explored the fucking journey to the cloud, covering the various steps and considerations involved. We learned about the importance of assessing readiness, defining a cloud strategy, building a migration plan, managing change and adoption, and the real-world examples of organizations that have successfully embarked on this journey.

The cloud journey is not a one-size-fits-all approach. It requires careful planning, a deep understanding of your organization's needs, and a commitment to continuous learning and improvement. By embracing the cloud, organizations can unlock the full potential of modern technology, drive innovation, and stay ahead in an ever-changing digital landscape.

So fuck it, get ready to embrace the cloud and conquer the fucking world!

Resources

1. Fuck the Cloud: A Comprehensive Guide to Cloud Computing (Herkimer Throckmorton, 2022)

2. Cloud Adoption Framework: Assessing Your Cloud Readiness (Microsoft, fuckin.com)

3. The Journey to Cloud - A Practical Guide (Amazon Web Services, fuckawsonline.com)

4. The Phoenix Project: A Novel About IT, DevOps, and Helping Your Business Win by Gene Kim, Kevin Behr, and George Spafford

DEVOPS AND CONTINUOUS INTEGRATION/CONTINUOUS DEPLOYMENT (CI/CD)

Exercises

1. Assess the readiness of your organization for cloud adoption using the Cloud Readiness Assessment Framework. Identify areas for improvement and develop a roadmap for your cloud journey.

2. Imagine you are the IT manager of a retail company. Define your cloud strategy, including goals, service model, and deployment model. Justify your choices based on the specific needs of your organization.

3. Using the lift and shift migration approach, plan the migration of an on-premises application to a public cloud platform of your choice. Consider factors such as dependencies, scalability, and security.

4. Develop a change management plan for migrating a critical business application to the cloud. Identify the potential challenges and risks associated with change and propose strategies to overcome them.

5. Research and analyze a real-world case study of a company that has successfully migrated to the cloud. Evaluate the impact of cloud adoption on their business and identify the key factors contributing to their success.

Remember, the cloud journey is not just a technical undertaking. It requires a mindset shift, collaboration, and continuous improvement. So embrace the challenges, learn from the fuck-ups, and enjoy the fucking journey to the cloud!

DevOps and Continuous Integration/Continuous Deployment (CI/CD)

Principles of DevOps

In this section, we will explore the principles of DevOps and how they contribute to the successful implementation of cloud computing. DevOps is a methodology that emphasizes collaboration, communication, and integration between development and operations teams. By breaking down silos and fostering a culture of continuous improvement, organizations can achieve faster delivery of software and services, improved reliability, and increased efficiency.

Background

The concept of DevOps emerged in response to the growing demand for agility and speed in software development and deployment. Traditionally, development and operations teams have operated separately, leading to bottlenecks, delays, and discrepancies between the two departments. DevOps aims to eliminate these inefficiencies by promoting a set of principles that enable seamless collaboration and integration.

The Three Ways

The Three Ways of DevOps, as introduced by Gene Kim in his book "The Phoenix Project," serve as a foundation for understanding the core principles of DevOps. Let's take a closer look at each of these ways:

1. The First Way: Systems Thinking

The First Way emphasizes a holistic approach to software development and delivery. It entails understanding the entire value stream, from idea to production, and optimizing it for flow, feedback, and continuous improvement. By focusing on the end-to-end process and identifying bottlenecks, waste, and dependencies, organizations can streamline their operations and deliver value to customers more effectively.

For example, consider a company developing a new mobile application. Instead of solely focusing on writing code, the First Way encourages teams to consider how the application will be deployed, monitored, and maintained in production. By involving operations early in the development process, potential issues can be identified and resolved upfront, reducing the likelihood of critical failures in production.

2. The Second Way: Amplify Feedback Loops

The Second Way revolves around creating fast and reliable feedback loops throughout the development and deployment cycle. Feedback loops enable teams to gather valuable insights, detect problems, and make informed decisions. By shortening the feedback loops, organizations can iterate quickly, learn from failures, and continuously improve their processes and products.

For instance, suppose a team is deploying a new version of a web application to a production environment. By implementing automated tests and continuous integration, the team can quickly identify any defects or regressions. This timely feedback allows them to address issues promptly, reducing the time and effort required for troubleshooting and resolving problems.

3. The Third Way: Culture of Experimentation and Learning

The Third Way emphasizes creating a culture that encourages experimentation, learning, and innovation. It involves fostering an environment where individuals can take risks, explore new ideas, and learn from both successes and failures. By promoting a growth mindset, organizations can drive continuous learning and improvement.

For example, imagine a company adopting a new infrastructure-as-code approach to manage their cloud resources. Instead of sticking to traditional methods, the Third Way encourages teams to experiment with new tools, techniques, and automation frameworks. Through experimentation, they can uncover more efficient and scalable solutions, leading to better resource utilization and enhanced performance.

Continuous Integration/Continuous Deployment (CI/CD)

To implement the principles of DevOps effectively, organizations often embrace continuous integration/continuous deployment (CI/CD) practices. CI/CD is a software development approach that combines automated testing, continuous integration, and continuous deployment to ensure the rapid, reliable, and frequent delivery of software updates and enhancements.

Continuous Integration

Continuous integration involves automatically integrating code changes from multiple developers into a shared repository. By doing so, integration issues and conflicts can be identified and resolved early in the development process. Continuous integration relies on automated build processes, version control systems, and automated testing to maintain the integrity and stability of the codebase.

For example, consider a team of developers working on a web application. Each developer contributes code to a central repository multiple times a day. Through automated build and testing processes, the team can detect and rectify any compatibility or integration issues promptly. This ensures that the codebase remains functional and ready for deployment at any given time.

Continuous Deployment

Continuous deployment takes continuous integration a step further by automating the release and deployment of code changes to production environments. The goal is to enable rapid, reliable, and low-risk software releases. Continuous deployment relies on extensive automation, testing, monitoring, and rollback strategies to ensure the stability and reliability of the software.

For instance, imagine a team working on a mobile application. With continuous deployment in place, every successful code change triggers an automated release and deployment process. Through extensive testing and monitoring, the team can minimize the risk of introducing critical issues into the production environment. If any issues arise, automated rollback mechanisms ensure that the application can be reverted to a stable state quickly.

Infrastructure as Code (IaC)

Infrastructure as Code (IaC) is a fundamental concept in DevOps that treats infrastructure configuration and management as code. With IaC, infrastructure components such as servers, networks, and databases are defined and provisioned using declarative configuration files. This approach enables organizations to automate and version their infrastructure, leading to improved consistency, scalability, and efficiency.

Benefits of IaC

Implementing IaC brings several benefits to organizations:

- **Version control:** Infrastructure configurations can be stored in version control systems, allowing teams to track changes, review history, and roll back to previous versions if necessary.

- **Reproducibility:** IaC enables the replication of infrastructure across environments, ensuring consistency and eliminating manual configuration errors.

- **Scalability:** With IaC, scaling infrastructure resources up or down becomes easier and more efficient, as the infrastructure definitions can be adjusted programmatically.

- **Automation:** IaC promotes the automation of infrastructure deployment and management, reducing errors and increasing operational efficiency.

Tools for IaC

There are various tools available for implementing IaC, including:

- **Terraform:** Terraform is a widely adopted open-source tool that enables infrastructure provisioning across different cloud providers using a simple declarative language.

- **AWS CloudFormation:** AWS CloudFormation is a service provided by Amazon Web Services (AWS) that allows you to define and provision infrastructure resources in a template file.

- **Azure Resource Manager:** Azure Resource Manager is a service provided by Microsoft Azure that enables infrastructure provisioning and management using JSON or YAML templates.

IaC Best Practices

To make the most of IaC, it is essential to follow some best practices:

- **Modularity:** Break infrastructure configurations into reusable modules, promoting consistency and reducing duplication.

- **Testing:** Implement automated testing of infrastructure configurations to validate their integrity and ensure they meet the desired requirements.

- **Documentation:** Maintain clear and up-to-date documentation of infrastructure configurations, making it easier for team members to understand and modify them if needed.

- **Collaboration:** Leverage version control systems and collaboration platforms to enable seamless collaboration and versioning of infrastructure configurations.

Monitoring and Logging

Monitoring and logging play a crucial role in ensuring the stability, performance, and availability of cloud services. By monitoring key metrics and logging relevant events, organizations gain insights into the health of their systems, identify issues, and proactively respond to potential incidents.

Monitoring

Monitoring involves collecting, analyzing, and visualizing various metrics and logs to gain visibility into the behavior and performance of systems and applications. It helps organizations identify trends, anomalies, and areas for optimization.

- **Key Metrics:** Organizations should monitor metrics such as response time, throughput, error rates, and resource utilization to assess the performance and reliability of their systems.

- **Alerting and Notification:** Establishing alerting mechanisms allows teams to be notified promptly when specific conditions or thresholds are met, enabling them to take immediate action.

- **Continuous Improvement:** By analyzing monitoring data, organizations can identify bottlenecks, inefficiencies, and areas for optimization, driving continuous improvement.

Logging

Logging involves capturing, storing, and analyzing events and logs generated by systems and applications. Logs provide detailed information about the behavior, state, and interactions within the system, aiding in troubleshooting, debugging, and compliance.

- **Structured Logs:** Structured log formats, such as JSON or key-value pairs, provide meaningful and machine-readable information that enables efficient log analysis and processing.

- **Centralized Log Management:** Aggregating logs from multiple systems into a centralized platform simplifies log retrieval, searching, and analysis.

- **Log Retention:** Organizations should define log retention policies that balance the need for historical analysis with storage costs and compliance requirements.

Troubleshooting and Incident Response

Monitoring and logging are integral to effective troubleshooting and incident response. By correlating monitoring data and analyzing logs, organizations can quickly identify the root cause of issues and respond accordingly.

- **Troubleshooting Process:** Establish a systematic approach to troubleshooting, including gathering relevant data, analyzing logs and metrics, and identifying potential causes.

- **Incident Response:** Develop predefined procedures and playbooks for incident response to ensure a consistent and efficient response to critical events.

- **Post-Incident Analysis:** Conduct post-incident analysis to learn from failures, improve processes, and prevent similar incidents in the future.

Conclusion

The principles of DevOps, such as Systems Thinking, Amplify Feedback Loops, and Culture of Experimentation and Learning, provide organizations with a framework for achieving seamless collaboration, continuous improvement, and efficient software delivery. By embracing DevOps principles and practices like continuous integration/continuous deployment and infrastructure as code, organizations can unlock the full potential of cloud computing and drive innovation in the digital landscape.

In the next section, we will explore cloud cost management strategies and techniques to optimize cloud spending and maximize return on investment. Let's delve into the world of cloud cost control, where we'll unveil the secrets to keeping your cloud expenses in check.

CI/CD Pipelines

CI/CD (Continuous Integration/Continuous Deployment) pipelines are essential in modern cloud computing environments. They provide a streamlined approach for developing, testing, and releasing software applications. In this section, we will dive deep into the principles, components, and practices of CI/CD pipelines.

Definition and Purpose

CI/CD pipelines are a set of automated processes that enable developers to integrate code changes, build applications, run tests, and deploy software to production environments rapidly and consistently. The primary goal of CI/CD is to eliminate manual steps and ensure the delivery of high-quality applications in an efficient, reliable, and repeatable manner.

Key Components

A typical CI/CD pipeline consists of several key components, each performing a specific task to support the software development lifecycle. Let's take a closer look at these components:

- **Source Code Repository:** This is where the application's source code is stored, version-controlled, and managed. Git, for example, is a popular distributed version control system used by many development teams.

- **Build System:** The build system compiles the source code, resolves dependencies, and generates executable artifacts. Tools like Maven, Gradle, and Ant are commonly used for building applications in various programming languages.

- **Testing Framework:** Testing is a crucial aspect of the CI/CD pipeline. It includes unit tests, integration tests, and end-to-end tests that validate the correctness and functionality of the application. Frameworks like JUnit, Selenium, and Cucumber support different types of testing.

- **Artifact Repository:** The artifact repository is a storage location where the compiled binaries, libraries, and other build artifacts are stored. Popular artifact repositories include Nexus, JFrog Artifactory, and Docker Registry.

- **Deployment Orchestrator:** This component manages the deployment process, configuring the infrastructure, provisioning resources, and orchestrating the deployment of the application to various environments.

- **Continuous Integration Server:** The CI server coordinates the different stages of the pipeline, automatically triggering builds, running tests, and generating reports. Jenkins, Travis CI, and GitLab CI/CD are popular CI server options.

CI/CD Practices

To ensure maximum efficiency and effectiveness, CI/CD pipelines follow several best practices. Let's discuss some of the key practices:

1. **Automated Build and Test Automation:** Every code change triggers an automated build process, ensuring that the application can be successfully compiled. Additionally, comprehensive test suites are executed automatically to catch any bugs or regressions.

2. **Version Control and Branching Strategy:** Effective version control and branching strategies enable teams to work collaboratively and manage code changes without conflicts. The widely used GitFlow approach allows for efficient feature development, bug fixing, and release management.

3. **Continuous Integration:** Developers frequently integrate their code changes into a central repository, triggering automated tests and builds. This practice greatly reduces integration issues, allowing teams to detect and fix issues early in the development cycle.

4. **Continuous Deployment:** Once the code changes pass all tests, they are automatically deployed to the production environment. This ensures that changes are rapidly and consistently released to end-users, reducing time-to-market and enabling continuous delivery of value.

5. **Infrastructure as Code (IaC):** The infrastructure, including servers, networks, and application dependencies, is provisioned and configured automatically using code-based definitions. Tools like Terraform and Ansible enable declarative infrastructure management, providing consistency and reproducibility.

6. **Monitoring and Alerting:** Continuous monitoring and alerting mechanisms are critical in ensuring application health and performance. Real-time metrics, logs, and alerts allow teams to detect and respond to issues promptly, improving overall system reliability.

Example Workflow

To illustrate the concept of CI/CD pipelines, let's consider an example workflow for a web application:

1. Developers write code changes and commit them to the Git repository.

2. The CI server automatically detects the code changes and triggers a build process.

3. The build system compiles the code, runs unit tests, and generates an executable artifact.

4. The artifact is stored in the artifact repository.

5. Automated integration tests are executed against the artifact to ensure its correctness.

6. If all tests pass, the application is deployed to a staging environment for further testing.

7. Manual or automated functional tests are performed in the staging environment.

8. Once the tests pass, the application is automatically deployed to the production environment.

9. Monitoring systems continuously monitor the application in production, providing feedback and alerting in case of any issues.

Throughout this workflow, the CI/CD pipeline ensures that the application is built, tested, and deployed automatically and consistently, allowing rapid and reliable software delivery.

Resources and Further Reading

To deepen your understanding of CI/CD pipelines, consider exploring the following resources:

- Books:

    - "Continuous Delivery: Reliable Software Releases through Build, Test, and Deployment Automation" by Jez Humble and David Farley.

    - "The DevOps Handbook: How to Create World-Class Agility, Reliability, and Security in Technology Organizations" by Gene Kim, Patrick Debois, John Willis, and Jez Humble.

- Websites and Blogs:

    - Atlassian's CI/CD Guide: https://www.atlassian.com/continuous-delivery/continuous-integration

    - ThoughtWorks' CI/CD Pipeline Guide: https://www.thoughtworks.com/continuous-integration-delivery-pipelines

    - Martin Fowler's CI/CD Article: https://martinfowler.com/articles/continuousIntegration.html

Remember, mastering CI/CD pipelines takes time and practice. Embrace the automation, collaboration, and continuous improvement mindset to unlock the full potential of your software development and deployment processes.

Before we move on to the next section, let's challenge ourselves with a practice exercise.

DEVOPS AND CONTINUOUS INTEGRATION/CONTINUOUS DEPLOYMENT (CI/CD)

Exercise: Setting up a CI/CD Pipeline

Imagine you are working on a team developing a microservices-based application. Your task is to set up a CI/CD pipeline using Jenkins as the CI server, Docker for containerization, and AWS Elastic Beanstalk for deployment.

Design and describe the steps involved in your CI/CD pipeline, including the integration, building, testing, and deployment processes. Consider how you would handle version control, automated tests, and rollback strategies. What additional tools or technologies would you incorporate into your pipeline to enhance its efficiency and reliability?

Take your time to brainstorm and document your solution. Once you're done, compare your approach with other team members or seek feedback from experienced professionals in the field.

Remember, the journey of writing a CI/CD pipeline starts with a single step!

Infrastructure as Code (IaC)

In the world of cloud computing, managing infrastructure can be a daunting task. Not only do you need to provision and configure servers, storage, and networking equipment, but you also have to ensure that they are properly maintained and can scale to meet the needs of your applications. This is where Infrastructure as Code (IaC) comes into play.

What is IaC?

At its core, Infrastructure as Code is the practice of managing and provisioning infrastructure resources through machine-readable configuration files, rather than manually configuring them. It allows you to describe your infrastructure using code, just like you would describe the behavior of a software application.

In the context of cloud computing, IaC enables you to define and control your entire infrastructure stack, including servers, storage, networking, and security settings, using declarative configuration files. These files can be versioned, shared, and reviewed, just like any other software code.

Why Use IaC?

Using IaC brings numerous benefits to cloud computing:

- **Consistency:** With IaC, you can ensure that your infrastructure is consistently provisioned and configured every time. You don't have to worry about manual errors or inconsistencies that can arise from human intervention.

- **Reproducibility:** Since your infrastructure is defined as code, you can easily reproduce it in different environments, such as development, testing, and production. This eliminates any potential discrepancies between environments and reduces the chances of unexpected issues.

- **Scalability:** IaC allows you to easily scale your infrastructure up or down in response to changing workload demands. You can define auto-scaling policies and let the code take care of the scaling process, ensuring your applications can handle varying levels of traffic without manual intervention.

Tools and Technologies

There is a wide range of tools and technologies available for implementing IaC. Here are some popular choices:

- **Terraform** - Terraform is an open-source IaC tool developed by HashiCorp. It provides a declarative language called HashiCorp Configuration Language (HCL) for defining infrastructure resources. Terraform supports a variety of cloud service providers, making it a versatile choice for managing infrastructure across different platforms.

- **AWS CloudFormation** - AWS CloudFormation is a service provided by Amazon Web Services (AWS) that allows you to define infrastructure resources as a CloudFormation template. It uses JSON or YAML syntax for creating stacks, which can be easily managed and updated using AWS tools and services.

- **Azure Resource Manager (ARM) Templates** - Azure Resource Manager is a service provided by Microsoft Azure for managing and provisioning Azure resources. ARM templates allow you to define infrastructure using a JSON or YAML-based declarative language. With ARM templates, you can deploy and manage resources as a single unit, making it easy to manage complex deployments.

These are just a few examples of the tools available for implementing IaC. Depending on your cloud provider and specific requirements, you may choose a different tool or technology.

Best Practices

When using IaC, it's important to follow best practices to ensure the successful implementation and management of your infrastructure. Here are some key practices to keep in mind:

- **Modularity:** Divide your infrastructure code into reusable modules and components. This allows for better organization, easier maintenance, and promotes code reusability across different projects or environments.

- **Version Control:** Just like traditional software code, your infrastructure code should be versioned using a version control system such as Git. This enables you to track changes, collaborate with others, and easily roll back to previous versions if needed.

- **Testing:** Implement testing practices for your infrastructure code to catch errors and misconfigurations before deploying to production. This can include automated tests to validate the correctness of your infrastructure definitions.

- **Documentation:** Document your infrastructure code to provide clarity and guidance for other team members. Include comments and annotations to explain the purpose of each resource and any specifics about their configuration.

Example: Provisioning a Web Application

To illustrate the power of IaC, let's consider an example of provisioning a web application in the cloud. We will use Terraform as the IaC tool of choice.

Assume we want to deploy a simple web application that consists of an Amazon EC2 instance, an Elastic Load Balancer, and a MySQL database. Using Terraform, we can define the infrastructure resources in a declarative manner:

```
resource ``aws_instance'' ``web'' {
  ami           = ``ami-XXXXX"
  instance_type = ``t2.micro"

  tags = {
    Name = ``web-instance"
  }
}
```

```
resource ``aws_elb'' ``web'' {
  name             = ``web-elb"
  availability_zones = ["us-east-1a", ``us-east-1b"]

  listener {
    instance_port     = 80
    instance_protocol = ``http"
    lb_port           = 80
    lb_protocol       = ``http"
  }
}

resource ``aws_db_instance'' ``web'' {
  engine         = ``mysql"
  instance_class = ``db.t2.micro"
  name           = ``web-db"
  username       = ``admin"
  password       = ``password"
}
```

In this example, we have defined an EC2 instance, an Elastic Load Balancer, and a MySQL database using Terraform's HCL syntax. We can then use the Terraform CLI to apply this configuration, which will create the specified resources in our cloud provider account.

By using IaC, we have eliminated the need for manual provisioning and configuration of these resources. We can simply update the code if we need to make changes and apply the configuration again to reflect those changes.

Conclusion

Infrastructure as Code is a powerful practice that allows you to treat your infrastructure like software code. By using IaC tools and following best practices, you can achieve consistency, reproducibility, and scalability in managing your cloud infrastructure. So, embrace the power of IaC and conquer the challenges of managing modern cloud deployments.

Remember, the cloud is your playground, and IaC is the magic wand that enables you to build, scale, and automate your infrastructure like a boss. So go forth, Code Masters, and conquer the world of cloud computing!

DEVOPS AND CONTINUOUS INTEGRATION/CONTINUOUS DEPLOYMENT (CI/CD)

Resources:

- Mitchell Hashimoto, Armon Dadgar. "Terraform: Up and Running." O'Reilly Media, 2017.
- AWS CloudFormation Documentation: https://aws.amazon.com/cloudformation/
- Azure Resource Manager Documentation: https://docs.microsoft.com/en-us/azure/azure-resource-manager/

Exercises:

1. Research and compare different IaC tools available in the market. Create a table listing their key features, supported cloud providers, and any limitations or caveats.
2. Set up a simple infrastructure using your chosen IaC tool. Try creating an EC2 instance, a load balancer, and a database. Test the provisioning process and make any necessary adjustments to the code.

Challenge:

Design an infrastructure using IaC that can automatically scale based on incoming traffic. Consider using serverless compute services and auto-scaling policies. Create a multi-tier architecture that can handle high loads and optimize cost efficiency. Provide a detailed diagram of your design and explain how all the components interact and scale dynamically.

Monitoring and Logging

In the world of cloud computing, monitoring and logging are essential practices to ensure the smooth operation and optimal performance of your systems. When dealing with complex and distributed architectures, it's crucial to have visibility into the health and behavior of your applications and infrastructure. This section will delve into the principles, tools, and best practices of monitoring and logging in the cloud.

Why Monitoring and Logging Matter

Monitoring involves the continuous observation of system components, such as servers, databases, networks, and applications, to detect any abnormalities or performance issues. It provides real-time insights into the health and availability of your resources, allowing you to detect and address problems before they impact your users.

Logging, on the other hand, involves the collection and storage of data related to system events, errors, and activities. It serves multiple purposes, including troubleshooting, debugging, compliance, and performance analysis. Logs provide a historical record of what happened in your system and can be invaluable in understanding and resolving issues.

Effective monitoring and logging practices can help you:

- **Real-time visibility**: Monitor the performance, availability, and utilization of your resources to ensure optimal operation.

- **Proactive issue detection**: Identify and address potential issues before they cause significant problems, minimizing downtime and user impact.

- **Troubleshooting and root cause analysis**: Use logs to analyze events leading up to an issue, helping you understand its root cause and take appropriate actions.

- **Capacity planning**: Monitor resource utilization over time to identify trends and plan for scaling or optimization.

- **Compliance and auditing**: Retain and analyze logs to meet regulatory requirements and perform security audits.

- **Performance optimization**: Analyze performance metrics to identify bottlenecks and optimize your system's efficiency.

Without monitoring and logging, you would be flying blind, unaware of critical issues and lacking the necessary data for analysis and improvement.

Monitoring Techniques

Monitoring in the cloud relies on a combination of infrastructure-level monitoring and application-level monitoring. Let's explore these techniques in more detail.

Infrastructure-level Monitoring Infrastructure-level monitoring focuses on the health and performance of your cloud infrastructure components, such as virtual machines, storage, and networks. It typically involves the following aspects:

- **Resource Monitoring:** Tracking resource utilization metrics like CPU, memory, disk space, and network traffic can help you identify performance bottlenecks, plan capacity, and optimize resource allocation.

- **Health Monitoring:** Checking the availability and responsiveness of your infrastructure elements ensures high availability and provides insights into potential issues. This can involve pinging servers, checking connectivity, or monitoring response times.

- **Alerting and Notification:** Setting up thresholds and alert triggers allows you to receive notifications when predefined conditions are met. For example, you might receive an alert when CPU usage goes above a certain threshold or when a server becomes unresponsive.

Cloud service providers offer built-in monitoring tools and APIs that facilitate infrastructure-level monitoring. For example, Amazon Web Services provides Amazon CloudWatch, Microsoft Azure has Azure Monitor, and Google Cloud Platform offers Stackdriver Monitoring.

Application-level Monitoring Application-level monitoring focuses on the performance and behavior of your applications and services. It involves measuring key performance indicators (KPIs) and collecting relevant data. Some of the common application-level monitoring techniques include:

- **Metrics and Tracing:** Collecting metrics on response times, throughput, error rates, and other application-specific metrics helps you monitor and optimize your application's performance. Tracing allows you to follow a request's journey through various components, enabling you to identify bottlenecks and optimize latency.

- **Log Aggregation:** Centralizing logs from different application components makes it easier to search, analyze, and extract valuable insights. Log aggregation tools, such as the Elastic Stack (Elasticsearch, Logstash, Kibana), Splunk, or CloudWatch Logs, provide scalable solutions for collecting, storing, and analyzing logs.

- **Distributed Tracing:** For highly distributed and microservices-based architectures, distributed tracing techniques, such as OpenTelemetry or Jaeger, enable you to track requests across services, even as they traverse different systems or components.

By combining infrastructure-level and application-level monitoring, you gain a comprehensive view of your system's health and performance, allowing you to make informed decisions and take necessary actions.

Log Management and Analysis

Logs play a crucial role in understanding system behavior, diagnosing issues, and ensuring compliance. However, managing and analyzing logs at scale can be challenging. Let's explore some best practices and tools for log management and analysis in the cloud.

Log Collection and Centralization To effectively manage logs, it's essential to centralize them in a scalable and searchable repository. This centralization allows you to aggregate logs from various sources, making it easier to analyze them collectively. Here are some common approaches to log collection and centralization:

- **Log Shippers:** Use log shippers like Filebeat, Fluentd, or Logstash to collect logs from different sources and forward them to a centralized location. These shippers support various log formats and integrations with popular log management systems.

- **Distributed Log Collection:** In highly distributed environments, deploying log collectors close to the log sources can help reduce network latency and improve scalability. Tools like Fluent Bit or Logagent enable efficient log collection in distributed architectures.

- **Log Management Systems:** Choose a suitable log management system that meets your requirements for scalability, searchability, and analysis capabilities. Popular options include Elasticsearch with Kibana (ELK Stack), Splunk, and Graylog.

By centralizing logs, you can easily access and analyze them, enabling effective troubleshooting, debugging, and compliance monitoring.

Log Analysis and Visualization Once you have centralized logs, the next step is to analyze and visualize the data to gain insights. Here are some techniques and tools for log analysis and visualization:

- **Search and Query:** Use query languages like Elasticsearch's Query DSL or Splunk's search language to search and filter logs based on specific criteria. These languages allow you to search for specific errors, patterns, or events of interest.

- **Dashboards and Alerts:** Create customizable dashboards in tools like Kibana or Splunk to visualize log data and track key metrics in real-time. Set up alerts based on predefined conditions to receive notifications when certain events occur.

- **Machine Learning-based Anomaly Detection:** Leverage machine learning algorithms to detect anomalies in log data automatically. These algorithms can learn normal patterns and behaviors, alerting you when abnormal events occur.

Log analysis and visualization give you the power to quickly identify issues, perform root cause analysis, and monitor system performance.

Challenges and Considerations

While monitoring and logging in the cloud offer immense benefits, there are several challenges and considerations to keep in mind:

Cost Management Monitoring and logging generate significant amounts of data, which can result in increased storage costs. It's crucial to balance the retention period and granularity of your logs with cost considerations. Define log retention policies and periodically review them to ensure cost-effective data storage.

Security and Compliance Monitoring and logging involve handling sensitive data. Ensure that appropriate security measures, such as encryption, access controls, and data protection mechanisms, are in place to protect your logs. Additionally, adhere to regulatory requirements and privacy standards when storing and analyzing logs.

Event Correlation and Noise Reduction When dealing with large-scale systems, logs from various components can generate an overwhelming amount of information. Implement mechanisms to correlate related events and reduce noise, enabling you to focus on critical events and abnormal behaviors.

Scaling and Performance   As your system grows, monitoring and logging must scale accordingly. Consider the scalability and performance limitations of your monitoring and logging tools, as they can impact the overall performance of your system.

Automation and Integration   Automating monitoring and logging processes can save time and effort. Use infrastructure-as-code tools, such as AWS CloudFormation or Terraform, to provision and configure monitoring resources consistently. Integrate monitoring and logging within your CI/CD pipelines to ensure continuous monitoring and feedback loops.

Conclusion

Monitoring and logging are critical practices in cloud computing that empower you to understand, troubleshoot, and optimize your systems. Through infrastructure-level monitoring, application-level monitoring, and effective log management, you gain insights into system health, performance, and behavior. By leveraging the right tools and best practices, you can ensure the smooth operation of your cloud-based applications, improve resource utilization, detect and mitigate issues, and deliver exceptional user experiences.

As you continue your cloud computing journey, be sure to embrace monitoring and logging as indispensable components of your overall cloud strategy.

The Fucking DevOps Revolution

In this section, we will dive into the exciting world of DevOps and explore how it has revolutionized the software development and deployment processes. DevOps, short for Development and Operations, aims to bridge the gap between software development and IT operations, fostering collaboration, efficiency, and continuous delivery of high-quality software applications. It's all about breaking down silos, tearing down walls, and getting shit done.

Principles of DevOps

DevOps is founded on a set of principles that guide its implementation and success. These principles, commonly referred to as the Three Ways of DevOps, provide a framework for achieving rapid, reliable, and scalable software delivery. Let's take a fucking look at them:

1. The First Way: Systems Thinking

DEVOPS AND CONTINUOUS INTEGRATION/CONTINUOUS DEPLOYMENT (CI/CD)

The First Way emphasizes the holistic view of the entire software delivery lifecycle. It encourages teams to understand the flow of work, identify bottlenecks, and optimize the end-to-end value stream. By focusing on the big picture and addressing systemic issues, we can eliminate waste, reduce lead time, and improve overall efficiency.

2. The Second Way: Amplify Feedback Loops

The Second Way emphasizes the importance of obtaining fast and frequent feedback to ensure continuous improvement. Through automated testing, monitoring, and telemetry, we can detect and rectify issues at the earliest possible stages. This enables us to deliver better software with fewer defects, enhancing customer satisfaction and loyalty. Feedback loops also foster a culture of collaboration, learning, and innovation.

3. The Third Way: Continual Experimentation and Learning

The Third Way embraces a culture of experimentation, iteration, and continuous learning. It encourages organizations to embrace failure as a means of learning and stay open to new ideas and solutions. By fostering a blameless culture and promoting knowledge sharing, we can create an environment that fosters innovation, creativity, and growth.

CI/CD Pipelines

Central to the DevOps revolution is the concept of Continuous Integration and Continuous Deployment (CI/CD) pipelines. CI/CD pipelines automate the software delivery process, enabling the rapid and reliable release of new features and bug fixes. These pipelines consist of a series of automated stages that build, test, and deploy applications. Let's explore each stage in the fucking pipeline:

1. Build

The build stage involves compiling and packaging the source code into executable artifacts. It ensures that the code is syntactically correct, compiles without errors, and adheres to coding standards. Automation tools, such as Jenkins or GitLab CI/CD, are commonly used to trigger the build process upon code changes and to handle build dependencies.

2. Test

The test stage involves running automated tests to verify the functionality and quality of the application. Different types of tests, such as unit tests, integration tests, and end-to-end tests, are conducted to catch bugs and ensure the application meets the specified requirements. Continuous testing helps identify issues early in the development process, preventing them from propagating further.

3. Deploy

The deploy stage involves the release and deployment of the application to a production environment or target server. This stage can vary depending on the architecture and infrastructure of the application. It may involve deploying to on-premises servers, virtual machines, or cloud-based platforms like AWS, Azure, or GCP.

4. Verify

The verify stage involves validating the deployed application to ensure it functions as intended in the production environment. It may include running additional tests or performing health checks to confirm that the application is working properly. Automated monitoring and logging tools help detect potential issues and enable fast troubleshooting.

5. Release

The release stage involves making the application available to end-users or customers. It may involve coordinating with marketing, support, and other business functions to ensure a smooth release process. Version control and tagging mechanisms are used to track and manage different versions of the application.

Infrastructure as Code (IaC)

Another crucial aspect of the DevOps revolution is Infrastructure as Code (IaC). IaC is an approach that enables the provisioning and management of infrastructure resources using code. Instead of manually configuring servers and network infrastructure, IaC allows us to define and maintain infrastructure configurations using declarative files. This offers numerous benefits:

1. Scalability and Consistency

IaC allows us to scale resources up or down as needed, ensuring optimal utilization while reducing costs. It also ensures that infrastructure configurations are consistent across different environments, eliminating potential issues due to configuration drift.

2. Version Control and Change Management

With IaC, infrastructure configurations and changes can be version controlled just like any other code. This provides a complete history of changes, making it easier to track and revert changes if necessary. It also enables collaboration and facilitates peer reviews.

3. Reproducibility and Automation

IaC enables the reproducibility of infrastructure setups across different environments, making it easier to create development, testing, and production environments that are identical. It also allows us to automate the provisioning and

DEVOPS AND CONTINUOUS INTEGRATION/CONTINUOUS DEPLOYMENT (CI/CD)

deployment of infrastructure, making it faster, more reliable, and less prone to errors.

Monitoring and Logging

Effective monitoring and logging are crucial components of a successful DevOps strategy. By monitoring application and infrastructure metrics, we can proactively identify performance bottlenecks, security vulnerabilities, and system failures. Logging enables us to capture and analyze application logs, aiding in troubleshooting, debugging, and auditing. Some key concepts and best fucking practices in monitoring and logging include:

1. Key Performance Indicators (KPIs)

Identifying the right KPIs helps us measure and track the health, performance, and efficiency of our applications and infrastructure. KPIs may include response time, error rate, resource utilization, and throughput. Dashboards and data visualization tools facilitate the monitoring and analysis of KPIs.

2. Alerting and Notifications

Setting up alerts based on predefined thresholds allows us to be promptly notified when abnormalities or critical events occur. This enables us to take immediate action to prevent or mitigate service disruptions. Alerting can be configured through integrated monitoring tools or custom scripts.

3. Log Aggregation and Analysis

Centralized log management systems, such as ELK Stack (Elasticsearch, Logstash, Kibana), help aggregate, index, and analyze logs from different sources. These tools provide powerful querying and filtering capabilities, making it easier to identify patterns, troubleshoot issues, and generate actionable insights.

4. Security Monitoring

Monitoring for security-related events and anomalies is vital for ensuring the integrity and security of our applications and systems. Intrusion detection systems, log analysis for security events, and regular vulnerability scanning are some key practices in security monitoring.

The Fucking DevOps Community

Embracing the DevOps revolution means joining a vast and vibrant community of practitioners, enthusiasts, and experts. The community offers a wealth of resources, knowledge sharing platforms, and best fucking practices to support and inspire your DevOps journey. Here are some valuable resources to explore:

1. DevOps Conferences and Events

Attending DevOps conferences and events, such as DockerCon, DevOpsDays, or AWS re:Invent, allows you to connect with industry leaders, learn from case studies and success stories, and stay up-to-date with the latest trends and technologies.

2. Online Communities and Forums

Engaging in online communities and forums, like Reddit's r/devops or Stack Overflow's DevOps tag, provides a platform to ask questions, share experiences, and seek advice from fellow DevOps practitioners. These communities often offer valuable insights, troubleshooting tips, and recommendations for tools and techniques.

3. Blogs and Publications

Following DevOps blogs and publications, such as The DevOps Handbook by Gene Kim, The Phoenix Project by Gene Kim and Kevin Behr, or publications from industry leaders like AWS, Microsoft, and Google, helps you stay informed about emerging practices, case studies, and thought leadership in the DevOps space.

4. Online Courses and Certifications

Completing online courses and earning certifications in DevOps-related domains, such as AWS Certified DevOps Engineer or Google Cloud Professional DevOps Engineer, demonstrates your expertise and commitment to continuous learning. Platforms like Udemy, Coursera, and A Cloud Guru offer a range of DevOps courses taught by industry experts.

Remember, in the DevOps community, sharing is caring. So, don't be afraid to contribute, ask questions, share your insights, and learn from others. Together, we can embrace the DevOps revolution and build a more efficient, reliable, and resilient software development ecosystem.

Exercises

Now that you've learned about the fucking DevOps revolution, it's time to put your knowledge into action. Here are some exercises to test your understanding:

1. Identify a bottleneck in a software delivery process you have experienced or read about. Apply the principles of DevOps to propose possible solutions to address the bottleneck.

2. Design a CI/CD pipeline for a web application. Consider the stages, tools, and practices necessary to ensure reliable and efficient software delivery.

3. Implement an IaC solution using a tool like Terraform or AWS CloudFormation. Provision and manage a cloud infrastructure resource, such as a virtual machine or a database, using code.

4. Build a monitoring and alerting system for a web application. Define key performance indicators, set up alerting rules, and implement a centralized logging solution.

5. Participate in a DevOps community or forum. Ask a question related to a challenge you are facing in your software delivery process and contribute to discussions by sharing your insights or experiences.

These exercises will not only help reinforce your understanding of the DevOps concepts and practices but also provide you with hands-on experience in implementing DevOps principles in real-world scenarios.

Additional Resources

To further explore the fucking DevOps revolution, here are some additional resources that you may find valuable:

- **Books**
    - "The DevOps Handbook: How to Create World-Class Agility, Reliability, and Security in Technology Organizations" by Gene Kim, Patrick Debois, John Willis, and Jez Humble
    - "Accelerate: The Science of Lean Software and DevOps: Building and Scaling High Performing Technology Organizations" by Nicole Forsgren, Jez Humble, and Gene Kim
    - "Site Reliability Engineering: How Google Runs Production Systems" by Betsy Beyer, Chris Jones, Jennifer Petoff, and Niall Richard Murphy

- **Websites**
    - `https://devops.com/` - DevOps.com, a leading online community and resource hub for DevOps professionals.
    - `https://cloudacademy.com/blog/category/devops/` - Cloud Academy Blog, featuring a wide range of DevOps-related articles, tutorials, and case studies.
    - `https://dev.to/` - Dev.to, an online community for programmers and developers, with a dedicated section for DevOps topics.

- **Tools**
    - **Jenkins** - A popular open-source automation server for building, testing, and deploying software projects.

- **GitLab CI/CD** - A complete DevOps platform that includes a built-in continuous integration and delivery system.

- **Terraform** - An infrastructure as code tool that allows you to define and manage cloud resources across multiple providers.

- **Prometheus** - An open-source monitoring and alerting toolkit that helps you capture and analyze time-series metrics.

- **ELK Stack** - An open-source log management stack that includes Elasticsearch, Logstash, and Kibana for centralized log analysis.

The DevOps revolution is ongoing, so stay curious, keep learning, and embrace the power of collaboration, automation, and continuous improvement. May the force of DevOps be with you!

Cloud Cost Management

Understanding Pricing Models

In the exciting realm of cloud computing, understanding pricing models is key to making informed decisions and optimizing costs for your cloud-based applications and services. In this section, we'll dive into the different pricing models offered by cloud service providers and explore their advantages, disadvantages, and real-world examples. So hold on tight, because we're about to navigate the treacherous waters of cloud pricing.

Pay-As-You-Go

One of the most common pricing models in the cloud computing world is the pay-as-you-go model. As the name suggests, you only pay for the resources you actually use. This model is ideal for workloads with variable demand and unpredictable usage patterns. For example, if you have an e-commerce website, you may experience higher traffic during the holiday season but lower traffic during other times of the year. With the pay-as-you-go model, you have the flexibility to scale up or down based on demand, and you're only charged for the resources you consume.

In this model, cloud service providers typically charge you based on the duration of resource usage. For example, with Amazon Web Services (AWS), you might be charged per hour for each instance of a virtual machine that you use.

Other resources, such as storage or data transfer, may be billed based on the amount of data you store or transfer.

The pay-as-you-go model is great for startups and small businesses, as it allows them to minimize upfront costs and scale their operations as they grow. However, it's important to monitor your usage regularly to avoid unexpected costs. A sudden spike in usage can result in a higher bill than anticipated. So, keep an eye on your usage and adjust your resources accordingly.

Reserved Instances

Another pricing model offered by cloud service providers is the reserved instances model. With this model, you commit to using a specific amount of cloud resources for a contracted duration, typically one to three years. In return for this commitment, you receive a significant discount compared to the pay-as-you-go rates. This model is ideal for workloads with a consistent, predictable demand.

Let's say you have a large e-commerce platform that requires a certain number of virtual machines to handle the incoming traffic. By reserving those instances for a specific period, you can save up to 75% compared to the pay-as-you-go rates. This can result in substantial cost savings over time.

However, keep in mind that reserved instances are less flexible than the pay-as-you-go model. If your workload decreases, you may end up paying for resources that you're no longer utilizing. On the other hand, if your workload increases beyond the reserved capacity, you may need to provision additional resources at the higher pay-as-you-go rates. It's crucial to strike the right balance and accurately forecast your resource requirements.

Spot Instances

For those with a sense of adventure and a willingness to embrace uncertainty, spot instances offer an intriguing pricing model. With this model, cloud service providers offer spare computing capacity at significantly reduced prices compared to the pay-as-you-go rates. However, there's a catch. Spot instances are available on a first-come, first-served basis, and the prices are determined by supply and demand.

Spot instances are excellent for workloads that can tolerate interruptions and don't require continuous availability. For example, if you're running a batch processing job that can be paused and resumed without significant impact, spot instances can be a cost-effective choice. You can save up to 90% compared to pay-as-you-go rates, but you need to be prepared for the possibility of your instances being reclaimed if the spot price rises above your bid price.

To make the most of spot instances, you need to carefully analyze historical price trends and bidding strategies. Cloud service providers often provide tools and APIs to help you automate the management of spot instances and optimize your bid prices. Keep in mind that spot instances are not suitable for all workloads, so make sure to evaluate their feasibility and potential risks before relying on them.

Resource Consumption Models

In addition to the above pricing models, some cloud service providers offer resource consumption models. These models allow you to purchase a certain amount of resources upfront at a discounted rate and consume them over time, similar to a prepaid plan.

This model is especially beneficial for workloads with steady resource consumption patterns. It offers cost savings by providing a discounted rate for the committed resources. For example, if you know that your application requires a specific amount of storage or compute capacity every month, you can purchase a resource consumption plan that matches your needs and enjoy significant savings compared to the pay-as-you-go rates.

Resource consumption models provide predictability and cost control, making them suitable for applications with well-defined resource requirements. However, they may not offer the same flexibility as other pricing models, so it's essential to carefully assess your workload's characteristics before committing to a resource consumption plan.

Hybrid and Custom Pricing Models

As the cloud computing landscape evolves, cloud service providers are introducing new pricing models to cater to specific needs. Hybrid pricing models, for example, offer flexibility by combining elements of different models. These models allow you to leverage both on-premises infrastructure and cloud resources, giving you the best of both worlds. With hybrid pricing, you can choose to pay for on-premises resources separately or integrate them into your overall cloud billing.

Cloud service providers also offer custom pricing models for organizations with unique requirements. This can include tailored pricing based on specific usage patterns, enterprise agreements, or special discounts for long-term commitments. Custom pricing models are typically negotiated directly with the cloud service provider, allowing you to optimize costs based on your specific needs.

Cloud Pricing Optimization

Now that you understand the various pricing models, it's essential to optimize your cloud costs by implementing cost management strategies. Here are a few tips to get you started:

- Monitor and analyze your resource usage regularly to identify opportunities for optimization.

- Leverage auto-scaling capabilities to dynamically adjust resources based on demand, minimizing both underutilization and overutilization.

- Utilize cloud cost management tools provided by cloud service providers to track and analyze your spending patterns.

- Consider using reserved instances for workloads with predictable usage and spot instances for flexible, non-critical workloads.

- Optimize your architecture and resource configurations to maximize efficiency and reduce costs.

By implementing these strategies, you'll be well on your way to maximizing cost savings and getting the most out of your cloud infrastructure.

Conclusion

Pricing models in the cloud computing world can be complex, but understanding them is crucial for optimizing costs and making informed decisions. Whether you choose the pay-as-you-go model for its flexibility, reserved instances for cost predictability, spot instances for cost savings, or custom pricing models for tailored solutions, there's a pricing model that suits your specific needs. By leveraging the right pricing model and implementing cost management strategies, you can conquer the challenges of cloud pricing and ensure that your resources are utilized efficiently and cost-effectively, ultimately leading to your cloud computing success.

So, my dear Gen-Z readers, go forth and conquer the world of cloud computing pricing like the badass cloud warriors that you are. While the pricing landscape may be ever-changing, armed with knowledge and a little bit of grit, you'll conquer the cost challenges and harness the full potential of the cloud. Now, let's continue our cloud journey and explore the exciting world of cloud infrastructure.

Cost Optimization Strategies

In the world of cloud computing, cost optimization is a crucial aspect that cannot be ignored. Organizations are always looking for ways to minimize their cloud expenses while maximizing the benefits and capabilities offered by cloud providers. In this section, we will explore various cost optimization strategies that can help you make the most out of your cloud investment.

Understanding Pricing Models

Before diving into cost optimization strategies, it's important to understand the pricing models offered by cloud service providers. Each provider has its own pricing structure, and understanding the nuances can help you make informed decisions.

1. **Pay-as-you-go** pricing: This model allows you to pay only for the resources you consume, typically on an hourly or per-minute basis.

2. **Reserved Instances (RIs)**: RIs provide a discounted pricing option for customers who commit to using a specific instance type and region for a predetermined period, usually one to three years. RIs can result in significant cost savings for workloads with predictable usage patterns.

3. **Spot Instances:** Spot instances allow you to bid on unused compute capacity, potentially offering significant cost savings. However, there is a risk of termination if the spot price exceeds your bid price.

4. **Savings Plans:** Savings Plans offer flexible pricing options for both compute and NoSQL database workloads, allowing you to save up to 72% compared to on-demand pricing.

5. **Managed Instance Groups:** In some cloud providers, you can leverage managed instance groups to automatically scale the number of instances based on demand. This dynamic scaling can optimize costs by ensuring you only pay for the resources you need at any given time.

It's important to regularly review your cloud resource usage and adjust your pricing model accordingly to find the best fit for your workload.

Cost Optimization Strategies

Now let's delve into some practical cost optimization strategies that can help you optimize your cloud spend.

1. **Rightsizing Instances:** Rightsizing involves matching your instance types and sizes to the actual resource requirements of your workload. By analyzing your usage patterns and performance metrics, you can identify instances that are

overprovisioned or underutilized. Downsizing or resizing these instances can lead to significant cost savings without sacrificing performance.

2. **Using Spot Instances:** Spot instances can be an excellent option for non-production workloads or workloads with flexible scheduling requirements. By leveraging spot instances, you can take advantage of unused compute capacity at heavily discounted prices. However, it's essential to have failover mechanisms in place to handle spot instance terminations.

3. **Implementing Auto Scaling:** Auto Scaling allows you to automatically adjust the number of instances based on demand. By scaling up during peak periods and scaling down during lower demand, you can eliminate wasted resources and reduce costs.

4. **Utilizing Reserved Instances:** For workloads with predictable usage patterns, purchasing Reserved Instances (RIs) can provide significant cost savings over on-demand pricing. Analyze your workload's long-term requirements to identify instances that can benefit from RI purchases.

5. **Applying Cost Tags and Resource Grouping:** Utilize cost tags provided by your cloud provider to accurately track resource costs. By tagging resources based on departments, projects, or applications, you can gain better visibility into cost distribution. Additionally, grouping resources that have similar characteristics can help optimize costs through efficient resource utilization and configuration.

6. **Monitor and Optimize Storage:** Regularly review and optimize your storage configurations. Remove any unnecessary files or objects, compress data when possible, and leverage lifecycle management policies to transition less frequently accessed data to lower-cost storage tiers.

7. **Implementing Serverless Architecture:** Serverless computing can provide significant cost savings by eliminating the need for provisioning and managing servers. Functions are executed on-demand, and you only pay for the compute resources used during that time.

8. **Analyzing and Reducing Data Transfer Costs:** Data transfer costs can quickly add up, especially when dealing with large volumes of data. Minimize unnecessary data transfers by optimizing data storage location, compressing data before transmission, and leveraging content delivery networks (CDNs) for efficient content distribution.

Tools and Best Practices

To support your cost optimization efforts, various tools and best practices are available:

1. **Cost Explorer and Budgets:** Leverage the cost management tools provided by your cloud provider, such as Cost Explorer and Budgets. These tools allow you to visualize and analyze your cloud expenses, set budget thresholds, and receive cost alerts.
2. **Monitoring and Logging:** Implement comprehensive monitoring and logging solutions to gain insight into your cloud resource usage, identify anomalies, and detect cost optimization opportunities.
3. **Infrastructure as Code (IaC):** Embrace Infrastructure as Code (IaC) principles by using frameworks like AWS CloudFormation or Azure Resource Manager. IaC allows you to define and provision your cloud infrastructure programmatically, making it easier to manage resources efficiently and avoid unnecessary costs.
4. **Continuous Cost Optimization:** Treat cost optimization as an ongoing process. Regularly review your usage patterns, adjust your infrastructure accordingly, and explore new pricing models and services offered by your cloud provider.

Real-World Example

Let's consider a real-world example to illustrate the effectiveness of cost optimization strategies.

Suppose a startup is developing a web application that experiences significant fluctuations in user traffic throughout the day. During peak hours, the application requires several instances to handle the load, while during off-peak hours, usage drops significantly.

To optimize costs, the startup decides to implement auto scaling for their compute resources. They set up policies to scale the instances based on CPU utilization. During peak hours, additional instances are launched to handle the increased traffic, ensuring optimal performance. Conversely, during off-peak hours, instances are scaled down to avoid unnecessary costs.

By implementing auto scaling, the startup can effectively reduce costs by paying only for the resources they need at any given time, rather than maintaining a fixed number of instances throughout the day.

Summary

Cost optimization is a critical aspect of cloud computing. Understanding the pricing models offered by cloud service providers, implementing effective strategies such as rightsizing instances, utilizing spot instances, and applying auto scaling can help you optimize costs while maintaining performance. Leveraging tools, best practices, and continuously monitoring your cloud resource usage will ensure ongoing cost optimization and maximize the value of your cloud investment. Remember, cost optimization is an iterative process that requires regular review and adjustment to stay on top of your cloud expenses. So get out there and conquer the cloud with your newfound cost optimization knowledge!

Budgeting and Cost Tracking Tools

Introduction

In the world of cloud computing, it's all about scalability, flexibility, and accessibility. But let's not forget about the bottom line! Budgeting and cost tracking are crucial aspects of managing your cloud resources effectively. In this section, we'll dive into the various tools and strategies that help you monitor and control your cloud costs. So, buckle up and get ready to tackle the financial side of the cloud!

Understanding Cloud Costs

Before we jump into the budgeting and cost tracking tools, it's important to understand the key factors that contribute to cloud costs. To effectively manage your expenses, you need to be aware of these factors and how they impact your bills. Here are a few things you should keep in mind:

Usage-based pricing

Unlike traditional IT infrastructure, cloud services typically follow a pay-as-you-go model. You only pay for the resources you use, which can be both a blessing and a curse. On the one hand, you have the freedom to scale your resources up and down as needed. On the other hand, if you're not careful, unexpected usage spikes can lead to skyrocketing costs.

Pricing models

Cloud service providers offer various pricing models to meet different needs. These models include on-demand pricing, reserved instances, and spot instances. Each comes with its own advantages and disadvantages.

On-demand pricing offers the flexibility to provision resources whenever you need them, but it tends to be the most expensive option. Reserved instances, on the other hand, require an upfront commitment but offer significantly lower prices for long-term usage. Spot instances allow you to bid on unused cloud capacity, offering potential cost savings, but there is a risk of termination if the price exceeds your bid.

Data transfer costs

One often overlooked aspect of cloud costs is data transfer. Transferring data into and out of the cloud can incur additional charges. This includes both incoming and outgoing traffic, so it's important to optimize your data transfer and choose the right pricing tier for your needs.

Budgeting Tools

Now that we have a clear understanding of the factors that influence cloud costs, let's explore the budgeting tools that can help you stay on top of your expenses.

Cloud cost calculators

Cloud service providers offer cost calculators that allow you to estimate your monthly bills based on your expected usage. These calculators take into account various parameters such as the number of instances, storage volumes, data transfer, and other services. They can be a useful starting point to get an idea of your potential costs before you actually deploy your applications.

Third-party cost management tools

In addition to the built-in cost calculators, many third-party tools specialize in cloud cost management. These tools provide more comprehensive analysis and reporting, allowing you to track your expenditure across multiple cloud providers and services. They often offer features such as granular cost breakdowns, cost allocation for different departments or projects, and alerts when costs exceed predefined thresholds.

Cost allocation tags

Cloud providers allow you to assign cost allocation tags to your resources. These tags act as metadata that help you categorize and track your costs based on different criteria, such as project, department, or application. By using cost allocation tags effectively, you can gain insights into the specific areas of your infrastructure that contribute the most to your bills, enabling you to optimize your spending.

Cost Tracking Tools

Budgeting is only the first step. The real challenge lies in tracking your actual costs and making data-driven decisions to optimize your expenditure. Here are some tools and techniques to help you with cost tracking:

Cloud provider billing dashboards

Cloud service providers offer detailed billing dashboards that provide an overview of your costs. These dashboards allow you to drill down into different service categories, visualize cost trends over time, and download cost reports. They often provide APIs that allow you to programmatically access the billing data, enabling integration with other cost tracking tools or custom analysis.

Real-time cost monitoring

To stay on top of your costs, it's important to monitor them in real-time. Many third-party tools provide real-time cost monitoring, allowing you to set up automated alerts when costs exceed certain thresholds. These tools can help you identify cost spikes and take immediate action to mitigate them.

Cost anomaly detection

In addition to real-time monitoring, some cost tracking tools leverage machine learning algorithms to detect cost anomalies. These algorithms analyze your historical cost data and identify abnormal patterns or unexpected shifts in spending. By proactively detecting anomalies, you can investigate and address potential cost inefficiencies or security vulnerabilities.

Cost Optimization Strategies

Now that you have the tools to budget and track your costs, let's explore some strategies to optimize your cloud spending:

Right-sizing your resources

One of the most effective ways to optimize costs is to right-size your resources. This means choosing the appropriate instance types, storage volumes, and networking configurations that meet your application's requirements without excessive over-provisioning. By regularly analyzing your resource utilization and making adjustments, you can eliminate wasted resources and reduce your bills.

Automated resource scheduling

Many applications have predictable usage patterns, with periods of high demand followed by periods of low or no activity. By leveraging automation tools and services, you can schedule your resources to turn on and off automatically based on these usage patterns. This allows you to save costs during idle periods and scale up when needed, without manual intervention.

Optimizing data transfer

As mentioned earlier, data transfer costs can add up quickly. To optimize these costs, you can leverage various techniques such as content caching, compression, and choosing the right pricing tier for your data transfer needs. Additionally, consolidating your data transfers and minimizing unnecessary data movement can help reduce costs.

Conclusion

Budgeting and cost tracking are essential for effectively managing your cloud expenses. By using the right tools and following cost optimization strategies, you can gain better control over your spending and ensure that the financial side of the cloud doesn't come as a nasty surprise. So, go ahead, embrace the power of the cloud, but always keep an eye on your wallet!

Reserved Instances and Spot Instances

In cloud computing, one of the key considerations is cost optimization. As companies migrate their workloads to the cloud, they need to find ways to reduce their expenses and make the most efficient use of resources. This is where reserved instances and spot instances come into play.

Understanding Reserved Instances

Reserved instances (RIs) are a pricing model offered by cloud service providers that allow customers to reserve compute capacity for a longer-term commitment, typically one to three years. By making this commitment, customers can significantly reduce their costs compared to on-demand instances.

When purchasing a reserved instance, customers have the option to choose between different payment models:

- **All Upfront Payment:** Customers pay the entire cost of the reservation upfront, resulting in the highest discount.

- **Partial Upfront Payment:** Customers pay a portion of the cost upfront and the remaining balance is paid in monthly installments.

- **No Upfront Payment:** Customers pay no upfront costs but commit to a higher monthly payment.

The savings achieved with reserved instances can be substantial, with discounts ranging from 30% to 75% compared to on-demand pricing. This allows businesses to optimize costs for their predictable workloads that require long-term or consistent usage.

Spot Instances: Cost Optimization through Flexibility

While reserved instances provide cost savings for long-term commitments, spot instances take a different approach to cost optimization by offering spare cloud capacity at significantly discounted prices.

Spot instances are available on a "price bidding" model, where customers bid on the hourly rate they are willing to pay for the instance. The spot price fluctuates depending on supply and demand, and customers are allocated instances as long as their bid exceeds the current spot price.

Spot instances are ideal for workloads that are flexible and can handle interruptions or sudden termination. Examples include batch processing, data analysis, and workload testing. By utilizing spot instances, businesses can achieve cost savings of up to 90% compared to on-demand instances.

Effective Use of Reserved and Spot Instances

To maximize cost savings and achieve a balance between reliability and affordability, businesses can employ various strategies:

- **Reserve Instances for Stable Workloads:** Reserved instances are best suited for predictable workloads that have consistent usage patterns. By reserving capacity for these workloads, businesses can realize substantial cost savings.

- **Spot Instances for Low-Priority Workloads:** Low-priority or non-essential workloads can be assigned to spot instances, taking advantage of the steep cost discounts. These workloads may experience interruptions but can be designed to handle them gracefully.

- **Combining RIs and Spot Instances:** By using a combination of reserved instances and spot instances, businesses can strike a balance between cost optimization and reliability. Reserved instances can handle the critical workloads, while spot instances can supplement capacity during peak usage or handle less critical tasks.

- **Monitoring and Automation:** To make the most of spot instances, businesses should monitor spot pricing and automatically adjust their bidding strategy to ensure they remain below the current spot price. Automation tools can help businesses optimize their usage and reduce costs further.

Real-World Example: Media Streaming Service

Let's consider the example of a popular media streaming service that experiences peak demand during evenings and weekends when users stream their favorite movies and TV shows. To handle this increased demand, the streaming service typically uses a combination of reserved instances and spot instances.

The reserved instances are used to handle the baseline load and ensure consistent availability and reliability. These instances are reserved well in advance to secure the capacity required.

During peak usage hours, the streaming service dynamically scales its infrastructure using spot instances. By bidding on spot instances, they are able to add additional capacity at highly discounted prices. However, the infrastructure is designed to gracefully handle the termination of spot instances, as it does not impact the service's overall availability.

This combination of reserved and spot instances allows the streaming service to optimize costs while maintaining a high-quality streaming experience for its users.

Caveats and Considerations

When using spot instances, there are some caveats and considerations to keep in mind:

- **Potential Interruptions:** Spot instances can be terminated with little to no notice if the spot price exceeds the bidder's maximum bid. Applications running on spot instances should be designed to gracefully handle interruptions, ensuring minimal impact on overall operations.

- **Spot Price Volatility:** Spot prices are determined by supply and demand, which can lead to price fluctuations. Businesses should monitor spot pricing trends to make informed bidding decisions and adjust bidding strategies accordingly.

- **Trade-off between Cost and Reliability:** While spot instances offer significant cost savings, they come with a trade-off in terms of reliability. Critical workloads that require guaranteed availability and stability should be assigned to reserved instances or a combination of reserved instances and spot instances.

Conclusion

Reserved instances and spot instances are two powerful mechanisms for cost optimization in cloud computing. By reserving capacity for predictable workloads and leveraging spare capacity at discounted prices, businesses can achieve substantial cost savings while maintaining the necessary flexibility and reliability.

It is important for businesses to understand their workload requirements, monitor pricing trends, and adopt strategies that strike the right balance between cost optimization and performance. With proper planning and utilization, reserved and spot instances can be valuable tools in harnessing the full potential of cloud computing.

Additional Resources

For further exploration of reserved instances and spot instances, the following resources may be helpful:

- AWS Reserved Instances Documentation: *https://docs.aws.amazon.com/AWSEC2/latest/UserGuide/reserved-instances.html*
- Google Cloud Preemptible VMs Documentation: *https://cloud.google.com/preemptible-vms*
- Azure Spot Virtual Machines Documentation: *https://docs.microsoft.com/en-us/azure/virtual-machines/spot-vms*

Exercises

1. Consider a web application that experiences a sudden surge in traffic during a specific time of the day. How can you leverage reserved instances and spot instances to optimize costs and handle the increased demand?

2. Research and compare the pricing models for reserved instances across different cloud service providers. How do they differ in terms of upfront payment options and associated discounts?

3. Analyze your own workload demands and identify potential candidates for spot instances. Discuss how you would design your application to handle spot instance interruptions.

BUDGETING AND COST TRACKING TOOLS

Remember, understanding the nuances of reserved instances and spot instances can greatly impact your cloud computing costs. Keep exploring and experimenting to find the optimal mix for your specific use case!

The Fucking Art of Cost Control

In the world of cloud computing, managing costs is a critical skill that can make or break a project. It's not just about the initial investment or the monthly bill, it's about optimizing resources, avoiding unnecessary expenses, and making smart decisions that align with your budget. Welcome to the fucking art of cost control in the cloud!

Understanding Pricing Models

Before diving into cost control strategies, it's important to understand the various pricing models offered by cloud service providers. These models determine how you pay for the resources you use, and they can have a significant impact on your costs.

Pay-As-You-Go The pay-as-you-go model, also known as on-demand pricing, is the most flexible but usually the most expensive option. With this model, you pay for the resources you consume on an hourly or per-second basis. It's a great choice for short-term or unpredictable workloads, but it can quickly add up if you're not careful.

Reserved Instances Reserved Instances let you reserve capacity for a fixed period, usually one to three years. By committing to a longer-term contract, you can save up to 70% compared to on-demand pricing. This model is ideal for workloads with predictable usage patterns or for applications that require sustained usage.

Spot Instances Spot Instances allow you to bid for unused computing capacity in the cloud. The prices are variable and can fluctuate based on supply and demand. While this model can result in significant cost savings, there's a risk of interruption if the spot price exceeds your bid. It's a good fit for workloads that can handle interruptions or for non-critical tasks.

Savings Plans Savings Plans provide flexibility similar to reserved instances but without the need for upfront payments or long-term commitments. They offer lower prices in exchange for a usage commitment, allowing you to save up to 72% compared to on-demand pricing. This model is well-suited for workloads with consistent usage but doesn't require reservations.

Compute Engine Compute Engine provides virtual machines (VMs) with predefined machine types and extended usage discounts. It offers committed use discounts, where you commit to use specific capacity for one or three years, or sustained use discounts, where you automatically get discounted rates for using instances for the majority of a month.

Cost Optimization Strategies

Now that you're familiar with the pricing models, let's explore some effective cost optimization strategies that can help you maximize your cloud budget without compromising on performance.

Right-Sizing One of the most fundamental cost optimization strategies is right-sizing your resources. This involves selecting compute instance sizes and storage options that align with your workload requirements. By choosing the right resource specifications, you can avoid overprovisioning and underutilization, leading to cost savings.

To determine the optimal size, monitor your resource utilization and performance metrics. Tools like AWS Trusted Advisor, Azure Advisor, and Google Cloud's Cost Optimization Explorer can provide insights into resource utilization and recommend right-sizing opportunities.

Auto Scaling Auto Scaling allows you to automatically adjust the number of compute instances based on demand. By dynamically scaling up during peak periods and scaling down during off-peak periods, you can ensure that you're only paying for the resources you need.

Implementing auto scaling requires defining scaling policies, which are rules that determine when and how to scale. These policies can be based on metrics like CPU utilization, network traffic, or custom application-level metrics. By setting up auto scaling, you can optimize your costs without sacrificing performance or availability.

Idle Resource Monitoring Idle resources can be a significant source of wasted costs. Identify and monitor resources that are consistently idle or underutilized. This includes compute instances, databases, and storage volumes that are not actively used.

Consider terminating or pausing idle resources when they're not needed. Schedule scripts or use automation tools to automatically shut down instances during periods of inactivity. By actively managing idle resources, you can reduce costs and make more efficient use of your cloud environment.

BUDGETING AND COST TRACKING TOOLS

Spot Instances and Spot Fleets Take advantage of the Spot Instances pricing model for workloads that can tolerate interruptions. Spot Instances offer significant cost savings, especially for non-critical or fault-tolerant applications.

Spot Fleets allow you to provision a mixture of On-Demand and Spot Instances within a single fleet. By using Spot Fleets, you can combine the cost savings of Spot Instances with the reliability of On-Demand Instances. This hybrid approach can optimize costs while maintaining high availability.

Data Transfer Optimization Data transfer costs can add up, especially if you have a large volume of inbound or outbound traffic. To optimize data transfer costs, consider the following strategies:

- Use content delivery networks (CDNs) to cache and deliver static content closer to end-users, reducing the amount of data transferred over long distances.

- Leverage compression techniques to reduce the size of data transferred over the network.

- Take advantage of cloud provider-specific options for free or reduced-cost data transfer between cloud services within the same region or availability zone.

By optimizing data transfer, you can minimize costs while ensuring optimal performance for your users.

Budgeting and Cost Tracking Tools

Tracking costs and staying within your budget is essential for effective cost control. Cloud service providers offer various budgeting and cost tracking tools that can help you monitor your spending and take proactive steps to manage costs.

AWS Budgets AWS Budgets allows you to set custom cost and usage budgets and receive alerts when your actual or forecasted costs exceed the specified thresholds. You can also set up automatic actions, such as sending notifications or triggering AWS Lambda functions, to proactively control your spending.

Azure Cost Management Azure Cost Management provides cost tracking and optimization capabilities across your Azure subscriptions. It offers budgeting features, cost reporting, and recommendations to help you identify cost-saving opportunities and optimize your resource usage.

Google Cloud Billing   Google Cloud Billing offers cost management solutions that help you monitor, analyze, and control your costs. It provides budget alerts, usage reports, and insights into your spending patterns. You can also use Google Cloud's Pricing Calculator to estimate costs before provisioning resources.

By leveraging these budgeting and cost tracking tools, you can gain visibility into your spending and take proactive measures to control costs.

The Fucking Art Made Practical

Now that we've covered the theory and strategies behind cost control in the cloud, let's explore a real-world scenario to put the fucking art into practice.

Scenario: E-commerce Application   You're working on an e-commerce application hosted on a cloud platform, and you want to optimize costs while maintaining performance and availability. Here's how you can apply the cost control strategies we discussed:

- Right-size your compute instances based on the application's resource requirements. Monitor CPU and memory utilization to ensure you're not overprovisioning or underutilizing resources.

- Implement auto scaling to dynamically adjust the number of instances based on demand. Scale up during peak periods, such as promotional campaigns or holiday seasons, and scale down during quieter periods.

- Identify and terminate idle resources, such as test or development instances, during non-working hours to save costs.

- Consider using Spot Instances for non-critical tasks, such as background processing or image rendering. Leverage Spot Fleets to combine Spot Instances with On-Demand Instances for fault-tolerant and cost-efficient workloads.

- Optimize data transfer by using CDNs to cache and deliver static content. Compress data and take advantage of cloud provider-specific data transfer options for reduced-cost or free transfers.

- Set up cost and usage budgets using the cloud provider's budgeting tools. Receive alerts when you approach or exceed your defined thresholds, and take appropriate actions to control spending.

BUDGETING AND COST TRACKING TOOLS

By implementing these strategies and continually monitoring and optimizing your resources, you can strike a balance between cost control and performance for your e-commerce application.

Caveat: Hidden Costs   While cost control is essential, it's important to be aware of potential hidden costs that may not be immediately apparent. Examples of hidden costs include:

- Data transfer costs between availability zones or regions within the same cloud provider.

- Ingress and egress costs for cloud storage services.

- Additional fees for premium support, extended service level agreements (SLAs), or specific service features.

Be sure to review the cloud provider's pricing documentation thoroughly and consider potential hidden costs when estimating and managing your budget.

Conclusion

Congratulations, you've mastered the fucking art of cost control in the cloud! By understanding the different pricing models, implementing cost optimization strategies, leveraging budgeting and cost tracking tools, and considering real-world scenarios, you're equipped to effectively manage your cloud costs and make informed decisions that align with your budgetary constraints.

Remember, cost control is an ongoing process. Regularly evaluate your resource utilization, monitor costs, and adjust your strategies as needed. With the right approach, you can conquer the cloud and keep your finances in check.

Recommended Resources

- FreeCodeCamp: "Control your AWS bill with these cost-saving techniques"

- YouTube: "AWS Reinvent 2019: Cost Optimization at Scale"

- Google Cloud Blog: "5 steps to better GCP cost management"

- Microsoft Docs: "Optimize costs in Azure"

Disaster Recovery and High Availability

Backup and Restore

In the fast-paced world of cloud computing, data is king. Businesses rely on their data for critical operations, and losing that data can be catastrophic. That's where backup and restore processes come into play. These processes ensure that data can be safely stored and retrieved in the event of an unexpected failure or disaster. In this section, we'll dive into the world of backup and restore in cloud computing and explore the best practices and strategies that can help you protect your valuable data.

Understanding Backup

Backup is the process of creating copies of data to ensure its availability and integrity. The primary goal of backup is to have a duplicate set of data that can be used to restore systems and applications in the event of data loss or corruption. Backup strategies can vary depending on the size and complexity of the data, the criticality of the systems, and the desired recovery time objectives (RTO) and recovery point objectives (RPO).

Backup Types

There are several types of backups commonly used in cloud computing:

1. Full Backup: This type of backup creates a copy of all data in the system. It provides a complete restoration point, but it can be time-consuming and resource-intensive.

2. Incremental Backup: In incremental backup, only the changes made since the last backup are saved. This approach reduces backup time and storage requirements but requires the previous full backup and all subsequent incremental backups to restore data completely.

3. Differential Backup: Differential backup captures the changes made since the last full backup. Unlike incremental backup, differential backup does not rely on previous backups, making it faster to restore data.

4. Snapshot: A snapshot provides a point-in-time copy of data. It captures the entire system state and can be used to revert to a specific configuration or recover from user errors. Snapshots are commonly used in virtualized environments and provide a quick restore option.

It's crucial to carefully select the appropriate backup type based on your specific requirements, considering factors such as data size, RPO, and RTO.

Backup Strategies

When designing a backup strategy for your cloud infrastructure, it's essential to consider factors such as cost, performance, and data protection. Here are some commonly used backup strategies:

1. On-Premises Backup: In this strategy, backups are stored in local storage systems within your premises. While it provides complete control over the data, it can be limited in terms of scalability and disaster recovery capabilities.

2. Cloud Backup: Cloud backup involves storing backups in remote cloud storage services provided by cloud service providers (CSPs). It offers flexibility, scalability, and off-site data protection. CSPs often offer managed backup services, taking care of backup administration, monitoring, and maintenance.

3. Hybrid Backup: The hybrid backup strategy combines both on-premises and cloud backup. It allows for faster data recovery from on-premises backups while leveraging cloud storage for off-site data protection and disaster recovery.

The choice of backup strategy depends on factors such as data sensitivity, compliance requirements, and budgetary constraints. It's crucial to assess your specific needs and consult with experts to determine the most effective strategy for your organization.

Restore Process

The restore process involves recovering data from backups and returning it to its original or desired state. The speed and reliability of the restore process are critical, especially during critical incidents or unplanned outages. Here are the key steps involved in the restore process:

1. Identify the Backup: Determine which backup contains the required data and select the appropriate backup source. It's essential to maintain accurate records of backups, including timestamps and descriptions, to facilitate easy identification.

2. Prepare the Environment: Set up the necessary infrastructure, such as servers, networking, and storage, to restore the data. Ensure that the environment matches the original or desired state.

3. Data Restoration: Copy the backup data to the appropriate location and restore it to the target systems. This step might involve transferring large volumes of data, so network bandwidth and data transfer speeds are crucial factors to consider.

4. Data Validation: Verify the integrity of the restored data and ensure that it matches the expected state. Data validation processes, such as checksum verification, can help identify any potential data corruption or loss during the restore process.

5. Testing and Verification: Once the data is restored, ensure that the systems and applications function correctly. Conduct comprehensive testing to validate the restore process and confirm that data is accessible and usable.

It is worth mentioning that backup and restore processes should be periodically tested to ensure their effectiveness. Regular testing helps identify any potential issues and allows for necessary adjustments and improvements.

Backup and Restore Best Practices

To ensure a robust backup and restore strategy, consider the following best practices:

- **Identify Critical Data**: Prioritize the backup of critical data that is essential for business operations. Identifying and classifying data based on its criticality can help allocate resources effectively.

- **Automate Backup Processes**: Utilize automation tools and scripts to schedule and perform backups consistently. Automation reduces the risk of human error and ensures backups are executed regularly.

- **Implement Multiple Copies**: Store multiple copies of backups in different locations to minimize the risk of data loss due to physical disasters or hardware failures.

- **Secure Backup Data**: Encrypt backup data to protect it from unauthorized access. Implement robust access controls, authentication mechanisms, and encryption techniques to ensure the confidentiality and integrity of backup data.

- **Monitor Backup Jobs:** Regularly monitor backup jobs and logs to ensure they are running successfully. Implement alert systems to receive notifications in case of backup failures or anomalies.

- **Regularly Test Restores:** Test the restore process periodically to validate the effectiveness of backups. Regular testing helps identify any potential issues and ensures that the restore process is reliable.

Following these best practices will help you establish a resilient backup and restore strategy and protect your data from unexpected incidents.

Real-World Example

Let's consider a scenario where an e-commerce website experiences a catastrophic server failure. The website relies on a cloud-based database to store customer information, order details, and inventory data. The company had implemented a backup strategy that includes daily full backups and hourly incremental backups.

To restore the website and recover the data, the IT team identifies the most recent full backup and the relevant incremental backups. They spin up a new server instance, prepare the environment, copy and restore the backup data, and validate the restored data using checksum verification.

Once the data is restored, they conduct extensive testing to ensure that the website is fully operational and the data is accurate. The restore process is successful, and within a few hours, the e-commerce website is back online, providing uninterrupted service to its customers.

Conclusion

Backup and restore processes play a vital role in safeguarding data in cloud computing. Understanding various backup types, implementing effective backup strategies, and following best practices are essential to protect your data from unexpected events and ensure business continuity.

Remember, your data is your life-blood in the digital age. Don't underestimate the value of a solid backup and restore strategy. It's better to be safe than sorry, so be proactive and make sure your cloud infrastructure is well-prepared for any data loss or corruption situation.

Multi-Region Deployment

In the world of cloud computing, multi-region deployment refers to the practice of deploying and running applications or services across multiple geographical regions simultaneously. This approach offers several advantages, including increased availability, improved performance, and enhanced disaster recovery capabilities. In this section, we will delve into the details of multi-region deployment and explore its benefits and challenges.

The Need for Multi-Region Deployment

As cloud computing continues to evolve and become an integral part of modern businesses, the need for high availability and low latency becomes more critical. In a single-region deployment, if a service or data center experiences an outage or significant network congestion, it can impact the availability and performance of the entire application. By spreading the workload across multiple regions, organizations can minimize downtime and ensure consistent performance even in the face of regional disruptions.

Design Considerations

When designing a multi-region deployment strategy, there are several key considerations to take into account:

- **Geographical distribution:** Choose regions that are strategically located to serve your target audience. Consider factors such as proximity to end users, regulatory requirements, and network connectivity.

- **Data replication and synchronization:** Ensure that data is replicated across regions in near real-time to maintain consistency. Use technologies such as database replication, caching mechanisms, content delivery networks (CDNs), or distributed file systems to achieve this.

- **Traffic routing:** Implement intelligent traffic routing mechanisms to direct user requests to the closest, least congested, or the most available region. DNS-based routing, global load balancers, or software-defined networking (SDN) technologies can assist in achieving efficient traffic routing.

- **Failover and disaster recovery:** Define failover mechanisms that automatically switch user traffic to a standby region in case of a region-wide outage. Regularly test and validate failover capabilities to ensure a seamless transition.

- **Data locality and regulatory compliance:** Assess regulatory requirements and consider data locality laws that govern the storage and processing of sensitive data. Ensure compliance by deploying resources in regions that meet the necessary compliance standards.

- **Cost considerations:** Multi-region deployments can significantly impact costs due to increased resource consumption and data transfer fees. Optimize resource utilization and carefully evaluate the associated costs to ensure cost-effectiveness.

Benefits of Multi-Region Deployment

Multi-region deployment offers several benefits, enabling organizations to provide a better user experience and enhance their overall service reliability. Some key advantages include:

- **Improved availability:** By distributing workload across multiple regions, organizations can ensure that their services remain available even if one or more regions experience outages or disruptions. This helps mitigate the impact of localized incidents and enhances service availability for end-users.

- **Enhanced performance:** Multi-region deployments enable organizations to reduce latency and improve response times by locating resources closer to end users. This is especially important for applications that require real-time interactions or have strict performance requirements.

- **Disaster recovery:** Multi-region deployment plays a crucial role in disaster recovery planning. By replicating data and applications across regions, organizations can quickly recover from regional failures or natural disasters, minimizing downtime and data loss.

- **Global scalability:** With multi-region deployment, organizations can easily scale their applications to different geographical locations based on user demand. This flexibility allows for easy expansion into new markets or handling peak loads during specific periods.

Challenges and Considerations

While multi-region deployment offers numerous benefits, it also presents certain challenges and considerations that organizations need to address:

- **Complexity and management:** Managing resources across multiple regions can be complex. Organizations need robust automation and management tools to streamline deployment, configuration, and monitoring processes.

- **Data consistency and synchronization:** Ensuring data consistency across multiple regions in near real-time can be challenging. Organizations must carefully design and implement data replication strategies to maintain data integrity and minimize conflicts.

- **Increased costs:** Operating in multiple regions can incur higher costs due to increased resource consumption, data transfer fees, and additional infrastructure requirements. Organizations need to carefully evaluate the cost implications and optimize their resource usage to contain expenses.

- **Compliance and regulatory challenges:** Multi-region deployments may introduce additional compliance and regulatory complexities. Organizations must navigate data protection laws, privacy regulations, and industry-specific requirements to ensure regulatory compliance.

- **Network connectivity and performance:** Achieving reliable and high-performance communication between regions can be challenging, especially when dealing with long distances and varying network conditions. Organizations should consider network proximity, bandwidth, and latency to design robust network architectures.

- **Operational dependencies:** Multi-region deployments introduce dependencies on various cloud service providers and geographical regions. Organizations need to assess the reliability, scalability, and availability of these providers to minimize operational risks.

Real-World Example: Netflix's Multi-Region Deployment

A notable example of a successful multi-region deployment is Netflix. As a global streaming platform, Netflix has implemented a multi-region strategy to ensure uninterrupted service availability for its millions of subscribers worldwide.

Netflix employs a distributed architecture that leverages multiple cloud providers and geographically dispersed regions. By replicating their content libraries and streaming infrastructure across different regions, Netflix can handle high traffic loads efficiently, provide a consistently smooth streaming experience, and mitigate the impact of regional outages.

The company utilizes traffic routing techniques to direct user requests to the optimal region based on factors such as network latency, available capacity, and local service availability. This ensures that users receive content from the closest and least congested server, minimizing buffering and latency issues.

In addition to the performance benefits, Netflix's multi-region deployment also enhances the company's disaster recovery capabilities. In the event of a regional outage or network disruption, traffic is automatically redirected to healthy regions, allowing users to continue streaming without disruption.

Conclusion

Multi-region deployment is a key element of modern cloud computing strategies. It offers organizations a way to achieve high availability, improved performance, and enhanced disaster recovery capabilities. However, it also introduces additional complexities and considerations that must be carefully addressed.

By designing and implementing a robust multi-region deployment strategy, organizations can ensure that their services are accessible, reliable, and performant, even in the face of regional disruptions. With careful planning, organizations can harness the power of multi-region deployment to deliver exceptional user experiences and drive business success in the cloud-enabled world.

Exercises

1. Consider a multinational e-commerce company that wants to expand its operations to multiple regions to cater to a global customer base. Explain how multi-region deployment can benefit the company in terms of availability, performance, and disaster recovery. Provide specific examples of scenarios where multi-region deployment would be advantageous.

2. Discuss the challenges and considerations associated with multi-region deployment, focusing on the complexity of managing resources, data consistency, increased costs, and compliance. Provide strategies or best practices to address these challenges.

3. Research and compare the multi-region deployment strategies of two major cloud service providers, such as Amazon Web Services (AWS) and Microsoft Azure. Identify key similarities and differences in their approaches and discuss the implications for organizations leveraging their services.

4. Explore the concept of hybrid cloud architecture, which combines private and public cloud deployments. Discuss how multi-region deployment can be integrated into a hybrid cloud environment to achieve optimal performance, scalability, and cost-efficiency. Provide a real-world example of an organization utilizing hybrid cloud with multi-region deployment.

5. Investigate the impact of network latency on multi-region deployment. Discuss the factors influencing network latency, such as geographical distance, network congestion, and service provider connectivity. Propose strategies to optimize network performance and reduce latency in a multi-region deployment scenario.

Additional Resources

- **Book:** "Architecting for Scale: High Availability for Your Growing Applications" by Lee Atchison.

- **Whitepaper:** "Architecting for the Cloud: Best Practices" by Amazon Web Services (AWS).

- **Article:** "Multi-Region and Multi-Availability Zone Architectures" by Microsoft Azure Documentation.

DISASTER RECOVERY AND HIGH AVAILABILITY

- **Webinar:** "Optimizing Multi-Region Cloud Deployments" by Google Cloud.

- **Blog Post:** "Multi-Region Active-Active Architectures and Service Design" by Netflix Technology Blog.

- **Case Study:** "How Airbnb Achieves Global Scale with AWS" by Amazon Web Services (AWS).

Remember, multi-region deployment is a powerful strategy that enables organizations to deliver highly available and performant services. With careful planning, thoughtful design, and continuous monitoring, organizations can conquer the challenges associated with multi-region deployment and unlock the full potential of the cloud.

Load Balancing and Failover

In the world of cloud computing, load balancing and failover are essential techniques for ensuring the availability, performance, and reliability of applications and services. In this section, we'll dive into the concepts behind load balancing and failover, explore different strategies and technologies, and discuss how they contribute to a resilient cloud infrastructure.

Load Balancing: Spreading the Load

When it comes to handling a high volume of user requests and distributing the workload across multiple servers or resources, load balancing comes to the rescue. The goal of load balancing is to evenly distribute incoming traffic, ensuring optimal utilization of resources, and preventing any single server from becoming overwhelmed.

There are different load balancing algorithms and techniques, each with its own strengths and advantages. Let's take a look at a few popular ones:

- **Round Robin:** This is the simplest and most common load balancing algorithm. It distributes requests evenly across a set of servers in a cyclic manner. Each new request is directed to the next server in line. While simple to implement, Round Robin does not take into account server load or capacity, which can lead to imbalanced distribution in some scenarios.

- **Weighted Round Robin:** To address the limitations of Round Robin, weighted load balancing assigns different weights to servers based on their capacity. Servers with higher capacity are assigned a higher weight, meaning they receive a more significant portion of incoming requests. This allows for better resource utilization and can prevent overloading of weaker servers.

- **Least Connections:** This algorithm directs new requests to the server with the Fewest active connections at the time. It ensures that the load is balanced based on the current workload of each server. However, it does not consider server capacity, which may lead to imbalances if servers have different processing power.

- **Dynamic Load Balancing:** This advanced load balancing technique takes into account real-time server metrics such as CPU utilization, memory usage, and network latency. By continuously monitoring server health and performance, dynamic load balancers can make intelligent decisions regarding traffic distribution. If a server becomes overloaded or starts to underperform, the load balancer can redirect traffic to healthier servers to maintain optimal performance.

Load balancers can be implemented as software or hardware appliances. They act as intermediaries between clients and servers, receiving incoming requests and intelligently routing them to designated backend servers.

Failover: No More Downtime

Every system, no matter how robust, is susceptible to failures. Failover is a mechanism that allows a system to automatically switch over to a standby or backup component in the event of a failure, ensuring the uninterrupted delivery of services.

In the context of cloud computing, failover techniques are employed to maintain high availability and minimize service disruption. When a failure is detected, whether it's a hardware failure, software crash, or network outage, failover mechanisms kick in to quickly and seamlessly transfer the workload and user requests to a redundant or standby system.

There are different approaches to implementing failover, depending on the specific requirements of the system:

- **Active-Passive Failover:** In this setup, there is a primary active system that handles all the workload and a passive standby system that remains idle. The standby system stays synchronized with the active system, replicating data and state in real-time. When a failure occurs, the standby system takes over and starts processing requests. This approach provides a straightforward failover mechanism, but it may result in underutilization of resources during normal operation.

+ **Active-Active Failover:** In an active-active setup, multiple active systems share the workload, each capable of handling requests independently. If one system fails, the remaining systems continue to handle the traffic, ensuring uninterrupted service. Active-active failover offers better resource utilization but requires careful load balancing and synchronization mechanisms to ensure consistency across multiple systems.

+ **Cloud-Based Failover:** Public cloud providers often offer built-in failover capabilities as part of their service offerings. By leveraging the provider's infrastructure and redundancy features, applications can be designed to seamlessly switch between different availability zones or regions in the event of a failure. This approach eliminates the need for managing and maintaining redundant hardware and systems, reducing costs and complexity.

Implementing failover requires careful planning, redundancy, and monitoring. It involves making critical decisions on the placement and configuration of backup systems, data replication methods, and failover triggers. Additionally, automated monitoring and alerting systems are vital for quick detection and response to failures.

Load Balancing and Failover in Action

Let's consider a real-world example to illustrate how load balancing and failover work together in a cloud computing environment.

Imagine an e-commerce website experiencing a surge in traffic during a holiday sale. To handle the increased load, the website employs load balancers to evenly distribute client requests across multiple backend servers. The load balancer uses a combination of round-robin and weighted round-robin algorithms to allocate traffic based on server capacity.

Unfortunately, one of the servers becomes overwhelmed due to an unexpected influx of requests. In this case, the load balancer, equipped with dynamic load balancing capabilities, detects the degraded performance and automatically reduces the traffic directed to the struggling server. The load balancer redirects the traffic to healthier servers, ensuring all requests are processed smoothly despite the isolated server's inadequacy.

Now, let's say that a hardware failure occurs on one of the servers. The server suddenly becomes unresponsive, causing the load balancer to detect the failure. Using a failover mechanism, the load balancer instantly redirects the traffic intended for the failed server to a redundant server, seamlessly resuming the service without any noticeable interruption for users.

In this way, load balancing and failover work in harmony, ensuring that applications and services in the cloud remain available, performant, and resilient against various failures.

Conclusion

Load balancing and failover are essential components of a robust cloud infrastructure. By evenly distributing the workload across multiple resources and seamlessly switching to backup components in the event of failures, organizations can achieve high availability, scalability, and reliability for their applications and services.

Whether it's balancing traffic using algorithms like round-robin or dynamically adjusting traffic based on server health, load balancers play a critical role in optimizing resource utilization and preventing overload.

Similarly, failover mechanisms, such as active-passive or active-active setups, provide the means to quickly recover from failures and maintain uninterrupted service delivery.

As cloud computing continues to evolve, load balancing and failover techniques will play an increasingly vital role in shaping the future of resilient and highly available systems.

Exercises

Exercise 1

Consider an online gaming platform that experiences an unexpected surge in traffic during a major gaming event. The platform uses a Round Robin load balancing algorithm to distribute user requests across multiple game servers.

1. Explain how the Round Robin algorithm works in the context of load balancing.

2. Discuss the potential limitations of the Round Robin algorithm and how they may impact the gaming platform during high traffic periods.

3. Propose an alternative load balancing algorithm that could better handle the increased load during gaming events.

Exercise 2

An e-commerce website is hosted in multiple regions to provide global availability. The website employs an active-passive failover mechanism, with a primary server handling incoming traffic and a backup server remaining idle.

1. Explain how an active-passive failover works and discuss its advantages and disadvantages compared to an active-active failover mechanism.

2. Outline the steps involved in detecting a failure and switching the traffic from the primary server to the backup server.

3. Suggest additional measures that could be taken to optimize resource utilization in an active-passive failover setup.

Resources

- Rouse, M. (2019). Load balancing. *SearchNetworking*. Retrieved from https://searchnetworking.techtarget.com/definition/load-balancer

- Kim, S. (2021). Load balancing algorithms for distributed systems. *Smashing Magazine*. Retrieved from https://www.smashingmagazine.com/2021/07/load-balancing-algorithms-distributed-systems/

- Microsoft Azure Documentation. (n.d.). *Traffic Manager*. Retrieved from https://docs.microsoft.com/en-us/azure/traffic-manager/

- Red Hat. (2021). *Chapter 7. Load balancing and high availability*. Retrieved from https://access.redhat.com/documentation/en-us/red_hat_enterprise_linux/7/html/load_balancer_administration/

Trick of the Trade

To ensure the effectiveness of load balancing and failover mechanisms, it's essential to regularly test and validate their functionality. Implementing automated tests and monitoring systems can help detect potential issues and ensure your infrastructure is ready to handle unexpected failures or traffic spikes.

Caveat

While load balancing and failover strategies contribute to the resilience and availability of cloud-based systems, they are not silver bullets. It's crucial to design applications with fault tolerance in mind, implementing redundancy, backup mechanisms, and proper error handling to minimize the impact of failures.

Remember: Load balancing and failover mechanisms are just components of a larger puzzle. Building scalable and reliable cloud systems requires a holistic approach, taking into account various factors such as architectural design, scalability, security, and monitoring.

Testing and Failback Procedures

In the world of cloud computing, where reliability and availability are paramount, testing and failback procedures play a crucial role. When implementing cloud-based solutions, organizations must ensure that their systems are thoroughly tested to identify and address any potential issues. Additionally, having well-defined failback procedures is essential for the seamless transition back to a previous state in the event of a failure or rollback. In this section, we will explore the importance of testing and failback procedures in cloud computing, discuss various testing strategies, and outline best practices for failback.

The Importance of Testing in Cloud Computing

Testing is an integral part of the software development life cycle. In the context of cloud computing, thorough and comprehensive testing becomes even more critical due to the distributed nature of cloud-based systems and the potential for complex interactions among various components. The primary goals of testing in cloud computing include:

- **Validation and Verification:** Testing helps validate that the cloud infrastructure, applications, and services meet the specified requirements and function as intended. It also ensures the verification of proper interactions between different components.

- **Identifying and Fixing Issues:** Testing helps uncover bugs, performance bottlenecks, security vulnerabilities, and other issues that may impact the stability and reliability of cloud-based systems. Timely identification and resolution of these issues are crucial for maintaining the integrity of the system.

- **Optimizing Performance:** By measuring and analyzing system performance under different loads, testing helps identify opportunities for optimization. This includes identifying performance bottlenecks, tuning system parameters, and optimizing resource allocation.

Testing Strategies in Cloud Computing

In cloud computing, several testing strategies are commonly employed to ensure the quality and reliability of cloud-based systems. Let's explore a few of these strategies:

1. **Functional Testing:** This strategy focuses on verifying that the system behaves as expected from a functional standpoint. It involves testing individual components, APIs, and interfaces, as well as end-to-end workflows to ensure correct functionality.

2. **Performance Testing:** Performance testing is crucial to evaluate the system's behavior under varying workloads and stress conditions. It involves load testing, stress testing, and capacity planning to ensure that the system can handle the expected user load and perform within acceptable performance thresholds.

3. **Security Testing:** Security testing aims to identify vulnerabilities and potential security risks in the cloud infrastructure and applications. It includes penetration testing, vulnerability scanning, and security code review to ensure the confidentiality, integrity, and availability of data and resources.

4. **Resilience Testing:** Resilience testing focuses on assessing the system's ability to recover from failures and disruptions. It involves simulating failure scenarios and validating that the system can continue to operate and recover within an acceptable time frame.

The selection and combination of testing strategies depend on the specific requirements and challenges of the cloud-based system being tested. It is important to design a comprehensive test plan that covers the various dimensions of testing to ensure a robust and reliable system.

Best Practices for Failback Procedures

Failback refers to the process of restoring operations to a previous state after a failure or rollback in the cloud environment. Having well-defined failback procedures is crucial for minimizing downtime, mitigating risks, and ensuring a smooth transition back to normal operations. Here are some best practices to consider when designing failback procedures:

- **Documentation and Communication:** Documenting and communicating failback procedures is essential for the entire team involved in cloud operations. Clearly outline the steps to be followed, the roles and responsibilities of team members, and the communication channels to be used during the failback process.

- **Automated Failback:** Whenever possible, automate failback procedures to reduce human error and accelerate the restoration process. Automation can include scripting failback steps, using infrastructure as code (IaC) tools for provisioning resources, and leveraging configuration management tools for consistent environment setup.

- **Testing Failback Procedures:** Just as testing is crucial for the initial deployment of cloud-based solutions, it is equally important to test failback procedures. Create a test environment that closely resembles the production environment and simulate various failure scenarios to validate the effectiveness of failback procedures.

- **Rollback and Redundancy:** Implementing rollback mechanisms and building redundancy into the system architecture can greatly simplify failback procedures. By ensuring that the system can easily revert to a previous known state, organizations can minimize potential data loss or service disruptions during the failback process.

- **Monitoring and Alerting:** Continuous monitoring of the cloud infrastructure and applications is crucial during the failback process. Implement monitoring and alerting mechanisms to detect any issues or anomalies promptly. This allows for timely intervention and remediation during failback.

By following these best practices, organizations can ensure a reliable and resilient failback process that minimizes downtime, mitigates risks, and helps restore normal operations as quickly as possible.

Real-World Example: Failback in a Cloud-Based E-commerce System

To illustrate the importance of failback procedures, let's consider a real-world example in the context of a cloud-based e-commerce system. The system experiences a critical failure that requires rolling back to a previous version. The following steps outline a failback procedure in this scenario:

1. **Identification and Analysis:** Detect the failure, analyze the impact, and determine the need for failback.

2. **Communication and Coordination:** Notify the relevant stakeholders, including the development team, operations team, and customer support, about the failback plan. Ensure clear communication channels are established and coordinated efforts are made throughout the process.

3. **Prepare the Failback Environment:** Set up a test environment that mirrors the production environment as closely as possible. This includes provisioning the required resources, databases, and application configurations.

4. **Data Backup and Restoration:** Ensure a recent backup of the data is available to avoid data loss. Restore the data to the failback environment.

5. **Deployment Rollback:** Roll back to the previous version of the application, codebase, or infrastructure configuration. Utilize version control systems or infrastructure provisioning tools to automate the rollback process.

6. **Testing and Verification:** Validate the failback environment by running appropriate tests to ensure that the system behaves as expected. This includes functional testing, performance testing, and security testing, among others.

7. **Monitoring and Risk Mitigation:** Continuously monitor the failback environment for any issues or anomalies. Implement risk mitigation measures, such as load balancing, to ensure the system can handle the expected workload.

8. **Gradual Traffic Restoration:** Gradually redirect the web traffic back to the failback environment, closely monitoring the system's performance and stability. Establish rollback criteria and procedures in case any issues arise during the restoration process.

9. **Post-Failback Analysis:** Once the system is fully restored, perform a post-failback analysis to identify the root cause of the failure and implement preventive measures for future incidents.

By following these steps, the e-commerce system can efficiently recover from the failure and ensure a smooth transition back to normal operations, thereby minimizing customer impact and revenue loss.

Summary

Testing and failback procedures are critical components of cloud computing, ensuring the reliability, availability, and recoverability of cloud-based systems. Thorough testing across functional, performance, security, and resilience aspects helps identify potential issues and optimize system performance. Well-defined failback procedures, coupled with documentation, automation, and testing, contribute to a seamless transition back to normal operations after a failure or rollback. By following best practices and leveraging real-world examples, organizations can enhance the robustness and resiliency of their cloud-based solutions.

The Fucking Safeguard of the Cloud

In the ever-changing landscape of cloud computing, ensuring the security and safety of your data is paramount. The fucking safeguard of the cloud refers to the measures and practices put in place to protect your valuable information from unauthorized access, breaches, and other potential threats. In this section, we will explore the various aspects of cloud security and discuss the strategies and tools that can help you maintain a robust and reliable cloud infrastructure.

Understanding Cloud Security

When it comes to cloud security, there are several key areas to consider. These include data protection, access control, network security, and threat detection. Let's dive deeper into each of these aspects and understand their significance in safeguarding the cloud.

Data Protection Data protection is the foundation of cloud security. It involves implementing strategies and mechanisms to ensure the confidentiality, integrity, and availability of your data. Encryption is a crucial aspect of data protection, as it helps protect your data from being intercepted or accessed by unauthorized individuals.

DISASTER RECOVERY AND HIGH AVAILABILITY 337

By encrypting your data, you can ensure that even if it falls into the wrong hands, it remains inaccessible without proper decryption keys.

In addition to encryption, data backups and disaster recovery plans are essential components of data protection. By regularly backing up your data and having a recovery plan in place, you can mitigate the impact of potential data loss or system failures.

Access Control   Access control refers to the mechanisms and policies that restrict access to your cloud resources. The goal is to allow only authorized individuals to access and modify your data and services. Access control lists, role-based access control, and multi-factor authentication are common practices used to enforce access control in cloud environments.

Implementing strong access control measures helps prevent unauthorized users from gaining access to your sensitive information and reduces the risk of data breaches.

Network Security   Network security focuses on protecting the communication channels between your cloud resources, your users, and the external world. It involves implementing secure network architectures, such as virtual private networks (VPNs) and firewalls, to safeguard your cloud infrastructure.

By establishing secure network connections, you can prevent unauthorized access to your cloud resources and protect your data from malicious activities, such as network attacks and data interception.

Threat Detection   Threat detection involves continuously monitoring your cloud environment for potential security threats and anomalies. This includes monitoring network traffic, system logs, and user activities to identify any suspicious behavior that may indicate a security breach.

By implementing robust threat detection mechanisms, such as intrusion detection systems and security incident and event management (SIEM) tools, you can quickly detect and respond to security incidents, minimizing the damage caused by potential breaches.

Best Practices for Cloud Security

Now that we've covered the key aspects of cloud security, let's discuss some best practices that can help you safeguard your cloud environment effectively.

Regular Security Audits   Performing regular security audits is crucial to identify vulnerabilities and weaknesses in your cloud infrastructure. Conducting penetration testing, vulnerability scanning, and compliance audits can help ensure that your systems are up to date and aligned with industry security standards.

By regularly assessing and fine-tuning your security measures, you can proactively address potential security risks and take necessary actions to mitigate them.

Secure Configuration Management   Proper configuration management is essential in maintaining a secure cloud environment. This involves hardening your cloud resources by disabling unnecessary services, applying security patches and updates, and enforcing secure configurations for your applications and systems.

By adopting secure configuration management practices, you can minimize the attack surface and reduce the likelihood of successful exploitation of vulnerabilities.

Employee Training and Awareness   Human error is still one of the leading causes of security breaches. Therefore, educating your employees about security best practices and raising awareness about potential threats is crucial. Regular training sessions and security awareness programs can help ensure that your workforce remains vigilant and follows secure practices while working with cloud resources.

By promoting a security-conscious culture, you can empower your employees to be the first line of defense against potential security threats.

Incident Response and Disaster Recovery   Having a well-defined incident response and disaster recovery plan is vital for minimizing the impact of security incidents and ensuring business continuity. This plan should detail the steps to be taken in the event of a security breach, including the roles and responsibilities of the incident response team, communication protocols, and recovery procedures.

By promptly responding to security incidents, containing the impact, and recovering from disruptions, you can minimize downtime and mitigate potential financial and reputational damage.

Real-World Example: Capital One Data Breach

To understand the importance of cloud security, let's take a look at a real-world example: the Capital One data breach in 2019. Capital One, one of the largest banks in the United States, suffered a massive data breach that exposed the personal information of over 100 million customers.

DISASTER RECOVERY AND HIGH AVAILABILITY

The breach occurred due to a misconfigured web application firewall in the cloud infrastructure. A cybercriminal exploited this vulnerability to gain unauthorized access to customer data stored in the cloud. The incident highlighted the criticality of proper security configurations and continuous monitoring in maintaining a secure cloud environment.

In the aftermath of the breach, Capital One implemented enhanced security measures and conducted a thorough review of their cloud infrastructure. They also cooperated with law enforcement agencies to bring the responsible party to justice. This incident serves as a reminder that even a minor misconfiguration can lead to significant breaches and emphasizes the need for robust cloud security practices.

Resources and Tools

When it comes to cloud security, several resources and tools are available to help you safeguard your cloud environment effectively. Here are some widely used resources and tools that you can explore:

- **Cloud Security Alliance (CSA):** CSA is an organization dedicated to defining and promoting best practices for secure cloud computing. They provide a comprehensive set of guidelines and frameworks for cloud security.

- **Security Information and Event Management (SIEM) Tools:** SIEM tools, such as Splunk and IBM QRadar, help monitor and analyze security event data from various sources to detect and respond to security incidents in real-time.

- **Intrusion Detection and Prevention Systems (IDPS):** IDPS tools, like Snort and McAfee Intrushield, provide real-time monitoring of network traffic to detect and prevent potential intrusions and attacks.

- **Encryption Tools:** Encryption tools, such as OpenSSL and VeraCrypt, help protect your data through various encryption algorithms and secure key management practices.

The Fucking Safeguard of the Cloud in a Nutshell

In conclusion, the safeguard of the cloud is an ongoing effort to protect your data and resources from potential security threats. By implementing strong data protection measures, access controls, network security protocols, and threat detection mechanisms, you can ensure the safety and integrity of your cloud infrastructure.

However, cloud security is not a one-off task. It requires continuous monitoring, regular security audits, and the adoption of best practices to adapt to evolving threats. By staying informed about the latest security trends, leveraging resources and tools, and implementing robust security measures, you can harness the full potential of the cloud technology while keeping your data safe and secure.

Remember, the fucking safeguard of the cloud is in your hands. Embrace it, master it, and conquer the cloud with confidence!

Future Trends in Cloud Computing

Edge AI and Fog Computing

Pushing AI to the Edge

As technology continues to advance, the possibilities for artificial intelligence (AI) are expanding at a rapid pace. One of the exciting advancements in AI is the concept of pushing AI to the edge. In this section, we will explore what it means to push AI to the edge, the advantages it brings, and the challenges that come along with it.

Understanding Edge Computing

Before diving into the topic of pushing AI to the edge, let's first understand the concept of edge computing. Edge computing refers to a decentralized approach of processing data and running applications closer to the source of data generation. Instead of relying solely on centralized cloud infrastructure, edge computing brings computational power and storage capabilities directly to the edge devices or close-by edge servers.

The edge devices could include smartphones, IoT devices, smartwatches, or even small servers located at the network edge. By processing data at the edge, it reduces the latency and bandwidth requirements for transmitting the data to the cloud, enables real-time data analysis, and enhances the overall performance of applications.

Advantages of Pushing AI to the Edge

Pushing AI to the edge offers several advantages that make it an increasingly popular choice for various AI applications. Let's take a look at some of these advantages:

1. **Reduced Latency:** With edge computing, AI models can be deployed directly on edge devices or edge servers, eliminating the need to send data to the cloud for processing. This significantly reduces the latency involved in data transmission and enables real-time decision-making. For applications like autonomous vehicles or industrial automation, low latency is crucial to ensure fast and accurate responses.

2. **Improved Privacy and Security:** When AI processing is done at the edge, sensitive data doesn't need to leave the device or local network. This helps address privacy concerns and reduces the risk of data breaches. For example, in medical applications, where patient data needs to be processed securely, pushing AI to the edge ensures compliance with stringent data privacy regulations.

3. **Bandwidth Optimization:** Transmitting large volumes of data to the cloud for processing can strain network bandwidth and increase costs. By performing AI computations at the edge, only relevant information or processed results are transmitted to the cloud, optimizing bandwidth usage and reducing data transfer costs.

4. **Offline Capabilities:** Edge AI allows applications to operate even in environments with limited or no internet connectivity. This is especially useful in remote areas, such as offshore oil rigs or remote mining sites, where maintaining constant connectivity to the cloud may not be feasible. Edge devices can continue running AI models locally, ensuring uninterrupted operations.

5. **Real-Time Decision-Making:** AI models deployed at the edge can quickly analyze and respond to data in real-time. This is essential for applications that require immediate actions or decisions, such as fraud detection, facial recognition, or predictive maintenance. With edge computing, AI can empower devices to make autonomous decisions without relying on cloud connectivity.

Challenges of Pushing AI to the Edge

While pushing AI to the edge brings numerous benefits, it also presents several challenges that need to be addressed. Let's discuss some of these challenges:

1. **Limited Computational Resources:** Edge devices typically have limited computational power and storage capacity compared to cloud servers. This

poses challenges in deploying and running complex AI models on resource-constrained devices. Optimizing AI algorithms for efficiency and developing lightweight models become crucial to ensure smooth operations.

2. **Data Variability and Heterogeneity:** Edge computing environments often deal with diverse data sources and formats. Integrating and processing data from different devices or sensors can be challenging due to the variability in data characteristics. AI models deployed at the edge must be adaptable to handle data heterogeneity and accommodate various input formats.

3. **Model Deployment and Management:** Managing AI models at the edge introduces complexities in model deployment, version control, and updates. With potentially thousands of edge devices deployed in the field, ensuring proper coordination and updating models can be challenging. Robust systems for model deployment, monitoring, and maintenance are necessary for effective edge AI management.

4. **Security and Trustworthiness:** Edge devices are more susceptible to physical tampering and security breaches compared to cloud servers. Securing edge devices, authenticating and verifying the integrity of AI models becomes crucial to prevent unauthorized access or manipulation. Additionally, ensuring the trustworthiness and fairness of AI models deployed at the edge is essential, especially in critical applications like autonomous vehicles or healthcare.

5. **Lack of Standardization:** The edge computing ecosystem is relatively new and lacks consistent standards and frameworks. This lack of standardization poses challenges in interoperability between edge devices, data compatibility, and development of portable AI models. Collaborative efforts from industry stakeholders are required to establish common frameworks and protocols for seamless edge AI adoption.

Real-World Applications

Pushing AI to the edge opens up a wide range of exciting real-world applications. Let's explore a couple of examples to better understand the practical implications of edge computing in AI:

1. **Autonomous Drones:** Edge AI enables drones to perform real-time object detection and avoidance, enabling them to fly autonomously without relying on continuous communication with the cloud. By processing video streams

on-board, drones can make split-second decisions even in dynamic environments, making them more reliable and efficient for applications like surveillance, delivery, or disaster response.

2. **Smart Cities:** Edge AI plays a crucial role in building smart cities. By deploying AI models on edge devices like traffic cameras, streetlights, or waste management sensors, cities can efficiently process real-time data and make decisions locally. For instance, intelligent traffic management systems using edge AI can analyze traffic patterns, adjust signal timings, and optimize traffic flow, all without significant delays caused by cloud connectivity.

Conclusion

The convergence of AI and edge computing opens up exciting possibilities for a wide range of applications. Pushing AI to the edge offers reduced latency, improved privacy, optimized bandwidth usage, offline capabilities, and enables real-time decision-making. However, challenges related to limited computational resources, data variability, model deployment, security, and lack of standardization need to be addressed to fully embrace the potential of edge AI. As technology continues to evolve, edge AI is set to revolutionize industries and pave the way for a smarter and more connected future.

As you can see, pushing AI to the edge has its advantages and challenges. By understanding the potential of edge computing, we can harness the power of AI and bring it closer to the data source, enabling real-time decision-making and unlocking the full potential of AI in various domains. So, let's continue our journey and explore more exciting trends in cloud computing!

Fog Computing Architecture

In this section, we will explore the architecture of fog computing, which is an emerging paradigm that extends the capabilities of cloud computing closer to the edge of the network. Fog computing addresses the limitations of cloud-centric models by bringing computation, communication, and storage resources closer to the devices and end-users. This section will cover the principles, components, and use cases of fog computing, highlighting its benefits and challenges.

Principles of Fog Computing

Fog computing follows several key principles that distinguish it from traditional cloud computing models. These principles are aimed at enabling low-latency and real-time applications, improving reliability, and reducing bandwidth consumption:

- **Proximity**: Fog computing places computing resources closer to the edge devices, reducing the distance and latency between data sources and computational services. This proximity enables quick response times for time-sensitive applications and reduces the reliance on centralized cloud services.

- **Distributed Architecture**: Unlike centralized cloud systems, fog computing adopts a distributed architecture, where resources are deployed across various fog nodes. These fog nodes are geographically dispersed and strategically located to provide localized services to the nearby devices.

- **Heterogeneity**: Fog computing accommodates a wide range of devices, including sensors, IoT devices, smartphones, and edge servers. Each device contributes its computational capabilities to form a heterogeneous network of fog nodes. This diversity in devices enables flexible resource allocation and efficient data processing at the edge.

- **Scalability**: Fog computing supports horizontal scalability, enabling the addition of more fog nodes as the network grows. This scalability allows fog computing environments to handle varying workloads and adapt to changes in demand without compromising performance.

- **Collaboration**: Fog nodes in the architecture collaborate and cooperate to perform computational tasks efficiently. By leveraging the capabilities of multiple fog nodes, fog computing can overcome resource limitations of individual devices and achieve better scalability and fault tolerance.

Components of Fog Computing

The architecture of fog computing consists of several components that work together to enable efficient computation and communication at the edge. Let's explore the major components:

- **Fog Nodes**: Fog nodes are the fundamental building blocks of the fog computing architecture. These nodes can be any computing device, such as routers, switches, gateways, or edge servers, that have sufficient computational capabilities, networking functionalities, and storage capacities. They are responsible for executing tasks and processing data at the edge of the network.

- **Fog Infrastructure:** The fog infrastructure refers to the underlying physical and virtual resources that support the fog computing environment. It includes the hardware and software components required to host fog nodes, such as servers, storage devices, networking equipment, and virtualization technologies.

- **Connectivity:** Connectivity plays a crucial role in fog computing, as it enables seamless communication between fog nodes and the devices they serve. This connectivity is established through wired and wireless networks, including cellular networks, Wi-Fi, Bluetooth, and Zigbee. Efficient and reliable connectivity ensures that data can be processed locally, reducing the need to transfer it to centralized cloud servers.

- **Data Management:** Fog computing requires efficient management of data generated and processed at the edge. This includes data storage, retrieval, and synchronization mechanisms. Fog nodes often leverage techniques such as edge caching, data replication, and distributed file systems to ensure data availability and reliability.

- **Security and Privacy:** With the increased distribution of computational resources, ensuring security and privacy in fog computing becomes critical. Fog nodes need to implement encryption, access control, and data integrity mechanisms to protect data and prevent unauthorized access. Privacy concerns related to data collection and processing at the edge should also be addressed.

- **Orchestration and Coordination:** Fog computing systems require effective orchestration and coordination mechanisms to manage the distribution of tasks and resources among fog nodes. This involves load balancing, resource allocation, and task scheduling algorithms that can dynamically adapt to changing network conditions and application requirements.

Use Cases of Fog Computing

Fog computing finds applications in various domains that require real-time data processing, low-latency communication, and local decision-making. Let's explore a few notable use cases:

- **Smart Cities:** Fog computing enables the deployment of smart city infrastructures, where sensors and IoT devices collect and process data in real-time. With fog nodes distributed throughout the city, applications such as intelligent transportation systems, smart grids, and environmental monitoring can provide faster response times, optimize resource utilization, and enhance the overall efficiency of urban services.

- **Industrial IoT:** In industrial settings, fog computing allows for real-time monitoring and control of equipment, reducing the reliance on cloud services for timely decision-making. By analyzing sensor data locally at the edge, industrial IoT applications can improve operational efficiency, detect anomalies, and enable predictive maintenance.

- **Healthcare:** Fog computing has transformative potential in healthcare, facilitating remote patient monitoring, real-time health data analysis, and efficient sharing of medical records. By leveraging edge devices and fog nodes, healthcare providers can enhance the quality of care, enable quicker response times, and ensure patient privacy and data security.

- **Autonomous Vehicles:** Fog computing plays a vital role in enabling autonomous vehicles by providing real-time data processing and decision-making capabilities at the edge. Fog nodes located alongside road infrastructure can process sensor data from vehicles, optimize traffic flow, and enable vehicle-to-vehicle communication for enhanced safety.

- **Retail:** In the retail industry, fog computing can support personalized customer experiences, accurate inventory management, and real-time analytics. By deploying fog nodes in stores, retailers can process data from surveillance cameras, analyze customer behavior, and deliver targeted promotions, improving customer satisfaction and operational efficiency.

Challenges and Future Directions

While fog computing offers numerous benefits, it also presents certain challenges and issues that need to be addressed:

- **Resource Constraints:** Fog nodes often have limited computational power, memory, and storage capacities. Optimizing resource utilization and designing efficient algorithms and protocols for constrained fog devices remain active areas of research.

- **Network Bandwidth**: The increased deployment of IoT devices and the growing demand for real-time applications generate huge amounts of data. Utilizing limited network bandwidth efficiently and prioritizing data transmission become critical challenges in fog computing environments.

- **Security and Privacy**: The distributed nature of fog computing introduces new security and privacy risks. Securing fog nodes, implementing robust authentication and access control mechanisms, and preserving the privacy of user data are ongoing challenges that require continuous innovation.

- **Interoperability**: As fog infrastructures are likely to be heterogeneous with varying devices and protocols, ensuring interoperability and seamless integration across different fog nodes remain a challenge. Standardization efforts and the adoption of open protocols can help overcome these interoperability issues.

Looking ahead, fog computing will continue to evolve and play a crucial role in enabling edge computing, IoT, and real-time applications. The integration of fog computing with emerging technologies such as 5G, AI, and blockchain holds immense potential for enhancing the performance, scalability, and capabilities of fog-enabled systems. However, addressing the challenges and ensuring the secure and efficient operation of fog computing architectures will be key to realizing the full potential of this paradigm.

Summary

In this section, we explored the architecture of fog computing, a paradigm that extends the capabilities of cloud computing to the edge of the network. We discussed the principles of fog computing, including proximity, distributed architecture, heterogeneity, scalability, and collaboration. We examined the components of fog computing, such as fog nodes, fog infrastructure, connectivity, data management, security, and orchestration. We also explored various use cases of fog computing, including smart cities, industrial IoT, healthcare, autonomous vehicles, and retail. Finally, we discussed the challenges and future directions of fog computing, highlighting resource constraints, network bandwidth, security, privacy, and interoperability as ongoing areas of focus. By embracing fog computing, organizations can unlock new opportunities for real-time data processing, low-latency communication, and localized decision-making, ultimately driving innovation and efficiency in various industries.

Use Cases and Challenges

Use cases of fog computing extend beyond the realm of traditional cloud computing, offering unique advantages in specific scenarios. However, along with these advantages come some challenges that need to be addressed for successful implementation. In this section, we will explore some prominent use cases of fog computing and discuss the associated challenges.

Use Cases of Fog Computing

1. **Industrial Automation:** Fog computing plays a significant role in industrial automation, where real-time data processing and low latency are critical. By deploying fog nodes near the industrial machinery, data can be processed locally, reducing the reliance on centralized cloud infrastructure. This allows for quicker decision-making, increased operational efficiency, and enhanced safety. For example, in a manufacturing plant, fog computing can be used to monitor machine health, predict failures, and trigger maintenance activities without the need for constant human intervention.

2. **Smart Cities:** Fog computing is a key enabler of smart cities, where various Internet of Things (IoT) devices generate massive amounts of data. By leveraging fog nodes deployed throughout the city, data processing and analysis can occur closer to the data sources, reducing data transfer to the cloud. This enables the real-time management and optimization of urban services such as traffic control, waste management, and energy distribution. For instance, fog computing can be

used to monitor traffic congestion and dynamically adjust traffic light timings for efficient traffic flow.

3. **Healthcare:** In the healthcare industry, fog computing can have life-saving implications. By bringing computation closer to the edge devices, healthcare providers can ensure real-time monitoring and analysis of patient data. This enables timely intervention and decision-making, even in situations where immediate response is critical. For example, fog computing can be used in remote patient monitoring systems to detect abnormalities in vital signs and send alerts to healthcare professionals in emergency situations.

4. **Autonomous Vehicles:** Fog computing is vital for the successful operation of autonomous vehicles. These vehicles generate colossal amounts of data that need to be processed in real-time to ensure safe and efficient navigation. By deploying fog nodes at strategic locations, such as traffic intersections or along highways, data processing can occur at the edge, improving response times and reducing dependence on the cloud. Fog computing can enable vehicles to make split-second decisions based on local data, such as detecting obstacles or avoiding accidents.

Challenges of Fog Computing

While fog computing provides numerous benefits, there are several challenges that must be addressed to ensure its successful implementation. Let's explore some of these challenges:

1. **Scalability:** As the number of fog nodes increases, managing the scalability of the fog computing infrastructure becomes crucial. Each fog node needs to efficiently allocate resources and handle the increasing workload. Additionally, ensuring seamless coordination between fog nodes and the centralized cloud infrastructure is necessary for optimal scalability.

2. **Security and Privacy:** Fog computing introduces additional security and privacy concerns due to the distributed nature of data processing. Securing data at the edge becomes vital to prevent unauthorized access or data breaches. Additionally, privacy concerns arise when sensitive data is processed locally on fog nodes. Implementing robust security measures and privacy-preserving techniques is essential in fog computing environments.

3. **Resource Management:** Efficient utilization of computing and storage resources of fog nodes is critical to maximize performance. Resource allocation algorithms need to dynamically adapt to changing workloads and optimize resource utilization. Efficient data placement and migration strategies are also necessary to balance the load and minimize latency in fog computing environments.

4. **Network Dynamics:** Fog computing relies on the connectivity between fog nodes, edge devices, and the cloud. The dynamic nature of these networks, with devices joining or leaving the network, can pose challenges in maintaining reliability and efficient communication. Ensuring seamless connectivity and addressing network heterogeneity are crucial to prevent disruptions in fog computing deployments.

5. **Standardization and Interoperability:** To foster widespread adoption and interoperability, standardization of fog computing architectures, protocols, and interfaces is essential. This promotes seamless integration of fog computing solutions across different domains and reduces vendor lock-in. Collaborative efforts among industry and academia are required to establish common standards in fog computing.

6. **Limited Resources at the Edge:** Edge devices often have limited computational power, energy, and storage capacity. This poses challenges in deploying resource-intensive applications on edge devices. Optimizing application design, resource allocation, and utilization are critical to overcome these limitations and ensure efficient use of edge resources.

Addressing these challenges will pave the way for the broader adoption of fog computing and unlock its full potential across various domains.

Further Reading

To delve deeper into fog computing and its use cases, challenges, and potential solutions, consider exploring the following resources:

- "Fog Computing: Concepts, Frameworks, and Technologies" by J. Rodrigues et al.

- "Fog for 5G and IoT" by M. Z. Shakir et al.

- "Security for Fog Computing: Challenges and Solutions" by R. Roman et al.

- "Resource Allocation Techniques for Fog Computing Networks" by M. S. Ali et al.

These resources provide valuable insights and research findings that can deepen your understanding of fog computing and its practical implications in various industries.

Exercise

Think of a specific industry or application where fog computing can be beneficial. Identify the challenges that may arise in implementing fog computing in that context and propose possible solutions.

The Fucking AI Revolution Continues

Artificial Intelligence (AI) has made tremendous advancements in recent years, revolutionizing various industries and fundamentally changing the way we live, work, and interact with technology. But guess what? The AI revolution isn't over yet. In this section, we will explore some of the exciting advancements and trends in AI that are shaping the future.

Natural Language Processing (NLP)

NLP is a branch of AI that focuses on understanding and processing human language. It enables machines to comprehend, analyze, and generate human language in a way that was once only possible for humans. NLP has already found its way into our lives through virtual assistants like Siri, Alexa, and Google Assistant. But hold your horses, there's a lot more to come.

One area where NLP is making significant strides is in the field of chatbots. Chatbots are computer programs that simulate human conversation, allowing users to interact with machines in a more natural and intuitive way. They are being used in customer service, healthcare, and even in education to provide personalized assistance and support. Imagine having a chatbot that can give you advice on your homework or help you study for an exam. The possibilities are fucking endless!

Another exciting development in NLP is sentiment analysis. This technique allows machines to understand and interpret human emotions expressed in text. It has applications in social media monitoring, customer feedback analysis, and even in detecting fake news and propaganda. With sentiment analysis, machines can gauge how people feel about a particular topic or product and provide timely insights for businesses and policymakers. Isn't that fucking awesome?

Computer Vision

Computer vision is another AI field that has seen remarkable progress in recent years. It focuses on giving machines the ability to perceive and understand visual content, just like humans do. With advancements in deep learning and neural networks, computer vision has become exceptionally powerful and is finding applications in various domains.

One of the most notable applications of computer vision is in autonomous vehicles. Self-driving cars rely heavily on computer vision to perceive and analyze the surrounding environment, detect objects, and make informed decisions. They use cameras and sensors to identify pedestrians, traffic signs, and other vehicles, ensuring a safe and efficient driving experience. The day when we can sit back and relax while our car drives itself is coming, my friends!

Computer vision is not limited to transportation. It is also being used in healthcare for medical imaging and diagnosis. Doctors can use AI-powered algorithms to analyze medical images such as X-rays and MRIs, assisting them in the detection and diagnosis of diseases. This technology has the potential to save lives and improve patient outcomes.

Machine Learning in Every Field

Machine learning, a subset of AI, is being incorporated into almost every industry and sector. Its ability to learn from data and make predictions or decisions based on patterns has made it a game-changer. Let's take a look at a few examples:

1. Finance: Machine learning is used for fraud detection, credit scoring, stock market prediction, and algorithmic trading. It can analyze large volumes of financial data and identify patterns that humans might miss. This helps financial institutions make better-informed decisions and prevent fraudulent activities.

2. Healthcare: Machine learning is transforming healthcare by aiding in diagnostics, drug discovery, personalized medicine, and patient monitoring. It can analyze medical records, genetic data, and electronic health records to provide insights and recommendations for better patient care.

3. Marketing: Machine learning is revolutionizing marketing by enabling targeted advertising, customer segmentation, and personalized recommendations. By analyzing customer behavior and preferences, it can help businesses tailor their marketing strategies to specific audiences, increasing sales and customer satisfaction.

4. Agriculture: Machine learning is being used in smart farming to optimize crop yield, monitor soil conditions, and predict pest outbreaks. By analyzing weather data, soil quality, and plant health, it can provide farmers with precise recommendations for irrigation, fertilization, and pest control.

The beauty of machine learning is that it can be applied to almost any field that deals with data. Its potential to automate tasks, improve decision-making, and drive innovation is truly remarkable.

Ethical Considerations

As the AI revolution continues to unfold, we need to address the ethical concerns surrounding its use. AI technologies can have both positive and negative impacts on society, and it is our responsibility to ensure that they are developed and used responsibly.

One major ethical consideration is privacy and data protection. As AI systems collect and analyze massive amounts of data, there is a risk of misuse and unauthorized access. We need robust laws and regulations to protect individuals' privacy and ensure the secure handling of personal data.

Another concern is fairness and bias in AI algorithms. AI systems are trained on historical data, which may contain biases and reflect societal prejudices. If not properly addressed, these biases can perpetuate discrimination and inequity. It is crucial to develop AI systems that are fair, transparent, and accountable.

Responsible AI development and use is also essential. Developers and policymakers need to consider the potential social, economic, and environmental impacts of AI technologies. They should involve diverse stakeholders and engage in ongoing dialogue to ensure that AI benefits everyone and does not exacerbate existing inequalities.

The future of AI holds immense possibilities and promises. The AI revolution is far from over, and as we move forward, we must prioritize ethical considerations and use AI as a tool for the betterment of humanity. So buckle up and get ready for the fucking ride of a lifetime as we witness the continued growth and impact of AI.

And remember, the power of AI lies in our hands, so let's use it wisely and responsibly.

Quantum Computing and Cloud

Introduction to Quantum Computing

Alright, buckle up, my fellow Gen-Z cloud conquerors, because we're about to dive into the mind-blowing world of quantum computing. Get ready to have your brains twisted like a pretzel as we explore the next frontier of computational power.

You see, traditional computers, the ones we're all familiar with, use bits to store and process information. These bits can either be in a state of 0 or 1, representing off or on, respectively. It's like a light switch that can only be in one of two positions.

But, quantum computing takes things to a whole new fucking level. Instead of bits, quantum computers use quantum bits, or qubits, which can be both 0 and 1 at the same damn time. Yeah, you heard me right. These qubits exist in what we call superposition, meaning they can be in a state of 0 and 1 simultaneously. It's like being in two places at once - the ultimate multitasking.

So, how the hell does this superposition thing work? Well, let me break it down for you. Qubits are typically represented using some cool-ass physics phenomenon, like trapped ions or superconducting circuits. These physical systems have properties that allow them to exist in multiple states at once.

But wait, there's more. Quantum computing also has another mind-blowing concept called entanglement. It's like a cosmic connection between qubits, where the state of one qubit depends on the state of another, no matter how far freaking apart they are. It's like having a telepathic bond with your friends, but on a quantum level. This entanglement can be used to perform calculations and solve problems that would take traditional computers billions of years to do. Talk about a quantum shortcut!

Now, before we get too excited, we need to address a couple of challenges. First off, quantum computers are still in their infancy. We're talking baby steps here, folks. They're highly susceptible to errors, and maintaining the delicate quantum states is no easy task. We need to keep those qubits isolated and free from any unwanted interference, which is easier said than done.

Secondly, quantum algorithms are a whole new ballgame. We can't just take our traditional algorithms and expect them to work on quantum computers. We need to develop new algorithms that leverage the power of quantum superposition and entanglement. It's like learning a brand-new language, but one that promises to unlock a world of possibilities.

Despite these challenges, quantum computing holds the promise of solving problems that are beyond the reach of classical computers. It's like having a god-like power to calculate things that were previously impossible. Quantum computers could revolutionize fields like cryptography, optimization, drug discovery, and even artificial intelligence. The possibilities are fucking endless!

So, my fellow cloud conquerors, get ready to embrace the quantum revolution. It's a wild ride, filled with mind-bending concepts and fascinating potential. Quantum computing is the future, and it's time for us to step into that future with our heads held high and our minds open to the limitless possibilities that await us.

Are you ready to unleash the power of qubits? Let's fucking go!

Quantum Computers in the Cloud

Quantum computing is a revolutionary field that harnesses the principles of quantum mechanics to perform computations that are exponentially faster than classical computers. These powerful machines have the potential to solve complex problems that are currently intractable for classical computers, such as factoring large numbers and simulating quantum systems. As quantum technology continues to advance, the concept of quantum computers in the cloud has emerged, offering users access to quantum computing resources and services remotely.

Introduction to Quantum Computing

Before diving into the realm of quantum computers in the cloud, let's briefly recap the fundamental principles of quantum computing. Quantum mechanics describes the behavior of matter and energy at the smallest scales, where particles exhibit wave-like properties and can exist in superposition states. A qubit, the fundamental unit of quantum information, can represent a 0, a 1, or any superposition of the two states simultaneously.

Quantum Computing Hardware

To grasp the concept of quantum computers in the cloud, it is crucial to understand the hardware elements that make up a quantum computer. Quantum computers rely on delicate and complex systems to manipulate qubits and perform quantum operations. These hardware components include:

1. **Qubits:** The building blocks of quantum computation, qubits can be implemented using a variety of physical systems such as superconducting circuits, trapped ions, or topological states.

2. **Quantum Gates:** Quantum gates are the equivalent of classical logic gates in quantum computing. They allow for the manipulation and transformation of qubits to perform calculations.

3. **Quantum Register:** A collection of qubits that can be used together to perform operations. Quantum algorithms often require multiple qubits to achieve computational advantages.

4. **Control Systems:** These systems control and stabilize the delicate quantum states of qubits, mitigating environmental and quantum noise that can lead to errors.

Challenges of Quantum Computers

Quantum computing is still in its infancy, and several challenges need to be overcome before it can be widely adopted. These challenges include:

1. **Quantum Error Correction:** Quantum systems are prone to errors due to environmental disturbances and decoherence. Developing effective error correction codes is crucial to maintaining the integrity of quantum computations.

2. **Scaling:** Quantum computers need to scale up to handle more qubits and perform complex calculations. However, increasing the number of qubits also amplifies the challenge of reducing errors and maintaining coherence.

3. **Quantum Algorithms:** Developing quantum algorithms that can harness the full potential of quantum computers is an ongoing research area. These algorithms must be designed to exploit the unique properties of qubits and quantum gates.

4. **Hardware Limitations:** The physical implementation of qubits and quantum gates face technical limitations, such as noise, gate errors, and finite coherence times. Overcoming these limitations is crucial for practical quantum computing.

Quantum Computers in the Cloud: Overview

Quantum computers in the cloud take advantage of the distributed nature of cloud computing to provide access to quantum resources remotely. With cloud-based quantum computing, users can leverage the power of quantum computers without the need for on-site hardware, allowing for rapid prototyping, algorithm development, and exploration of quantum capabilities.

Benefits of Quantum Computers in the Cloud

The integration of quantum computers in the cloud offers numerous benefits to users:

1. **Accessibility:** Quantum computers in the cloud democratize access to this cutting-edge technology. Users can access quantum hardware and software resources remotely, without the need for substantial financial investment or specialized infrastructure.

2. **Rapid Development:** Cloud-based quantum computing platforms enable researchers and developers to accelerate the development and testing of quantum algorithms and applications. The cloud provides an environment for iterating and refining quantum code without the need for local quantum hardware.

3. **Scalability:** Cloud-based platforms can accommodate the vast computational demands of quantum algorithms. Users can easily scale their computing resources to meet the requirements of their applications, such as increasing the number of qubits or accessing multiple quantum computers simultaneously.

4. **Collaboration:** Quantum computers in the cloud foster collaboration among researchers and developers. Multiple users can access the same quantum resources, sharing insights, and working together to advance the field of quantum computing.

Cloud-Based Quantum Computing Platforms

Several cloud providers have emerged, offering quantum computing services and platforms. Let's explore some of the prominent players in the cloud-based quantum computing landscape:

1. **IBM Quantum Experience:** IBM offers the IBM Quantum Experience platform, which provides access to their quantum processors and simulators. Users can write quantum programs using Qiskit, IBM's open-source quantum development framework, and execute them on IBM's quantum computers in the cloud.

2. **Amazon Braket:** Amazon Web Services (AWS) launched Amazon Braket, a fully managed quantum computing service. It allows users to experiment with different quantum hardware providers, including IonQ, Rigetti, and D-Wave, through a unified interface.

3. **Microsoft Azure Quantum:** Microsoft Azure Quantum provides a cloud-based ecosystem for quantum development. Users can access simulators, development tools, and quantum hardware from partners such as Honeywell Quantum Solutions, IonQ, and Quantum Circuits Inc.

4. **Google Quantum Computing:** Google's quantum computing initiative, known as Google Quantum Computing, offers access to their quantum processors through the Quantum Computing Service. Users can write quantum algorithms in Cirq, an open-source framework, and execute them on Google's quantum hardware.

Use Cases for Quantum Computers in the Cloud

Cloud-based quantum computing has the potential to address various computational challenges. Here are a few prominent use cases:

1. **Quantum Simulation:** Quantum computers can simulate quantum systems and materials with unprecedented accuracy. This capability has applications in drug discovery, materials science, and optimization problems.

2. **Cryptography and Security:** Quantum computers have the potential to break conventional cryptographic systems. By leveraging quantum-resistant algorithms and developing quantum cryptography protocols, cloud-based quantum computing can enhance data security.

3. **Optimization and Machine Learning:** Quantum algorithms, such as the Quantum Approximate Optimization Algorithm (QAOA), can tackle optimization problems faced by industries like logistics, finance, and supply chain management. Quantum machine learning is another emerging field that utilizes quantum algorithms to improve pattern recognition and data analysis.

4. **Quantum Chemistry:** Quantum computers can accurately simulate chemical reactions, aiding the development of new drugs, catalysts, and materials. Cloud-based quantum computing allows researchers to explore and optimize quantum chemical processes effectively.

Limitations of Quantum Computers in the Cloud

While cloud-based quantum computing offers exciting possibilities, it is essential to be aware of its limitations:

1. **Qubit Limitations:** Current quantum computers have a small number of qubits, and their coherence times are limited. This restricts the complexity of calculations and the size of problems that can be solved.

2. **Noise and Errors:** Quantum systems are susceptible to noise and errors due to environmental factors and imperfect hardware. These errors can propagate and compromise the results of quantum computations.

3. **Availability and Cost:** Access to quantum computing resources may be limited due to high demand. Additionally, quantum computing services can be expensive, especially for resource-intensive calculations.

4. **Development Complexity**: Quantum programming and algorithm design can be highly complex, requiring specialized knowledge and skills. The learning curve for quantum development can be steep for newcomers.

Conclusion

Quantum computers in the cloud hold immense promise for advancing the field of quantum computing and making this powerful technology accessible to a broad range of users. While challenges and limitations remain, cloud-based quantum computing platforms enable researchers, developers, and businesses to explore quantum algorithms, develop quantum applications, and accelerate advancements in this cutting-edge field. By harnessing the power of quantum computers in the cloud, we can unlock new possibilities and pave the way for quantum supremacy in solving complex real-world problems.

Impacts and Limitations

Cloud computing has revolutionized the way businesses and individuals interact with technology. It has brought numerous benefits and possibilities, but it also has its fair share of limitations. In this section, we will examine the impacts of cloud computing and discuss its limitations.

Impacts of Cloud Computing

Scalability and Elasticity: One of the significant impacts of cloud computing is its ability to provide scalability and elasticity. With cloud services, users can easily scale up or down their resources based on their needs. This flexibility allows businesses to handle sudden surges in traffic or accommodate dynamic workloads without the need for major infrastructure investments. For example, during major shopping events like Black Friday, e-commerce websites can scale up their server capacity to ensure smooth customer experiences.

Cost Efficiency: Cloud computing has transformed the way businesses manage their IT budgets. Traditional on-premises infrastructure requires large upfront investments in hardware and software licenses, along with ongoing maintenance costs. In contrast, cloud computing follows a pay-as-you-go model, allowing businesses to pay only for the resources they use. This cost-effective approach eliminates the need for excessive spending on expensive IT infrastructure, making it accessible to organizations of all sizes, including startups and small businesses.

Collaboration and Remote Work: The cloud has facilitated seamless collaboration and remote work environments. With cloud-based productivity tools and applications, teams can work on shared documents in real-time, regardless of their physical locations. This has significantly improved productivity and efficiency for businesses, especially in today's increasingly remote and globally distributed workforce.

Data Accessibility and Availability: Cloud storage services have made data access and availability more convenient. Users can access their files and data from anywhere with an internet connection. This accessibility has transformed the way we store, share, and access information. Additionally, cloud providers offer robust backup and disaster recovery capabilities, ensuring data resilience and minimizing downtime in case of system failures or outages.

Innovation and Rapid Deployment: Cloud computing has given rise to innovation and rapid deployment of new applications and services. Developers can leverage cloud platforms and services to build, test, and deploy applications more quickly and efficiently. This has resulted in a vibrant ecosystem of third-party applications and services, enabling businesses to continually evolve and adapt to changing market demands.

Limitations of Cloud Computing

While cloud computing offers numerous benefits, it is important to recognize its limitations and potential challenges:

Dependency on Internet Connection: Cloud computing heavily relies on a stable and fast internet connection. Without internet access, users may face difficulties accessing cloud services and data. This could be problematic in areas with limited or unreliable internet connectivity. It is crucial for businesses to consider backup plans or alternative solutions in case of internet outages.

Data Security and Privacy Concerns: Storing sensitive data on a third-party cloud provider's infrastructure raises security and privacy concerns. Although cloud providers implement strong security measures, such as encryption and access controls, data breaches are not unheard of. It is essential for businesses to carefully evaluate the security practices of their chosen cloud providers and implement additional security measures such as data encryption and regular security audits.

Vendor Lock-In: Moving applications and data to the cloud involves vendor dependence. Once a business adopts a particular cloud platform, it can become challenging to switch to a different provider due to data compatibility, platform-specific features, and integration complexities. This can limit flexibility and potentially increase costs in the long run. It is essential for businesses to consider the scalability and portability of their cloud deployments to minimize vendor lock-in.

Performance and Latency: The performance of cloud applications and services may be impacted by network latency and distance from the cloud data centers. Users far from the data centers may experience slower response times and decreased performance. This latency can be critical for applications requiring real-time data processing, such as online multiplayer gaming or high-frequency trading. It is crucial for businesses to consider the location of their cloud data centers and the proximity to their target users.

Data Transfer and Bandwidth Costs: Cloud providers often charge for data transfer and bandwidth usage. For businesses with substantial data transfer requirements, especially for data-intensive workloads like media streaming or big data analytics, these costs can accumulate quickly. Careful consideration should be given to data transfer costs and the selection of the appropriate cloud service plans to mitigate unexpected expenses.

Regulatory and Compliance Challenges: Depending on the industry and location, businesses may face regulatory and compliance challenges when adopting cloud computing. Industries like healthcare and finance have strict regulations regarding data privacy, security, and residency. Cloud providers need to comply with these regulations, but it is ultimately the responsibility of the business to ensure compliance with applicable laws and regulations.

Despite these limitations, cloud computing continues to offer significant advantages over traditional on-premises infrastructure. To overcome these challenges, businesses should carefully evaluate their specific requirements, choose reputable cloud providers, implement best security practices, and develop contingency plans to ensure smooth cloud operations.

Real-World Example: Netflix and Cloud Scalability

Netflix is an excellent example of how cloud scalability can revolutionize an industry. The streaming giant migrated its IT infrastructure to the cloud to accommodate its rapidly growing user base and streaming demands. By leveraging cloud computing, Netflix can dynamically scale its infrastructure in real-time, scaling up during peak usage hours and scaling down during off-peak periods, ensuring a seamless customer experience. This scalability allows Netflix to deliver high-quality streaming content to millions of users worldwide without major infrastructure investments.

Resources

To delve deeper into the impacts and limitations of cloud computing, consider exploring the following resources:

- Armbrust, M., Fox, A., Griffith, R., Joseph, A. D., Katz, R. H., Konwinski, A., ... & Zaharia, M. (2010). *A view of cloud computing*. Communications of the ACM, 53(4), 50-58.

- Mell, P., & Grance, T. (2011). *The NIST definition of cloud computing*. National Institute of Standards and Technology, Information Technology Laboratory.

- Gartner. (2020). *Gartner Hype Cycle for Cloud Computing*. Retrieved from https://www.gartner.com/en/documents/3986424/hype-cycle-for-cloud-computing-2020

- AWS Trusted Advisor. (n.d.). *What is a well-architected framework?* Retrieved from https://aws.amazon.com/architecture/well-architected/

Key Takeaways

Cloud computing has ushered in a new era of technological possibilities, allowing organizations to scale and innovate rapidly. The impacts of cloud computing include scalability, cost efficiency, collaboration, data accessibility, and rapid deployment. However, there are limitations to consider, such as internet dependency, security concerns, vendor lock-in, performance issues, data transfer costs, and regulatory compliance challenges. Understanding these impacts and limitations is crucial for businesses to make informed decisions and maximize the benefits of cloud computing.

The Fucking Quantum Leap

Dive into the mind-bending world of quantum computing, where the laws of classical physics take a backseat and the future of technology is being rewritten. In this section, we'll explore the potential and limitations of quantum computing, its integration with the cloud, and the exciting possibilities it holds for the future.

Introduction to Quantum Computing

Quantum computing is a revolutionary approach to computation that leverages the principles of quantum mechanics. Unlike classical computers that rely on bits—units of information represented by either a 0 or a 1—quantum computers use quantum bits, or qubits, which can exist in a superposition of states. This means that a qubit can simultaneously represent 0 and 1, opening the door to parallel processing and exponentially increasing computing power.

Quantum Computers in the Cloud

Integrating quantum computing into the cloud is an emerging trend that allows researchers, scientists, and developers from around the world to access and use quantum resources remotely. Cloud providers are leading the charge by offering quantum computing services, providing the necessary infrastructure, and democratizing the quantum leap. For instance, IBM Quantum Experience and Amazon Braket are two prominent cloud services that provide access to real quantum hardware.

Impacts and Limitations

The potential impacts of quantum computing are vast and far-reaching. Some of the most notable applications include:

- **Cryptography and Security:** Quantum computers can potentially break many of the encryption algorithms used today, leading to a need for new quantum-resistant cryptography solutions.

- **Optimization and Simulation:** Quantum algorithms can address complex optimization and simulation problems, enabling advancements in fields such as materials science, drug discovery, and supply chain management.

- **Machine Learning and AI:** Quantum machine learning algorithms have the potential to outperform classical algorithms, allowing for more accurate predictions and faster data processing.

- **Quantum Chemistry:** Quantum computers can simulate the behavior of molecules, leading to advancements in drug design and renewable energy research.

However, quantum computing is not without its limitations. Some of the key challenges include:

- **Quantum Error Correction:** Qubits are highly susceptible to errors due to decoherence and noise. Quantum error correction techniques aim to address this issue but are still in the early stages of development.

- **Scalability:** Building large-scale quantum computers with thousands or millions of stable qubits is a significant engineering feat that still requires breakthroughs in hardware design and fabrication.

- **Quantum Algorithms:** Developing efficient quantum algorithms for a wide range of applications is an ongoing research area. Many algorithms are still in their infancy and require optimization.

- **Access and Education:** Quantum computing is a rapidly evolving field, and there is a shortage of skilled experts. Access to quantum resources and educational materials needs to be democratized to foster widespread adoption.

The Fucking Quantum Leap

To better understand the power of quantum computing, let's dive into a simple example: factoring large numbers. Factoring large numbers is a computationally intensive problem that plays a crucial role in encryption algorithms. Traditional computers struggle to factorize large numbers efficiently, but quantum computers excel at it, posing a potential threat to encryption.

For instance, Shor's algorithm, a famous quantum algorithm, can factorize large numbers exponentially faster than classical algorithms. This breakthrough has implications for the security of systems that rely on classical encryption, such as online banking and secure communication.

However, the quantum leap provided by quantum computing comes with a catch. Shor's algorithm and other quantum algorithms are not applicable to all types of problems. They tend to outperform classical algorithms only for specific use cases, making it crucial to identify and develop quantum-ready applications.

Furthermore, quantum computers are error-prone, and errors tend to accumulate as computations become more complex. Quantum error correction techniques are being developed to mitigate these errors, but their effectiveness is still a topic of ongoing research. Achieving the stability and reliability required for large-scale quantum computing remains a significant challenge.

Resources and Further Reading

To explore quantum computing further and keep up with the ongoing developments, here are some recommended resources:

- **IBM Quantum Experience**: Access IBM's quantum computing systems and learn quantum programming through their cloud-based platform. Visit: `https://quantum-computing.ibm.com/`.

- **Amazon Braket**: Dive into quantum computing using Amazon Web Services (AWS) and explore a range of quantum hardware. Visit: `https://aws.amazon.com/braket/`.

- "**Quantum Computing for Computer Scientists**" by Noson S. Yanofsky and Mirco A. Mannucci: This book provides an in-depth introduction to the principles of quantum computing and algorithms. Available online and in print.

- "**Quantum Computing: An Applied Approach**" by Jack Hidary: This book focuses on practical quantum computing, explaining various algorithms and their real-world applications. Available online and in print.

The field of quantum computing is evolving rapidly, and staying up to date with the latest research and advancements is essential. Embrace the uncertainty and explore the limitless possibilities of the fucking quantum leap!

Blockchain and Distributed Ledger Technology (DLT)

Overview of Blockchain

Blockchain is a revolutionary technology that has gained significant attention in recent years. It is the underlying technology behind cryptocurrencies like Bitcoin, but its potential applications extend far beyond digital currencies. In this section, we will provide an overview of blockchain technology, explaining its fundamental concepts, structure, and characteristics.

What is Blockchain?

At its core, a blockchain is a decentralized and distributed ledger that records transactions or any digital information in a secure and transparent manner. Unlike traditional centralized databases, which require a central authority for verification

BLOCKCHAIN AND DISTRIBUTED LEDGER TECHNOLOGY (DLT)

and validation, blockchain employs a consensus mechanism to achieve trust and immutability.

The term "blockchain" comes from the way data is stored in the system. Transactions are grouped into blocks, which are then linked together in a chain-like structure using cryptographic hashes. Each block contains a unique identifier called a hash, as well as the hash of the previous block, creating an unbroken chain of blocks.

Key Elements of Blockchain

To understand how blockchain works, we need to examine its key elements:

- **Decentralization:** Blockchain operates in a decentralized manner, with no central authority controlling the system. Instead, it relies on a network of nodes or computers that work together to maintain and update the blockchain's integrity.

- **Consensus Mechanism:** Consensus is crucial in a blockchain network to establish agreement among nodes on the validity of transactions. Different consensus mechanisms, such as Proof of Work (PoW) and Proof of Stake (PoS), are used to verify and validate transactions and ensure the security and immutability of the blockchain.

- **Cryptographic Hashing:** Cryptographic hash functions play a vital role in blockchain technology. They convert data of arbitrary size into a fixed-size string of characters, representing the digital fingerprint or hash value of the data. Any change in the data will result in a completely different hash, enabling detection of tampering or data corruption.

- **Immutability:** Once a block is added to the blockchain, it becomes nearly impossible to modify or delete the information stored within it. The decentralized nature of blockchain, along with cryptographic techniques, ensures the immutability of the data, making it highly secure against fraud or unauthorized changes.

- **Smart Contracts:** Smart contracts are self-executing contracts with predefined rules and conditions encoded within the blockchain. They automatically enforce the terms of an agreement, eliminating the need for intermediaries and reducing the potential for disputes. Smart contracts have extensive applications beyond financial transactions, ranging from supply chain management to decentralized applications (dApps).

Blockchain Applications

Blockchain technology has the potential to transform various industries and revolutionize traditional processes. Here are some prominent applications of blockchain:

- **Financial Services:** Blockchain has disrupted the financial industry by enabling faster and more secure cross-border transactions, reducing fees, and eliminating intermediaries. It also enables the tokenization of assets, making financial markets more accessible and efficient.

- **Supply Chain Management:** Blockchain enhances transparency and traceability in supply chains, enabling better product provenance and reducing counterfeiting. It allows for real-time tracking of goods, ensuring the integrity of the supply chain network and enhancing consumer trust.

- **Healthcare:** Blockchain can improve interoperability and security in healthcare systems by securely storing and sharing patient data. It ensures the integrity of medical records, facilitates medical research, and enables secure sharing of electronic health records between healthcare providers.

- **Voting Systems:** Blockchain-based voting systems can provide a more secure and transparent method for conducting elections. The tamper-resistant nature of blockchain ensures the integrity of voting records, reducing the risk of fraud and manipulation.

- **Digital Identity Management:** Blockchain can provide a decentralized and secure solution for managing digital identities. It allows individuals to have control over their personal data and reduces the risk of data breaches and identity theft.

Challenges and Limitations

Despite its potential, blockchain technology still faces several challenges and limitations that need to be addressed:

- **Scalability:** The scalability of blockchain remains a significant challenge, especially for public blockchains. As the number of transactions increases, the consensus mechanism and the size of the blockchain can become barriers to efficiency and speed.

- **Energy Consumption:** Some blockchain networks, particularly those that use Proof of Work for consensus, consume a substantial amount of energy. This environmental impact is a concern and could hinder the widespread adoption of blockchain technology.

- **Regulatory and Legal Issues:** The regulatory landscape for blockchain technology is still evolving, with governments worldwide grappling with how to regulate cryptocurrencies, smart contracts, and decentralized applications. Legal issues, such as data privacy and intellectual property rights, also need to be addressed.

- **Interoperability:** As blockchain networks grow in number and diversity, achieving interoperability between different blockchains becomes crucial. Interoperability would enable seamless integration and communication between various blockchain platforms, fostering collaboration and innovation.

In summary, blockchain technology holds immense promise across a wide range of industries, offering secure and transparent transactions, reduced costs, improved efficiency, and increased trust. However, addressing the challenges associated with scalability, energy consumption, regulation, and interoperability is necessary for the widespread adoption of blockchain in the future.

For further exploration of blockchain technology, we recommend the following resources:

- *Mastering Blockchain: Unlocking the Power of Cryptocurrencies, Smart Contracts, and Decentralized Applications* by Imran Bashir.

- *Blockchain Basics: A Non-Technical Introduction in 25 Steps* by Daniel Drescher.

- *Blockchain Revolution: How the Technology Behind Bitcoin and Other Cryptocurrencies Is Changing the World* by Don Tapscott and Alex Tapscott.

Now that you have a solid overview of blockchain technology, let's dive deeper into other exciting advancements in cloud computing. Stay tuned for the remaining chapters of this book!

Blockchain in Cloud Computing

Blockchain technology has gained significant attention in recent years due to its potential to revolutionize various industries. One area where blockchain shows great promise is in cloud computing. In this section, we will explore how blockchain can be utilized in cloud computing, its benefits, challenges, and potential applications.

Understanding Blockchain

Before diving into the specifics of blockchain in cloud computing, let's briefly recap what blockchain technology is. At its core, blockchain is a distributed, decentralized, and immutable ledger. It consists of a chain of blocks, each containing a list of transactions. These transactions are securely recorded and linked together using cryptographic hashes.

Blockchain operates on a peer-to-peer network, where participants (or nodes) maintain a copy of the entire blockchain. Transactions are validated and added to the blockchain through a consensus mechanism, such as proof-of-work or proof-of-stake. Once a block is added to the blockchain, it becomes virtually impossible to alter or tamper with the recorded transactions, providing an inherently transparent and trustworthy system.

Benefits of Blockchain in Cloud Computing

Integrating blockchain into cloud computing can unlock several benefits, addressing some of the challenges faced by traditional cloud solutions. Here are a few key advantages:

Enhanced Security: Blockchain technology can enhance the security of cloud computing by providing secure and tamper-proof storage for sensitive data. The decentralized nature of the blockchain eliminates the reliance on a single central authority, reducing the risk of a single point of failure or malicious attacks. Additionally, the use of cryptographic algorithms ensures data integrity and confidentiality.

Improved Trust and Transparency: Cloud computing often involves multiple participants, including service providers, customers, and third-party auditors. Blockchain can enhance trust and transparency among all parties by providing a shared and immutable record of transactions and activities. This enables efficient auditing and dispute resolution, reducing the need for intermediaries and increasing overall transparency.

Increased Data Control: Traditional cloud computing often requires users to relinquish control of their data to service providers. With blockchain, users can retain control over their data while still using cloud services. Blockchain-based identity management systems allow users to manage access permissions and selectively share data with other participants, ensuring data privacy and control.

Reliable Smart Contracts: Smart contracts, which are self-executing agreements with predefined conditions, can be implemented on a blockchain. These contracts can automate various tasks in cloud computing, such as service provisioning, billing, and SLA enforcement. By leveraging blockchain-based smart contracts, cloud service providers can ensure reliable and transparent execution of agreements, minimizing the need for manual intervention.

Challenges and Limitations

While blockchain holds great promise for cloud computing, there are several challenges and limitations that must be addressed:

Scalability: Blockchain technology, especially public blockchains like Bitcoin and Ethereum, currently face scalability challenges. The consensus mechanisms and the need for all nodes to validate transactions limit the number of transactions processed per second. As cloud computing involves handling large volumes of data and transactions, scalability becomes a critical factor.

Performance: The decentralized nature of blockchain comes at the cost of performance. The process of reaching consensus and maintaining a distributed ledger requires significant computational resources. As a result, the transaction processing speed and overall network performance of blockchain-based cloud solutions may be slower compared to centralized systems.

Regulatory and Legal Concerns: The regulatory landscape around blockchain is still evolving, with varying degrees of acceptance and understanding across different jurisdictions. Cloud computing utilizing blockchain may face legal challenges related to data privacy, compliance, and intellectual property rights. Addressing these concerns requires collaboration between regulatory authorities and industry stakeholders.

Applications of Blockchain in Cloud Computing

Blockchain technology opens up several exciting possibilities for cloud computing. Here are some potential applications:

Decentralized Cloud Storage: Traditional cloud storage relies on centralized data centers. With a blockchain-based decentralized storage system, data can be distributed across a peer-to-peer network, ensuring redundancy, privacy, and high availability. Examples of blockchain-based cloud storage platforms include Storj, Sia, and Filecoin.

Secure Identity Management: Blockchain-based identity management systems enable users to have control over their online identities. These systems can tackle the challenge of managing multiple identities across different cloud services, providing a unified and secure identity management solution.

Auditing and Compliance: Blockchain's transparent and tamper-proof nature makes it an ideal tool for auditing and compliance in cloud computing. All cloud transactions and activities can be recorded on the blockchain, enabling easy auditing, accurate billing, and compliance with regulatory requirements.

Edge Computing and Blockchain: Edge computing, which involves processing data closer to the source rather than in centralized data centers, can benefit from blockchain technology. Blockchain can provide a trust layer for interconnecting edge devices, ensuring secure and reliable communication and data exchange.

Conclusion

Blockchain technology has the potential to transform various aspects of cloud computing. By enhancing security, improving trust and transparency, and enabling new applications, blockchain can address some of the challenges faced by traditional cloud solutions. However, scalability, performance, and regulatory considerations must be carefully addressed for widespread adoption of blockchain in cloud computing. With ongoing developments and advancements, blockchain is poised to revolutionize the way we think about and utilize cloud computing.

Decentralized Storage and Computing

In the world of cloud computing, where data is stored and processed on remote servers, the concept of centralized control seems to be the norm. However, with the rise of decentralized technologies, such as blockchain and distributed ledger technology (DLT), the landscape is shifting towards a more distributed approach. In this section, we will explore the idea of decentralized storage and computing and its potential impact on cloud computing.

Understanding Decentralization

To understand decentralized storage and computing, we need to first grasp the concept of decentralization itself. In a centralized system, there is a single entity or authority that controls the storage and processing of data. This means that all the data is stored in a single location and is managed by a central authority. On the other hand, in a decentralized system, the storage and processing of data are distributed across multiple nodes or computers. There is no central authority, and each node in the network participates in the storage and verification of data.

Decentralized storage and computing aim to eliminate the reliance on a single entity or authority. Instead, they distribute data and computing tasks across a network of computers, making the system more resilient, transparent, and secure.

Decentralized Storage

Decentralized storage is a method of storing data across a network of computers, each contributing a small part of their storage capacity to the overall system. Unlike traditional centralized storage systems where data is stored on dedicated servers, decentralized storage systems use a peer-to-peer network to distribute and replicate data across multiple nodes.

One key advantage of decentralized storage is its inherent redundancy. Since data is stored across multiple nodes, even if some nodes fail or go offline, the data remains accessible from other nodes. This makes the system more resistant to failures and ensures high availability.

Decentralized storage also offers enhanced security and privacy. With traditional storage systems, data is stored in a central location, making it a target for attacks. In a decentralized storage system, data is distributed and encrypted, making it more difficult for unauthorized users to gain access.

One example of a decentralized storage system is the InterPlanetary File System (IPFS). IPFS uses a distributed hash table (DHT) to store and retrieve files in a peer-to-peer network. By breaking files into small chunks and assigning unique identifiers to each chunk, IPFS ensures that files are retrievable even if some nodes are offline.

Decentralized Computing

Decentralized computing, also known as distributed computing, involves distributing computational tasks across multiple nodes in a network. This approach allows for parallel processing, increasing computational power and speed.

In a decentralized computing system, tasks are divided into smaller sub-tasks and assigned to different nodes for processing. Once completed, the results are combined to derive the final output. This distributed approach offers several benefits, including improved scalability, fault tolerance, and resource utilization.

Blockchain technology is often associated with decentralized computing. In a blockchain network, consensus algorithms such as proof of work (PoW) or proof of stake (PoS) are used to validate and execute computations. Each node in the network participates in the computational process, ensuring transparency and security.

An example of decentralized computing is Ethereum, a blockchain platform that allows for the execution of smart contracts. Smart contracts are self-executing agreements with the terms of the agreement directly written into code. By distributing the computational load across the network, Ethereum enables the execution of complex decentralized applications (dApps).

Benefits and Challenges

Decentralized storage and computing offer a range of benefits over their centralized counterparts. Some of the key advantages include:

- **Resilience:** Decentralized systems are more resilient to failures and attacks since there is no single point of failure or control.

- **Fault Tolerance:** By distributing data and tasks, decentralized systems can continue to function even if some nodes or components fail.

- **Transparency:** Decentralized systems provide greater transparency as the storage and computation processes are visible to all participants in the network.

- **Enhanced Security:** The distributed nature of decentralized systems makes them more resistant to attacks and unauthorized access.

- **Improved Privacy:** Decentralized storage and computing can provide better privacy by encrypting data and limiting access to authorized parties.

However, decentralized storage and computing also present their own set of challenges:

- **Scalability:** As more nodes join a decentralized network, scalability becomes a concern. The system needs to handle the increased load and ensure efficient coordination between nodes.

- **Data Consistency:** In a decentralized storage system, ensuring data consistency across multiple nodes can be challenging. Synchronization mechanisms and consensus protocols are necessary to maintain a consistent view of data.

- **Energy Consumption:** Some decentralized systems, especially those that rely on proof of work consensus algorithms, can consume significant energy resources. This is a concern from both an environmental and economic perspective.

Real-World Examples

Decentralized storage and computing have already found applications in various real-world scenarios. Here are a few examples:

- **Filecoin:** Filecoin is a decentralized storage network that incentivizes individuals to rent out their spare storage space. Users can store and retrieve files using Filecoin's native cryptocurrency as a medium of exchange.

- **Golem:** Golem is a decentralized computing platform that enables users to rent out their idle computing power for tasks such as rendering CGI or executing complex computations. It allows individuals and organizations to utilize distributed computing resources at a lower cost.

- **Sia:** Sia is a decentralized cloud storage platform that allows users to rent and store data across a distributed network of nodes. The platform uses smart contracts to facilitate trustless and secure transactions.

These examples demonstrate the practical application of decentralized storage and computing, bringing the advantages of the technology to users and developers, and paving the way for the future of cloud computing.

Conclusion

Decentralized storage and computing are disrupting the traditional centralized models in the realm of cloud computing. By distributing data and computational tasks across a network of computers, these technologies offer increased resilience, transparency, and security. While there are challenges to overcome, the real-world applications and the potential for innovation make decentralized storage and computing an exciting area to watch in the future of cloud computing.

Ultimately, as cloud computing continues to evolve, decentralized technologies will play a crucial role in shaping the way data is stored, processed, and accessed.

Embracing the benefits and addressing the challenges will pave the way for a more secure, transparent, and inclusive cloud computing ecosystem.

So, get ready to witness the fucking revolution of decentralized storage and computing in the cloud! It's time to take control and distribute power. The cloud is no longer just a fluffy place in the sky; it's a battleground for innovation and disruption. Embrace the decentralized future and conquer the cloud!

The Fucking Power of Blockchain

Blockchain technology has emerged as a revolutionary concept with the potential to disrupt various industries. It was initially popularized by Bitcoin, the first cryptocurrency, but its applications extend far beyond digital currencies. In this section, we will explore the fucking power of blockchain and its impact on cloud computing.

Understanding Blockchain

At its core, a blockchain is a decentralized and distributed ledger that records transactions across multiple computers, creating an immutable and transparent record. Each transaction is bundled into a block and linked to previous blocks, forming a chain of blocks. This decentralized nature eliminates the need for a central authority, making it resistant to fraud or manipulation.

Blockchain Principles

To fully grasp the fucking power of blockchain, it's crucial to understand its underlying principles. Here are a few key concepts:

1. **Decentralization** Blockchain operates on a peer-to-peer network where participants, known as nodes, have equal rights and responsibilities. This decentralized structure ensures that no single entity controls the network, enhancing transparency and resilience.

2. **Immutability** Once a transaction is added to the blockchain, it becomes nearly impossible to alter or delete. The use of cryptographic hashing and consensus mechanisms ensures the integrity and immutability of the data stored on the blockchain, making it a reliable source of information.

3. **Transparency** Blockchain provides unparalleled transparency as all transactions are visible to all participants of the network. This transparency fosters trust and accountability, making it ideal for applications where transparency is paramount, such as supply chain management or voting systems.

4. **Security** Blockchain employs advanced cryptographic techniques to secure transactions and prevent unauthorized access. Each transaction is digitally signed, and consensus mechanisms like proof-of-work or proof-of-stake ensure the validity of the transactions, making the blockchain highly secure.

Blockchain in Cloud Computing

Cloud computing and blockchain technology are a match made in heaven. The decentralized, transparent, and secure nature of blockchain complements the scalable, flexible, and accessible nature of cloud computing. Let's explore how blockchain can enhance various aspects of cloud computing:

1. **Data Security and Privacy** Blockchain can significantly enhance data security and privacy in the cloud. By using blockchain as a decentralized identity and access management solution, users can securely authenticate and access cloud resources without relying on a trusted third party. This eliminates the risks associated with centralized identity systems and provides users with full control over their data.

2. **Decentralized File Storage** Traditionally, cloud storage relies on centralized servers, making it vulnerable to data breaches and outages. By utilizing blockchain, cloud storage can become decentralized, with files distributed across a network of nodes. This enhances data redundancy, reduces the risk of data loss, and mitigates the impact of server failures.

3. **Smart Contracts for Service Agreements** Smart contracts, self-executing agreements stored on the blockchain, can revolutionize the way cloud services are delivered and managed. Instead of relying on traditional service-level agreements, smart contracts can automatically enforce the terms of service, ensuring transparency and trust between the cloud provider and the user.

4. **Auditing and Compliance** With blockchain, auditing and compliance in the cloud become more efficient and transparent. Since every transaction and modification is recorded on the blockchain, auditors can easily trace data access,

system changes, and user actions, ensuring compliance with regulations and standards.

Challenges and Considerations

While the fucking power of blockchain in cloud computing is tremendous, it is essential to address some challenges and considerations:

1. Scalability   Blockchain networks often face scalability issues. As the number of transactions increases, the network may become slower and less efficient. This challenge requires innovative solutions, such as sharding or off-chain transactions, to ensure the scalability of blockchain-based cloud applications.

2. Energy Consumption   Proof-of-work consensus mechanisms, like those used in Bitcoin, consume significant amounts of energy. This carbon footprint poses environmental concerns. However, the development of energy-efficient consensus algorithms, like proof-of-stake, is underway to address this issue.

3. Regulatory and Legal Implications   Blockchain technology is still relatively new, and its deployment in cloud computing raises regulatory and legal considerations. Issues such as cross-border data transfer, privacy regulations, and intellectual property rights need to be carefully addressed to ensure compliance and avoid legal disputes.

Real-World Examples

To understand the potential of blockchain in cloud computing, let's explore two real-world examples:

1.   Supply Chain Management   Blockchain can revolutionize supply chain management by providing end-to-end transparency and traceability. By integrating cloud-based IoT sensors and blockchain technology, companies can track the movement of goods, validate authenticity, and verify compliance with regulations. This ensures efficiency, reduces fraud, and enhances customer trust.

2.   Decentralized Cloud Storage   Projects like Filecoin and Storj leverage blockchain technology to offer decentralized cloud storage services. Users can rent out their spare storage space and earn cryptocurrency, while others can securely

BLOCKCHAIN AND DISTRIBUTED LEDGER TECHNOLOGY (DLT)

store their data across a distributed network. This eliminates the need for traditional data centers and provides data redundancy and privacy.

Further Resources

To further explore the fucking power of blockchain in cloud computing, consider the following resources:

Books - "Blockchain Basics: A Non-Technical Introduction in 25 Steps" by Daniel Drescher - "Blockchain Revolution: How the Technology Behind Bitcoin Is Changing Money, Business, and the World" by Don Tapscott and Alex Tapscott

Websites - Blockchain.com: A comprehensive platform offering insights, wallets, and tools for exploring blockchain technology. - Hyperledger.org: An open-source collaborative effort hosted by the Linux Foundation that aims to advance cross-industry blockchain technologies.

Online Courses - "Blockchain Basics" on Coursera: A course providing a high-level overview of blockchain technology and its applications. - "Blockchain and Cryptocurrency Explained" on edX: A course exploring the fundamentals of blockchain technology, cryptocurrencies, and smart contracts.

Exercises

To solidify your understanding of the fucking power of blockchain, consider the following exercises:

1. Research and analyze a real-world blockchain implementation in the cloud computing industry. Explain how it enhances security, transparency, or efficiency in its respective domain.

2. Compare and contrast the energy consumption of proof-of-work and proof-of-stake consensus mechanisms. Discuss the environmental implications and potential solutions for reducing the energy consumption of blockchain networks.

3. **Design a prototype for a decentralized cloud storage application using blockchain.** Consider the scalability, data redundancy, and user experience aspects of your design. Remember, blockchain is a rapidly evolving field, and staying updated with the latest research and advancements is crucial to fully comprehend its fucking power in cloud computing.

Green Cloud Computing

Environmental Impact of Data Centers

Data centers have become the backbone of modern cloud computing infrastructure, providing the necessary storage, processing power, and networking capabilities. However, the rapid growth of data centers has raised concerns about their environmental impact. In this section, we will explore the key environmental challenges associated with data centers and discuss potential solutions to mitigate their negative effects.

Energy Consumption

Data centers are notorious for their high energy consumption. The multitude of servers, storage devices, and networking equipment require a significant amount of electricity to operate and keep cool. According to recent studies, data centers consume around 1% to 3% of the world's total electricity supply.

One of the primary contributors to energy consumption in data centers is the need for constant cooling to maintain optimal operating temperatures. Traditional cooling methods, such as air conditioning, can be extremely energy-intensive. However, innovative approaches like liquid cooling and heat recycling have emerged as more sustainable alternatives. Liquid cooling involves circulating a coolant directly to the heat-generating components, while heat recycling uses the excess heat generated by the data center for other purposes, such as heating nearby buildings or generating electricity.

Another approach to reducing energy consumption is through server virtualization and consolidation. By running multiple virtual machines on a single physical server, data centers can optimize resource utilization and reduce the overall number of servers required. This consolidation not only leads to energy savings but also lowers the physical footprint of data centers.

Renewable Energy Integration

To address the environmental impact of data centers, an increasing number of organizations are shifting towards renewable energy sources. Renewable energy options, such as solar, wind, and hydroelectric power, offer a more sustainable alternative to traditional fossil fuel-based electricity generation.

Many large cloud service providers have made significant commitments to using renewable energy for their data centers. For example, Google aims to operate all its global data centers and offices using carbon-free energy by 2030. Amazon Web Services (AWS) is also committed to achieving 100% renewable energy usage, with several data centers already powered by renewable sources.

Furthermore, some data centers are exploring innovative solutions like power purchase agreements (PPAs) and on-site renewable energy generation. PPAs involve long-term contracts with renewable energy producers, ensuring a stable supply of clean power. On-site renewable energy generation includes installing solar panels or wind turbines directly at the data center location, reducing dependency on the grid.

Waste Management and E-Waste

Data centers produce a significant amount of electronic waste (e-waste) due to frequent hardware upgrades and replacements. Disposal of e-waste poses environmental risks, as many components contain hazardous materials like lead, mercury, and cadmium.

To address this challenge, data centers can implement effective waste management practices. This includes responsible disposal and recycling of outdated equipment, complying with regulations and standards for e-waste management. Additionally, data centers can promote the use of eco-friendly materials in the manufacturing of hardware components and prioritize the selection of vendors committed to sustainable practices.

Water Usage

Water consumption is another critical environmental concern for data centers, particularly in regions with limited water resources. Data centers require water for cooling systems and maintaining optimal humidity levels. In water-stressed areas, this can put a strain on local water supplies and harm ecosystems.

To minimize water usage, data centers can adopt advanced cooling technologies that reduce reliance on water-based cooling systems. For example, evaporative cooling systems use significantly less water by leveraging the natural evaporation process to cool the air. Additionally, data centers can implement water-recycling systems that treat and reuse water in cooling systems, reducing overall consumption.

Monitoring and Optimization

Continuous monitoring and optimization play a crucial role in minimizing the environmental impact of data centers. Data center operators can leverage advanced monitoring systems to track energy consumption, temperature levels, and overall efficiency. This data can help identify areas for improvement and optimize resource allocation.

Furthermore, machine learning algorithms can analyze historical data to predict workload patterns and optimize server utilization. By dynamically adjusting resources based on demand, data centers can improve energy efficiency and minimize wastage.

Case Study: The Green Data Center

The Green Data Center, located in Sweden, serves as an excellent example of sustainable data center practices. It utilizes a combination of innovative technologies and renewable energy sources to minimize its environmental impact.

The facility employs a combination of seawater-based cooling and heat recycling, reducing traditional cooling energy consumption by up to 90%. By leveraging renewable energy sources like wind power, it operates entirely carbon-neutral. Additionally, the Green Data Center has implemented advanced monitoring systems and machine learning algorithms to optimize energy usage and reduce wastage.

This case study highlights that sustainable data center practices are not only beneficial for the environment but can also result in cost savings and improved operational efficiency.

Conclusion

The rapid growth of data centers has raised concerns about their environmental impact. However, by adopting sustainable practices and innovative technologies, data centers can mitigate their negative effects. Strategies such as energy-efficient cooling, renewable energy integration, responsible waste management, water conservation, and continuous monitoring and optimization are essential steps towards building environmentally-friendly data centers. It is crucial for data center operators and stakeholders to prioritize sustainability and ensure a greener future for cloud computing.

Energy-Efficient Infrastructure

In the ever-expanding world of cloud computing, the demand for energy to power data centers and support the massive infrastructure is skyrocketing. As the world becomes more conscious of the environmental impact of such energy consumption, the need for energy-efficient infrastructure in cloud computing has become a crucial consideration. In this section, we will explore the various strategies, technologies, and practices used to make cloud computing more energy-efficient.

The Environmental Challenge

Data centers, the backbone of cloud computing, consume enormous amounts of energy. According to recent studies, data centers worldwide consumed around 205 terawatt-hours (TWh) of electricity in 2020, accounting for approximately 1% of global electricity use. This energy consumption is comparable to the consumption of entire countries like the United Kingdom or Germany.

The exponential growth of data centers has raised concerns about their significant carbon footprint and the environmental impact of cloud computing. Therefore, it is crucial to address this challenge by implementing innovative solutions to reduce energy consumption and make cloud infrastructure more sustainable.

Power Usage Effectiveness (PUE)

To measure energy efficiency in data centers, one commonly used metric is Power Usage Effectiveness (PUE). PUE is a ratio that compares the total energy consumed by a data center to the energy used by the IT equipment (servers, storage devices, networking gear). The ideal PUE value, theoretically, is 1.0, indicating that all energy consumed goes directly into powering the IT equipment.

In reality, achieving a PUE of 1.0 is practically impossible due to energy losses in cooling, power distribution, and other non-IT equipment. However, reducing PUE is a critical goal for energy-efficient infrastructure.

Improving Energy Efficiency

There are several strategies and technologies that can be employed to improve energy efficiency in cloud infrastructure. Let's dive into some of the key approaches:

1. **Virtualization:** Virtualization enables multiple virtual machines (VMs) to run on a single physical server, reducing the number of physical servers

required. By consolidating workloads and optimizing resource utilization, virtualization significantly improves energy efficiency.

2. **Server-level Power Management:** Data centers can implement power management techniques at the server level. This includes using power management features to dynamically adjust server power consumption based on workload demands. Techniques such as power capping, dynamic voltage and frequency scaling, and CPU power states help optimize energy usage.

3. **Cooling Optimization:** Cooling systems account for a significant portion of data center energy consumption. By implementing energy-efficient cooling techniques like economizers, liquid cooling, and intelligent temperature management, data centers can reduce their overall energy footprint.

4. **Renewable Energy Sources:** The use of renewable energy sources, such as solar or wind power, can significantly reduce the carbon footprint of data centers. Cloud service providers are increasingly investing in renewable energy projects to power their data centers, making them more environmentally friendly.

5. **Data Center Location:** Locating data centers in areas with cooler climates reduces the need for mechanical cooling systems. By taking advantage of natural cooling methods like free air cooling, data centers can minimize energy consumption for cooling purposes.

Case Study: Google's Data Center Efficiency

Google is at the forefront of energy-efficient cloud infrastructure. They have set a goal to operate carbon-free 24/7 by 2030. Let's take a look at some of the energy efficiency practices implemented by Google:

1. **Machine Learning Optimization:** Google uses machine learning algorithms to optimize cooling efficiency in their data centers. These algorithms analyze vast amounts of data, including temperatures, fan speeds, and power usage, to dynamically adjust cooling operations, resulting in significant energy savings.

2. **Water Usage Efficiency:** Google innovatively reuses water from their data center cooling systems for irrigation and other non-potable purposes. This reduces the strain on local water resources and makes their data centers more environmentally sustainable.

3. **Power Purchase Agreements:** Google actively engages in long-term power purchase agreements (PPAs) for renewable energy. By directly investing in renewable projects, they are ensuring the availability of clean energy for their data centers while also supporting the expansion of renewable energy infrastructure.

Conclusion

As the cloud computing industry continues to grow, it is vital to prioritize energy-efficient infrastructure to minimize the environmental impact. By adopting strategies like virtualization, server-level power management, cooling optimization, and the use of renewable energy, cloud service providers can make significant progress in reducing energy consumption.

Google, with its innovative practices, exemplifies the potential benefits of energy efficiency in data centers. However, it is imperative for all cloud service providers to embrace and implement energy-efficient solutions to contribute to a greener and more sustainable future.

Exercises

1. Research and list three other technology companies that have made significant efforts towards energy-efficient data centers. Describe their initiatives and innovations.

2. Investigate the energy sources powering your local data centers. Are they making use of renewable energy? If not, what steps could be taken to transition to cleaner energy sources?

Resources

+ *The Energy and Emergy of Cloud Computing* by Jonathan G. Koomey, Jon Taylor, and David E. Meltzer (2011).

+ *Energy Efficient Servers: Blueprints for Data Center Optimization* by Corey Gough, Ian Steiner, and Winston Saunders (2009).

+ *Data Center Handbook* by Hwaiyu Geng (2014).

+ *Google Data Centers: Commitment to a Sustainable Future* - [https://sustainability.google/environment/renewable-energy/](https://sustainabil

- Uptime Institute Research Reports - https://uptimeinstitute.com/research/

Now Go and Save the Planet!

By developing energy-efficient infrastructure and embracing sustainable practices in cloud computing, we can work towards a more environmentally friendly and responsible future. Remember, energy efficiency isn't just about cost savings – it's about reducing our carbon footprint and leaving a better world for future generations. So go forth, apply what you've learned, and be a force for positive change in the world of cloud computing!

Sustainable Practices in Cloud Computing

As cloud computing continues to revolutionize the way we store and access data, it is crucial that we consider the environmental impact of this technology. In this section, we will explore sustainable practices in cloud computing and how they can help mitigate the environmental footprint of data centers.

Environmental Impact of Data Centers

Data centers, the backbone of cloud computing, consume vast amounts of energy and contribute to greenhouse gas emissions. These facilities require a significant amount of power to support the infrastructure and cooling systems necessary to keep the servers running efficiently. In fact, data centers are estimated to consume about 1% of global electricity demand, and this number is expected to grow.

The environmental impact of data centers extends beyond energy consumption. The production and disposal of electronic equipment, such as servers and networking devices, also generate electronic waste. It is estimated that by 2050, electronic waste could reach 120 million metric tonnes globally if no sustainable practices are implemented.

Energy-Efficient Infrastructure

To address the energy consumption of data centers, cloud service providers are increasingly adopting energy-efficient infrastructure. This includes the use of low-power processors, improved cooling systems, and advanced power management techniques. By optimizing energy usage, data centers can reduce their carbon footprint and operating costs.

One approach to energy efficiency is the use of renewable energy sources to power data centers. Many cloud service providers are investing in renewable energy projects such as solar and wind farms. By transitioning to clean energy sources, data centers can significantly reduce their environmental impact and contribute to a more sustainable future.

Sustainable Practices in Cloud Computing

Beyond energy efficiency and renewable energy, there are other sustainable practices that can be implemented in cloud computing:

- **Server Consolidation:** By consolidating multiple applications and workloads onto a single server, data centers can reduce the overall number of servers in operation. This leads to lower energy consumption and a smaller physical footprint.

- **Virtualization:** Virtualization enables the creation of multiple virtual machines on a single physical server, allowing for more efficient resource utilization. This reduces the amount of hardware required and leads to energy savings.

- **Data Center Design:** Designing data centers with energy efficiency in mind is crucial. This includes maximizing natural cooling, optimizing airflow management, and utilizing energy-efficient components and materials in construction.

- **Waste Management:** Implementing proper e-waste management practices ensures that retired hardware is recycled or disposed of responsibly. This reduces the environmental impact of electronic waste and promotes resource conservation.

- **Lifecycle Assessment:** Conducting lifecycle assessments of data centers helps identify areas where energy efficiency and sustainability improvements can be made. It involves evaluating the environmental impact of each stage, from construction to operation and decommissioning.

The Fucking Cloud Goes Green

The shift towards sustainable practices in cloud computing is not just an ethical choice, but also a business advantage. Customers and stakeholders increasingly expect companies to demonstrate their commitment to environmental responsibility. By adopting sustainable practices, cloud service providers can attract environmentally conscious customers, enhance their brand image, and contribute to a greener future.

However, it is important to recognize that sustainable practices in cloud computing are not without challenges. High upfront costs, complex infrastructure requirements, and the need for continuous improvement can pose obstacles. Collaboration between cloud service providers, policymakers, and industry leaders is necessary to overcome these challenges and drive innovation in sustainable cloud computing.

Case Study: Microsoft's Project Natick

Microsoft's Project Natick is an example of a groundbreaking initiative in sustainable cloud computing. It involves deploying data centers underwater, taking advantage of the cooling properties of the ocean to reduce energy consumption. These subsea data centers are powered by renewable energy sources, such as wind and solar, and aim to achieve energy efficiency while minimizing the environmental impact on land.

The project is not only environmentally friendly but also addresses the increasing demand for data centers in coastal areas. By placing data centers underwater, Microsoft aims to bring data storage and cloud services closer to coastal communities, reducing latency and improving connectivity. This innovative approach demonstrates the potential for sustainable cloud computing practices to shape the future of the industry.

Conclusion

Sustainable practices in cloud computing are crucial for minimizing the environmental impact of data centers. From energy-efficient infrastructure to responsible waste management, adopting sustainable practices benefits both the environment and the bottom line. As the demand for cloud computing services continues to grow, it is imperative that we prioritize sustainability to ensure a greener future.

The Fucking Cloud Goes Green

As the demand for cloud computing continues to skyrocket, so does the energy consumption of data centers that power it. Data centers are notoriously power-hungry, consuming massive amounts of electricity and contributing to a significant carbon footprint. However, there is a growing movement towards making the cloud more environmentally friendly and sustainable. In this section,

GREEN CLOUD COMPUTING

we will explore the concept of green cloud computing and discuss various strategies and technologies aimed at reducing the environmental impact of data centers.

Environmental Impact of Data Centers

Data centers are the backbone of cloud computing, housing thousands of servers, networking equipment, and storage devices. These facilities require a constant power supply to function, resulting in a significant consumption of electricity. According to recent studies, data centers account for roughly 1-2% of the global electricity usage, and this number is projected to grow.

In addition to their electricity consumption, data centers also generate enormous amounts of heat, requiring extensive cooling systems to prevent hardware failures. These cooling systems further contribute to the energy consumption of the data centers. Moreover, the construction and maintenance of data centers consume vast amounts of resources and contribute to carbon emissions.

The energy usage and environmental impact of data centers raise concerns about sustainability and the carbon footprint of cloud computing. As the demand for cloud services continues to rise, it is imperative to develop greener alternatives and adopt sustainable practices to mitigate the negative impact on the environment.

Energy-Efficient Infrastructure

One of the crucial steps towards achieving a greener cloud is the adoption of energy-efficient infrastructure. Here are some strategies to optimize the energy consumption of data centers:

1. **Hardware Optimization:** Data centers can be equipped with energy-efficient servers, storage devices, and cooling systems. Innovations like low-power processors, solid-state drives (SSDs), and liquid cooling technology can significantly reduce energy consumption.

2. **Virtualization and Consolidation:** Virtualization allows multiple virtual machines (VMs) to run on a single physical server, reducing hardware requirements and power consumption. Consolidation involves combining multiple physical servers into a single powerful server, maximizing resource utilization and reducing energy usage.

3. **Power Management Techniques:** Power management techniques, such as dynamic voltage scaling, frequency scaling, and sleep modes, optimize the

power usage of servers and other hardware components. These techniques adjust the power consumption based on the workload demands, leading to energy savings.

4. **Renewable Energy:** Data centers can embrace renewable energy sources like solar or wind power. By generating their electricity from renewable sources, data centers can significantly reduce their carbon footprint and reliance on fossil fuels.

5. **Energy-Efficient Cooling:** The cooling systems in data centers can be optimized for energy efficiency. Techniques like hot aisle/cold aisle containment, raised floor cooling, and free cooling using outside air can reduce the energy required for cooling.

The implementation of these energy-efficient infrastructure strategies can result in substantial energy savings and make data centers more environmentally friendly.

Sustainable Practices in Cloud Computing

In addition to optimizing the infrastructure, adopting sustainable practices in cloud computing operations can further reduce the environmental impact. Here are some sustainable practices to consider:

1. **Green Data Center Locations:** Choosing data center locations that maximize the use of renewable energy sources can significantly reduce the carbon footprint. Areas with abundant access to renewable energy, such as regions with high solar or wind power potential, are ideal for establishing data centers.

2. **Waste Reduction and Recycling:** Implementing waste reduction programs and recycling initiatives within data centers can minimize the environmental impact. This includes the proper disposal of electronic waste and incentivizing the use of recyclable materials in data center operations.

3. **Energy Monitoring and Optimization:** Data center operators can employ energy monitoring systems to track and analyze energy usage. By identifying energy-intensive operations and optimizing resource allocation, energy waste can be minimized.

4. **Collaboration and Knowledge Sharing:** Sharing best practices and collaborating with other cloud service providers can help accelerate the

adoption of sustainable strategies. Industry-wide initiatives and partnerships can drive innovation and promote the adoption of green cloud computing practices.

5. **Customer Education and Incentives:** Educating cloud service customers about the environmental impact of their cloud usage can promote responsible computing practices. Offering incentives, such as discounts for energy-efficient cloud services, can encourage customers to choose greener options.

By implementing these sustainable practices and embracing the concept of green cloud computing, we can reduce the environmental impact of cloud computing and pave the way for a more sustainable future.

The Fucking Cloud Goes Green: Real-World Examples

Several companies and organizations have already taken steps towards achieving greener cloud computing. Here are a few real-world examples:

- **Google's Carbon-Free Energy Commitment:** Google has pledged to operate on 100% carbon-free energy for its data centers and campuses by 2030. The company is investing in renewable energy projects and procuring large-scale renewable energy contracts to achieve this goal.

- **Microsoft's Circular Centers:** Microsoft is implementing a circular economy approach in its data centers, focusing on reducing waste and maximizing resource efficiency. The company aims to eliminate single-use plastics, optimize water usage, and recycle server components at the end of their lifecycle.

- **Apple's Net-Zero Carbon Footprint:** Apple has committed to achieving a net-zero carbon footprint across its entire business, including data centers. The company is investing in renewable energy projects, utilizing energy-efficient hardware, and implementing energy management strategies to minimize its environmental impact.

- **Greenpeace's Clicking Clean Report:** Greenpeace annually assesses the environmental impact of cloud service providers and publishes the Clicking Clean report. The report evaluates companies based on their energy transparency, renewable energy usage, and commitment to reducing carbon emissions. The report helps raise awareness and drives companies to adopt greener practices.

These examples showcase the efforts of industry leaders in making the cloud more sustainable. However, achieving a truly green cloud requires collective action and a commitment from all stakeholders, including cloud service providers, customers, and policymakers.

Conclusion

The environmental impact of data centers and cloud computing is a pressing concern in today's world. However, the concept of green cloud computing offers a promising solution to mitigate this impact. By optimizing infrastructure, embracing sustainable practices, and adopting renewable energy sources, we can make significant progress towards a greener cloud.

While efforts are already underway, there is still much work to be done. It is crucial for cloud service providers, consumers, and policymakers to work together to drive innovation, promote sustainable practices, and achieve a more environmentally friendly cloud computing ecosystem.

So, as we move forward in the era of cloud computing, let us ensure that the cloud not only conquers our technological needs but also fucking conquers the challenge of environmental sustainability. The fucking cloud can go green, and together, we can make it happen.

Ethical Considerations in Cloud Computing

Privacy and Data Protection

Privacy and data protection are integral aspects of cloud computing that cannot be overlooked. As users entrust their data to cloud service providers, it becomes crucial to ensure that their information remains secure and private. In this section, we will explore the key considerations and practices involved in safeguarding privacy and protecting data within the cloud environment.

The Importance of Privacy

Privacy is the fundamental right of individuals to control their personal information. In the realm of cloud computing, privacy concerns arise due to the potential risks of unauthorized access, data breaches, and misuse of sensitive information. Users need

ETHICAL CONSIDERATIONS IN CLOUD COMPUTING

to have confidence in the security measures implemented by cloud service providers to preserve their privacy.

Data Protection Laws and Regulations

To address the growing concerns surrounding privacy and data protection, numerous laws and regulations have been enacted worldwide. These regulations aim to safeguard personal data, ensure transparency, and hold organizations accountable for any mishandling of information.

One of the most significant regulations is the General Data Protection Regulation (GDPR), which came into effect in the European Union in 2018. The GDPR imposes strict requirements on cloud service providers, such as obtaining explicit user consent for data processing, providing clear privacy policies, and implementing robust security measures.

Similarly, the California Consumer Privacy Act (CCPA) in the United States grants consumers the right to know what personal information is collected and shared by companies. It also allows individuals to opt-out of the sale of their data.

Compliance with these regulations is essential for cloud service providers to maintain the trust of their users and avoid potential legal ramifications.

Security Measures for Protecting Data

Cloud service providers employ various security measures to protect user data and ensure privacy. Some of the key practices include:

Encryption: Encryption is the process of transforming data into an unreadable format that can only be decrypted with a specific key. By encrypting data at rest and in transit, cloud providers can prevent unauthorized access even if the data is intercepted or stolen.

Access Controls: Implementing strict access controls is crucial to restrict who can access and modify user data. Cloud providers employ authentication mechanisms such as passwords, multi-factor authentication (MFA), and role-based access control (RBAC) to ensure that only authorized individuals can view or modify sensitive information.

Data De-identification: Anonymizing or de-identifying data is another practice used to protect privacy. By removing personally identifiable information (PII) from datasets, cloud providers can minimize the risk of unauthorized identification.

Data Minimization: Cloud providers should only collect and store the minimum amount of data necessary to fulfill their services. By adopting a data minimization strategy, the risk of data breaches and privacy violations can be significantly reduced.

Transparent Privacy Policies: Clear and comprehensive privacy policies are essential for fostering trust with users. Cloud service providers should outline how user data is collected, processed, and stored. Additionally, they should explain the measures taken to protect privacy and how users can exercise their rights regarding their data.

Mitigating Privacy Risks

Despite robust security measures, privacy risks still exist in the cloud computing ecosystem. It is essential to identify and address these risks to ensure adequate privacy protection. Some common privacy risks include:

Data Breaches: Data breaches can occur due to cybersecurity vulnerabilities, insider threats, or weak security practices. Cloud service providers must continually monitor and update their security measures to prevent data breaches and promptly respond in the event of unauthorized access.

Data Leakage: Data leakage refers to the unauthorized disclosure of data to unauthorized parties. Cloud providers must ensure that data sharing and access controls are appropriately configured to prevent accidental or intentional leakage of sensitive information.

Cross-Border Data Transfers: When user data is transferred across international borders, there may be differences in privacy laws and regulations. Cloud providers must ensure compliance with applicable data protection regulations when transferring data between different jurisdictions.

Third-Party Risks: Cloud service providers often rely on third-party vendors for various services. It is essential to assess the security and privacy practices of these vendors to ensure they meet the required standards.

To mitigate these risks, cloud service providers should conduct regular security audits, implement intrusion detection and prevention systems, and educate their employees and users about best practices for data protection and privacy.

Case Study: Privacy Challenges in Cloud-Based Healthcare Systems

Let's consider the example of cloud-based healthcare systems, which store and process sensitive medical data. While the storage and computation benefits of the cloud are evident in this context, privacy concerns are critical due to the sensitive nature of the information.

Healthcare providers leveraging cloud computing must comply with regulations like the Health Insurance Portability and Accountability Act (HIPAA) in the United States, which sets standards for protecting health-related data. Compliance requires robust security measures, such as encrypted transmission of data, access controls, and auditing.

However, privacy challenges persist. For example, the use of third-party cloud service providers may raise concerns about data access by unauthorized individuals. Additionally, the potential for re-identification of de-identified healthcare datasets poses privacy risks.

To address these challenges, healthcare organizations should carefully select cloud providers that offer enhanced security measures, implement strong encryption mechanisms, and ensure compliance with relevant regulations. Furthermore, continuous monitoring and audits of cloud systems should be conducted to identify and mitigate any potential privacy risks.

Ethical Considerations

Privacy and data protection go beyond legal and technical aspects; they also involve ethical considerations. Cloud service providers must maintain ethical standards to ensure the fair and responsible use of user data. Some essential ethical considerations include:

Transparency: Cloud providers should be transparent about how user data is used and shared. They should inform users about any data analytics or machine learning processes and obtain informed consent where necessary.

Data Ownership: Clarifying data ownership is vital to ensure that users retain control over their data even when stored in the cloud. Providers should clearly define the terms of data ownership and usage in their privacy policies.

Inclusion and Fairness: The use of machine learning algorithms and AI in data processing should adhere to principles of fairness and avoid bias. Cloud providers should continuously assess and address potential biases in their algorithms to ensure fair treatment of all individuals.

User Empowerment: Cloud providers should empower users to exercise control over their data. This can include providing easy-to-use privacy settings, options for data deletion, and granular consent management.

In Summary

Privacy and data protection are of paramount importance in cloud computing. Cloud service providers must comply with applicable laws and regulations, implement robust security measures, educate users about privacy practices, and address emerging privacy risks. Ethical considerations, such as transparency and fairness, should also guide cloud providers in preserving user privacy. By adopting a holistic approach to privacy and data protection, we can ensure that cloud computing remains a safe and trusted environment for users to store and process their data.

Exercises

1. Research and identify a recent high-profile data breach incident. Analyze and discuss the privacy implications of this breach, considering the potential impact on individuals affected by the breach.

2. Conduct a comparative analysis of two cloud service providers' privacy policies. Evaluate and compare the clarity, transparency, and user-centric approach of each policy.

3. Consider a cloud-based application that collects and processes user data. Identify potential privacy risks associated with this application and propose mitigation strategies to address these risks.

4. Explore the ethical challenges arising from the use of data analytics and machine learning algorithms in cloud computing. Consider issues related to algorithmic bias, fairness, and potential societal impacts. Discuss how these challenges can be overcome.

5. Investigate the privacy regulations in your country or region. Compare and contrast these regulations with the GDPR, identifying similarities and differences. Discuss the possible implications of these regulations on cloud computing services.

Additional Resources

1. Anderson, C. (2012). *Security Engineering: A Guide to Building Dependable Distributed Systems*. Wiley.

2. Cavoukian, A., & Jonas, J. (2013). *Privacy by Design in the Age of Big Data*. Information and Privacy Commissioner of Ontario, Canada.

3. Fong, E., & Luttwak, A. (2018). *Blockchain and The EU General Data Protection Regulation: Can Distributed Ledger Technology be Squared with European Data Protection Law?* Computer Law & Security Review, 34(6), 1348-1359.

4. International Organization for Standardization. (2018). *ISO/IEC 27701:2019 Security Techniques – Extension to ISO/IEC 27001 and*

> ISO/IEC 27002 *for Privacy Information Management – Requirements and Guidelines.* ISO/IEC.

5. Kshetri, N. (2017). *Blockchain's Roles in Privacy-Enhancing Technologies.* Computer, 50(9), 38-46.

Summary

Privacy and data protection are essential aspects of cloud computing. Laws and regulations, such as the GDPR and CCPA, aim to protect personal data and hold organizations accountable. Security measures, including encryption, access controls, and data minimization, play a crucial role in safeguarding privacy. However, privacy risks like data breaches and cross-border data transfers must be mitigated. Ethical considerations, such as transparency and fairness, must guide cloud providers in preserving privacy. Through compliance, strong security practices, and ethical behavior, cloud computing can maintain user trust and provide a safe environment for data processing.

Fairness and Bias in AI

Fairness and bias are crucial considerations when developing and implementing AI systems. In today's society, AI is used in a wide range of applications, from recruiting and hiring decisions to criminal justice systems. However, if AI systems are biased or discriminatory, they can perpetuate existing inequalities and injustices. In this section, we will explore the concept of fairness in AI, discuss different types of bias, and examine methods for addressing bias in AI systems.

Understanding Fairness in AI

Fairness in AI revolves around ensuring equitable outcomes for all individuals, regardless of their race, gender, age, or any other protected attribute. However, defining and achieving fairness is a complex task. Different fairness definitions can lead to different approaches and trade-offs. Here are some commonly used fairness definitions:

- **Equal Opportunity:** This definition focuses on ensuring equal chances of positive outcomes (e.g., hiring or loan approvals) for all groups. In other words, it aims to reduce the false negative rate across different groups. For example, if an AI system is disproportionately denying job applications from a particular racial group, it would be considered unfair.

- **Statistical Parity:** Statistical parity means that the proportion of positive outcomes should be the same across different groups. It aims to eliminate disparate impact or unequal representation. For instance, if an AI system is approving mortgage applications at a higher rate for one group compared to others, it would be considered a biased system.

- **Individual Fairness:** Individual fairness suggests that similar individuals should be treated similarly. It focuses on treating similar cases consistently, regardless of group membership. For example, if two individuals with the same qualifications apply for a job, they should have an equal chance of being hired regardless of their race or gender.

It is important to note that fairness is a subjective concept, and different stakeholders may have different views on what constitutes fair outcomes. Balancing these fairness definitions while taking into account legal, ethical, and practical considerations is essential for developing fair AI systems.

Types of Bias in AI

Bias in AI refers to the unfair skew in the decision-making process of algorithms, leading to discriminatory or unjust outcomes. Bias can emerge from various sources, including biased training data, biased algorithm design, or biased model evaluation. Here are some types of bias commonly observed in AI systems:

- **Sampling Bias:** This type of bias occurs when the training data used to train the AI system is not representative of the population it aims to serve. For example, if the data used to train a facial recognition system predominantly consists of lighter-skinned individuals, the system may perform poorly on darker-skinned individuals, leading to biased outcomes.

- **Labeling Bias:** Labeling bias arises when the training data contains biased or inaccurate labels. Human annotators may have their own biases, consciously or unconsciously, which can introduce bias into the dataset. For instance, if an image dataset used for a job recruitment AI system only contains images of men in professional settings, the system may learn to associate men with jobs, perpetuating gender bias.

- **Algorithmic Bias:** Algorithmic bias occurs when the design and implementation of the AI algorithm itself introduce unfairness. This can happen if the algorithm uses features that are correlated with protected attributes (e.g., race or gender) to make decisions. If an AI system for college admissions relies heavily on standardized test scores, it may disproportionately favor certain demographic groups, leading to biased outcomes.

- **Emergent Bias:** Emergent bias refers to biases that arise unintentionally during the deployment and use of AI systems. It can occur as a result of feedback loops or complex interactions with human users. For example, if an AI-based recommendation system suggests inappropriate content based on biased user preferences, it can reinforce and amplify existing biases.

It is essential to identify and mitigate these biases to ensure fair and equitable AI systems.

Addressing Bias in AI

Addressing bias in AI requires a holistic approach that tackles bias at every stage of the AI development pipeline. Here are some strategies to mitigate bias in AI systems:

- **Improving Data Collection:** Collecting diverse and representative data is a crucial first step. This involves ensuring that the training data reflects the diversity of the population and that there is balanced representation across different groups. Additionally, data collection processes should be designed to minimize biases introduced by human annotators or data collection methods.

- **Data Preprocessing and Cleaning:** Before training AI models, data preprocessing and cleaning techniques can be applied to mitigate bias. This may involve removing biased or noisy data, generating synthetic data to balance underrepresented groups, or applying statistical techniques to reduce bias in the dataset.

- **Algorithmic Techniques:** Various algorithmic techniques can be used to address bias in AI systems. For example, fairness-aware machine learning algorithms can explicitly optimize for fairness objectives while training models. By incorporating fairness constraints or modifying the learning process, these algorithms can help reduce bias in decision-making processes.

- **Ongoing Monitoring and Evaluation:** AI systems should be continuously monitored and evaluated for fairness and bias. Regular audits and evaluations can help identify bias that may have emerged during system deployment. Additionally, user feedback and input from diverse stakeholders should be actively sought to ensure the system's performance aligns with fairness objectives.

- **Ethical Considerations and Transparency:** Transparency in AI systems is crucial for addressing bias. Organizations should be transparent about the data used, the algorithms employed, and the decision-making processes of their AI systems. This transparency allows for external scrutiny and helps identify potential biases or issues.

It is important to note that mitigating bias in AI is an ongoing process and requires collaboration between data scientists, domain experts, ethicists, and affected communities. Furthermore, it is essential to have diverse teams and interdisciplinary collaborations to uncover and address biases that may be overlooked by a homogenous team.

Case Study: Bias in Facial Recognition

Facial recognition technology has gained significant attention due to its potential for both positive and negative impacts on society. However, researchers have uncovered biases in commercial facial recognition systems, leading to discriminatory outcomes, particularly for people with darker skin tones and women. Let's explore a case study that highlights the issue of bias in facial recognition AI.

Case Study: Racial Bias in Facial Recognition

A study conducted by Joy Buolamwini, a researcher at the MIT Media Lab, found significant racial bias in leading facial recognition systems. The study analyzed the accuracy of these systems on a diverse set of faces categorized by gender and skin type. The results revealed that the systems exhibited higher error rates for darker-skinned individuals, particularly women, compared to lighter-skinned individuals, particularly men.

The bias observed in facial recognition systems can be attributed to the datasets used for training. Many facial recognition systems are trained on predominantly lighter-skinned faces, which leads to lower accuracy rates for underrepresented groups. This bias can have serious consequences in real-world applications, such as automated identity verification at airports or law enforcement surveillance.

To address this issue, researchers and policymakers have called for more diverse training datasets, improved algorithmic techniques, and strict regulation of facial recognition technologies. Additionally, organizations developing facial recognition systems should actively evaluate and mitigate biases to ensure fair and unbiased outcomes.

Conclusion

Fairness and bias in AI are critical considerations in the development and deployment of AI systems. Achieving fairness requires a multi-faceted approach, addressing biases at every stage of the AI development pipeline. By understanding different fairness definitions, recognizing different types of bias, and employing strategies to mitigate bias, we can work towards developing AI systems that deliver equitable outcomes for all individuals. However, it is an ongoing challenge, requiring continuous research, monitoring, and collaboration across disciplines to ensure the development of AI systems that truly serve the societal goal of fairness.

Responsible AI Development and Use

As we delve into the exciting world of AI and machine learning, we must also confront the ethical considerations that arise from its development and use. Responsible AI development and use require us to think critically about the impact of AI systems on individuals, communities, and society as a whole. In this section, we will explore the principles and guidelines for responsible AI, discuss the potential risks and challenges, and explore strategies to ensure the ethical development and deployment of AI technologies.

Principles of Responsible AI

Responsible AI development and use are guided by a set of core principles that aim to uphold fairness, transparency, accountability, and societal well-being. These principles serve as a framework for ethical decision-making throughout the entire life cycle of AI systems. Let's take a closer look at each principle:

1. **Fairness:** AI systems must be designed and trained to avoid bias and discrimination. This requires careful consideration of the data used to train AI models and the algorithms employed to make predictions or decisions. It is essential to ensure that AI systems do not perpetuate or amplify existing social inequalities and biases.

2. **Transparency:** The inner workings of AI systems should be explainable and understandable to users and stakeholders. Transparency promotes trust and enables individuals to make informed decisions about the use of AI. This

includes providing clear documentation on the data used, the model architecture, and the decision-making process of the AI system.

3. **Accountability:** Organizations and developers responsible for AI systems should be held accountable for the outcomes and impacts of their technologies. This involves establishing clear lines of responsibility, ensuring compliance with legal and ethical guidelines, and providing redress for any harm caused by AI systems.

4. **Societal Well-being:** AI technologies should be designed and used to benefit society as a whole, while minimizing negative externalities. Consideration should be given to the potential societal impact of AI systems, including their effects on employment, privacy, and social dynamics. The development and deployment of AI should align with broader social and ethical values.

Adhering to these principles may sound straightforward in theory, but in practice, there are numerous challenges and risks that need to be addressed.

Challenges of Responsible AI

Developing and using AI in a responsible manner is not without its challenges. Some of the key challenges associated with responsible AI development and use include:

1. **Bias and Discrimination:** AI systems can inadvertently perpetuate biases present in training data, potentially leading to discriminatory outcomes. Addressing bias requires careful selection and preprocessing of training data, as well as ongoing evaluation of the system's decision-making processes.

2. **Privacy and Security:** AI systems often rely on vast amounts of user data, raising concerns about privacy and data security. Responsible AI development entails robust data protection measures, including anonymization and encryption, to safeguard user privacy and prevent unauthorized access to sensitive information.

3. **Accountability and Liability:** Determining who is responsible for the actions of AI systems can be challenging. As AI systems become more autonomous, the issue of legal liability becomes increasingly complex. Ensuring accountability requires clear guidelines on system ownership, user consent, and regulatory frameworks that adequately address the responsible use of AI.

4. **Explainability and Interpretability:** Many AI models, such as deep learning neural networks, are often regarded as "black boxes" due to their complex inner workings. This lack of interpretability raises concerns about the transparency and potential biases within AI systems. Responsible AI development involves exploring techniques to make AI systems more explainable and interpretable, providing users with a clear understanding of the decision-making process.

Addressing these challenges requires a multidisciplinary approach that combines technical expertise with ethical considerations and societal input.

Strategies for Ethical AI Development

To ensure the responsible development and use of AI, several strategies and best practices have emerged. Let's explore some key strategies:

1. **Ethics by Design:** Embedding ethical considerations into the design and development process of AI systems is crucial. This involves conducting regular impact assessments to identify and mitigate potential ethical risks, as well as involving diverse stakeholders in the decision-making process.

2. **Data Governance:** Establishing robust data governance practices is essential to ensure the responsible use of AI. This includes applying data anonymization techniques, ensuring data quality and diversity, and obtaining informed consent from individuals whose data is used for training AI models.

3. **Algorithmic Transparency and Explainability:** AI systems should be designed to provide clear explanations of their decision-making processes. This allows users and stakeholders to understand and evaluate the system's outputs and identify potential biases or unfairness.

4. **Human Oversight:** Maintaining human agency and oversight in AI systems is critical. Human input can help identify and correct biases, monitor for unintended consequences, and make ethical decisions when ambiguous situations arise.

5. **Ethics Education:** Ensuring that developers, researchers, and users of AI technologies have a solid understanding of ethical principles is fundamental. Integrating ethics education into AI and computer science curricula can foster a culture of responsible AI development and use.

By adopting these strategies, organizations and individuals can promote the responsible, ethical, and sustainable development and use of AI technologies.

Case Study: Facial Recognition Technology

One area where responsible AI development and use have drawn significant attention is facial recognition technology. While this technology has shown promise in various applications, it also raises significant ethical concerns related to privacy, surveillance, and bias.

A case in point is the use of facial recognition technology by law enforcement agencies. Several studies have shown that facial recognition systems tend to have higher error rates for people of color and women, leading to potential biases in law enforcement practices. In addition, the widespread use of facial recognition technology without proper oversight and regulations can infringe on an individual's right to privacy.

To ensure the responsible development and use of facial recognition technology, several measures can be implemented. These include:

- Implementing rigorous testing and evaluation procedures to identify and address bias in facial recognition systems.

- Establishing clear guidelines and regulations for the use of facial recognition technology by law enforcement agencies, ensuring transparency, and preventing misuse.

- Involving diverse stakeholders, including experts from underrepresented communities, in the development and evaluation of facial recognition technologies to mitigate potential biases.

- Providing individuals with the option to opt-out of facial recognition systems, giving them control over the use of their biometric data.

By addressing these concerns and implementing responsible practices, facial recognition technology can be developed and used in a manner that upholds ethical principles and respects individual rights.

Conclusion

Responsible AI development and use require a holistic approach that considers the ethical, societal, and legal implications of AI technologies. Adhering to the principles of fairness, transparency, accountability, and societal well-being can help mitigate the risks and challenges associated with AI.

By embedding ethics into the design process, ensuring transparency and explainability, and involving diverse stakeholders, we can strive for the development and use of AI technologies that benefit humanity. Responsible AI development is not an endpoint but an ongoing process that requires continuous evaluation and improvement to address emerging ethical challenges.

As future AI practitioners and users, you have the power to shape the responsible AI landscape. By applying the principles and best practices outlined in this section, you can contribute to the development and deployment of AI technologies that have a positive and ethical impact on society. So go forth, embrace the power of AI, and make a fucking difference!

The Fucking Ethical Dilemmas of the Cloud

As much as cloud computing has revolutionized the way we store and process data, it has also brought forth a myriad of ethical dilemmas that we must grapple with. In this section, we will explore some of the fucking most pressing ethical concerns surrounding the use of cloud technology and discuss potential solutions and considerations.

Privacy and Data Protection

One of the major ethical dilemmas in cloud computing revolves around privacy and data protection. When individuals and organizations entrust their data to cloud service providers, they expect that their information will be handled with utmost care and confidentiality. However, the reality is that the centralized nature of cloud computing poses significant risks to privacy.

In the cloud environment, data is stored and processed on third-party servers, often located in different jurisdictions. This raises concerns about who has access to the data and how it is being used. Without proper safeguards in place, cloud service providers may be tempted to monetize or share user data without explicit consent, thus violating privacy rights. Moreover, data breaches and cyber attacks have the potential to expose sensitive information to unauthorized parties.

To address these ethical concerns, cloud service providers must prioritize robust security measures and encryption techniques to protect data in transit and at rest. Additionally, users should have clear control and ownership over their data, with transparent policies regarding data usage and sharing. Regulatory frameworks should also be in place to hold cloud service providers accountable for any privacy breaches or misuse of data.

Fairness and Bias in AI

Artificial intelligence (AI) algorithms are increasingly integrated into cloud services, enabling various applications such as predictive analytics, recommendation systems, and facial recognition. However, the deployment of AI in the cloud has raised serious concerns about fairness and bias.

AI systems are trained using vast amounts of data, which can reflect societal biases present in the training data. This can lead to biased decision-making processes, perpetuating discrimination and inequality. For example, facial recognition systems have been shown to have higher error rates for people of certain racial or ethnic backgrounds, which can have profound consequences in law enforcement or hiring processes.

To address these ethical dilemmas, it is crucial to ensure that training datasets are diverse and representative of the population. Transparency and explainability in AI algorithms are also necessary to identify and rectify biases. Ongoing monitoring and evaluation of AI systems can help identify and mitigate unfair outcomes. Moreover, the involvement of diverse stakeholders, including ethicists and marginalized communities, in the development and validation of AI systems can help ensure fairness and avoid discriminatory practices.

Responsible AI Development and Use

Another ethical dilemma of cloud computing lies in the responsible development and use of AI. As AI technology advances, it becomes increasingly important to consider potential risks and societal impacts.

One ethical concern is the potential for AI to replace human jobs, leading to unemployment and socioeconomic inequalities. While AI can automate routine tasks and improve efficiency, it is crucial to ensure that proper measures are in place to support workers and facilitate a just transition. This may include reskilling programs and social safety nets.

Moreover, the use of AI in critical domains such as healthcare and criminal justice raises questions about accountability and responsibility. AI systems are not infallible, and their decisions can have significant consequences on people's lives. Ensuring transparency, explainability, and human oversight in AI decision-making processes is crucial to avoid any undue harm or negligence.

To address these ethical dilemmas, there is a need for interdisciplinary collaboration, involving experts from various domains such as ethics, law, and social sciences. International standards and guidelines for responsible AI development and deployment can provide a framework for ethical practices. Additionally, public dialogue and engagement can help shape the development and use of AI technologies in a manner that respects societal values and priorities.

The Fucking Ethical Dilemmas of the Cloud: A Call for Action

As cloud computing continues to evolve and shape our digital landscape, addressing the ethical dilemmas it presents becomes increasingly urgent. Privacy, fairness, responsible development, and use of AI are just some of the key concerns that demand attention from both cloud service providers and the wider society.

To navigate these ethical dilemmas, it is crucial to establish clear guidelines and standards for ethical cloud computing practices. This includes robust privacy policies, transparency in AI algorithms, and mechanisms for accountability and recourse in case of ethical violations. Education and awareness among cloud service providers, users, and policymakers are essential to ensure responsible and ethical decision-making.

In conclusion, as we harness the power of the cloud, we must also confront the ethical challenges it poses. By addressing these dilemmas head-on, we can create a cloud ecosystem that is not only technologically advanced but also respects privacy, promotes fairness, and upholds ethical values. Ultimately, it is through collective action and a commitment to ethical practices that we can build a fucking cloud that benefits everyone.

Index

-effectiveness, 32, 72, 153, 181, 241
-gritty, 15

a, 1–5, 7–22, 24, 25, 27–45, 47, 48, 50–60, 62–65, 67–69, 71–80, 84–89, 91–93, 95, 96, 99–101, 103–111, 115–128, 130–132, 136–139, 141–143, 145–155, 157–172, 174, 176–187, 189–204, 206–213, 215–218, 220–224, 227–235, 237, 239–247, 249–277, 282–288, 290, 292–297, 299–302, 304, 306, 307, 309–311, 313–317, 319–325, 327–341, 343, 344, 346, 348, 349, 352–356, 359, 360, 362, 363, 365–367, 369, 370, 372–377, 379–383, 385, 387–389, 391, 392, 396–407

ability, 10, 11, 13, 14, 17, 44, 52, 53, 55, 56, 59, 61, 64, 68, 91, 106, 122, 145, 148, 160, 206, 209, 217, 240, 260, 352, 353

abstraction, 67, 77, 164
academia, 351
accelerate, 136, 221, 223, 253, 360
access, 1, 2, 4, 5, 7–11, 14–17, 20–22, 24, 31, 33, 34, 37, 54–59, 62, 68–70, 75–77, 79, 85, 86, 112, 122, 125, 126, 145, 148, 162, 165, 180, 181, 197–200, 202, 206, 207, 210–212, 215, 241, 247, 267, 271, 290, 291, 308, 336, 337, 339, 350, 354, 356, 357, 364, 373, 377, 386, 392, 395, 397, 405
accessibility, 14, 15, 34, 37, 54–57, 306, 363
account, 170, 286, 307, 322, 398
accountability, 182, 232, 235, 237, 377, 401, 405–407
accuracy, 151, 400
ACID, 154
act, 75, 86, 95, 180, 307, 328
action, 26, 75, 100, 130, 207, 210, 221, 222, 240, 295, 296, 308, 392, 407
activity, 11, 57, 207, 308

adaptability, 54
addition, 55, 68, 153, 184, 195, 206, 255, 300, 307, 308, 325, 337, 389, 390, 404
address, 15, 16, 33, 43, 49, 51, 56, 57, 62, 63, 74, 112, 121, 176, 179, 180, 192, 198, 210, 232, 234, 236, 237, 257, 261, 263, 267, 271, 274, 288, 296, 308, 323, 332, 338, 354, 355, 359, 372, 378, 381, 383, 386, 393–396, 400, 405–407
addressing, 42, 47, 64, 88, 130, 159, 196, 235, 237, 261, 293, 348, 351, 369, 370, 376, 397, 401, 404, 407
adjustment, 170, 305
admin, 197
administration, 70
administrator, 95
adopting, 27, 28, 31, 33, 79, 133, 176, 208, 211, 275, 338, 382, 385, 386, 388, 390, 392, 396, 404
adoption, 15, 102, 103, 232, 235, 270–272, 340, 351, 369, 372, 389
advance, 232, 235, 236, 311, 356, 379
advantage, 17, 32, 48, 52, 126, 181, 206, 248, 256, 259, 260, 263, 315, 357, 373, 387, 388
adventure, 242, 269, 299
advertising, 353
advice, 352
affordability, 310
aftermath, 339

afterthought, 216
age, 3, 59, 321, 397
aggregate, 290
agility, 10, 54, 95, 260, 270, 274
ai, 237
aid, 229
aim, 235, 373, 388, 393, 397, 401
air, 123, 380, 381
alerting, 231, 297, 329
Alex Tapscott, 379
algorithm, 184, 199, 330, 357, 365, 398
algorithms, 63, 75, 121, 183, 184, 186, 204, 217, 228–236, 264, 308, 327, 329, 330, 350, 353–355, 360, 365, 378, 382, 396, 398, 406, 407
allocation, 12, 33, 41, 51–54, 57, 77, 79, 170, 172, 183, 222, 234, 264, 307, 350, 351, 382
allure, 37
alternative, 56, 155, 159, 177, 268, 381
amount, 53, 122, 161, 162, 170, 240, 291, 299, 300
analysis, 71, 112, 122, 125, 185, 198, 228, 229, 236, 241, 254, 288, 290, 291, 295, 307, 308, 341, 350, 352, 396
annotation, 232
anomaly, 198
answer, 20, 237
app, 159
appetite, 18
application, 4, 14, 20, 25, 27, 51, 53, 54, 71, 75, 103, 105–108, 110, 111, 115, 137–139,

Index

142, 147, 150, 156, 159, 161, 167, 169, 170, 172, 173, 181, 184–187, 191, 192, 197, 221, 222, 227, 232, 240, 256–258, 260–270, 274–276, 283, 285, 288, 290, 292–295, 297, 300, 304, 307, 308, 314, 316, 317, 322, 339, 351, 352, 375, 396
approach, 17, 32, 47, 53, 56, 62, 69, 72, 78, 92, 96, 99, 106, 108, 125, 127, 131, 160, 167, 183, 184, 203, 208, 209, 216, 239, 254, 256, 259, 261, 262, 270–272, 274, 275, 283, 310, 315, 317, 322, 341, 373, 380, 387, 388, 396, 399, 401, 403, 404
architecting, 256
architecture, 33, 38, 67, 80, 82–87, 93, 94, 99, 105–107, 131, 133, 138, 148, 153, 178, 187, 256, 260, 261, 263, 264, 287, 294, 324, 344, 345, 349
archival, 72
archive, 72, 267
archiving, 72, 148, 267
area, 228, 255, 352, 370, 375, 404
armor, 207
array, 10, 235, 247, 255
arsenal, 150, 169, 254
art, 11, 313, 316, 317
aspect, 52, 109, 160–162, 207, 302, 304, 306, 336
ass, 59, 99, 355
assessment, 259, 267, 269

asset, 234
assistance, 352
atmosphere, 33
attack, 210, 338
attacker, 210, 211
attention, 15, 37, 366, 370, 400, 404, 407
attribute, 151, 397
audit, 198, 268
auditing, 162, 198, 295, 377
audits, 14, 56, 63, 215, 268, 338, 340, 394, 395
authentication, 56, 62, 120, 162, 337
authenticity, 378
authority, 366, 372, 373, 376
authorization, 197
auto, 52, 170–172, 178, 179, 263, 265, 287, 304, 314
automate, 51, 93, 96, 122, 168, 169, 234, 259, 286, 294, 300, 353, 406
automating, 234, 235, 275
automation, 48, 95, 110, 128, 235, 259, 275, 298, 308, 314, 336, 349
availability, 32, 53, 55, 57, 62, 64, 75, 79, 84, 112, 136, 137, 144, 149, 153, 168, 169, 176, 183–186, 190, 192, 197, 200, 204, 208, 239, 245, 247, 253, 254, 264, 277, 287, 311, 314–316, 322, 324, 325, 327, 328, 330–332, 336, 373
awareness, 271, 338, 407
AWS, 138, 241, 242, 255, 294, 296
Azure, 138, 149, 246, 255

baby, 1, 120, 355

back, 7, 8, 11, 14, 31, 34, 54, 119, 120, 169, 183, 321, 332, 334–336, 353
backbone, 7, 65, 73, 80, 96, 128, 159, 177, 193–196, 380
backend, 328, 329
backseat, 363
backup, 3, 11, 56, 62, 72, 86, 267, 268, 318–321, 328–332
balance, 41, 44, 152, 184, 291, 299, 310, 312, 317, 350
balancer, 185, 186, 329, 330
balancing, 20, 85, 110, 183–187, 190–192, 240, 327, 329, 330, 332
ballgame, 355
band, 34
bandwidth, 99, 119, 120, 125–127, 341, 344, 345, 349
bank, 8, 18
banking, 365
bar, 254
barrier, 75, 204
base, 30, 54, 112, 161, 189, 362
baseline, 311
basic, 4, 145, 194, 212
basis, 8, 31, 299, 313
bat, 8
battleground, 376
bay, 58, 120
beach, 33
beast, 1
beauty, 353
beginning, 87, 102, 125, 216
behavior, 93, 132, 162, 171, 172, 198, 207, 233, 277, 278, 283, 287, 290, 292, 337, 353, 356, 397

being, 2, 17, 34, 47, 53, 55, 63, 103, 126, 128, 185, 217, 333, 336, 352, 353, 355, 363, 365, 401, 405
benefit, 11, 31, 126, 128, 153, 232, 240, 271, 272, 405
Berners-Lee, 4
betterment, 354
Bias, 398
bias, 232, 235, 237, 354, 396–401, 404
bid, 300, 306, 310, 313
bidding, 300, 310, 311
bill, 299, 313
billing, 300, 308
birth, 3, 4, 7, 9
bit, 57, 59, 120, 301
bitch, 2
blanket, 212, 214, 216
blend, 32
blessing, 306
blink, 86
block, 69, 73, 75, 85, 87, 119, 148–151, 207, 367, 376
blockchain, 15, 253, 255, 348, 366–372, 376–380
blood, 321
blueprint, 111, 153
bond, 355
book, 274, 369
booking, 24, 163
boot, 220
border, 378, 397
boss, 286
bottleneck, 296
boutique, 18
brain, 93, 121, 170, 172, 229
branch, 234, 352
brand, 355, 388

breach, 59, 63, 181, 203, 215, 337–339, 396
breakthrough, 4, 232, 365
breeze, 160
bridge, 292
brother, 121
browser, 4
browsing, 159
bucket, 137
budget, 222, 308, 313–317
budgeting, 306, 307, 315–317
buffering, 13, 53, 76, 324
build, 8, 10, 18, 21, 24, 85, 92, 99, 106, 121, 177, 182, 217, 225, 234, 242, 244, 254, 255, 265, 275, 286, 296, 407
building, 4, 10, 20, 32, 76, 80, 107, 109, 110, 113, 136, 137, 141, 147, 151, 160, 167, 176, 181, 187, 229, 235, 270, 272, 382
bunch, 119
burden, 12, 21, 222
business, 3, 5, 8, 10–13, 15, 18, 30, 31, 58–60, 62, 72, 120, 178, 202, 211, 241, 245, 246, 250, 261, 263, 267, 294, 321, 325, 338, 387
buzzword, 44

cache, 147
caching, 85, 264–266, 309
calendar, 268
call, 119, 120, 355
camp, 220
capability, 53, 178, 229, 254
capacity, 13, 52, 53, 75, 132, 150, 161, 177, 183, 240, 299, 300, 306, 310–313, 324, 329, 351, 373
capital, 11, 13
capture, 229, 295
car, 5, 87, 353
carbon, 12, 255, 378, 383, 386, 388, 389
care, 14, 18, 67, 108, 109, 353, 405
case, 58, 71, 72, 75, 92, 112, 159, 183, 237, 261, 268, 270, 296, 313, 329, 382, 400, 404, 407
Cassandra, 154
catalog, 249
catch, 254, 293, 299, 365
categorization, 210
category, 229
cater, 19, 242, 243, 250, 300
cause, 210, 278, 291
caution, 3
center, 2, 17, 74, 80, 82–87, 119, 322, 380, 382
centralization, 290
centralizing, 95, 290
chain, 367, 370, 376–378
challenge, 32, 39, 56, 120–122, 126, 212, 231, 232, 254, 261, 282, 297, 307, 365, 378, 381, 383, 392, 401
change, 4, 131, 132, 271, 272, 276
changer, 7, 9, 10, 44, 48, 51, 106, 118, 353
characteristic, 151
charge, 222, 364
chat, 138
chatbot, 352
check, 6, 86, 186, 279, 317
checking, 113, 186
checksum, 321

choice, 21, 25, 27, 48, 105, 142, 156–158, 160, 168, 169, 241, 256, 261, 285, 313, 319, 341, 387
choose, 2, 21, 32, 55, 56, 59, 62, 74, 111, 150, 154, 240, 245, 246, 255, 270, 284, 300, 301, 307, 309, 362
choosing, 48, 55, 80, 151, 159, 308, 309, 314
ciphertext, 199
city, 123
clarity, 396
classification, 229, 234
click, 249
clicking, 4
client, 107, 184, 203, 329
climate, 241
cloud, 1–3, 7–22, 24, 28, 31–65, 67–80, 83–87, 91, 92, 96, 106, 109, 110, 113–115, 118–121, 125–130, 132–134, 136, 138, 139, 141, 144, 145, 147–154, 159–170, 172, 177–183, 185–187, 190–204, 206–208, 210–216, 220–223, 225, 233–237, 240–243, 245–247, 249, 250, 253–260, 262–266, 268–273, 275, 277, 279, 283–288, 290–292, 294, 296, 298–302, 304–310, 312–314, 316–319, 321, 322, 324, 325, 327–330, 332–341, 344, 345, 349–351, 354–364, 369–372, 375–380, 382, 383, 385–397, 405–407

Cloud Spanner, 255
club, 58, 86
cluster, 71, 74, 79, 109, 111
clustering, 85
code, 4, 20, 24, 67, 107, 115, 131, 132, 137, 138, 141, 144, 169, 173, 240, 258, 260, 261, 263, 264, 266, 274–276, 283, 286, 294, 296
codebase, 275
coffee, 3
collaboration, 8, 10, 12, 14, 20, 27, 33, 47, 273, 274, 292–294, 298, 349, 363, 400, 401, 407
collection, 4, 63, 182, 197, 234, 288, 290
color, 404
column, 151
columnar, 159
combination, 42, 54, 62, 115, 162, 186, 194, 236, 288, 311, 329, 333, 382
come, 2, 15, 39, 45, 48, 57, 59, 85, 101, 120, 175, 176, 182, 299, 309, 318, 349, 352
commerce, 8, 10, 18, 30, 50, 52, 74, 161, 170, 181, 185, 187, 210, 257, 264, 265, 270, 298, 316, 317, 321, 329, 331, 335, 336
commitment, 255, 272, 296, 299, 306, 387, 392, 407
commodity, 94
communication, 5, 8, 42, 73, 74, 76, 82, 94, 111, 122, 126, 193, 210, 234, 267, 268, 271, 273, 338, 344–346, 349,

Index

351, 365
community, 3, 31–33, 45–47, 270, 295–297
company, 12, 50, 51, 54, 74, 76, 79, 207, 210, 215, 269, 270, 274, 275, 321, 324, 325
compatibility, 78, 167, 259, 261, 265, 275
competition, 51, 246
complexity, 11, 12, 253, 260, 261, 263, 270
compliance, 14, 18, 32, 33, 37, 39, 40, 47, 58, 59, 63, 64, 72, 129, 198, 234, 246, 255, 267–271, 278, 288, 290, 319, 338, 363, 377, 378, 395, 397
component, 68, 74, 87, 92, 145, 148, 151, 153, 328
compression, 72, 222, 223, 309
compromise, 208
computation, 128, 344, 345, 350, 394
compute, 17, 133, 170, 172, 177–179, 243, 246, 287, 300, 304, 314
computer, 3, 7, 8, 65, 165, 217, 229–234, 352, 353, 356
computing, 1–3, 7–19, 21, 24, 28, 31, 33, 37, 40, 41, 44, 45, 47, 48, 51–57, 59–61, 63–65, 67, 68, 71, 73–76, 78, 80, 83–85, 87, 89, 92, 96, 103, 106, 110, 115, 118–121, 125–130, 133, 136, 137, 141–145, 148–151, 153, 154, 159, 164–169, 172–179, 182–184, 187, 190, 192, 193, 196, 197, 199, 201–204, 207, 211, 212, 216, 223, 225, 233–237, 239, 241, 242, 246, 247, 249, 250, 253–256, 259, 260, 263, 265, 268, 269, 271, 273, 283, 286, 287, 292, 298–302, 304, 306, 309, 312, 313, 318, 321, 322, 325, 327–330, 332, 333, 336, 341, 343–352, 354–366, 369–380, 382, 383, 385–392, 394–397, 405–407
concept, 4, 8, 15, 40, 45, 47, 60, 73, 122, 125, 128, 132, 133, 151, 152, 154, 164, 167, 191, 237, 274, 341, 355, 356, 372, 376, 389, 391, 392, 397, 398
concern, 17, 31, 56, 59, 62, 161, 212, 354, 381, 392, 406
conclusion, 9, 12, 54, 109, 339, 407
concurrency, 151
conditioning, 380
conduct, 268, 271, 321, 394
conferencing, 95
confidence, 59, 340, 393
confidentiality, 32, 126, 197, 200, 204, 208, 336, 405
configuration, 99, 103, 139, 283, 286, 294, 329, 338
configure, 39, 96, 100, 141, 170, 180, 207
confusion, 4
congestion, 128, 322
conjunction, 206
connection, 2, 8, 34, 56, 74, 76, 120, 126, 355

connectivity, 32, 56, 73, 76, 91, 111, 122, 126, 181, 193, 194, 196, 349, 351, 388
conquer, 12, 18, 28, 44, 48, 51, 54, 59, 60, 73, 85, 110, 114, 118, 119, 148, 151, 167, 177, 182, 192, 197, 199, 223, 246, 255, 262, 272, 286, 301, 305, 317, 327, 340, 376
consensus, 367, 376–378
consent, 63, 182, 405
conservation, 382
consideration, 126, 171, 216, 270, 354, 383
consistency, 69, 151, 154, 169, 255, 259, 264, 286
console, 180
consolidation, 12, 79, 380
conspiracy, 57
construction, 389
consultation, 267
consumer, 228
consumption, 12, 52, 264, 300, 345, 369, 380–383, 385, 386, 388, 389
container, 103, 105–107, 109, 110, 112, 113, 115, 118, 119, 133, 167–169, 177, 179, 255
containerization, 92, 96, 106, 109, 113, 114, 116, 167, 177
contender, 242, 254
content, 9, 23, 50, 53, 68, 70, 71, 85, 133, 148, 178, 185, 187–190, 234, 241, 309, 324, 352, 362
context, 65, 78, 95, 96, 131, 148, 164, 190, 192, 199, 203, 211, 223, 283, 328, 332, 335, 352, 394
contingency, 362
continuity, 11, 62, 72, 211, 321, 338
contrast, 12, 154, 223, 396
control, 14, 19–21, 31, 32, 37–41, 44, 52, 57, 59, 61, 63, 69, 79, 93, 95, 96, 98–100, 105, 112, 148, 151, 162, 171, 180, 181, 197–199, 204, 206, 207, 270, 275, 279, 283, 294, 300, 306, 309, 313, 315–317, 336, 337, 353, 376, 377, 392, 405
controller, 93–95, 100
convenience, 21, 119
convergence, 344
conversation, 352
coolant, 380
cooling, 12, 84, 86, 380–383, 385, 386, 388, 389
coordination, 48, 121, 124, 350
cop, 183
copy, 321
core, 10, 12, 14, 22, 48, 88, 100, 106, 199, 217, 265, 274, 283, 366, 370, 376, 401
corporation, 12, 178
correction, 365
corruption, 321
cost, 2, 8, 13, 15, 17, 20, 27, 31–34, 37, 39, 41, 44, 47, 51–54, 68, 72, 79, 125, 132, 136, 141, 144, 153, 172, 176–179, 181, 222, 223, 241, 256, 259, 260, 263, 265, 266, 268, 270, 271, 279, 287, 291, 300–310,

Index 417

312–317, 319, 363, 382
country, 396
couple, 47, 143, 162, 163, 195, 271, 343, 355
course, 379
cousin, 37
crash, 328
creation, 77, 87, 88, 115, 123, 147, 151, 164
creativity, 110, 293
credit, 353
criticality, 271, 339
crop, 353
cropping, 132
cryptocurrency, 376, 378
cryptography, 355
culture, 271, 273, 275, 293, 338
curse, 306
custom, 295, 300, 301, 308, 314, 315
customer, 18, 30, 32, 39, 40, 53, 60, 74, 75, 91, 153, 162, 181, 182, 197, 202, 203, 210, 211, 215, 228, 234, 236, 270, 293, 321, 336, 339, 352, 353, 362, 378
customization, 31, 32, 37, 40, 47
cutting, 8, 10, 220, 360
cyberbullying, 228
cybercriminal, 339
cybersecurity, 180, 235
cycle, 183, 240, 274, 332, 401

daemon, 107
damage, 181, 215, 338
Dan Faggella - Provides, 237
dance, 87, 120
Daniel Drescher, 379

data, 1–3, 8, 10–12, 14, 15, 17, 18, 22, 24, 31–34, 37–40, 51, 55–65, 68, 69, 71–76, 80, 82–87, 94–96, 99, 100, 112, 119, 120, 122–129, 131, 132, 136–138, 145, 148–154, 156, 159–162, 178, 180–182, 193, 196, 198–204, 207, 210–213, 215, 217, 220, 221, 223, 228–230, 232–234, 236, 239–241, 244–247, 255, 258, 261, 264, 267–270, 278, 288, 290, 291, 295, 306–309, 315, 318, 319, 321, 322, 329, 336–341, 344, 346, 349, 350, 353, 354, 363, 367, 372, 373, 375–383, 385–390, 392–398, 400, 405, 406
database, 18, 70, 73, 131–133, 138, 141, 152–154, 156, 159–163, 180, 181, 187, 240, 244, 246, 255, 257, 260, 263–266, 285, 286, 296, 321
dataset, 235
date, 126, 147, 177, 216, 296, 338, 366
day, 1, 13, 119, 198, 210, 275, 304, 353
de, 178, 395
deal, 17, 39
deallocation, 172
debt, 263
debugging, 144, 278, 288, 290, 295
decentralization, 372
decision, 21, 122, 124, 128, 217, 233–236, 267–269, 344,

346, 349, 350, 353, 398, 401, 406, 407
decryption, 337
dedication, 255
deduplication, 17
defense, 59, 206, 207, 338
definition, 103, 105, 111, 155, 159
degradation, 75, 184
degree, 56
delivery, 15, 50, 80, 85, 125, 133, 147, 159, 177, 187, 189, 190, 273, 274, 292, 293, 296, 297, 328, 330
deluge, 122
demand, 10, 13, 16, 18, 19, 22, 24, 31, 39, 52–54, 73, 96, 99, 122, 125, 130, 136, 145, 153, 170, 172, 177, 178, 189, 241, 265, 274, 298, 299, 306, 308, 310, 311, 313, 314, 382, 383, 388, 389, 407
denormalization, 154
department, 307
dependence, 17, 57, 350
dependency, 48, 363
deploy, 2, 10, 20, 21, 24, 37, 110, 113, 115, 132, 138, 139, 153, 154, 166, 240, 242, 245, 247–249, 254, 255, 285, 294, 307
deploying, 21, 67, 105, 107, 109–111, 113–115, 167–169, 172, 176, 177, 222, 223, 255, 274, 294, 321, 349–351, 388
deployment, 20, 21, 24, 31, 32, 45, 51, 85, 103–106, 108–111, 113, 115, 123, 126, 132, 138, 139, 141, 168, 169, 223, 234–237, 240, 249, 270, 274–276, 292, 294, 295, 321–325, 327, 344, 363, 378, 401, 405, 407
depth, 186, 187
design, 55, 154, 187, 260, 263, 287, 327, 332, 333, 351, 398, 405
desire, 20, 271
desktop, 77
destination, 74, 86
detail, 80, 105, 131, 250, 288, 338
detection, 11, 17, 62, 198, 208, 210, 211, 229, 231, 234, 295, 329, 336, 337, 339, 353, 394
develop, 10, 14, 20, 63, 222, 270, 354, 355, 360, 362, 365, 389
developer, 106, 176, 197, 246, 275
development, 3, 10, 14, 15, 20, 21, 24, 25, 27, 28, 96, 103, 106, 109, 121, 136, 139, 141, 142, 167, 217, 223, 228, 231, 232, 234, 235, 237, 240, 260, 270, 273–275, 292–294, 296, 332, 352, 354, 357, 378, 399, 401–407
device, 8, 34, 55, 57, 74, 76, 77, 87, 94, 100, 119
diagnosis, 231, 236, 353
diagram, 154, 287
dialogue, 354, 407
difference, 405
digit, 240
dilemma, 406

diligence, 2
dimension, 121
disaster, 8, 11, 55, 62, 80, 119, 167, 245, 318, 322, 325, 337, 338
discipline, 212
discount, 299
discovery, 110, 236, 248, 353, 355
discrimination, 354, 406
disk, 69, 161
displacement, 235
disposal, 12, 381, 386
disruption, 56, 261, 270, 325, 328, 376
distance, 17, 120
distress, 228
distribution, 148, 183, 184, 187, 201, 383
dive, 3, 7, 15, 19, 34, 37, 42, 51, 57, 80, 85, 87, 106, 110, 114, 119, 125, 142, 145, 148, 159, 177, 185, 193, 199, 208, 212, 241, 242, 292, 298, 306, 318, 327, 336, 354, 365, 369
diving, 102, 186, 302, 313, 341, 356, 370
Docker, 105–107, 109, 110, 115, 167, 177
Docker, 107, 115
document, 4, 14, 159, 160, 283
documentation, 141, 317, 336
domain, 96, 98, 152, 154, 190, 191, 193, 225, 400
dominance, 255
Don Tapscott, 379
download, 308
downtime, 3, 62, 112, 169, 234, 266, 322, 334, 338

drift, 294
drink, 183
drive, 5, 136, 236, 246, 253, 272, 275, 325, 353, 388, 392
driving, 10, 233, 349, 353
drug, 236, 353, 355
duo, 5, 109
durability, 72, 148, 149
duration, 299
dynamic, 5, 41, 57, 71, 99, 132, 160, 170, 216, 329, 351

e, 10, 12, 18, 30, 50, 52, 74, 161, 170, 181, 185, 187, 210, 257, 264, 265, 270, 298, 316, 317, 321, 329, 331, 335, 336, 381
ease, 160
eavesdropping, 76
ecosystem, 87, 122, 246, 254, 296, 376, 392, 394, 407
Edgar F. Codd, 151
edge, 8, 10, 15, 54, 119–121, 125–130, 189, 220, 229, 233, 236, 341–345, 348–351, 360
education, 5, 33, 98, 352
effectiveness, 32, 72, 153, 181, 189, 206, 231, 241, 304, 320, 332, 365
efficiency, 8, 10, 12, 14, 27, 31, 32, 41, 44, 53, 79, 92, 96, 106, 123, 125–127, 132, 136, 144, 152, 164, 169, 170, 172, 176–179, 217, 221, 234, 256, 259, 260, 263, 265, 270, 273, 287, 292, 293, 295, 349, 363, 369,

420   Index

378, 382, 385, 387, 388, 406
effort, 10, 20, 249, 260, 265, 274, 339, 379
elasticity, 11, 31, 34, 37, 53, 85
electricity, 380, 381, 388, 389
element, 177, 199, 325
Eliezer Yudkowsky, 237
email, 12, 265, 268, 269
embedding, 405
emergency, 350
emotion, 227, 228
emulation, 78, 164
encryption, 11, 14, 17, 18, 56, 57, 59, 62, 72, 112, 120, 161, 199–204, 215, 267, 291, 337, 365, 395, 397, 405
end, 181, 188, 254, 274, 293, 294, 299, 344, 378
endpoint, 132, 405
energy, 12, 255, 351, 356, 369, 378, 380–383, 385–390, 392
enforcement, 339, 400, 404, 406
engagement, 407
engine, 107, 167, 240
entanglement, 355
enterprise, 7, 77, 95, 136, 245, 246, 254, 300
entertainment, 5, 9, 13, 228
entity, 151–153, 372, 373, 376
entrepreneur, 18
environment, 19, 24, 32, 34, 39, 41, 45, 50, 57, 63, 64, 78, 80, 103, 107, 110, 115, 124, 126, 131, 137, 164, 167, 179, 181, 191, 197, 198, 201, 204, 208, 211, 212, 228, 249, 256, 258, 260, 261, 263–266, 271, 274–276, 293, 294, 314, 321, 329, 334, 337–339, 353, 382, 388, 389, 392, 396, 397, 405
equalizer, 8
equipment, 11, 39, 73–76, 80, 84–87, 381, 383, 386
era, 3, 19, 85, 130, 148, 363, 392
Eric Schmidt, 8
error, 95, 99, 132, 295, 332, 338, 365, 400, 404, 406
essence, 99
essential, 6, 27, 47, 56, 61, 62, 74, 76, 80, 83, 84, 102, 106, 112, 122, 130, 150, 152, 153, 162, 177, 185, 187, 195, 197, 201, 204, 206, 220, 223, 229, 232, 235, 249, 253, 259, 263, 265, 267–269, 277, 287, 290, 300, 301, 309, 315, 317, 319, 321, 327, 330, 332, 337, 338, 350, 351, 354, 359, 366, 378, 382, 393–395, 397–400, 407
evaluation, 398, 405, 406
evaporation, 381
event, 55, 131, 132, 137–139, 141, 169, 185, 210, 260, 318, 325, 328, 330, 332, 338
evolution, 3, 7, 99
exam, 55, 352
example, 10–15, 18, 20, 32, 33, 39, 52–55, 74–76, 95, 111, 120, 123, 131, 132, 138, 147, 153, 161, 162, 169, 179–181, 183–185, 191, 192, 197, 210, 215, 222, 228, 254, 255, 257, 260,

Index

263, 264, 268–271, 274, 275, 285, 286, 289, 298, 300, 304, 311, 324, 329, 335, 338, 349, 350, 362, 365, 381, 382, 388, 394, 395, 406
exception, 153
exchange, 122
execution, 103, 131, 132, 137, 141, 144, 165, 176, 262, 269
exercise, 282
exfiltration, 211
expenditure, 307
experience, 11, 24, 53, 74–76, 112, 119, 162, 163, 169, 178, 185, 217, 245, 249, 254, 270, 297, 298, 311, 323, 324, 353, 362
experiment, 275
experimentation, 275, 293
expert, 118
expertise, 20, 32, 39, 47, 255, 260, 270, 296, 403
explainability, 405, 406
Explainable AI, 235
exploitation, 211, 338
exploration, 79, 133, 241, 312, 357, 369
explorer, 6
extension, 245
extent, 261
extraction, 229
eye, 59, 86, 299, 309

face, 4, 11, 31, 33, 60, 62, 126, 147, 226, 322, 325, 378
fact, 128
factor, 56, 62, 337
Failback, 334

failback, 332, 334–336
failover, 160, 186, 327–332
failure, 8, 11, 33, 185, 186, 293, 318, 321, 328, 330, 332, 334–336
fairness, 64, 121, 232, 235, 354, 396–398, 401, 405–407
fame, 120
fan, 120
farm, 120
farming, 353
fashion, 4, 18
faster, 14, 118, 126, 130, 144, 160, 177, 189, 236, 273, 295, 355, 365
fault, 136, 137, 168, 169, 185, 186, 191, 239, 315, 332, 373
favor, 268
fear, 57, 59, 62, 170, 183
feasibility, 267, 300
feature, 34, 170, 172, 177, 180, 229, 230
feed, 159
feedback, 228, 268, 269, 274, 283, 293, 352
fertilization, 353
festival, 120
field, 8, 14, 15, 19, 96, 125, 204, 216, 228, 229, 232, 283, 352, 353, 355, 360, 366, 380
file, 69, 70, 73, 131, 132, 139, 145, 147, 148
filter, 86, 206
filtering, 129, 204, 206, 229
finance, 218
finding, 210, 353
fine, 59, 69, 162, 172, 185, 206, 262, 338
fire, 86

Firebase, 138
firewall, 204, 206, 207, 339
fit, 20, 302, 313
flash, 54, 161
flaw, 211
fleet, 315
flexibility, 8–10, 12, 13, 17–21, 23, 27, 32, 44, 48, 54–57, 63, 79, 80, 95, 98, 125, 127, 128, 153, 155, 160, 163, 167, 169, 179, 181, 241, 245, 246, 254, 256, 259, 260, 264, 265, 271, 298, 300, 301, 306, 312
flow, 94, 123, 180, 181, 274, 293
fluctuate, 13, 313
Fluentd, 112
fly, 132
focus, 2, 10, 12, 14, 18, 20–22, 24, 28, 54, 67, 132, 136, 138, 144, 153, 160, 172, 176, 180, 240, 255, 260, 270, 291, 349
fog, 121, 344, 345, 347–352
food, 159
footprint, 12, 245, 247, 378, 380, 383, 386, 388, 389
force, 193, 253, 298
forefront, 102
form, 94, 109, 111, 115, 148, 194, 212, 229
format, 110, 167
formation, 229
formula, 199
forth, 14, 49, 110, 119, 120, 177, 286, 301, 405
fortress, 31
forum, 297
forwarding, 93–95, 99, 100
fossil, 381
foster, 293, 351
foundation, 4, 7, 22, 73, 76, 84, 167, 182, 197, 274, 336
framework, 107, 138, 139, 197, 206, 271, 292, 401, 407
Frankenstein, 121
fraud, 353, 376, 378
freedom, 19, 110, 125, 142–144, 180, 306
frequency, 17
friend, 1–3, 57, 59, 120
front, 75, 181
frontier, 354
fuck, 1, 13, 272, 273
fuckin, 13–15
fucking, 1–3, 5, 9, 13, 19, 21, 44, 48, 57, 61, 64, 85, 87, 99–102, 114, 116, 118, 119, 125, 130, 134, 142–144, 159, 193, 197, 204, 212, 214, 216, 233, 235, 236, 250, 253–255, 269, 272, 273, 292, 295–297, 313, 316, 317, 336, 340, 352, 354, 355, 366, 376, 378–380, 392, 405, 407
fuel, 37, 381
function, 120, 126, 131, 132, 137, 138, 204
functionality, 65, 71, 138, 139, 173, 176, 195, 267, 271, 293, 332
fundamental, 15, 54, 57, 68, 74, 80, 145, 151, 161, 193, 199, 204, 216, 229, 314, 356, 366, 392
future, 3, 6, 12, 15, 17, 51, 62, 64, 96, 99, 121, 125, 144, 177,

190, 209, 211, 217, 231, 236, 269, 330, 344, 349, 354, 355, 363, 369, 375, 376, 382, 385, 387, 388, 391, 405
gadget, 2
game, 7, 9, 10, 15, 44, 48, 51, 106, 118, 119, 254, 255, 330, 353
gaming, 74, 187, 330
gap, 235, 292
gatekeeper, 199
Gen-Z, 354
gender, 397, 400
Gene Kim, 274, 296
Gene Kim, 296
generation, 201, 341, 381
giant, 85, 162, 178, 254, 362
go, 2, 4, 8, 11, 13, 21, 31, 54, 87, 110, 115, 120, 129, 151, 158, 161, 171, 177, 182, 222, 239, 245, 250, 262, 286, 298–301, 306, 309, 313, 355, 373, 392, 395, 405
goal, 128, 220, 229, 256, 260, 275, 327, 337, 383, 401
goddamn, 262
gold, 212
good, 33, 116, 161, 237, 313
governance, 33, 47, 63, 271
government, 32, 59, 123, 124
grade, 246
Grafana, 112
granularity, 291
graph, 159
grasp, 107, 116, 143, 173, 183, 193, 217, 229, 239, 356, 372, 376
green, 389, 391, 392
grid, 229
grit, 301
ground, 10
group, 111, 171, 172, 204
growth, 10, 14, 15, 30, 54, 60, 236, 275, 293, 354, 380, 382, 383
guest, 78, 164, 165
guidance, 186
guide, 19, 292, 396, 397

hand, 4, 10, 11, 21, 53, 58, 77, 78, 85, 86, 95, 107, 115, 125, 128, 161, 170, 184, 197, 208, 222, 223, 288, 299, 306, 373
handling, 63, 72, 74, 87, 109, 128, 138, 182, 183, 185, 291, 327, 331, 332, 354
happen, 14, 108, 392
hardware, 2, 8, 10–14, 22, 32, 34, 39, 53–55, 65, 66, 73, 77, 78, 80, 85–87, 94, 164, 165, 180, 184–186, 221, 223, 269, 328, 330, 356, 357, 364, 381, 389
harm, 235, 381, 406
harmony, 330
hash, 147, 367
hashing, 376
hassle, 10, 21
hate, 228
head, 407
headache, 2, 141
header, 100
healing, 112, 248

health, 75, 112, 113, 162, 186, 228, 240, 277, 287, 288, 290, 292, 294, 295, 330, 349, 353
healthcare, 11, 32, 33, 39, 55, 128, 218, 228, 234, 236, 237, 255, 270, 349, 350, 352, 353, 394, 395, 406
heart, 65, 85, 99, 107, 164, 179, 224, 230, 233
heat, 380, 389
heating, 380
hell, 1, 2, 8, 355
help, 18, 31, 48, 58, 62, 75, 119, 120, 168, 180, 183, 193, 198, 222, 223, 228, 237, 246, 252, 259, 269, 271, 288, 294, 297, 300, 302, 305–309, 314–316, 318, 321, 332, 336–339, 352, 353, 382, 386, 405–407
Heroku, 28
heterogeneity, 122, 349, 351
high, 19, 32, 53, 55, 57, 62, 72, 74, 75, 77–79, 84, 93, 136, 137, 144, 148, 150, 153, 168, 169, 176, 178, 183, 185–187, 190, 191, 215, 221, 223, 228, 239–241, 245, 247, 254, 266, 268, 287, 292, 308, 311, 315, 322, 324, 325, 327, 328, 330, 355, 362, 373, 379, 396
highlight, 118, 128, 272
highway, 4
hippie, 31
hiring, 397, 406
history, 9, 162, 294

holiday, 170, 298, 329
home, 55, 70, 120
homework, 58, 352
hop, 169
hospitality, 241
host, 18, 77, 103, 107, 164, 165, 167
hosting, 10, 18, 70, 71, 210, 241
house, 12, 31, 39, 80, 263
human, 64, 217, 229, 230, 233–235, 237, 259, 349, 352, 406
humanity, 354, 405
humidity, 381
hybrid, 31, 32, 41–44, 62, 94, 125, 126, 254, 261, 270, 300, 315
hyperparameter, 220, 223
hypertext, 4, 7
hypervisor, 77–80, 86, 87, 91, 164, 165

IaC, 283
idea, 8, 21, 119, 274, 307
ideal, 31, 37, 40, 107, 110, 148, 160, 240, 298, 299, 377
identification, 210, 231, 395
identifier, 145, 147, 151, 367
identify, 41, 52, 63, 132, 207, 208, 211, 227, 229, 231–235, 259, 267, 269, 271, 274, 277, 278, 291, 293, 295, 308, 315, 320, 332, 336–338, 353, 365, 382, 394–396, 399, 406
identity, 133, 377, 400
image, 107, 115, 132, 137, 147, 167, 229, 231, 234, 254, 265, 388
imaging, 231, 353
immutability, 367, 376

Index

impact, 5, 6, 8, 9, 12, 13, 15, 56, 60, 62, 112, 154, 162, 187, 208, 209, 211, 222, 228, 232, 233, 235, 237, 265, 267–269, 288, 292, 306, 311, 313, 322, 324, 332, 336–338, 354, 376, 377, 380–383, 385–392, 396, 401, 405

impartiality, 235

implement, 17, 18, 31, 32, 39, 41, 62, 112, 126, 132, 183, 207, 234, 297, 304, 362, 381, 385, 394–396

implementation, 43, 47, 91, 92, 147, 237, 271, 273, 285, 292, 349, 350, 390

importance, 12, 60, 74, 92, 128, 162, 170, 179, 189, 192, 195, 196, 202, 204, 207, 215, 237, 272, 293, 332, 335, 338, 395

important, 3, 9, 21, 64, 85, 90, 113, 119, 122, 124, 126, 141, 144, 152, 154, 161, 173, 176, 185, 186, 210, 222, 237, 265, 267, 269, 271, 285, 299, 302, 306–308, 312, 313, 317, 333, 361, 388, 398, 400, 406

improvement, 211, 262, 269, 272–275, 288, 293, 298, 382, 388, 405

in, 1–5, 7–15, 17, 18, 21, 26, 30–34, 36–39, 41, 47, 48, 51–65, 69–80, 83–87, 89, 91–96, 98–103, 105–107, 109, 110, 112–115, 119–128, 130–134, 137–139, 141, 144, 145, 147–154, 159–163, 165–170, 172, 176–187, 190–192, 195–200, 202–204, 206–217, 221–223, 225, 226, 228–237, 240–242, 245–247, 249, 250, 252–255, 258–261, 263–272, 274–279, 283, 285–301, 304, 306–308, 311–313, 316–319, 321, 322, 325, 328–332, 334–340, 343, 344, 346, 348–358, 360, 362, 363, 365–367, 369, 370, 372, 373, 375–383, 385–388, 390, 392–402, 404–407

inactivity, 314

inadequacy, 329

incident, 198, 208–211, 235, 278, 338, 339, 396

inconsistency, 267

increase, 10, 73, 161

independence, 55, 57

individual, 11, 48, 85, 100, 141, 151, 404

industry, 32, 33, 63, 106, 110, 123, 236, 237, 242, 246, 255, 267, 296, 338, 350–353, 362, 379, 385, 388, 392

inequality, 406

inequity, 354

infancy, 3, 355, 356

inference, 221–223

influx, 163, 329

information, 1, 3–5, 7, 11, 14, 15, 17, 18, 35, 56, 57, 62, 69, 74, 100, 126, 128, 129, 153, 159, 163, 182, 185,

186, 200, 204, 212, 216, 228, 229, 231, 236, 267, 278, 291, 321, 336–338, 354, 356, 366, 376, 392–394, 405
infrastructure, 2, 4, 10–15, 18–22, 24, 31–34, 37–42, 44, 45, 48, 50–53, 55, 65, 67, 72, 73, 76, 77, 79, 80, 84, 87, 88, 91–93, 96, 100, 103, 105, 106, 122, 124, 125, 130, 132, 136–138, 141, 144, 149, 152, 153, 167, 169, 170, 172, 176, 178, 180, 185, 189, 190, 193–196, 204, 207, 212, 213, 220, 223, 234, 239–242, 245, 247, 250, 253–256, 258–261, 264, 266, 269–271, 275, 283, 285–290, 292, 294–296, 300, 301, 306, 307, 311, 319, 321, 324, 327, 330, 332, 336, 338, 339, 341, 349, 350, 362, 364, 380, 383, 385, 386, 388–390, 392
initiative, 388
innovation, 7, 10, 12, 14, 37, 47, 54, 60, 130, 236, 246, 253, 255, 260, 272, 275, 293, 349, 353, 375, 376, 388, 392
input, 72, 403
installation, 20, 21, 160
instance, 10, 12, 17, 18, 53, 55, 107, 131, 138, 149, 151, 153, 161, 165, 167, 180, 192, 204, 270, 274, 276, 285, 286, 308–310, 314, 321, 364, 365
institution, 39, 40
integrating, 33, 48, 237, 249, 265, 275, 378
integration, 32, 33, 42, 51, 122, 141, 236, 245, 246, 253, 254, 273–275, 293, 308, 348, 351, 357, 363, 382
integrity, 11, 61, 126, 151, 152, 154, 197, 200, 201, 204, 208, 270, 275, 295, 336, 339, 376
intelligence, 14, 15, 121, 217, 233, 236, 237, 355
interaction, 69, 193, 230, 234
interception, 337
interest, 229
interference, 355
internet, 1, 2, 7, 8, 13, 15, 16, 21, 34, 56, 57, 71, 75, 96, 120, 122, 125, 145, 363
interoperability, 32, 33, 122, 245, 349, 351, 369
interpretability, 235
interruption, 313, 330
intervention, 132, 217, 228, 309, 349, 350
intrusion, 17, 62, 394
invention, 5, 7
inventory, 18, 30, 31, 74, 264, 269, 321
investigation, 198, 210
investment, 10, 20, 39, 40, 48, 52, 279, 302, 305, 313
involve, 62, 185, 258, 261, 291, 294, 354, 395
involvement, 406
irrigation, 353

Index   427

isolation, 77, 79, 80, 91, 92, 105, 167, 169
issue, 17, 61, 237, 378, 400
it, 1–5, 7–10, 13–15, 17, 20–23, 25, 27–29, 31, 34, 36–40, 42, 43, 46–49, 51, 55–57, 59–62, 64, 65, 74, 78, 80, 85, 87, 92, 99–101, 106–108, 110, 112, 114–116, 119, 120, 122, 124, 126, 128, 129, 131, 137, 141, 142, 144, 145, 147–150, 152–154, 159–162, 167, 169–171, 173, 177, 180, 183–186, 190, 192, 199, 200, 203, 204, 206, 212, 214, 215, 220–223, 229, 231, 232, 234, 236, 237, 239–242, 249, 250, 253–256, 258, 260, 261, 263, 265–272, 274, 277, 285, 287, 290, 292, 294–296, 299–302, 306–308, 311, 313, 317, 319, 322, 323, 325, 327, 328, 330, 332, 336, 337, 339–342, 344, 345, 347, 353–356, 359–361, 363, 365, 373, 376–378, 383, 385, 386, 388, 389, 392, 400, 401, 404–407
iteration, 293

job, 235
John McCarthy, 8
journey, 2, 5, 19, 106, 110, 180, 181, 199, 246, 269–273, 292, 295, 301, 344
Joy Buolamwini, 400

jurisdiction, 15, 63
justice, 339, 397, 406

Kevin Behr, 296
key, 16, 22, 25, 28, 32, 42, 43, 45, 46, 54, 65, 77, 80, 82–84, 87–89, 94, 105, 108, 110, 122, 126, 128, 132, 145, 148, 151, 153, 159, 160, 168, 173, 187, 193, 199, 201–204, 208, 209, 213, 214, 217, 219, 224, 229, 231, 242–246, 250, 254, 260, 268, 270, 277, 285, 295, 297, 298, 306, 309, 319, 322, 323, 325, 336, 337, 345, 348, 364, 367, 370, 373, 374, 376, 380, 392, 393, 402, 403, 407
kid, 119
killer, 20
kind, 57, 121
king, 318
kingdom, 199
knowledge, 4, 18, 59, 118, 192, 197, 215, 221–223, 241, 262, 271, 293, 295, 296, 301, 305

label, 229
labeling, 232
labor, 232
lack, 344
land, 388
landscape, 5, 8, 12, 13, 44, 54, 58, 128, 159, 180, 187, 189, 207, 208, 220, 250, 253, 266, 267, 272, 300, 301, 336, 358, 405, 407

language, 131, 198, 217, 233, 234, 255, 352, 355
laptop, 55
latency, 17, 39, 72, 74, 85, 119, 121, 125–129, 141, 144, 148, 149, 176, 185, 187, 221, 236, 239–241, 245, 247, 254, 263, 322, 324, 341, 344–346, 349, 350, 388
law, 58, 339, 400, 404, 406, 407
layer, 4, 48, 59, 74, 77, 78, 100, 184, 185, 206
lead, 152, 167, 170, 181, 215, 235, 265, 267, 293, 306, 339, 397, 406
leader, 255
leadership, 296
leap, 2, 364–366
learn, 6, 19, 147, 217, 233, 268, 273–275, 296, 353
learning, 10, 14, 55, 124, 128, 134, 167, 178, 183, 217, 220, 228–230, 233, 239, 242, 254, 255, 272, 275, 293, 296, 298, 308, 352, 353, 355, 382, 396, 401
ledger, 366, 370, 376
legacy, 167, 266, 268, 269
level, 8, 13, 19–22, 32, 37, 38, 48, 67, 69, 77, 78, 93, 95, 103, 105, 148, 149, 180, 185, 186, 204, 206, 217, 228, 288–290, 292, 314, 354, 355, 377, 379, 385
leverage, 13, 15, 17–19, 21, 32, 37, 42, 48, 50, 52, 53, 57, 64, 73, 79, 95, 104, 141, 148, 181, 198, 246, 248, 260, 261, 263, 264, 300, 308, 309, 355, 357, 378, 382
leveraging, 10, 11, 23, 28, 33, 38, 47, 53, 55, 56, 85, 91, 96, 103, 125, 127, 144, 147, 153, 162, 169, 176, 178, 181, 189, 207–209, 220, 223, 233, 235, 241, 249, 253, 259, 270, 271, 292, 301, 308, 312, 316, 317, 336, 340, 362, 381
Lexi, 18
library, 24, 178, 189
life, 3, 34, 37, 123, 321, 332, 350, 401
lifecycle, 201, 235, 267, 293
lifetime, 354
lift, 256–260, 271
light, 229, 354
lighting, 231
lightning, 120
likelihood, 274, 338
limit, 17, 110
line, 13, 170, 306, 338, 388
link, 4, 74, 100, 151
liquid, 380
list, 24, 370
listing, 241
living, 124
load, 20, 24, 53, 75, 76, 84, 85, 110, 132, 161, 169, 170, 183–187, 190–192, 240, 265, 304, 311, 327, 329, 330, 332, 350
localization, 229
location, 8, 10, 14, 17, 34, 55, 86, 137, 198, 229, 373
lock, 2, 17, 31, 33, 37, 56, 57, 59–62, 64, 141, 144, 176, 351, 363

Index

lodging, 241
log, 112, 198, 210, 290–292, 295
logging, 112, 113, 132, 207, 277, 278, 287, 288, 291, 292, 294, 295, 297
logic, 138
logs, 162, 198, 277, 278, 290, 291, 295, 337
look, 5, 7, 18, 34, 43, 47, 65, 101, 117, 128, 147, 159, 161, 178, 183, 189, 191, 194, 195, 213, 220, 233, 241, 243, 251, 267, 271, 274, 292, 327, 338, 341, 353, 401
loop, 268
loss, 8, 11, 181, 321, 336, 337, 377
lot, 1, 59, 87, 269, 352
loyalty, 234, 293
luxury, 48

machine, 2, 7, 10, 14, 53, 69, 77–79, 103, 106, 109, 128, 134, 164, 165, 178, 217, 228, 229, 233, 239, 254, 255, 283, 296, 308, 349, 353, 382, 396, 401
machinery, 349
magic, 85, 87, 99–102, 119, 159, 286
mainframe, 1, 2, 7
maintainability, 263
maintenance, 11, 12, 14, 20, 21, 39, 40, 62, 234, 268, 349, 389
making, 2, 4, 14, 20, 21, 25, 37, 46, 62, 78, 99, 100, 106–108, 110, 112, 115, 122, 124, 128, 149, 152, 153, 157, 160, 169, 176, 199, 217, 228, 233–236, 240, 241, 256, 260, 261, 263, 265, 269, 271, 290, 294, 295, 298, 300, 301, 307, 308, 313, 329, 344, 346, 349, 350, 352, 353, 360, 365, 373, 376, 377, 388, 392, 398, 401, 406, 407
manageability, 95
management, 10, 12, 14, 20, 24, 30, 31, 33, 39, 48, 51, 63, 70, 72, 77, 79, 91, 92, 95, 96, 100, 103–106, 109, 110, 112, 115, 121–123, 132, 136, 138, 145, 147, 148, 151, 153, 159, 168, 176, 190–192, 197, 199, 201–204, 259, 264, 266, 267, 279, 285, 290, 292, 300, 301, 307, 316, 338, 349, 377, 378, 381, 382, 385, 386, 388
manager, 154
ManagerID, 154
managing, 10, 21, 22, 32, 33, 40, 48, 51, 67, 70, 76, 79, 80, 86, 93, 95, 107–111, 113–115, 126, 137, 160, 162, 167, 168, 177, 180, 189, 190, 209, 240, 264, 265, 271, 272, 283, 286, 290, 306, 309, 313, 314, 317, 350
manifest, 110–112
manipulation, 151, 229, 376
manner, 13, 95, 148, 183, 285, 366, 402, 404, 407
manufacturing, 234, 349, 381
map, 4, 190

mapping, 91
market, 53, 54, 93, 144, 176, 228, 235, 242, 255, 353
marketing, 218, 234, 294, 353
marketplace, 24, 162, 241
match, 178, 377
matter, 2, 8–10, 14, 328, 355, 356
maze, 4
mean, 59
meaning, 34, 61, 106, 131, 204, 355
means, 10, 14, 57, 86, 170, 180, 293, 295, 308, 330, 372
measure, 200, 295
mechanism, 186, 265, 328, 330, 331, 367
media, 3, 7, 9, 11, 53, 120, 136, 159, 169, 228, 311, 352
medicine, 236, 353
medium, 12
memory, 53, 161, 165, 210
message, 137, 138
metadata, 69, 72, 147, 148, 307
metal, 77
method, 184, 373
methodology, 273
metric, 386
middle, 120, 185
migration, 32, 167, 190, 256, 258–262, 265, 266, 269–272, 350
million, 178, 241, 338, 386
mind, 18, 30, 36, 79, 114, 119, 121, 133, 139, 196, 200, 204, 232, 249, 252, 285, 291, 299, 300, 306, 311, 332, 354, 355, 363
mindset, 273, 275
minimization, 397
minute, 1, 2, 57
misconfiguration, 339
mishandling, 393
mission, 85
misuse, 354, 392, 406
mitigation, 396
mix, 32, 313
mixture, 315
mode, 94
model, 2, 11, 13, 20, 21, 24, 32, 45, 52, 53, 69, 138, 145, 160, 220–223, 239–241, 245, 270, 271, 298–302, 306, 310, 313, 315, 344, 398
modeling, 152, 153, 241
modification, 377
moment, 15, 184
money, 10, 170
monitor, 52, 75, 77, 112, 123, 126, 132, 162, 172, 178, 198, 231, 235, 262, 268, 291, 299, 306, 308, 312, 314–317, 349, 353
monitoring, 11, 41, 51, 79, 84, 112, 113, 120, 132, 141, 162, 186, 192, 198, 204, 207, 231, 234, 235, 240, 268, 271, 275–278, 287–295, 297, 305, 308, 317, 327, 329, 332, 337, 339, 340, 350, 352, 353, 382, 395, 401, 406
monster, 121
month, 300
motherfucker, 86
motion, 230
move, 2, 59, 92, 96, 187, 241, 259, 282, 354, 392
movement, 309, 378, 388
movie, 162, 178

Index   431

moving, 256, 260
multi, 17, 33, 34, 47–51, 56, 62,
    139, 216, 287, 321–325,
    327, 337, 401
multiplayer, 119
multitasking, 355
multitude, 12, 42
muscle, 121
music, 120
myriad, 34, 405

name, 59, 147, 154, 191, 298
nature, 34, 55, 58, 110, 132, 228,
    332, 350, 351, 357, 376,
    377, 394, 405
navigation, 350
need, 4, 8, 11–14, 20–23, 32–34,
    39, 46, 49, 52, 53, 55, 67,
    76, 78, 86, 107, 108, 110,
    111, 120–122, 125–129,
    132, 136, 137, 148, 153,
    157, 159, 161, 167, 176,
    178, 180, 193, 228, 261,
    264, 268, 270, 271, 286,
    299, 300, 304, 306, 309,
    314, 322, 323, 339, 342,
    344, 347, 349, 350,
    354–357, 367, 368, 372,
    376, 378–380, 383, 388,
    392, 402, 407
negligence, 406
neighborhood, 180
network, 56, 65, 68, 69, 73–77, 79,
    82, 84, 86–88, 90–96, 99,
    100, 111, 112, 119–121,
    125, 126, 128, 129, 149,
    170, 179, 180, 183, 184,
    187, 193–197, 204, 206,
    207, 236, 239, 241, 244,
    246, 247, 253, 255, 314,
    322, 324, 325, 328, 336,
    337, 339, 341, 344, 349,
    351, 373, 375–379
networking, 39, 73–76, 80, 84–87,
    91, 92, 94–96, 99, 101,
    102, 110, 111, 113, 115,
    125, 133, 141, 183, 184,
    193, 194, 196, 239, 242,
    244, 246, 254, 255, 283,
    308, 380, 386
neutrality, 255
newfound, 305
news, 352
Nick Bostrom, 237
night, 59
nightmare, 121
nitty, 2, 15, 180
node, 109, 350, 373
noise, 229, 291
normalization, 152
notch, 59
note, 55, 64, 185, 210, 398, 400
notification, 63
number, 24, 53, 76, 122, 132, 161,
    168, 170, 172, 180, 184,
    222, 304, 307, 314, 350,
    378, 380, 381
nutshell, 197

object, 68, 69, 73, 85, 145, 147, 148,
    229, 230, 234, 260
observation, 287
occur, 62, 138, 295, 350
ocean, 388
off, 13, 52, 53, 304, 308, 314, 340,
    354, 355, 362, 378
offer, 17, 21, 28, 31, 32, 39, 40, 52,
    54, 62, 70, 72, 77, 91, 92,

94, 95, 103, 109, 110, 121, 139, 145, 151, 153, 157, 159, 160, 162, 165, 168, 169, 173, 175, 176, 188, 190, 205, 206, 219, 221–223, 234, 289, 291, 296, 299, 300, 306–308, 315, 362, 374, 375, 378, 381, 395
offering, 8, 11, 48, 106, 149, 155, 166, 242, 254, 306, 310, 349, 356, 358, 364, 369, 379
offloading, 14, 126, 185
on, 2, 4, 7–22, 24, 28, 30–32, 37, 39, 42, 44, 45, 48, 52–56, 58–60, 62–64, 67, 75, 77–80, 86–88, 92, 94–96, 100, 103–107, 109, 111, 112, 115, 116, 119–122, 125, 128, 130, 132, 136, 138, 144, 145, 147, 150–154, 156, 159–162, 164, 167–170, 172, 173, 176–178, 180, 181, 183–185, 187, 189, 190, 192, 197, 199, 201, 203, 204, 206, 208, 211, 216, 217, 220–223, 228, 232–234, 236, 237, 239–243, 245, 246, 249, 254–257, 259–262, 264–272, 274–276, 279, 282, 284, 287, 288, 291–295, 297–301, 304–311, 313, 314, 316, 318, 319, 321, 324, 328–330, 333, 341, 349–357, 362, 365, 373, 376, 377, 379–382, 388, 389, 396, 398, 400, 401, 404–407
one, 2, 4, 17, 20, 21, 48, 50, 55, 60, 61, 71, 86, 106, 110, 154, 162, 180, 185, 186, 191, 204, 210, 229, 232, 242, 249, 250, 260, 266, 272, 299, 306, 309, 329, 330, 338, 340, 354, 355
online, 10, 18, 24, 50, 71, 153, 162, 181, 187, 189, 228, 241, 296, 321, 330, 365
operating, 20, 77, 78, 103, 106, 131, 164, 165, 167, 380, 386
operation, 47, 126, 193, 287, 292, 348, 350
opportunity, 260
optimization, 34, 48, 52, 85, 141, 220, 223, 259, 266, 271, 277, 302–305, 309, 310, 312, 314, 315, 317, 355, 382, 385
option, 20, 22, 46, 161, 306, 309, 313
orchestration, 33, 42, 47–51, 92, 96, 106, 107, 109–113, 115, 127, 168, 169, 255, 349
order, 75, 153, 177, 264, 321
organization, 12, 32, 37–39, 53, 58, 257, 258, 260–262, 266–272, 319
origin, 189
other, 2–5, 10, 11, 21, 53, 55, 57, 58, 65, 68–71, 74, 77, 78, 80, 85, 86, 95, 96, 107, 109–111, 115, 121, 125, 128, 131, 133, 138, 154, 161, 164, 165, 167, 168,

170, 184–187, 197,
206–208, 212, 222, 223,
229, 231, 240, 245, 248,
254, 261, 263, 267, 268,
283, 288, 294, 298–300,
306–308, 336, 353, 365,
369, 373, 380, 383, 387,
397
out, 2–4, 6, 8, 53, 58–60, 86, 115,
120, 161, 169, 180, 262,
301, 302, 305, 306, 378
outage, 55, 56, 322, 325, 328
output, 72, 373
overhead, 78, 80, 136, 183, 240
overlay, 111
overload, 184, 330
overprovisioning, 53, 314
oversight, 235, 237, 404, 406
overview, 121, 186, 308, 366, 369, 379
owner, 246
ownership, 40, 61, 63, 405

PaaS, 21
pace, 92, 118
package, 103, 106, 107, 115, 177
packaging, 109, 167
packet, 74, 100
pain, 99
panacea, 186
para, 78
paradigm, 8, 67, 128, 136, 344, 348, 349
paradigms, 54, 125
parallel, 71, 185, 373
part, 6, 9, 10, 130, 187, 189, 190,
269, 322, 332, 373
partitioning, 180
partner, 39

party, 14, 32–34, 36, 37, 45, 57, 183,
265, 266, 307, 308, 339,
377, 395, 405
past, 13, 14
patching, 160, 240
path, 1, 74, 86
patient, 11, 33, 55, 236, 270, 350, 353
pattern, 217, 233
pay, 2, 8, 11, 13, 31, 53, 54, 125, 145,
170, 178, 222, 239, 245,
298–301, 306, 310, 313
payment, 18, 264, 309
peace, 18
peak, 13, 18, 24, 34, 39, 40, 52, 53,
75, 185, 264–266, 270,
304, 311, 314, 362
peer, 294, 373, 376
penetration, 338
people, 4, 58, 59, 170, 228, 352, 400,
404, 406
perception, 229
performance, 17, 37, 39–41, 51, 53,
54, 68, 72, 74, 75, 77, 78,
80, 83, 85, 87, 128, 129,
132, 147, 148, 150, 152,
154, 155, 159, 161, 162,
172, 178, 183–187, 190,
192, 217, 222, 223, 233,
234, 236, 241, 259–266,
268, 271, 275, 277, 287,
288, 290–292, 295, 297,
304, 305, 312, 314–317,
319, 322, 325, 327, 329,
336, 341, 348, 350, 363,
372
performant, 240, 325, 327, 330
period, 291
permission, 197

persistence, 185
person, 227
personnel, 13, 231
pest, 353
Peter Norvig, 237
phase, 221
phenomenon, 355
photo, 147
physics, 355, 363
picture, 293
piece, 86, 107, 242
pipeline, 399, 401
pixel, 229
place, 3, 32, 33, 56, 57, 59, 126, 161, 180, 187, 210, 215, 276, 291, 336, 337, 376, 405, 406
placement, 329, 350
plaintext, 199
plan, 39, 86, 172, 210, 222, 261, 266, 267, 270, 272, 300, 333, 337, 338
plane, 94, 95, 99, 100
planet, 255
planning, 92, 123, 132, 171, 231, 259, 262, 265, 269, 272, 312, 325, 327, 329
plant, 349, 353
platform, 10, 11, 20, 21, 23, 24, 47, 50, 51, 62, 74, 106, 107, 115, 124, 131, 132, 138, 162, 167, 168, 189, 228, 239, 242, 245, 246, 250, 253, 254, 256, 260–264, 270, 316, 324, 330, 379
play, 3, 5, 15, 71, 74–76, 80, 86, 96, 99, 121, 125, 184, 190, 197, 207, 221, 235, 277, 290, 309, 318, 321, 330, 332, 348, 375, 382, 397
player, 242
playground, 148, 286
playing, 8, 14, 119
plethora, 250
plugin, 138, 211
point, 9, 86, 93, 95, 107, 307, 404
policy, 95, 182, 198, 396
pollution, 123
pool, 8, 16, 75, 145, 183, 185, 186, 192
pooling, 33, 38
popularity, 44, 110, 158, 177
population, 406
port, 74, 184
portability, 2, 60, 61, 63, 64, 169
portion, 184
position, 229
positive, 12, 354, 400, 405
possibility, 62
post, 11, 198, 211
posture, 62, 214
potential, 8, 11, 12, 37, 44, 52, 63, 64, 98, 102, 113, 122, 123, 125, 127, 130, 132, 136, 144, 177, 184, 187, 196, 207, 208, 210, 216, 219, 232, 234–237, 246, 250, 253, 263, 265, 272, 274, 277, 294, 300, 301, 306–308, 312, 317, 320, 327, 332, 336–340, 344, 348, 351, 353–355, 359, 361, 363–366, 368, 370–372, 375, 376, 378, 380, 385, 388, 392, 393, 395, 396, 400, 401, 404–406

Index

power, 2, 6, 7, 9, 10, 12, 15, 19, 21, 24, 28, 34, 35, 37, 47, 51, 53, 64, 65, 73, 84–86, 104, 106, 117, 119, 121, 124, 125, 132, 136, 141, 151, 153, 162, 169, 172, 177–179, 183, 184, 199, 207, 220, 223, 234, 239, 241, 242, 246, 247, 253, 255, 285, 286, 291, 298, 309, 325, 341, 344, 351, 354, 355, 357, 360, 365, 373, 376, 378–381, 383, 385–388, 405, 407
powerhouse, 121
practice, 147, 154, 185, 212, 282, 283, 286, 316, 321, 402
predictability, 13, 300, 301
prediction, 353
preprocess, 229
preprocessing, 220, 223
presence, 186, 245, 246
present, 157, 219, 235, 374, 406
presentation, 8
preservation, 267–269
pretzel, 354
prevention, 394
price, 2, 7, 300, 306, 310, 313
pricing, 150, 154, 222, 223, 239, 245, 253, 298–302, 304, 306, 307, 309, 312–315, 317
principle, 122, 198, 401
print, 59
priority, 95, 180
privacy, 2, 11, 14, 15, 31–33, 37, 39, 40, 56, 57, 59, 62–64, 121, 122, 128, 129, 182, 199, 232, 234, 268, 291, 344, 349, 350, 354, 373, 377–379, 392–397, 404–407
privilege, 198
pro, 262
problem, 47, 167, 217, 233, 237, 365
procedure, 335
process, 1, 14, 24, 53, 71, 74, 77, 85, 95, 106, 107, 115, 120, 125, 128, 132, 136–138, 141, 152, 153, 167, 183, 199, 210, 212, 217, 220, 221, 223, 229, 232, 240, 241, 249, 256, 259–265, 267–269, 271, 274–276, 293, 294, 296, 297, 305, 317, 319, 321, 334, 354, 381, 394, 396, 398, 400, 405
processing, 7, 53, 63, 71, 72, 75, 87, 119, 120, 122, 125–128, 132, 136–138, 160, 178, 182, 184, 217, 221, 229, 233, 234, 236, 255, 264, 265, 341, 346, 349, 350, 352, 372, 373, 380, 397
product, 153, 234, 352
production, 265, 274–276, 294, 386
productivity, 10, 55, 56, 176, 177
professional, 106, 246
profile, 396
program, 93, 95
programmability, 95, 99
programming, 131, 138, 217, 240
progress, 226, 228, 352, 385, 392
project, 10, 55, 241, 307, 313, 388
proliferation, 130, 204
Prometheus, 112
promise, 355, 360, 369–371, 404

proof, 377, 378
propaganda, 352
property, 163, 378
propose, 296, 352, 396
protection, 14, 32, 56, 57, 59, 63, 79, 182, 206, 212, 234, 291, 319, 336, 337, 339, 354, 392–397, 405
protocol, 93, 94
prototyping, 357
provider, 2, 3, 11, 14, 15, 17, 18, 20, 31, 32, 39, 45, 48, 50, 55–63, 67, 91, 92, 139, 180, 203, 210, 265, 284, 286, 300, 302, 317, 377
provision, 19, 34, 53, 141, 178, 299, 306, 315
provisioning, 12, 79, 93, 240, 259, 283, 285, 286, 294, 308, 316
proximity, 349
public, 4, 31–40, 42, 44, 62, 124, 180, 231, 270, 407
purchase, 13, 300
purchasing, 10, 309
purpose, 94, 266
push, 130, 138
puzzle, 242

quality, 53, 88, 123, 229, 231, 241, 263, 292, 293, 311, 333, 353, 362
quantization, 222
quantum, 15, 121, 354–360, 363–366
qubit, 355, 356
query, 153, 154, 191
question, 3, 297
queue, 137

quo, 3

race, 87, 397
range, 19, 21, 29, 31, 37, 57, 89, 107, 128, 136, 146, 151, 158, 160, 174, 180, 217, 224, 229, 230, 232, 233, 241–244, 246, 247, 250, 255, 272, 284, 296, 343, 344, 360, 369, 374, 397
rate, 295, 300, 310
re, 2, 3, 5, 18, 57–59, 85, 86, 102, 106, 115, 119–121, 124, 130, 136, 159, 161, 163, 178, 179, 181, 245, 246, 256, 283, 296, 298, 299, 306, 313, 314, 316, 317, 354, 355, 395
reach, 11, 37, 74, 128, 355, 386
read, 59, 148, 197, 296
readiness, 269, 270, 272
reading, 4, 118, 167, 262
reality, 383, 405
realization, 102
realm, 37, 121, 159, 182, 197, 204, 242, 298, 349, 356, 375, 392
reason, 11, 217
recipient, 74
recognition, 217, 227, 228, 233, 234, 400, 401, 404, 406
recommendation, 234
reconstruction, 231
record, 2, 62, 151, 288, 376
recourse, 407
recoverability, 336
recovery, 8, 11, 62, 80, 167, 245, 322, 325, 337, 338
recycling, 380–382

Index

reduction, 2, 15, 51, 52, 54, 129, 270
redundancy, 8, 11, 48, 55, 56, 62, 86, 152, 185, 186, 247, 329, 332, 373, 377, 379
reengineering, 63
refactoring, 263–266, 269, 271
referee, 86
refining, 217
regard, 204
region, 17, 321–325, 327, 396
registry, 109
regulation, 369, 400
rehosting, 256, 259
relationship, 3, 128, 151, 153
release, 275, 276, 294
reliability, 62, 64, 112, 120, 121, 126, 127, 153, 160, 186, 241, 247, 263, 269, 273, 275, 310–312, 315, 319, 323, 327, 330, 332, 333, 336, 345, 351, 365
reliance, 236, 349, 373, 381
reminder, 339
removal, 229
rental, 162
replatform, 262
replication, 51, 70, 264, 329
reporting, 307, 315
repository, 275, 290
representation, 88, 165
representative, 406
reproducibility, 286, 294
reputation, 182, 215
request, 75, 131, 141, 183, 185, 192
rescue, 18, 170, 327
research, 3, 4, 96, 98, 228, 241, 351, 365, 366, 380, 401
researcher, 400

resilience, 11, 12, 33, 332, 336, 375, 376
resiliency, 72, 336
reskilling, 235, 406
resolver, 191, 192
resource, 11, 12, 33, 34, 38, 41, 45, 51, 52, 54, 57, 75, 77, 79, 80, 91, 92, 106, 128, 131, 132, 164, 167, 169, 170, 177, 178, 183–186, 190, 222, 234, 263–266, 275, 292, 295, 296, 299, 300, 302, 305, 308, 314, 315, 317, 330, 349–351, 373, 380, 382
response, 75, 126, 128, 137, 141, 170, 183–185, 208–211, 222, 235, 264, 265, 274, 278, 295, 329, 338, 350
responsibility, 14, 354, 388, 406
responsiveness, 183, 186
rest, 17, 161, 405
restaurant, 5
restore, 211, 318–321, 334
restructuring, 263
result, 39, 172, 192, 260, 291, 299, 313, 382, 390
retail, 54, 234, 257, 270, 349
retention, 63, 268, 291
retirement, 267–269
retrieval, 145
return, 279, 299
revenue, 336
review, 55, 182, 211, 267, 268, 291, 302, 305, 317, 339
revocation, 201
revolution, 9, 119, 125, 295–298, 354, 355, 376

revolutionizing, 35, 218, 233, 236, 353
ride, 7, 48, 115, 121, 169, 354, 355
right, 3, 20, 21, 58, 59, 80, 105, 119, 120, 144, 151, 159, 170, 254, 270, 292, 295, 299, 301, 307–309, 312, 314, 317, 354, 392, 404
rightsizing, 304
rise, 2, 7, 51, 73, 106, 212, 234–236, 389
risk, 8, 11, 17, 31, 56, 58, 62, 122, 207, 214, 215, 259, 261, 275, 276, 306, 313, 337, 354, 377
road, 180
roadmap, 270
robin, 329, 330
robustness, 336
role, 15, 71, 73–76, 80, 87, 91, 95, 96, 99, 100, 113, 151, 154, 183, 190, 192, 197, 199, 207, 231, 232, 235, 277, 290, 321, 330, 332, 337, 348, 349, 365, 375, 382, 397
rollback, 112, 275, 276, 332, 334, 336
rolling, 112, 113, 169, 335
room, 1, 180
root, 210, 278, 291
rotation, 201
route, 180
routing, 74, 75, 180, 184, 185, 324, 328
row, 151
rubber, 34
rule, 217
run, 65, 71, 78–80, 87, 103, 106, 107, 109, 110, 115, 131, 167, 177, 178, 249
running, 2, 14, 74, 75, 78, 85, 88, 107, 164, 167, 168, 170, 180, 185, 245, 293, 294, 321, 341, 380
runtime, 20, 103, 107, 112, 131

safeguard, 11, 17, 56, 234, 246, 336, 337, 339, 340, 393
safety, 231, 336, 339, 349, 406
sale, 13, 54, 161, 329
satellite, 241
satisfaction, 228, 234, 268, 293, 353
sauce, 86
saving, 170, 255, 315, 350
say, 20, 95, 137, 161, 183, 186, 270, 330
scalability, 2, 8, 9, 11–13, 15, 19, 21, 23, 31, 32, 34, 37, 39, 41, 44, 47, 48, 51–54, 72, 79, 80, 83–85, 91, 95, 98, 99, 105, 106, 122, 125, 127, 128, 131, 132, 136–138, 141, 144, 145, 147, 153, 155, 159, 160, 163, 169, 176–179, 181, 187, 191, 220, 223, 240, 241, 246, 254, 256, 259, 260, 263–265, 270, 271, 286, 292, 306, 330, 348–350, 362, 363, 369, 372, 373, 378
scale, 2, 7, 8, 10, 11, 13, 14, 18, 19, 21, 24, 31, 34, 39, 40, 51, 53, 54, 80, 87, 110, 118, 125, 136, 145, 148, 151, 153, 161, 168–170, 172, 177, 178, 189, 198, 222,

223, 231, 236, 239–242,
245, 246, 264, 265, 270,
286, 287, 290–292, 294,
298, 299, 304, 306, 309,
314, 362, 363, 365
scaling, 10, 13, 20, 52, 53, 67, 79, 85,
107–110, 113, 115, 132,
136, 154, 160, 161,
168–172, 178, 179, 190,
240, 248, 263, 265, 266,
287, 304, 314, 362
scanning, 295, 338
scenario, 21, 50, 71, 74, 95, 138,
170, 184, 222, 268, 316,
321, 335
scene, 8, 229
schedule, 308
scheduling, 115
schema, 153, 154
scheme, 9, 88
science, 3
scientist, 4, 8
scope, 270
scoring, 353
season, 170, 298
second, 192, 240, 313, 350
secret, 18, 86, 199
section, 3, 9, 13, 19, 31, 33, 37, 42,
45, 47, 48, 54, 57, 60, 61,
64, 65, 73, 84, 85, 87, 92,
95, 96, 99, 103, 105, 106,
110, 113, 114, 124, 125,
128, 145, 151, 155, 159,
167, 177, 179, 186, 192,
193, 196, 199, 204, 212,
216, 223, 242, 246, 250,
269, 272, 273, 279, 282,
287, 292, 298, 302, 306,
318, 322, 327, 332, 336,
344, 349, 360, 363, 366,
370, 376, 380, 383, 386,
388, 392, 397, 401, 405
sector, 353
security, 2, 11, 12, 14, 15, 17, 18,
31–33, 37–40, 44, 47, 51,
56, 57, 59, 62, 64, 75, 76,
79, 80, 84, 86–88, 91, 92,
95, 105, 106, 112, 113,
120, 122, 126–128, 131,
133, 144, 153, 161, 162,
167, 180, 181, 197, 198,
200, 201, 203–216, 231,
234, 246, 255, 259, 267,
270, 271, 283, 291, 295,
308, 336–340, 344, 349,
350, 362, 363, 365, 372,
373, 375, 377, 393–397,
405
segmentation, 79, 112, 353
selection, 220, 223, 235, 236, 333,
381
self, 103, 106, 112, 167, 248, 377
sender, 74
sense, 221, 299
sensitivity, 319
sensor, 229
sentiment, 228, 352
separation, 95, 100, 180
series, 148, 267
server, 4, 13, 18, 65–67, 73, 75–77,
80, 86, 87, 107, 120, 126,
128, 161, 164, 183–186,
257, 264, 266, 294, 321,
324, 327, 329–331, 377,
380, 382, 385
serverless, 54, 67, 73, 136, 138–144,
173, 175–177, 179,
253–255, 260, 263–265,

287
service, 2, 3, 8, 13–15, 19–21,
    32–34, 39, 45, 48, 52–56,
    58–60, 62, 74, 75, 88, 91,
    92, 95, 110, 132, 149, 150,
    153, 160, 161, 169, 170,
    177, 178, 185, 190, 203,
    206, 210, 240, 241, 248,
    255, 259, 265–270, 289,
    295, 298–300, 302, 304,
    306–308, 311, 313, 315,
    321–324, 328, 330, 352,
    377, 385–388, 392–396,
    405–407
session, 55, 185
set, 10, 18, 20, 24, 39, 43, 58, 78, 90,
    110, 132, 162, 168, 176,
    197, 204, 207, 224, 240,
    244, 246, 247, 252, 254,
    258, 263, 274, 292, 297,
    304, 308, 315, 344, 374,
    400, 401
setting, 137, 180, 249, 270, 314
shape, 6, 159, 177, 388, 405, 407
sharding, 378
share, 1, 3–5, 7, 14, 33, 34, 45, 53,
    101, 106, 120, 147, 192,
    214, 296, 360, 405
sharing, 7, 10, 14, 17, 47, 70, 77,
    147, 293, 295–297, 405
shift, 8, 256–260, 271, 273, 387
shine, 255
shit, 2, 85, 86, 119, 120, 292
shop, 170
shopping, 52, 75, 153, 185, 270
Shor, 365
shortcut, 355
show, 159, 178, 228
sibling, 4

side, 58, 203, 306, 309
significance, 73, 336
silver, 332
simplicity, 132, 259
simulation, 233
Singapore, 123, 124
Siri, 352
site, 357
situation, 60, 120, 321
size, 21, 53, 148, 185, 222, 229, 245,
    272, 308, 314, 319
skew, 398
skill, 152, 235, 269, 313
skin, 400
sky, 15, 110, 376
smartphone, 55
smoothie, 32
snapshot, 107
society, 232, 354, 397, 400, 401,
    405, 407
software, 2, 8, 11, 12, 20, 21, 27, 32,
    34, 39, 53–55, 77, 86, 87,
    94, 95, 103, 106, 107, 125,
    164, 167, 180, 185, 240,
    249, 254, 263, 268, 269,
    273–275, 283, 286, 292,
    293, 296, 297, 328, 332
soil, 353
solution, 10, 27, 28, 31, 37, 41, 44,
    51, 106, 109, 128, 145,
    148, 162, 167, 185, 283,
    296, 297, 377, 392
solving, 47, 217, 233, 355, 360
soul, 65
source, 74, 106, 115, 125, 128, 129,
    132, 138, 229, 236, 249,
    255, 314, 341, 344, 376,
    379
sovereignty, 15

Index 441

space, 241, 254, 296, 378
span, 29, 99
specific, 19, 21, 28, 31, 32, 34, 37, 39, 40, 42, 45, 47, 48, 55, 56, 58, 59, 62, 63, 87, 92, 94, 96, 105, 107, 131, 132, 137–139, 141, 151, 153, 156, 159, 161, 170, 172, 180, 185, 197, 204, 207, 217, 220, 229, 230, 255, 260, 263, 264, 267, 284, 299–301, 307, 313, 319, 328, 333, 349, 352, 353, 362, 365
speech, 228, 254
speed, 74, 120, 169, 221, 259, 274, 319, 373
spend, 302
spending, 10, 52, 279, 307–309, 315, 316
spike, 170, 299
spot, 222, 299–301, 304, 306, 309–313
spread, 86, 121, 168
stability, 275, 277, 365
stack, 184, 190, 256, 283
stage, 293, 294, 399, 401
stake, 59, 377, 378
standard, 255
standardization, 344, 351
start, 18, 107, 141, 144, 153, 176, 180, 271
starting, 307
startup, 10, 14, 52, 136, 177, 178, 245, 304
state, 11, 108, 110, 111, 115, 123, 176, 186, 270, 276, 278, 319, 332, 334, 354, 355
status, 3, 186

step, 172, 258, 261, 265–268, 275, 290, 307, 355
stock, 353
storage, 7, 15, 17, 18, 24, 31, 32, 39, 52, 53, 63, 65, 68–74, 77, 80, 82, 84–87, 113, 119, 120, 122, 125, 128, 129, 132, 133, 145–151, 160, 161, 165, 201, 202, 239, 241–243, 246, 247, 254, 255, 257, 260, 261, 268, 283, 288, 291, 300, 307, 308, 314, 341, 344, 350, 351, 372–378, 380, 388, 394
store, 2, 10, 14, 18, 24, 32, 59, 62, 65, 68, 71, 85, 120, 125, 128, 151, 153, 159, 160, 162, 202, 203, 212, 240, 241, 244, 270, 321, 354, 379, 386, 394, 396, 405
storing, 2, 55, 58, 69, 85, 119, 126, 145, 148, 189, 241, 278, 291, 373
strain, 189, 381
strap, 110, 204
strategy, 17, 33, 56, 126, 185, 187, 256, 257, 259–261, 269, 270, 272, 292, 295, 319–322, 324, 325, 327
stream, 13, 274, 293, 311
streaming, 13, 23, 24, 53, 75, 76, 119, 126, 159, 161, 162, 169, 178, 179, 187, 189, 241, 311, 324, 325, 362
stroll, 120
structure, 13, 61, 145, 152, 302, 366, 367, 376
Stuart Russell, 237

student, 55
study, 55, 92, 228, 352, 382, 400
stuff, 2, 85
style, 262
sub, 373
subfield, 217, 233
subnet, 180, 181
subsea, 388
subset, 353
success, 37, 128, 169, 292, 296, 301, 325
suite, 79, 243, 247, 248, 254, 255
summary, 15, 255, 369
sunshine, 2
superposition, 355, 356
supply, 299, 310, 313, 377, 378
support, 14, 94, 122, 165, 197, 223, 228, 234, 237, 246, 255, 271, 294, 295, 303, 352, 383, 406
suppression, 86
supremacy, 360
supreme, 159
surface, 338
surge, 11, 18, 54, 161, 169, 170, 329, 330
surprise, 309
surrounding, 353, 354, 393, 405
surveillance, 59, 228, 230, 231, 400, 404
sustainability, 12, 255, 382, 388, 389, 392
sweat, 172
Sweden, 382
switch, 2, 17, 55, 56, 62, 63, 75, 94, 100, 169, 328, 354
switching, 60, 330
synchronization, 51, 126, 127, 268
synergy, 245

syntax, 286
system, 4, 7, 11, 12, 20, 30, 62, 65, 69, 77, 103, 106, 107, 110, 115, 120, 128, 131, 147, 153, 164, 165, 167, 170, 187, 193, 197, 203, 207, 210, 211, 217, 231, 234, 260, 263, 268, 269, 278, 287, 288, 290–292, 295, 297, 328, 333, 335–337, 367, 372, 373, 378

table, 2, 74, 94, 107, 116, 137, 151–154
tablet, 55
tag, 2, 7
tagging, 294
tailor, 18, 48, 353
taking, 2, 14, 32, 55, 260, 388, 398
talk, 57, 58, 86, 116, 120, 160
target, 172, 260, 294, 373
task, 131, 228, 340, 355, 397
team, 10, 20, 39, 55, 210, 211, 268, 269, 274–276, 283, 321, 338, 400
tech, 130, 254
technique, 78, 164, 184, 352
technology, 9, 12–15, 54, 57, 80, 87, 92, 96, 99, 109, 121, 123, 124, 130, 148, 177, 193, 223, 232, 235–237, 266, 268, 272, 284, 340, 344, 353, 356, 360, 363, 366, 368–372, 375–379, 386, 400, 404–406
telemetry, 293
temperature, 382
tenant, 34

Index 443

term, 8, 20, 24, 245, 268, 300, 306, 310, 313, 367
termination, 306, 311
test, 24, 172, 261, 293, 296, 332, 333
testing, 14, 77, 109, 187, 258, 259, 261, 265, 271, 275, 276, 293, 294, 320, 321, 332, 333, 336, 338
text, 227, 228, 254, 352
the United States, 3, 338
theft, 57
theory, 316, 402
thing, 15, 59, 355
thorough, 265, 267–269, 271, 332, 339
thought, 296
threat, 11, 204, 208, 210, 211, 336, 339, 365
thrive, 13, 15
throughput, 241, 295
tier, 150, 185, 287, 307, 309
Tim Berners-Lee, 4
time, 3, 10, 11, 13, 14, 20, 33, 41, 53, 75, 76, 95, 99, 107, 114, 123, 125, 126, 128, 130–132, 136, 138, 141, 144, 149, 167, 170, 172, 176, 183–185, 198, 221–223, 231–234, 236, 240, 249, 259, 265, 270, 274, 275, 283, 287, 293, 295, 296, 300, 304, 308, 341, 344–346, 348–350, 354, 355, 362, 376
timeline, 261
tip, 183, 259
titan, 255

today, 7–9, 11, 12, 54, 93, 212, 246, 392, 397
tolerance, 136, 137, 168, 169, 186, 191, 239, 332, 373
tomorrow, 120
ton, 85
tool, 105, 106, 109, 150, 165, 169, 171, 284, 285, 296, 354
toolkit, 106
toolset, 148
top, 4, 48, 59, 77, 87, 88, 160, 161, 180, 305, 307, 308
topic, 138, 186, 341, 352, 365
topology, 74, 88, 91, 100
tornado, 120
traceability, 378
track, 2, 62, 121, 132, 162, 198, 207, 231, 271, 294, 295, 307, 308, 378, 382
tracking, 172, 230, 231, 306–309, 315–317
traction, 4, 47, 96
trade, 154, 176, 265, 397
trading, 353
traffic, 11, 13, 18, 23, 52–54, 75, 76, 86, 91, 94, 95, 100, 123, 132, 161, 169, 170, 172, 178, 180, 181, 183–185, 187, 189–192, 204, 206, 207, 231, 266, 287, 298, 304, 307, 314, 315, 324, 325, 327, 329–332, 337, 350, 353
train, 15, 169, 178, 220, 254
training, 211, 217, 220–223, 234, 235, 252, 253, 255, 271, 338, 398, 400, 406
transaction, 151, 376, 377
transfer, 4, 17, 61, 72–74, 76, 120,

150, 193, 196, 223, 306, 307, 309, 315, 328, 363, 378
transformation, 136, 236, 253, 269
transit, 17, 161, 405
transition, 79, 261, 265, 267, 269, 332, 334, 336, 406
translation, 234
transmission, 63, 76, 129
transparency, 63, 234, 235, 237, 372, 375–378, 393, 396, 397, 401, 405–407
transport, 184
transportation, 123, 218, 353
travel, 55, 119, 128
treat, 286, 382
treatment, 236
trend, 364
trick, 41
trigger, 132, 137, 138, 228, 349
troubleshooting, 12, 99, 112, 196, 274, 278, 288, 290, 294, 295
trust, 2, 33, 47, 181, 182, 207, 234, 235, 367, 369, 372, 377, 378, 393, 397
tune, 172
tuning, 220, 223, 262, 338
tuple, 151
turbocharger, 87
turn, 37, 107, 308
turning, 9
turtle, 120
type, 58, 63, 150, 151, 156, 319, 400

unavailability, 62
uncertainty, 299, 366
understanding, 4, 18, 21, 37, 59, 64, 85, 92, 102, 105, 119, 130, 144, 148, 154, 163, 167, 194, 195, 199, 207, 208, 219, 228, 232, 234, 270, 272, 274, 288, 290, 296–298, 301, 302, 307, 313, 317, 344, 351, 352, 379, 401
undertaking, 273
underutilization, 53, 314
unemployment, 406
unit, 167, 293, 356
universe, 199
university, 154
up, 1, 2, 4, 7–10, 12–15, 18–20, 24, 30, 31, 34, 39, 47, 48, 53, 54, 58, 59, 85, 87, 101, 106, 115, 119, 120, 125, 126, 130, 131, 137, 145, 159, 161, 162, 169, 170, 177, 178, 180, 187, 207, 216, 236, 239, 240, 242, 245, 249, 254, 258, 294–299, 304, 306, 308, 309, 313–315, 321, 337, 338, 343, 344, 354, 356, 362, 366, 371
update, 112, 132, 152, 182, 286
updating, 17
upfront, 10, 11, 13, 18, 20, 32, 39, 40, 52–54, 178, 245, 274, 299, 300, 306, 388
upload, 120, 132, 147
upskilling, 235
usage, 17, 41, 119, 125, 132, 162, 222, 234, 264, 267, 271, 298–300, 302, 304–309, 311, 315, 316, 344, 362, 381, 386, 389, 405
use, 2, 4, 11, 13, 14, 17, 20, 21, 25,

28, 29, 31, 32, 35, 42, 44,
51, 54, 71–75, 78, 89, 92,
96, 99, 101, 103, 105, 106,
109, 121–123, 125, 128,
136–138, 143–146, 148,
149, 151, 158, 159, 162,
166, 170, 171, 174, 185,
217, 219, 229, 235–237,
239, 261, 270, 285, 286,
298, 306, 309, 313, 314,
316, 344, 347, 349, 351,
353, 354, 359, 364, 365,
373, 376, 381, 385–387,
395, 396, 401–407
user, 11, 24, 39, 53, 54, 76, 112, 122,
126, 132, 136, 147,
160–163, 169, 178, 185,
187, 189, 191, 192, 197,
198, 200, 228, 233, 234,
245, 268, 292, 304,
323–325, 327, 328, 330,
337, 362, 377, 378, 393,
395–397, 405
utility, 8
utilization, 11, 12, 34, 41, 52, 54, 71,
75, 79, 80, 91, 92, 131,
164, 167, 170, 178, 184,
186, 263–266, 275, 292,
294, 295, 304, 308, 312,
314, 317, 327, 330, 350,
351, 373, 380, 382

validation, 265, 367, 406
validity, 377
value, 144, 159, 160, 274, 293, 305,
321
variability, 344
variable, 298, 313
variety, 32, 54, 55, 68, 104, 122, 131,
142, 148, 149, 160, 161,
195, 242
vector, 210
vehicle, 231
velocity, 122
vendor, 17, 31, 33, 37, 56, 57,
59–62, 64, 141, 144, 176,
268, 351, 363
verification, 321, 366, 373, 400
verify, 268, 293, 294, 378
versatility, 35, 117, 159, 166
version, 77, 112, 274, 275, 294, 335
victim, 59
video, 23, 53, 75, 76, 95, 119, 126,
178, 229, 230, 254
view, 51, 142, 290, 293
viewing, 13, 162
viewpoint, 231
village, 5
virtualization, 12, 38, 39, 66, 73,
77–80, 86–93, 103, 164,
167, 380, 385
visibility, 162, 277, 287, 316
vision, 217, 229–234, 352, 353
visionary, 8
visit, 4, 186
visualization, 290, 291, 295
vital, 71, 73, 76, 99, 177, 190, 199,
207, 230, 235, 295, 321,
329, 330, 338, 350, 385
voice, 136, 234
volume, 122, 126, 148, 315, 327
voting, 377
vulnerability, 210, 295, 338, 339

wallet, 309
wand, 286
warehouse, 85, 255
wastage, 41, 382

waste, 12, 123, 274, 293, 381, 382, 386, 388
water, 381, 382
wave, 121, 356
way, 3–5, 7, 9, 12–15, 17, 20, 21, 35, 48, 52, 54, 57, 59, 87, 92, 106, 109, 114, 115, 119, 125, 130, 138, 151–154, 161, 166, 167, 169, 172, 176, 192, 197, 198, 212, 269, 301, 325, 330, 344, 351, 352, 360, 367, 372, 375–377, 386, 391, 405
wealth, 295
weapon, 18
weather, 353
web, 4, 10, 20, 32, 53, 71, 136, 137, 180, 185, 186, 191, 192, 257, 266, 274, 275, 285, 297, 304, 339
website, 10, 18, 54, 71, 132, 161, 170, 185, 186, 210, 241, 298, 321, 329, 331
weight, 184
well, 3, 11, 40, 51, 59, 64, 149, 155, 192, 210, 232, 255, 269, 300, 301, 311, 321, 332, 334, 338, 367, 401, 405
whole, 1, 2, 48, 87, 103, 121, 269, 354, 355, 401
willingness, 299
win, 120
wind, 381, 387, 388
word, 57
work, 3, 5, 8, 12–14, 35, 47, 55, 57, 65, 76, 80, 85, 86, 106, 121, 122, 128, 130, 173, 184, 194, 222, 269, 271, 293, 329, 330, 345, 355, 377, 378, 392, 401
workforce, 338
working, 10, 55, 112, 152, 159, 161, 170, 171, 185, 204, 275, 276, 294, 316, 338
workload, 53, 132, 150, 161, 168, 183–185, 243, 299, 300, 302, 312, 314, 322, 327, 328, 330, 350, 382
world, 1, 2, 5, 7–9, 11, 12, 15, 18, 23, 25, 26, 33, 34, 37, 41, 42, 45, 47, 48, 51, 54, 58, 65, 73, 75, 76, 80, 86, 87, 92, 99, 102, 103, 105, 106, 110, 114, 117–119, 121, 123–125, 128, 130, 133, 143, 145, 147, 148, 154, 155, 158, 159, 162, 163, 166, 169, 177, 179–181, 183–185, 192, 193, 195, 196, 199, 202, 204, 210, 212, 215, 216, 221, 222, 228, 232, 241, 242, 245, 247, 250, 251, 255–257, 263, 269, 271, 272, 279, 286, 287, 292, 297, 298, 301, 302, 304, 306, 313, 316–318, 321, 325, 327, 329, 332, 335, 336, 338, 343, 354, 355, 360, 363, 364, 375, 378, 383, 391, 392, 400, 401
write, 20, 138, 141, 197

year, 298
yield, 353

Milton Keynes UK
Ingram Content Group UK Ltd.
UKHW021125111124
451035UK00016B/1222